To Sov. & Jackie Sherman

So goes the world!

With best holiday wishes.

David

Jan. 1, 1991

LABOR LAWS IN THE MIDDLE EAST

TRADITION IN TRANSIT

DAVID ZISKIND, J.D., PH.D.

LITLAW FOUNDATION
P.O. BOX 36663
LOS ANGELES, CALIFORNIA 90036

Library of Congress Catalog Number 90-070809
ISBN 9615761-5-4 (Hardbound)
9615761-6-2 (Softbound)

CONTENTS

In Memory of

NATHAN and DORA

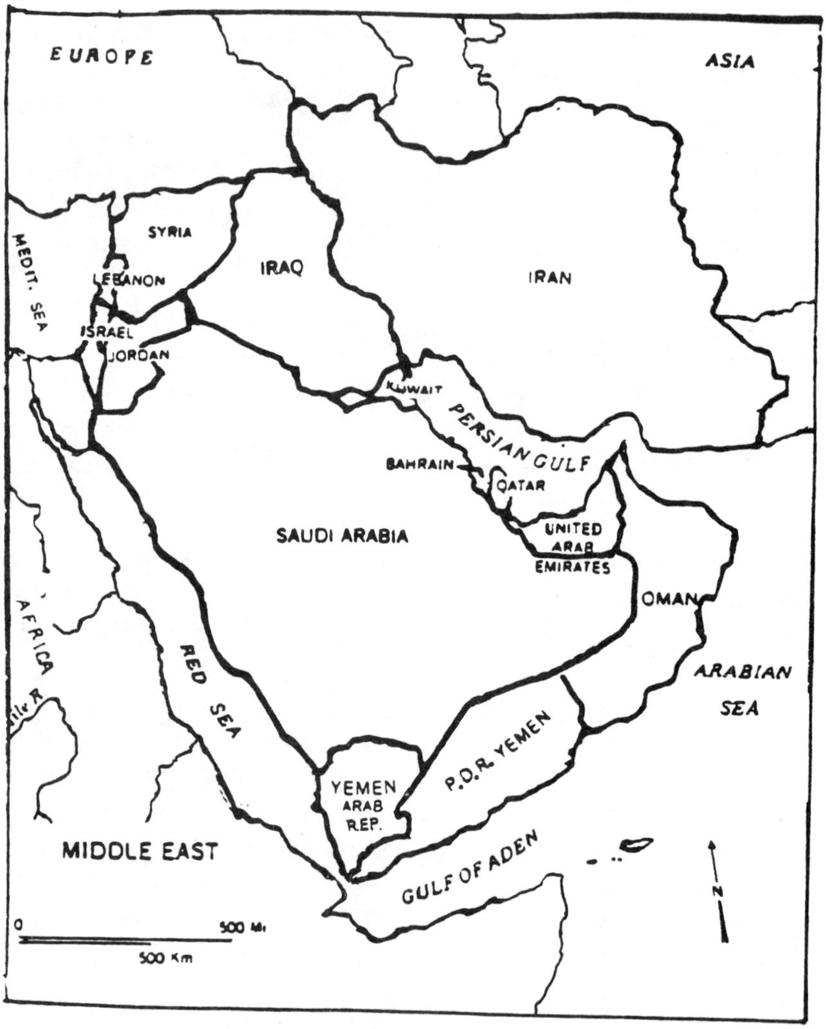
EUROPE
ASIA
SYRIA
MEDIT. SEA
LEBANON
IRAQ
IRAN
ISRAEL
JORDAN
KUWAIT
PERSIAN GULF
BAHRAIN
QATAR
SAUDI ARABIA
UNITED ARAB EMIRATES
OMAN
AFRICA
RED SEA
ARABIAN SEA
P.D.R. YEMEN
YEMEN ARAB REP.
MIDDLE EAST
GULF OF ADEN
N
0
500 Mi
500 Km

PREFACE

Friends jump in where angels fear to tread. Readers of my writings on the Labor Provisions in Constitutions suggested in complimentary comment, that I should broaden my outlook and encompass all labor legislation. When I proposed to deal with the Middle East, I counted only 14 countries and 13 of them had labor codes. Naively I thought it would not be a Herculean task to cover their labor laws as well as their constitutions. Soon I learned otherwise.

The labor laws of the Middle East are not confined to single documents called labor codes. A much larger body of Royal decrees, ministerial orders, and administrative regulations defy categorization or even discovery. In the rapidly changing conditions of the Middle East, officials have refrained from supplying documents that might be deemed controversial or that might prove embarrassing. Even when requested by the International Labour Organization (ILO) to submit required reports, many governments have failed to respond with information pertinent to their official conduct. Fortunately, not all was hidden or obscure.

The method of my research was to exhaust the rather voluminous literature on segments of my study and to supplement that by interviews with officials and scholars who had hands-on contact with labor policies and events in the Middle East.

There is considerable printed literature on the political and economic developments of Middle East countries in the libraries of the University of California at Los Angeles, the Library of Congress in Washington, and the Library of the International Labour Office in Geneva. Those wells of information are deep and constantly refreshed. I have listed most of the sources I have relied upon in footnotes to my text. Constitutions, labor codes, treaties and other laws are for the most part published in English; and I arranged for translations when necessary. I have referred extensively to the provisions of legal documents as well as to commentaries by other scholars.

The resources of the International Labour Office are invaluable, probably indispensable, to comparative labor law research. I have plumbed their treasure-hold through personal interviews with many of their staff members in Geneva. Alan Gladstone, the director of the Labor Law and Labor Administration Department of the ILO, offered his personal guidance and advice, and his gracious secretary, Lucille L. Turner, arranged for my consultations with numerous ILO experts. I was given unstintingly of the knowledge and records of J. M. Servais in the Office of the Director General, Edward Yemin, Chief of the Labor Law and Labor Relations Branch, N. Sarraf in the Application of Standards Branch, M. Ouldamar of the Labor Administration Branch, P. Bangasser of the Management Development Branch, and T. N. Bendahoo of the Social Security Department. Fortunately for me (though sadly for Middle East countries), the ILO Regional Office for Arab States was compelled for security reasons to leave its Beirut offices and to operate out of Geneva. There, I had the opportunity to interview S. Dajani, the Director of that Regional Office, and his staff members, N. Khoury and N. Atasi. They not only were acquainted with Arabic governmental officials and their labor laws, but they had spent years working on labor problems in Arab countries. Their insights were profound.

I was privileged also to confer with David Dorr of the ILO staff, who has extensive knowledge of the labor laws of Israel and with Professor Ruth Ben-Israel whose writings on Israeli Labor Law are encyclopedic.

My consultations with representatives of Middle East countries in their Washington Embassies and my correspondence with Ministers of Labor and Social Affairs in their home offices were fruitful in only a few instances. The microfiche series, entitled the Joint Publications Research Service, did contain English translations of some official statements and other reports that first appeared in Arabic and Hebrew.

PREFACE

I have pondered long over the evaluation of the data I have gathered. It is impossible to accumulate all the information extant on labor laws (an ever changing subject), and it may suffice for labor law comparisons to deal only with major topics. It is far more important for comparative purposes to observe the application of labor laws than to record their text; yet the social impact of the laws is most difficult to ascertain. I have tried to check my personal biases and to report what others have seen through their own cultural eyes.

Prefaces customarily release informants of all responsibility for what is written. I hereby make such acknowledgment. The inadequacies (and possible inadvertent inaccuracies) in my presentation of labor law and situations in the Middle East are due to my own limitations, not to those gracious enough to share their understandings with me.

I wish to acknowledge further my great indebtedness to Antonia Powell for her excellent legal research which has provided me with firm stepping stones on many a path. Dr. Ellen Berg and Felicitas Hinman have also given me valuable editorial assistance.

David Ziskind

Los Angeles, California
April, 1990

I. INTRODUCTION

The Middle East has been a market place of civilizations, full of familiar calls and thoughtful silences. I view it as a grand procession of peoples moving between Africa and Asia, penetrated at times by Europeans, but pulsating with a momentum of its own. Modern nations of the Middle East assert themselves as old members of the human family with something to say about life today.

The current Middle East is, most prominently, a conclave of oil rich and oil poor nations, a melange of Islamic, Hebrew, and Christian influences, an arena for competitive Arab-Jewish political games, a Third World center for super-power manipulation. It is, in my present concern, primarily an area in which several million human beings are working. I do not profess that my point of attention is more important than that of others. I merely find it exciting to explore aspects of labor as facets of the human condition which throb wherever they are found.

Workers are actors on a stage prepared for them; most are given scripts, but many ad-lib as the mood moves them. Workers are everywhere, and they do whatever happens. One digs a trench for rain water to flow into a field; another hammers nails into the frame of a home; another rolls out dough to make bread or a cake; another pulls a switch to send light into darkness; another rings a bell to bring pupils into a classroom; another creates a poem that links a mind with a heart. They do it alone or with others; and for each other. They do it as they have been taught, or as their imagination suggests; as they have been ordered and directed, or as they will. In the Middle East, there are millions of such workers; and their governments have wrought ways to enable them to work fruitfully. What the constitutions and laws of those nations say about that is the subject of this book.

There are many ways of looking at workers. Each of them is a separate human being. Abdul al Hakkim and Issac ben Abraham are both Middle East farmers, maybe scientists, but they are individual persons. Novelists and poets are best qualified to depict their peculiarities. I intend to glance across a broad landscape and I must, therefore, devote my energies to generalizations about workers.

Since labor law is my specialization, I see workers in groups, ranging from the totality of all workers, as embraced by some constitutions, to special groups of factory workers, farm workers, underground workers, railroad workers, home workers, truck drivers, and sailors, as designated in legislation. At times, even narrow laws cover all women or all child workers. At other times, laws are myopic, notably with respect to the many workers they exempt. I try to see more clearly how every body of workers is affected.

Work involves the whole of mankind. Work is not just toil—the movement of hands or the designing of a mind. Everyone engages in work—instinctively, imitatively, or creatively. Even the so-called idle, or the players, perform a deliberate role in society. We attempt to differentiate among workers with loose-fitting terms like blue collar and white collar workers, and rank-and-file and managerial workers. To count workers or to place them functionally, we set them off in agricultural, manufacturing, commercial, service, and informal sectors; we designate them as private, public, and mixed employees, or we label them as machine operators, dancers, tool and die men, inventors and investors. In political and philosophical discussion, much thoughtful analysis is given to the proletariat, to bourgeois, capitalist, and communal workers; and in sociological treatises there is much effort to distinguish lower, middle, and upper classes. I do not spurn such taxonomy; it is useful; however, I am concerned with what happens to workers in any and every path of life. That is an approach to what is happening to all of humanity.

This book, being a study confined to the Middle East, takes note of special conditions of work in that area of the world. Tribal farming and nomadic animal husbandry have been basic support systems resisting change in the Middle East. New industry and public administration demand skills and personnel not readily available. Women and traditional relationships are beset with disturbing modernization.

Simultaneously, as elsewhere, Middle East workers are also husbands, wives, and children, citizens and aliens, worshipers and warriors. They are tossed about in the sweep of society or lost in the voids of public apathy. Their work, indispensable to the development of the Middle East, is usually the most engrossing activity in their individual lives. With these factors in mind, all Middle East governments seek to safeguard and reward workers for their efforts.

For a great many years, the nations of the Middle East relied upon custom and the oral communication of norms concerning labor. Religious and secular leaders heard grievances and settled controversies. Written documents to which they could refer were rare. In time, tribal arrangements became traditional. They determined communal or extended family work relationships; they allocated tasks to be performed by members; they set the mode and degree of compensation; and they provided the satisfactions of personal accomplishments. Religious precepts molded or preserved such customary labor law and inspired more formal legislation. With the expansion of trade and political domains, and the formation of urban centers, rulers issued written decrees; and with the advance of modern commerce and industry, social legislation and codes followed. What effect these legal measures have had on the lives of workers has been a matter of some research and much conjecture. I shall endeavor to list and to comment upon the legal provisions undertaken by the several Middle East governments as they have sought to enrich the lives of workers.

Chapter 1

HISTORICAL ANTECEDENTS

Before launching into a detailed examination of what contemporary governments have provided, I believe it would be helpful to observe historical antecedents to their action.

One can trace throughout the long traditions of the Middle East a promise of a better life for people who labor. On clay tablets and papyrus scrolls, ancient men inscribed a record of works accomplished, including how the doers were or should have been rewarded. The legal codes of Lipit Ishtar (in Assyria, 1930 B.C.)[1] and Hammurabi (in Babylonia, 1752 B.C.)[2] told of the wages ordered by the Gods, Anum and Enlil, to be paid a farm laborer, a herdsman, a barber, a surgeon, a sailor, and a stonecutter. These were labor laws, later supplanted by new revelations of the word of God. Hebrews declared that Jehovah had ordained one day of rest in seven (Bible, Exod. 20:9). The Prophet Isaiah cried out against the exploitation of workers, "They shall not build for others to inhabit; nor plant for others to eat" (Isaiah, 65:22). Luke, the disciple of Christ, admonished, "The worker earns his pay" (Luke, 10:7), and the Apostle Paul exhorted, "Masters, be just and fair to your slaves knowing that you too have a Master in heaven" (Co.4:1). The Prophet Muhammed noted, in the revealed words of Allah, "To men is allotted what they earn, and to women what they earn" (Koran, Sura IV:32). Down the ages, these norms were repeated and are still proclaimed.

Precepts of how workers are to be treated stand out as beacons in the dawn of unrecorded or dimly defined ages. Over a span of

[1] Godfrey R. Driver, ed., Assyrian Laws, Oxford, Clarendon Press, 1935; Erasmus Steele, The Code of Lipit-Ishtar, 7 Am. Journal of Archaeology 432.

[2] Robert F. Harper, The Code of Hammurabi, 2d. ed., Chicago, Univ. of Chicago Press, 1904.

many centuries, nomads and farmers moved across the lands of the Middle East and established communal life. Tribal leaders and their followers created binding alliances. Many Gods were invoked to provide protection or to bestow legitimacy upon rulers and their states. Almost no contemporaneous records of the activities of those peoples or their governments survive. The few early written histories relate what had been transmitted orally. Archeological findings confirm only a portion of the reported events. Oral traditions, nonetheless, reflect social behavior and are a validating source of information about early governmental institutions.

The kingdoms of Mesopotamia, Assyria, Babylon, and Egypt demonstrated the imagination and ingenuity of peoples in fashioning elaborate regulatory systems, and their traditional practices lingered for a long time. However, in seeking to identify the most significant influences upon the development of government and labor relations in the Middle East, I leap over much of the early "history" of the area. The roots were nourishing, but later growth was more distinctive and determinate. A discerning analysis of the Middle East governments may commence with the city states in Syria-Palestine. That still leaves two millennia of history for perusal—a task more manageable. I confine my overview to the two most prominent peoples in the area—the Hebrews and the Arabs. Their principal response to the labor problems they encountered, in Biblical times and later, lay a foundation for an understanding of their very recent efforts to encapsulate their philosophies and regulations in modern constitutions and statutes.

HEBRAIC LABOR LAW

The labor of the primitive inhabitants of the Middle East was, as far as we can tell, relatively simple, yet with an increasing division of tasks. Early records mention tillers of the soil who grew wheat, barley, grapes, olives, and dates; hewers of wood who felled trees, made cabinets, and built temples; potters who made clay vessels; stone cutters and masons who created monuments;

metal workers who made bronze implements and gold ornaments; fishers and sailors of the sea. We are told that women spun threads of wool and flax, and made fabrics for garments. They also drew water from wells and baked bread. Some served as wet nurses. Religious functionaries, warriors, rulers and their entourage also performed their traditional services. Still we know very little about the conditions under which those workers labored.[3]

The Bible repeatedly reminds us that a great many people were poor, and it refers to slaves, bondsmen, bondsmaids, and hired servants. What portion of the population fell into each category is unknown. Many workers were paid for their services, but how much has rarely been recorded. There are references to contracts of employment for one or several years; yet more often there is indicated a hire for a day or a particular task. The Bible has provided rules of behavior and clues to the plight of workers; but early histories depicting labor conditions are absent or meager.[4]

Biblical Commandments

The first five books of the Bible, called the Pentateuch, or the Torah, constitute the law of the Hebrews. They intermingle religious and secular commandments that show how the devout are to "walk with the Lord." In addition to the texts quoted above on a day of rest and the equitable treatment of workers, the Bible contains a number of passages concerning workers and the poor. Illustrative are the following:

> "You shall gain your bread by the sweat of your brow " (Gen.3:19).
>
> "You shall not keep back the wages of a man who is poor and needy, whether a fellow countryman or an alien. . .Pay him his wages on the same day before sunset for he is poor and his heart is set on them" (Deut.24:15; also Lev.19:13).

[3] N. Gross, ed., Jewish Economic History, Jerusalem, 1975.

[4] The New English Bible, Oxford Univ. Press, Oxford, 1970; The Holy Bible, Univ. of Oxford and Cambridge, 1885. S. Wittmayer Baron, A Social and Religious History of the Jews, 2nd ed., New York, Columbia Univ. Press, 1952; Marcus Arkin, Aspects of Jewish Economic History, Jewish Publication Society of America, Philadelphia, 1975

> "You have six days to labor and do all your work. But the seventh day is a Sabbath of the Lord your God; that day you shall not do any work, you, your son, or your daughter, your slave or your slave-girl, your cattle or the alien within your gates" (Exod. 20-10; also Lev. 23:3,24,25).

With respect to slaves, there are additional provisions.

> "When your brother is reduced to poverty, and sells himself to you, you shall not use him to work for you as a slave. . .You shall not drive him with ruthless severity" (Lev.25:39, 42-43).
>
> "When a man strikes his slave or slave girl in the eye and destroys it, he shall let the slave go free in compensation for the eye" (Same for a tooth) (Exod. 21:26-27).
>
> "You shall not surrender to his master a slave who has taken refuge with you" (Deut. 23:15).
>
> "When you buy a Hebrew slave, he shall be your slave for six years, but on the seventh he shall go free and pay nothing" (Exod. 21:2; Deut. 15:12).
>
> "If he is married, his wife shall go out with him" (Exod.21:3).
>
> "If the servant should say, I love my master, I will not go free, then his master shall bring him to the Judges . . . and the man shall be his slave for life" (Exod. 21:5-6; Deut. 15:17).
>
> "When a man sells his daughter into slavery, she shall not go free as a male slave may . . .If he assigns her to his son, he shall allow her the rights of a daughter." (Exod. 21:8,9).
>
> "If he takes another woman, he shall not deprive the first of meat, clothes and conjugal rights, and if he does not provide her with these three things, she shall go free without any payment" (Exod. 21:10-11).
>
> "When you set him free, do not not let him go empty handed; be generous to him because the Lord your God has blessed you" (Deut.15:13,14).
>
> "Remember that you were slaves in Egypt and the Lord, your God, redeemed you" (Deut.15:15).
>
> "You shall hallow the 50th year and proclaim liberation in the land for all its inhabitants" (Lev. 25:10).

On aid to the poor and hungry who undoubtedly included laborers, the Bible enjoins believers to make specific provision.

> "When you gather the grapes from your vineyards, do not glean afterwards. What is left shall be for the alien, the orphan and the widow" (Deut. 24:21).
>
> "When you reap the harvest in your field and forget a swath, do not go back to pick it up; it shall be left for the alien, the orphan and the widow" (Deut. 24:19).
>
> "The poor will always be with you in the land and for that reason I command you to be open handed with your countrymen." (Deut. 15:11).

The extent to which Biblical precepts on labor were observed in ancient Israel and Judea has not been recorded. There were periods in which Jewish commandments were abandoned; and prophets implored the wayward to return to the Torah, stressing the care of those in need. Amos, claiming to be only a herdsman and a gatherer of fruit, lamented the mistreatment of the poor. Isaiah sounded a critical call for social justice. The teachings of learned Jews (called the Early Sages including the outstanding Rabbi Hillel) urged consecration to Biblical admonitions protective of laborers.[5] But political realities were often neither compliant nor benevolent.

There are references to multitudes engaged in building and trades, without explanation of the terms under which they worked. The chroniclers of the Book of Kings stated that King Solomon, in constructing the Temple at Jerusalem and his own palace, levied out of Israel "thirty thousand men"; he dispatched ten thousand a month, rotating one month in Lebanon and two months at home; he had "threescore and ten thousand that bare burdens" and "fourscore thousand hewers in the mountains"; he had three thousand and three supervisors "who ruled over the people that wrought the work." King Hiram of Tyre supplied his own servants to fell trees of cedar and fir, and to float them by sea to Solomon. King Solomon spent seven years building the Temple and thirteen years building his own house, both in great size and splendor. What happened to those who labored on those wondrous edifices? The Bible mentions only that Solomon gave

[5] A. Melamat, "The Period of the Judges" in The World History of the Jewish People, Hott. Ben-Sasson, Harvard Univ. Press, Cambridge, 1976.

Hiram large quantities of wheat and pure oil; and in Israel he "raised a levy" (1 Kings 5: 1-17).

Other records note that the royal workforces of the time were obtained by conscription (corvee) and were subjected to forced labor.[6] How they were compensated is unknown. When Solomon died his son Rehoboam, was confronted at his coronation with the cry of the congregation of Israel, "Thy father made our yoke grievous; now therefore make thou the grievous service of thy father, and his heavy yoke which he put upon us, lighter, and we will serve thee." Old men advised Rehoboam to "speak good words to them, then they will be thy servants forever"; however, he arrogantly replied to the congregation, ". . . whereas my father made your yoke heavy . . . I will add to your yoke; my father also chastised you with whips, but I will chastise you with scorpions". (1 Kings 12: 3-18)

The man sent by Rehoboam to oversee the labor tribute was stoned to death by "all Israel". And soon the kingdoms of Israel and Judah were torn with strife and remained asunder.

The destruction of the Second Temple (ca 70 A.D.) terminated the rule of the Hebrews in the Middle East, except for those communities of Jews permitted by Gentile and Muslim rulers to govern themselves.[7]

The Mishna and the Talmud.

For many years the Biblical commandments remained only oral traditions. Early tablets and scrolls (lost in time) were recited and interpreted by Rabbis. Many teachings of the sages were transcribed; however, not until about 200 A.D. was a renowned codification of Biblical law, the Mishna, completed by Rabbi Judah the Patriarch.[8] That was followed by the publication of the Talmud. The words of the Bible and the commentaries of a succession of scholars were compiled in a Palestinian

[6] A. F. Rainey, "Compulsory Labour Gangs in Ancient Israel," Israel Exploration Journal, Vol.20, pp. 191-202 (1970).

[7] A. Buchler, The Economic Conditions of Judea After the Destruction of the Second Temple, London, 1912.

[8] Philip Blackman, translator, Mishna, Misna Press Ltd, London, 1951.

Talmud (about 375 A.D.) and a Babylonian Talmud (540 A.D.). These served as texts for study by the devout.

As the primary text for rabbinical instruction of pious Jews, the Talmud presented interpretations of Biblical commandments and their application to secular as well as sacred situations. In the Mid-Eastern enclaves of Jews, the reported teachings of Rabbis on how labor should be treated set forth the traditional doctrines of Hebraic labor law. Selected samples, from the Babylonian Talmud,[9] follow.

(1) Labor, in itself, was extolled.

"Great is work, for it honors the workman". Nedarim, 49b. Rabbi Hayya said, "A man who lives from the labor (of his hands) is greater than the one who fears heaven. For with regard to . . . the man who lives from his own work, it is written: When thou eatest the labor of thy hands, happy shalt thou be, and it shall be well with thee. Happy shalt thou be in this world, and it shall be well with thee in the world to come. But of the man that fears heaven, it is not written, and it shall be well with thee" Berakoth, 41.

"Work is a splendid thing to make one warm" Gittin, 321. ". . .Do not say, 'I am a priest and a great man and it is beneath my dignity'. The greatest man is not degraded by honest work" Baba Bithra, 455.

(2) The obligation of the laborer to work diligently and properly was also stressed.

A Rabbi, consulted while he was working on a scaffold, replied, "I cannot come down because I am hired by the day" Exod. XIII,1. Another who ignored a salutation while he was ploughing explained, "I hired myself out for the day, so I was of the opinion that I had no right to interrupt my work" Taan., 23 a,b. A day worker may not work the night before and thereby diminish his work for his employer. Dammai, 26b. "A gardener who spoiled his work may be fired without

[9] I. Epstein, ed., The Babylonian Talmud (trans), London, Sonsino Press, 1961.

warning—the same for a butcher, cupper, town scribe" Baba Mez'm 625.

(3) Payment for labor was set forth for occupations of the times and in the manner of the day.

"According to the labor is the reward" Alot-Mishna, V,6. A harvest laborer hired for a denarius (coin) a day and paid in advance; but who is worth a sela (4 denarii) a day, should receive a sela a day. The excess is regarded as usury. However, if he is hired for the season at one denarius a day and paid in advance, the employer may have the benefit of the difference. Baba Bathra, 353.

A hiring retracted may lead to resentment; but no legal redress. However, if workers go to the scene of the labor, if drivers engaged to carry a load of grain go to the place and are prevented from performing, find no grain, or if laborers hired to plough go and find a swamp unfit for ploughing, they must be paid in full. Baba Mez'ia, 441.

"Raising or caring for cattle may be for a stipulated amount of money and the head of cattle and a share of profit" Baba Mez'ia, 68a.

"A man may not commission a tradesman on a half profit basis. . .unless he pays him a wage as a worker" Baba Mez'ia, Mishma, 397.

"The worker in the vineyard may eat grapes, but not figs. If he is collecting his master's figs, he may eat figs but not grapes." Rabbi Elazar said he may not eat more than his day's wage "but the sages say that the words in Deuteronomy xxxiii, 24 'at his own pleasure' show that he may." On the other hand, the Biblical words, 'thou shalt not put any in thy vessel' is interpreted strictly when the laborer is filling his master's vessels. Ki Teze, 255f, 121b.

"Who defers paying the wages of a hired laborer transgresses five commandments of the Torah: 'Thou shalt not oppress thy neighbor', Lev. xix,13. 'Neither shalt thou rob him'. Ibid. 'Thou shalt not oppress a hired servant that is poor and needy'. Deut. xxiv, 14; 'The wages of a hired servant shall not abide with thee all night until the morning'. Lev. supra; 'In his day shalt thou give him his hire', Deut. 24 and

'Neither shall the sun go down upon it'. ibid. Baba Mez'ia iiia."

(4) With respect to hours of work and meals.

It was said, "Everything depends on local custom, to commence early or to work late, to supply food, to provide amelish" Baba Mez'ea, 476.

(5) Talmudists made some inconsonant references to poverty as they saw it.

The compassionate and worldly-wise said, "all other sufferings in one pan, and poverty in the other, and the scales would balance" Exod., R. Mishpatim, xxi, 12, 14; also, "Worse is poverty in a man's house than fifty plagues" B.B. 116a. Another seeking to preserve faith among those in dire need wrote, "Elijah said, God looked about among all good qualities to give to Israel, and he found nothing better than poverty. So people say, 'Poverty suits Israel as a red bridle suits a white horse' " Hag. 9b.

(6) Many provisions in the Talmud relating to labor relations, pertinent to their day, call for further interpretation.

(1) "The first hour of the day is the mealtime for gladiators, the second for robbers, the third for heirs, the fourth for laborers, the fifth for all other people" (Shabbath 1,36). Was this poetic rumination or recital of a norm? (2) "A man may not hire a laborer on the condition that the son (of the laborer) should gather the gleanings after him" (Pe'ah, 27). Was that a restriction upon child labor? (3) Wages were to be paid from the Temple Funds for the "learned men who taught the priests the laws of ritual slaughter," for "book readers in Jerusalem" and for the "women who wove the (Temple) curtains." Were they public employees? (4) The "judges of Civil Law in Jerusalem" were paid 99 maneh a month out of Temple Funds, and it is stated, 'If they were not satisfied, they were given an increase" (Kathuboth II, 673). Did that imply collective negotiation?

(7) Slavery, as recognized in the Bible, was further defined and delimited in the Talmud.

A distinction was made between Israelites who were enslaved and Gentile slaves. The former, purchased or bound over by court judgment, were to be freed after six years of service (Exod. 21: 2) and not forced to do shameful tasks such as washing the master's feet or conveying him in a sedan; nor should he be obliged to do work other than his usual occupation (Mech., 75 a,b). The Hebrew master may not eat clean bread and his Hebrew slave eat mouldy bread; nor may the master sleep on soft cushions and the slave on straw (Ked. 20a). The Gentile slave must be circumcised with his consent or be sold (Job, 48b). He was exempted from wearing phylacteries or reciting the liturgy. He was not counted in the requirement of a quorum of ten for prayer (Ber. III,3); nor was he given the funeral honors bestowed upon Israelites (Ber. 11, 7).

Other general norms reflected a more critical view of slavery. A half slave works one day for his master and one day for himself (Pesaheim, 467). The master who kills a slave shall be punished (Mech. 83a); and if he knocks out a slave's tooth or eye, the slave shall go free. (Mech 85a). Freedom could also be obtained by purchase, a certificate of manumission (Kid, 1,3), or by the last will of a master (Pe'ah, Meshoah 8,17).

In the great dispersion of Jews that ensued upon the fall of the Temples, a devotion to the Book continued, and many discourses upon the Law were written. Learned Rabbis, known as the Gemara, recorded their commentaries upon the Mishna, and another group of respected Rabbis, known as the Geonim, became noted for their responses to inquiries from perplexed Jews. Their teachings were augmented by the writings of the famed Maimonides and other Talmudic scholars.

Maimonides, regarded as the outstanding Jewish philosopher of the Middle Ages, wrote a code of conduct for pious Jews. He referred to Biblical texts, with extrapolations pertinent to his time. Typical are these comments.[10]

> If a laborer is hired to water a field and rain comes, he is paid only for the work performed; but if a river overflows, he is paid his wages in full because it was heaven that helped him.
>
> A tiller of the soil, accustomed to great exertion, when he finishes before the end of the day is paid for a full day because he would be weakened by lack of work.
>
> A worker is enjoined not to deprive his employer of the benefit of his work by idling away his time.
>
> A hired man who takes an oath that he has not received his hire is to be paid.

Thus Biblical injunctions pertaining to labor were interpreted by the learned in the Talmud and other rabbinical writings. They were recorded along with lengthy treatises of a theological nature; which for generation after generation served as the text books of Hebraic study. As civilization advanced, commentators elaborated upon the labor provisions of the Torah in an increasingly humane spirit. The limitations upon the taking of slaves, the obligation to treat them justly, and the injunctions to free slaves were stressed. Rules for fair treatment of hired servants were recognized as terms of a covenant with God. These religious and secular precepts became premises from which Talmudists and observing Jews formulated rules for dealing with ever changing labor situations.[11]

THE LAWS OF MIDDLE EAST CONQUERORS

Assyrians, Persians, Romans and Babylonians, in succession took over Jerusalem as well as other parts of the Middle East. They had legal systems of their own including labor regulations. Undoubtedly, there was an interaction between the old and new norms of conduct every time a government was supplanted. However, their influences upon recent constitutional and statu-

[10] Jacob J. Rabinowitz, trans. Code of Maimonides. Vol.13, Ch.IX-XXIII on Hiring. Yale Univ. Press. New Haven, 1949.

[11] Israel H. Weisfeld, Labor Legislation in the Bible and Talmud, Yeshiva Univ. Press. New York, 1974.

tory provisions in the Middle East are only dimly discernible and therefor I give them only a passing nod.

THE LAW OF THE CHRISTIAN CRUSADERS

The Christian crusades brought to the Middle East a number of rulers who carried with them the labor rules of feudalism.

In their religious thinking they undoubtedly recognized the labor norms propounded by Christ's apostles Luke and Paul, acknowledging the worth of each worker and imploring masters to give their servants what is just. How they applied those precepts has not been recorded. Church advisors of crusaders probably referred them to biblical parables for guidance on master and servant relationships.

The Christian kings, however, perceived secular law as principles governing a feudal society. Their legal concepts and judgments were primarily concerned with fealty between lords and vassals. Armed assistance, in large and small conflicts, was the most important service rendered and the granting of fiefs in land was the chief form of compensation. Formal civil law dealt essentially with land ownership, marriage, dowries, and inheritance among the royalty, the nobility, the barons, knights and landed gentry. Labor by peasants, household servants, and to a large extent by artisans and traders, was not deemed of sufficient importance to require written laws.

An early codification of the law of the Crusaders is known as the Assises de Jerusalem.[12] In the year 1109, the Christian princes and barons who had conquered Jerusalem chose as their king, Duke Godfrey of Boullion. It is said he took counsel with the patriarchs and wise men from various lands and asked each about the usages and customs of his country. These were recorded; then Godfrey ordered them to be read and examined. With the consent of his followers, he decreed that the Assises be maintained as the law of the realm in Jerusalem.

[12] Assises de Jerusalem ou Recueil des Ouvrages de Jurisprudence composes pendant le XIII siecle dans les Royaumes de Jerusalem et de Chypre. Paris. Imprimerie Royale MDCCCXLIII

There were few provisions in the Assises de Jerusalem pertaining to serfs, the most numerous workers at that time. Certain restrictions were noted. Serfs had no power to sell, give, or rent their possessions. They could not plead in court. Serfs owed the king military service for two days a week. They apparently labored at the unrestrained will of the owners of the land to which they were attached. The extent of their servitude may be inferred from the code provision that forbade their masters to imprison them for more than three days.

Slavery was encountered by crusaders and though many came from lands that had abolished that institution, the Assises de Jerusalem continued to recognize the slavery (of Latins, Christians, Jews, Samaritans, Syrians, and Saracens). Fugitive slaves had to be returned; but those who became Christians were given their liberty. Manumission was also accredited.

Although artisans and traders were a vital part of the population, it was not seen necessary to refer to their conditions of work or employment in the Assises de Jerusalem.

A later legal code of feudalism, called the Assises of Romania,[13] was formulated in the 14th century for the principality of Achaia or Morea (comprising what is now the Greek archipelago), and it reflected usages throughout the Middle East. It differed in some respects from the Jerusalem Assises; but it was similarly sparse with respect to the work of serfs or other servants and artisans. The lord of a serf, it specified, could allow him to engage in trade with personal responsibility; but if the serf failed to pay his debts, the creditor who had his goods sold and who had him imprisoned was required to leave him a pair of oxen and an ass (presumably to resume his customary farming).

The crusaders were apparently more interested in conquest than in evangelism and when overcome by the Muslims, they left no distinctive doctrines as a tradition in the labor law of the Middle East.

[13] John L. Lamonte, ed. The Assizes of Romania. Philadelphia Univ. of Pennsylvania Press, 1949.

HISTORICAL ANTECEDENTS

ISLAMIC LABOR LAW

For over a thousand years, Islam has been the dominant cultural ingredient in the Middle East. It has been a pervasive force in the transformation of many social institutions—simple agricultural communities, mercantile cities, warring societies, political empires, reclusive enclaves, and bustling centers of world trade and finance. Labor relations in Muslim countries have been myriad and kaleidoscopic. At all times, Islamic rulers have claimed to remain constant in their faith; and portions of the sacred law, known as the Shariah, have been applied to secular relationships, including labor relations.

A bird's-eye view of the spread of Islam (from 610 to 1949 A.D.) may help set the stage on which governments laid down the law we wish to observe. Starting from two tiny towns, Medina and Mecca, Islam reached out to all of the Arabian Peninsula, Persia, and Turkey, and across Northern Africa to and including Spain. Christian Europe sought to roll it back in unsuccessful crusades. Not until Muslims inhabited Spain for over 800 years was it possible to expel them. Then after the growth of new empires, the British and the French seized footholds in Egypt and Algiers and established protectorates over most of the Arab Sultanates. World War I brought the defeat of the Ottoman Empire. England, in honoring some of its supporters, promised Palestine to the Jews, and with the sanction of the League of Nations, Israel became a new state. The rest of the Arab states asserted their independence and proclaimed their laws, including labor law, in the spirit of Islam.

In 610 A.D., the Prophet Muhammed announced his first revelation of the divine word of Allah. He founded a faith in which every man and woman owed primary allegiance to Allah and undertook to live in all respects as Allah had dictated. The Prophet was the human being through whom Allah spoke, and Allah's message was recorded in the Koran. Muhammed spread the gospel in Mecca and Medina to an increasing number of believers, even over the violent opposition of non-Muslims. His rule was personal and direct though frequently in consultation with his followers. After his death, the Prophet's teachings and exemplary acts, as recalled by his companions, were preserved in documents called the Sunna. The Koran and the Sunna became the basic texts of Islamic jurisprudence.

Little was recorded about labor conditions at the time. Farmers, artisans, and merchants were dominant members of the community; but slaves and hired servants, in unknown numbers, were relied upon. (Muhammed was, for a period, the leader of a camel caravan carrying goods to distant markets.) Historians have referred to the presence of many poor and to Muhammed's recognition that all persons were equal before God and were to be treated justly.

The Koran

The Koran is a spiritual document (the revealed word of Allah) set forth in poetic verses.[14] They contain some precepts that may be regarded as labor laws, but they were presented as spiritual commandments. They lead to rewards in the hereafter as well as on earth. The performance of work and the doing of good deeds were not particularly differentiated. The following are selected examples of Koranic labor provisions.

> "Man is made for toil and struggle. Let him not boast of ease and wealth. He will be called to account for all his doings. Let him use his God-given faculties and tread the steep path that leads to Heaven's Heights" (Sura XC:1-20).
>
> "The life of this world is but a plan and a pastime, but if you believe and fear Allah and avoid evil, He will grant you your wages and will not ask you (to give up) your wealth" (Sura XLVII:36).
>
> "To men there is a reward for what they have earned (and likewise) to women there is a reward for what they have earned, and ask Allah of His Bounty" (Sura IV:32).
>
> Many other passages refer to the essential requirement of justice, in the conduct of Muslim persons. Even those "abased in the land" are to be recipients of justice and might even be elevated as leaders (Sura XXVIII:4-5).

[14] A. Yusuf Ali, trans., The Holy Qur'an, Amana Corp., Brentwood, Md., 1983.

Slavery was a common source of labor; but the Koran contained verses that promoted manumission.

"And what will explain to thee the path that is steep? It is freeing the bondsman" (Sura XC:12,13).

"And a believing slave shall be freed" (Sura IV:92).

"For expiation. . .give a slave his freedom" (Sura V:89).

"It is righteousness. . .to spend of your substence . . . for the ransom of slaves" (Sura II:177).

"And if any of your slaves ask for a deed in writing (to enable them to earn their freedom for a certain sum) give them such a deed" (Sura XXIV:33).

The Sunna

The other fundamental compendium of Islamic teaching, the Sunna, reported a great many sayings of Muhammed.[15] Among these, there were a number that dealt with employment, the payment of workers and the treatment of slaves. Illustrative of the manner in which Muhammed had applied the tenets of Islam to the laborers of his day are the following portions of the Sunna. (The English translation may not convey all nuances apparent to the devout Muslim).

(a) The Prophet encourages the hiring of the pious and the honest but not "anybody who demands it earnestly" (par. 461, 462).

(b) The Prophet had shepherded sheep for compensation (par.463).

(c) The Prophet hired pagans "if necessary or if no Muslim was available" (par. 464,465).

(d) An employee for a term of several years need not have the nature of his work spelled out (par. 466).

(e) Wages may be taken for the repair of a wall about to fall (par. 467).

(f) The Prophet employed Muslims for more than he paid others, for that was his blessing to bestow upon whomever he wished (par. 468).

[15] Dr. Muhammad M. Khan, Sahil Al Bukhari, Vol. 3, Islamic Univ., Al Medina al Munauwaq, Pakistan, 1971.

(g) The Prophet said Allah would be an antagonist on the Day of Resurrection to persons who made a covenant in his name and were treacherous, who sold a free person and ate his price, or who employed someone and took full work from him but did not pay him for his labour (par. 470).

(h) The Prophet said that when employees worked part of the time and then abandoned their tasks and others completed the tasks the employer should pay the latter the wages of the former for "the light of guidance they have accepted willingly" (par. 471).

(i) Three men, trapped in a cave by a rock that fell across the entrance, asked Allah to rescue them. When one explained he had fed his parents before his children, the rock shifted a little; when another said he preserved the chastity of a niece whom he desired, the rock shifted only a little more; and when the third told that after one of his employees wasn't paid, he invested the unpaid wages and got much property thereby, but later he gave the hired man his camels, cows, sheep and slaves to please Allah, the rock shifted completely and the three got out walking (par. 472,526).

(j) When the Prophet told certain men to give charity; they took work as porters to earn two hand-fulls of food which they gave to charity; and now they have one-hundred thousand Dinars (par. 473).

(k) The Prophet said Muslims should abide by the conditions of their agreements (par. 473).

(l) It is permissible for a Muslim to work as an employee for pagans in a land of infidelity (par. 475).

(m) It is legal for a teacher of the Quran or for one who heals the sick by reciting divine speech to receive compensation for his tuition (par. 476).

(n) The Prophet ordered payment be given one who had cupped him, and the Prophet interceded with the latter's masters to reduce his taxes (par. 477-481).

(o) The Prophet regarded as illegal "the price of a dog, the earnings of a prostitute and the charges taken by a soothsayer" (par.482,483).

(p) The Prophet said, "Nobody has ever eaten a better

meal than that which he has earned by working with his own hands" (par. 286.)

(q) The Prophet said, "One would rather cut and carry a bundle of wood on his back than ask somebody who may or may not give him" (par. 288).

(r) "The Prophet concluded a contract with the people of Khaibar to utilize the land on the condition that half the products of fruits or vegetation would be their share" (par. 521,524, 881).

(s) The Prophet said, "He who cultivates land that does not belong to anybody is more rightful (to own it") (par. 528).

(t) The Prophet said "a servant is a guardian of his master's property and is responsible for it" (par. 592).

(u) The Prophet said, that when one manumits his share of a jointly possessed slave, "it is essential for him to manumit the slave completely if he has sufficient money. Otherwise he should look for some work for the slave (to earn what would enable him to emancipate himself) without overburdening him with work" (par. 682).

(v) When one says a slave is for Allah, he frees him (par. 707-709).

(w) The Prophet said, "Your slaves are your brethren upon whom Allah has given you authority. So if one has one's brethren under one's control, one should feed them with the likes of what one eats and clothe them with the like of what one wears. You should not overburden them with what they cannot bear, and if you do so, help them (in their hard job)" (par. 721).

(x) The Prophet said it is obligatory for a master to give a slave a writing of emancipation if he knows the slave has money or property (par.735).

Upon the death of Muhammed, there followed a succession of rulers, selected from his companions and adherents, to lead the faithful in accordance with the words of the Koran. They ruled over multitudes of persons, in many lands, and under ever changing geo-political circumstances. A very brief mention of significant periods may indicate the development of law and labor regulation.[16]

From 661 to 1258, there was a rapid territorial expansion of Islamic rule, extending from the Middle East to Spain, followed by some contraction and cultural consolidation. Caliphs issued new rules of government. Qadis rendered judgment in cases that came before them. Religious leaders, the Ulama, vied with the lay governors for control of Islamic society and though the Ulama were unable to acquire all the governmental power that they desired, they did achieve an acceptance of the principle that Islamic law must be observed.

Ijma, Qijas, Ijtihad

Orthodox (Sunni) scholars established four schools of law—the Hanafi, Maliki, Shaf'i, and the Hanbali.[17] Despite theological differences, they all accepted the four classical sources of Islamic law—the *Koran*, (the word of Allah), the *Sunna* (the words and deeds of Muhammed), the *Ijma* (doctrines reached by consensus among pious, legal scholars), and the *Qijas* (rules for new situations arrived at by analogy with the norms in the foregoing, and accepted by the scholars). Some heterodox Muslims (the Ibadi and the Shi'a) propounded variant theological doctrines not particularly pertinent to labor law.

Scholars wrote glosses on the Koran and Sunna and other treatises on Islamic jurisprudence. They developed a process of legal reasoning, called Ijtihad or independent reasoning, by jurists who applied Islamic precepts to major questions raised in novel situations.

By 923 A.D. leading Islamic jurists reached the opinion that the legal system was complete; Islam was all sufficient, all encom-

[16] Kemal A. Faruki. The Evolution of Islam. Constitutional Theory and Practice. National Publishing House Ltd. Karachi. 1971. Same. The Constitutional and Legal Role of the Umma. Ma'Aref Ltd. Karachi. 1979.

[17] They differed essentially on rules of succession for Islamic leadership, and on the relationship between religious leaders (the imams) and secular leaders (the caliphs). Their teachings on religious practices (such as prayer, pilgrimage, taxes, charitable endowments, marriage, divorce, inheritance) differed in ways that were not designed to affect labor relations.

passing, and omni-competent; and after centuries of intellectual struggle over the law, nothing more need be said. So there was "a closing of the gates of Ijtihad," and for a few hundred years Caliphs and jurists refrained from approving new rules of law by analogy with the old, and relied upon the sacred Islamic sources for their rulings as explained by the recognized schools of law.

Over the years, the faithful in Islam developed several religious sects—(principally the Sunni and the Shi'a; but also the Wahhabi, the Ibadi, the Bahai and some lesser or presently inactive groups). These sects influenced the selection of rulers and the ritualistic practices of Islam. Fundamental tenets concerning prayers, fasting, a pilgrimage to Mecca, the giving of charity, and the payment of a tax to the community became universal pillars of the religion. Rules of personal relationships in the family, marriage, divorce and inheritance; and rules of trade relationships in selling, buying and renting were enunciated as religious as well as secular requirements. Some norms of labor relations were included along with the other doctrines as ways in which man must serve Allah. The Shariah was the encompassing law of Islam, and the history of Islam has been replete with endless discussion of the role of the Shariah in the lives of Muslims. The differences among Islamic sects did not significantly affect the principles governing labor.[18]

The era 1258 to 1500 saw a multiplicity of Islamic kingdoms and principalities, at times warring with each other and on occasion joining in a common purpose against outsiders, such as the Christian crusaders. The legal scholars, "the men of the pen" extolled the sacred law. Except for some attempts to introduce elements of mysticism, they left the Shariah as it was. In this period, Muslim communities were governed by absolute Islamic

[18] I have been unable to find any significant difference on labor law in the doctrines of the Sunni and Shi'ite sects. An early difference in their treatment of a female slave who bore a child to her master is no longer of importance. See Joseph Schact. The Origins of Muhammedian Jurisprudence. Clarendon Press. Oxford 1950, pp 264-5. The recent enactment of labor law in predominantly Shi'ite Iran and Sunni Iraq, as indicated below, show no marked disparities.

rulers, not known for any special concern over labor law. Day-to-day labor patterns were set by employers and custom.

The following era, 1500 to 1800, was characterized by the emergence of three imperial Islamic states—the Safani, Ottoman, and Mughal. Government was institutionalized, centrally and peripherally. Hierarchical officials administered the Shariah with such adaptations to new situations as they found desirable.

From 1800 to 1925, European powers made political inroads into Muslim nations. The French, Russians and British occupied Muslim territories or obtained treaties giving the Europeans control over foreign trade and international relations. New legislation after 1826 contracted the sphere of adjudication in Shariah courts.

Majelle

Toward the height of the Ottoman Empire, a constitution (the Majelle) was formulated to establish a constitutional monarchy (1876).[19] It contained many specific rules for the letting or hiring of servants, laborers and artisans, such as the following.

> "468 . . . the hired person until the hire is paid can refuse to do the work."
>
> "482. If no agreement has been made for a deferred payment of a person hired to do work, and he is a person who causes a change by his work, like a tailor, dyer or washer, there is a right to keep possession of the thing delivered to him to do the work on for his pay."
>
> "483. For a hired person, who does not cause any change by his work, like a porter and a sailor . . . if the property is destroyed in his hands, when he keeps possession of it, he pays compensation."
>
> "495. In case someone hires a workman to do a day's work, from sunrise to Asr (prayer time two hours before sunset) or to sunset, in calculating the time of work, effect is given to that which is the custom of the town."
>
> "565. If someone employs a workman without naming the

[19] C.R. Tyser, trans., The Majelle, All Pakistan Legal Decisions, Lahore, 1901.

> wage, if there is a known daily wage, he gives the known wage. If not, he gives a wage equivalent to the work."
>
> "566. . . . the hiring of a wet nurse, in accordance with a custom for her clothes to be made, is permitted, and if the sort of clothes . . . has not been described, clothes of a middling quality must be given."
>
> "568. . . . a master hired to teach . . . has a right to the wage by being ready and willing to teach, whether the pupil studies or not."
>
> "569. When a man give his son to a master of a trade that he may learn an art . . . (without stipulating a wage) it is done according to what is the use and custom in the town."
>
> "571. When a person has been hired to do a work himself that is to say to do it by his personal work, he cannot employ another in his place."
>
> "576. It is not necessary for the hirer to feed the person hired. Unless there is a custom in the town."

The Majelle constitution established a limited constitutional monarchy over the entire Ottoman empire. It was put into effect for only several years, but it continued as a legal code in several Middle East countries (notably in Jordan).

There are many Koranic verses which do not mention workers, but which if applied broadly to human beings would create a social situation in which employers and employees might interact in an uniquely Islamic fashion. The Koran mandates that everyone should share the surplus of his good fortune (over and above his own needs) with those whose needs are not met. The surplus must not be retained; and payment by every Muslim of an annual tax (Zakat) to the community shall create a fund in which those in need shall have a "right" to partake. Additional distributions of a charitable nature must be given by all the faithful to the poor. In business dealings, certain rules must be obeyed. All contracts must provide for an exchange of equivalent values; the strong must not take advantage of the weak. Interest is not to be received on advances of money. Observance of these tenets by believers shall result in rewards both in this life and in the everlasting hereafter.

The extent to which Islamic religious principles were practiced by employers in the Middle East has not been elucidated in historical documents. It is possible that religious morality prompted pious employers at various times to treat their employees in a compassionate and magnanimous manner; but there is no indication of the extent, if any, that Muslim government or Islamic society distinguished itself by more humanitarian labor policies than were characteristic of other governments of the time. Rulers varied from despots to enlightened sponsors of science and learning. The spirit of the Shariah, however, promoted charity and compassion as a moral imperative.

Regardless of the large number of governmental permutations in the Middle East, scholarly disputations have wrestled with the interpretation of the Koran and Sunna.[20] They have even questioned whether one might overrule the other. How to resolve ambiguities was explored extensively. Consensus was obtained over the addition of the Ijma, and flexibility was gained in the analogical application of the strictly sacred classical sources to new situations (Qijas). Although the closing of the gates of Ijtihad retained doctrinal purity for years, and the primacy of the Shariah has always been maintained, labor law has undergone transformations throughout the Middle East. Slavery was eliminated by rules of manumission and humane considerations prescribed in the Koran. Master and servant relations generally were spelled out anew, under the influence of a miscellany of spiritual, economic and political interests.

Islamic accommodation to modern world developments took many forms. Imperial decrees, still affirming the Shariah as Islamic law, made allowances for custom and State necessity. Commercial and labor law followed established secular practices.

[20] Duncan MacDonald. Development of Muslim Jurisprudence and Constitutional Theory, Darf Publishing, London, 1985. Abdulrahman Abdul Kadir Kurdi. The Islamic State. Mansell Publishing Ltd. London and New York. 1984. S. Faroog Hassan. The Islamic Republic, Law and Economy. Aziz Publishers. Lahore, 1984. Kemal A. Faruki. The Evolution of Islamic Constitutional Theory and Practice. National Publ. House, Karachi, 1971. M. Khadduri and H. Liebesny, eds., Law in the Middle East. Middle East Institute. Washington, Vol.1, Ch.3.

To avoid even the appearance of an abandonment of the Shariah, several legalistic techniques were utilized. The jurisdiction of the judges in the Shariah (Qadi) courts was held aloof from many secular matters which were then adjudicated by other officials, often under the influence of other legal systems. The administration of justice was also entrusted to trade guilds and, in rural areas, to tribal rulers. Some qadis found a way around strict provisions of the orthodox Shariah by resorting, at times quite arbitrarily, to secular decrees of the rulers. Even some of the traditional Islamic rules relating to marital status, inheritance and pious foundations were consciously altered by legal decrees or verbal stratagems. In the field of labor law, slavery was eventually forbidden. Master and servant relationships followed custom. The moral values of the Koran and the Sunna were relegated to the personal lives of the pious.

In the inter-war years (1925 to 1945), Western influences penetrated Islamic thought and stimulated demands for independence in Muslim nations. By 1971, all the Muslim states in the Middle East had achieved independence, as monarchies or republics. The Shariah was declared basic to their law. However, secular codes were adopted, including labor codes. The extent to which the codes reflected norms of the Shariah will be commented upon below.

In 1948, Palestine, under a British mandate, was partitioned by the United Nations, and Israel was set apart as a homeland for Jews. Although family and religious concerns of Christians and Muslims were assigned to religious courts, labor relations were left to the Israeli civil courts. Unfulfilled desires of both Arabs and Jews led to warfare; and many aspects of human relations including labor relations have been left unsettled.

The Hebraic and Islamic labor law precepts recounted above were stored as sacks of seed or kegs of wine in the warehouses of the Middle East, available to congregants in succeeding generations. Adherents of Judaism and Islam have made many selections. Early labor norms were formulated when labor was essentially agricultural, with an outcropping of artisan, mercantile and maritime workers. They were reviewed in light of the industrial revolution. Painstakingly, scholars in both religions have distinguished between the word of God and interpretations, between divine revelation and mortal comprehension. The extent to which modern constitutions, labor codes, supplemental statutes and treaties have reflected historical antecedents will be disclosed in later chapters.

HEBRAIC LAW REFERENCES

Primary Sources

Holy Bible	The Holy Bible, King James version. American Bible Society. New York, 1958.
Mishna	Mishna, Philip Blackman, tr. London, Mishna Press Ltd. 1951.
Talmud	The Babylonian Talmud. I. Epstein, ed. London, Soncino Press, 1961.
Maimonides	Code of Maimonides. J.J. Rabinowitz, tr. New Haven, Yale Univ. Press, 1949.

Treatises

A. Melamat, "The Period of the Judges" in the World History of the Jewish People, H.H. Ben-Sasson, Harvard Univ. Press, Cambridge, 1976.

N. Gross, ed., Jewish Economic History, Jerusalem, 1975.

Marcus Arkin, Aspects of Jewish Economic History, Jewish Publication Society of America, Philadelphia, 1975.

Israel H. Weisfeld, Labor Legislation in the Bible and the Talmud, Yeshiva Univ. Press, New York, 1974.

M. Smith, Palestinian Parties and Politics that Shaped the Old Testament, N.Y. & London, 1971.

A.F. Rainey, "Compulsory Labour Gangs in Ancient Israel," Israel Exploration Journal, Vol.20, p.191-202, 1970.

M. Roth, The Laws in the Pentateuch & Other Essays, Edinburgh & London, 1966.

S. Wittmayer Baron, A Social and Religious History of the Jews, 2nd ed., Columbia Univ. Press, New York, 1952.

HISTORICAL ANTECEDENTS

L. Finkelstein, Jewish Self-Goverment in the Middle Ages, New York, 1924.

A. Buchler, The Economic Conditions of Judea After the Destruction of the Second Temple, London, 1912.

ISLAMIC LAW REFERENCES

Primary Sources

Koran	A. Yusuf Ali, trans., The Holy Qur'an, Amana Corp., Brentwood, Md., 1983.
Sunna	Dr. Muhammad M. Kan, Sahil Al Bukhari, Vol. 3, Islamic Univ., Al Medina al Munauwaq, Pakistan, 1971.
Majelle	The Majelle. C.R. Tyser, tr. Lahore, 1901.

Treatises

Leonard Binder, Islamic Liberalism: A Critique of Development Ideologies, Univ. Chicago Press, Chicago, 1988.

Sayed Hassan Amin, Islamic Law in the Contemporary World, Royston Ltd., Glasgow, 1985.

Pierre Rondot, "Islam et Declaration des Droits de L'Homme, Defense National, Jan., 1985.

Khalid M. Ishaq, "Islam and Law in the Twenty-First Century," Islamic & Comparative Law Quarterly, Vol.5, No.3-4, 1985.

Duncan MacDonald, Development of Muslim Theology, Jurisprudence & Constitutional Theory, Darf Publishing, London, 1985.

Origin & Development of Islamic Law (Series: Law in the Middle East, Vol.1) AMS Press, New York, 1984.

Khalid Ishaq, "State & Constitution in Islam," Islamic Comparative Law Quarterly, Vol.4, No.1-2, May-June, 1984.

Majid Khadduri, The Islamic Conception of Justice, John Hopkins Univ. Press, Baltimore, 1984.

Abdulrahman A.K. Kurdi, The Islamic State: A Study Based on the Islamic Holy Constitution, Mansell Publishing Ltd., London & NY, 1984.

S. Farooq Hassan, The Islamic Republic: Politics, Law & Economy, Aziz Publishers, Lahore, 1984.

Tahir Mahmood, "The Islamic Law on Human Rights", Islamic & Comparative Law Quarterly, Vol. IV, No.1-2, 1984.

Ibrahim Tokhais, Social Justice in Islamic Law, Univ. Microfilms Int'l., Ann Arbor,1982.

Noel J. Coulson, Conflicts & Tensions in Islamic Jurisprudence, Univ. of Chicago Press, Chicago & London, 1982.

Kemal Faruki, The Constitutional and Legal Role of the Umma, Ma'Aref Ltd., Karachi, 1979.

Anwar Bez, "Civil & Political Rights in Islam," Al-Ithihad, Jan-April, 1977.

Kemal Faruki, The Evolution of Islam in Constitutional Theory and Practice, National Publishing House, Ltd, Karachi, 1971.

W. 'Arafat, "The Attitude of Islam to Slavery," Islamic Quarterly, Vol.10, 1966.

Joseph Schact, An Introduction to Islamic Law, Clarendon Press, Oxford, 1964.

J.N.D. Anderson, Islamic Law in the Modern World, N.Y. Univ. Press, 1959

M.S. Husaini, The Constitution of the Arab Empire, Orientalia, Lahore, 1959.

Richard Nolte, "The Rule of Law in the Arab Middle East," The Muslim World; Vol. XLVIII, No.4, October, 1958.

Majid Khadduri and Herbert Liebsny, eds. Law in the Middle East, Vol. 1, Origin and Development of Islamic Law, The Middle East Institute, Wash. D.C., 1955.

Joseph Schact, The Origins of Muhammadian Jurisprudence, Clarendon Press, Oxford, 1950.

Chapter 2

THE MODERN MILIEU

All the nations now in the Middle East have striven to preserve their traditions; but events in and out of two World Wars have propelled them into currents of a changing universe. Try as they might to frame their individual destinies, they have been engulfed in a sputtering world constantly placing them in the midst of new scenes. Even if we confine our attention to how those countries have dealt with the plight or well being of their workers, we must delve into a myriad of interacting factors. There is a Middle East atmosphere in which labor problems are formed and solutions are devised.

The enveloping forces are innumerable; but some stand out prominently and a few brief descriptions may offer a backdrop for comprehending and comparing the labor laws of the Middle East. I have selected several significant aspects of the over-all situation and will endeavor to delineate, in very succinct form, those which appear meaningful and influential in the current of labor laws in the region.

Focal topics for this introductory exposition are 1 - the emergence of the several countries, 2 - the place of labor law in their legal systems, 3 - the tremendous in-pouring of oil revenue, 4 - the hectic distribution of the labor force, 5 - the dislocation of migrant workers, 6 - thc turmoil of religious strife, 7 - the devastation of coups and ongoing wars, and 8 - the purposeful planning for national development. Regardless of the individualities of the several Middle East governments, they all share these features.

THE EMERGENT GOVERNMENTS

Preliminary to our consideration of the present governments in the Middle East, we should designate which countries constitute, for our purpose,the Middle East. In public discourse, the Middle East has been set off as a portion of the world with common cultural traits, located generally to the south and east of the Mediterranean; but the inclusion or exclusion of states has varied with the interests and perspectives of each commentator. If religion were a prime consideration in my view of the region, several countries along the north of Africa and the European entrance to Asia would necessarily be included in my reference to the Middle East. Surely, Egypt and Turkey should be noted for their profound influences upon the rest of the Muslim states. Yet I have found the labor laws of those two countries better placed in the contexts of Africa and Europe, and I shall recall their impact upon Middle East countries only peripherally. The cluster of Middle East countries that lends itself to more intimate and immediate relationships in the field of labor law are those that abut upon the Persian Gulf or that lie within the Arabian Peninsula. These are, alphabetically, Bahrain, Iran, Iraq, Israel, Jordan, Kuwait, Lebanon, Oman, Occupied Palestine, Qatar, Saudi Arabia, Syria, United Arab Emirates, Yemen Arab Republic, and the People's Democratic Republic of Yemen.

Most of these governments acquired an independent status after World War II. Iran, Iraq, Lebanon, and Syria somewhat earlier, but others as late as 1971. Each has claimed to be a sovereign entity. Each has its own labor law, with distinguishing characteristics. All of the current Middle East peoples have histories going back to antiquity, but governments of recent origin.

The Arab States

Bahrain.

The islands that make up Bahrain were dominated by ancient Assyrians, Babylonians, Persians, from 2000 B.C. to a century and a half into the Christian era when the Portuguese took over. They were overthrown by Persians, who after another 150 years were disestablished by the current ruling Arab dynasty. The British entered into treaty arrangements protecting the local rulers from Iranian claims, thereby extending the influence of the

British Empire for another century, until the United Nations granted Bahrain full independence in 1971. Bahrain adopted the first written constitution for its Kingdom in 1973. Since its National Assembly was dissolved in 1975, it has been ruled by decree of the Amir. Its current Head of State is Amir Shaik Isa Bin-Sulman al Khalifa, of a dynasty in existence since 1783.

Iraq

Over 3000 years ago, the Sumerians forged a civilization in the land between the Tigris and Euphrates rivers. They merged with Akkadians, and later Babylonians. Arabs laid siege and the land became part of the Ottoman Empire for many centuries. In the first World War, the British seized control of Iraq, only to be ousted by a revolution (1920-21). The League of Nations created a mandate over it which was administered by the British for the next decade. After independence, an Iraqi monarchy ruled precariously until Iraq joined the United Arab Republic (1958). Another revolution, led by the Arab Baath Socialist Party (1968), proclaimed the present "Democratic Socialist State," "in the spirit of Islam." The current Head of State is President Saddam Hossein.

Jordan

The Fertile Crescent, a part of which is now Jordan, was, from 2000 B.C. on, the land of numerous invasions and rulers. With the rise of Islam, it was governed (except for a period in the 12th century when Crusaders were in power) by Caliphs and Sultans until the end of the First World War. At the close of that war, the victorious Great Britain controlled the Middle East and assigned Transjordan to an Emir, subject to the advice and guidance of the British. Full independence was granted to the Hashemite Kingdom of Transjordan in 1946. Under the constitution of Jordan, the King and a Parliament now issue laws, administered by Ministers and interpreted by a judiciary in separate religious and regular courts. The current Head of State is King Hussein ibn Talah.

Kuwait

Little has been recorded about Kuwaiti early history. In the 18th century, tribal rulers formed a council for security against the Ottoman and Persian military forces which had made inroads from time to time. In the 1890s, facing imperialist designs of Britain, Russia, and France, the Kuwaiti Sheik chose a protectorate under Great Britain. British and other non-Arab persons were placed under the jurisdiction of a British court. Kuwait established its independence in 1961 and promulgated a constitution in 1963 providing for a Sheikdom with a legislature and a judiciary. The Parliament was dissolved by the ruling Emir in 1986, and the dynasty of the Shabak sheiks has continued to reign. The current Head of State is Amir Sheikh Jaber Ahmad Al-Sabah.

Lebanon

The Lebanese government reflects centuries of crisscrossing merchants and their rivaling rulers. As early as 3000 B.C., Phoenicians governed Lebanon. Assyrians, Babylonians, Persians, Macedonians and Selencids (in turn) ruled until the Romans annexed Lebanon. The Roman Emperor Constantine adopted Christianity and when the Empire was split (395 A.D.), Lebanon came under Byzantine rule. From 636-1258, it was under Islamic sovereigns who permitted Christian Maronites and Melchites and Muslim Druzes some autonomy in personal matters. The Christian Crusaders held sway from 1096-1291 and were followed by Muslim Mamelukes and Ottoman Turks. After an 1860 massacre of Christians by Druzes, France, Great Britain, Russia, Austria and Prussia met with Turkey and reunified Lebanon under a Christian governorship which lasted until 1915. France was given a League of Nations mandate over Lebanon in 1920, and Lebanon received independence in 1943. By agreement, then, the President of Lebanon was to be a Maronite Catholic, the Prime Minister, a Sunni Muslim, and the Speaker of the Chamber, a Shi'ite Muslim. The influx of Palestinian refugees from Israel introduced new Arab influences. The population growth of Shi'ites created further imbalance. Tribal rivalries for power led to the formation of nongovernment militias (Christian Phalangists, Muslim Druzes, Sunnis and Shi'ites), each marking off its own turf and warring with the others to take over more territory. Syrian and Israeli military involvement and the continued presence of their forces have created zones of control. Only recently has a Parliament, unable to gather a quorum for several years, been able to establish a new government of consensus. Its current Head of State is President Elas Hrawi.

Oman

Oman was part of the Persian Empire from the 7th to the 4th centuries B.C., and under Arab tribal chiefs thereafter. Colonial powers interposed their influences. The Portuguese controlled its coast from 1508 to 1659; Turks and Persians came in intermittently; and Great Britain followed from 1891 to 1971. At various times, religious Imams fought with secular Sultans to rule. A British-backed coup in 1970 established the current Sultanate of Oman. The present Head of State is Sultan Qabus Bin Shaik Jaber al-Ahmad, of a dynasty in existence since 1749.

Qatar

For centuries, Qatar was a tiny part of the Ottoman Empire and in the 19th century it fell under the rule of Bahrain. Along with other Gulf States, it entered into treaties of protection with Great Britain. It became part of a Trucial system established by the British in the Gulf. In 1916, the Sheik of Qatar agreed not to dispose of his territory or enter into foreign government relationships without British consent, in return for Great Britain's protection against any aggressor. A Provisional Constitution of Qatar was adopted in 1970 and it was supplanted by an Amended Provisional Constitution of 1972. It remains an Emirate, with a Consultative Council that recommends legislation. Its current Head of State is Amir Shaik Khalifah Bin-Hamed al Thani.

Saudi Arabia

Arabia containing the two holiest cities of Islam, Mecca and Medina, was, for a great many years, segmented among many tribes. Most of the tribes were nomadic; a few ruled remote urban centers. The Saudi family with the support of converts to a new Islamic faith, the Wahhabi, conquered almost all of Arabia and parts of Syria and Iraq. Defeated by Ottoman Empire forces, the Saudis took refuge in Kuwait. With the deterioration of the Ottoman Empire at the turn of the 20th century, they recaptured Arabia; and in 1932 they formed the Kingdom of Saudi Arabia. They embraced the province of Hejaz which had acquired a constitution in 1926; but Saudi Arabia has never adopted a formal constitution. Political and economic power has been distributed among members of the Saudi family in a government of patrimonial kingship. The current Head of State is King Khalid ibn Abdul Aziz al Saud.

Syria

Having emerged from its rulers of antiquity, modern Syria has been unique under many successive constitutions. Its Ottoman constitution (1876) was followed by another under France's mandate (1920), then by its first republican constitution (1930) and a constitution, drafted by the Bath Socialist Party in 1950. That contained several social and economic rights of citizens, including a guarantee of work and social insurance. It was set aside by a coup in 1951, replaced by a 1953 constitution, and in 1954 the 1950 constitution was restored. In 1959, Syria merged with Egypt in the United Arab Republic, which lasted only a year. Syria then adopted provisional constitutions, (1960, 1963, 1964, 1966, 1969) interspersed with coups and revolutions. Syria suffered numerous coups (1949, 1951, 1954, 1962, 1963, 1965, 1970) and it endured several periods of constitutional suspension (1939, 1949, 1951, 1954, 1960, 1966, 1973). It formed a Federation of Arab States with Egypt and Libya in 1971. However, in 1973, the Federation disbanded and Syria, by referendum, approved its current constitution (technically replacing its constitution of 1969). Its current Head of State is President Hafez Al-Assad.

United Arab Emirates

Independent Sheikdoms, along the Arabian coast of the Persian Gulf, were part of the Ottoman Empire and later fell under the successive dominations of Portugal, Iran and Great Britain. Britain had the sheiks sign a General Treaty (for the Cessation of Plunder and Piracy by Land and Sea) under which they became the Trucial States subject to the supervision of a British Political Agent. The trust obligations were terminated in 1968. The sheiks of Bahrain and Qatar split away, and in 1971, seven Sheikdoms—Abu Dhabi, Dubai, Sharjah, Ajman, Umm al-Qwain, Ras al-Khaimah, and Fujawah—formed the United Arab Emirates. They adopted a Provisional Constitution (1971) which has been repeatedly extended. Offices in the national government are shared by representatives of the various emirates, with a preponderance of authority in the rulers of the oil states of Abu Dhabi and Dubai. Each emirate retains internal control, but the national government has broadened its powers. Family members of the regional sheiks occupy the high posts of government. The current Head of State is Shaik Zayed Bin Sultan al-Nahayen

Yemen Arab Republic

After centuries of rule by Ottoman Sultans and Imams, Yemen was governed by local Imams—both spiritual and temporal rulers. Shifting rivalries of royalist tribes led to a coup (with Egyptian support) and a republic was established in 1962. A Provisional Constitution of the YAR was promulgated in 1964. Civil war broke out; and an Interim Constitution of 1965 was replaced by a Permanent Constitution in 1970. That was suspended in 1974 and a brief Provisional Constitution has been promulgated. The current Head of State has been Abdullah Saleh.

People's Democratic Republic of Yemen

Once the Kingdom of Sheba, Yemen was conquered by Muslims in 632 A.D. The Ottomans took control in 1517 and exercised it until the British occupied the southern area in 1839 as a crown territory of Aden. Tribal Islamic rule was preserved until the British withdrew in 1967. Revolutionary Yemeni forces established a republic in 1970. Political turmoil and internal fighting continued. Ultimately, with the support of the USSR in 1978, the Yemen Socialist Party created a Marxist State in the PDRY. Its current Head of State is Ali Nasser Mohammed.

The Persian State

Iran

Persian empires in Iran go as far back as the reigns of Cyrus the Great (549 B.C.) and Alexander the Great (330 B.C.); and they were followed by absolutist dynasties of the Parthians and Sassinians. Arab conquest in 641 A.D. introduced Islam which has continued to be the dominant religion to the present time (except for a period in the 13th and 14th centuries when Mongols under Genghis Khan and others held sway). A long succession of Islamic dynasties ultimately culminated in the rule of Pahlavi Sheiks. In 1905, there was popular demand for a Constitution and a Fundamental Law; a Constitution was ratified in 1906. It provided for the formation of legislative and judicial bodies and a guarantee to Persians of equality before the law, and protection of person, goods, homes and honor. The last Sheik was deposed in a revolution led by the Ayatollah Ruhollah Khomeini in 1979. The monarchy was replaced by a constitutional Islamic republic, under which Khomeini was given life tenure as the country's religious leader, and he was endowed with extensive governmental powers. His death has left uncertain how his policies of Islamic fundamentalism will be continued. The current Head of State is President Hashemi Rafsanjani.

The Hebrew State

Israel

The ancient Jewish kingdoms of Jerusalem and Judah were overcome by a succession of conquerors (Assyrians in 701 B.C. and 586 B.C., Babylonians in 605 B.C., Persians in 539 B.C., Romans in 70 A.D., and Islamic rulers in 1187 A.D.). When the Ottoman Empire was dismembered after World War I, Palestine was placed under a British mandate by the League of Nations. In 1948, Israel was established by the United Nations as an independent country. Its existence or integrity has been challenged by Arab countries, with open warfare in 1948-49 and intermittent military engagements in 1967, 1973-74, 1978, 1982-85. Since 1967, Israel has occupied the West Bank of the Jordan, Gaza,and East Jerusalem. Of all the Arab states, only Egypt has signed a peace treaty with Israel; other Middle East countries have entered into disengagement agreements. The current Head of State is President Chaim Herzog.

The Occupied Territories

Sages referring back to the 4th millennium B.C. tell of numerous patriarchs, kings, and tribal leaders (Hebrews, Canaanites, Philistines, Moabites, Miduanites, Ammonites, and Aramians) at war over the control of ancient towns in Palestine. Except for several military reversals, Jews ruled Jerusalem and Judah from about 2000 B.C. to the destruction of their Temples in 586 B.C. and 70 A.D. For brief periods thereafter, Assyrians, Persians, Romans, and Mamelukes extended their conquests to those cities. With the spread of Islam, Palestine came under its domain; and from the 1200s A.D. to the end of World War 1, the area was embraced within the Ottoman Empire.

British armies took Jerusalem in 1917, and Great Britain ruled Palestine under mandates from the League of Nations and the United Nations until 1948. The Balfour Declaration (1917) stated Great Britain would use its best endeavors to facilitate the establishment of a national home for the Jewish people in Palestine, without prejudice to the civil and religious rights of existing non-Jewish communities. Many efforts to reconcile the differences amongst resident Arabs and Jews were rejected by one or both of the contenders. The UN terminated the British mandate and divided Palestine between Israel and Jordan.

Arab and Jewish hostilities have continued, and in 1967, the Israeli army seized a Gaza Strip from Egyptian territory, a West Bank from Jordan, and East Jerusalem from local Arabs. These areas are now referred to as Israeli Occupied Territories, ruled by military regulations within Israeli law.

LEGAL SYSTEMS AND LABOR LAW

Legal systems in the several counties of the Middle East differ in several respects—in their substantive norms of human conduct, in the religious or philosophical premises they follow, and in their institutions and procedures for the administration of justice. In all of these aspects, labor laws have received special attention.

The separate norms prescribed for labor relations are still embedded in general systems of law. Each system is characterized by the manner in which laws are created, the ways in which law is taught, the principles by which judges decide disputes, and the institutions which administer and enforce laws. Over the years, new countries have accepted and modified the legal systems of other political powers. European colonial powers brought to the Middle East primarily two legal systems (the British common law system and the French or Continental civil law system). They imposed upon their colonies or mandated lands those qualities of their systems that appeared to them to serve their own interests best.

On attaining independence, most Middle East countries retained portions of the common law and civil law systems along with their indigenous practices. The religious orientations of Judaism and Islam were preserved with varying degrees of commitment and application—influenced strongly by political and economic preferences. The present legal systems of the Middle East reflect the universal desire of new governments to assert their individuality as well as their religious loyalties; and in the field of labor law, the modern governments have all adapted their systems to the needs of changing labor situations.

The Muslim countries all proclaim their observance of the Shariah, but, in varying degrees, they have adopted aspects of the common law or civil law systems. All have combined the substantive provisions of their labor laws into a Labor Code; and from time to time they have added separate statutes relating to labor relations. The manner in which each system operates—in adopting laws, in administering regulations, in judging disputes and in disposing of violations—has differed idiosyncratically; but the predominant characteristics of each system and its labor laws have been acknowledged by each government as follows:

The Arab States

Bahrain

Bahrain states it follows English jurisprudence as well as Islamic law. These it expresses essentially through codes. A Labor Law and a Social Insurance scheme, adopted in 1976, form the basis of its labor relations regulations.

Iraq

The Iraqi legal system, originally based on the Shariah, passed through a British common law period, took on features of the French civil law, and since the 1960s has resorted to Islamic norms and modern codes. It has a Labor Code and a number of separate labor statutes (Appendix).

Jordan

The sources of law in Jordan are declared to be the Islamic Shariah, as interpreted by the Hanafi school, and the country's constitution, legislation, custom, and judicial precedents. A Labor Code was enacted in 1960 and amended thereafter. In 1978, a Social Security Act, and in 1984, a Public Employees (Pensions) Act were added.

Kuwait

The primary sources of Kuwaiti law are found in Islamic law, constitutional law, and legislation, including codes influenced by Egyptian and French law. The country has a Labor Code and a series of other labor laws (Appendix).

Lebanon

The legal system of Lebanon has been based upon a policy of preserving the religious laws of Muslims and Christians for purely personal affairs and of following a civil law system for commercial or contractual matters. With respect to labor, the legislature enacted a Labor Law in 1946, and added a number of supplemental statutes until recently (Appendix).

Oman

The sources of law in Oman are Islamic law, intertribal agreements, and legislation, including many codes. The Ibadhi school of Islamic law prevails; but the Shi'a minority is allowed to administer its own rules. Tribunals to enforce codified laws parallel the Shariah courts. The Sultan of Oman has decreed a Labor Code and a few other labor laws (Appendix); still no constitution.

Qatar

Islamic law is the main source of law in Qatar. The country's constitution has been supplemented by several codes, including the Labor Law of 1963. A Labor Court has special jurisdiction over labor disputes.

Saudi Arabia

The legal system of Saudi Arabia is said to be based upon the Shariah, as interpreted by the Hanabali school. However, tribal customs and foreign trade practices have been accepted as inherent in the law, and modern legislation has been added to the extent that it can be reconciled with traditional Islamic principles. A Labor and Workers Law was decreed in 1969, a Social

Insurance Law in 1970, a Civil Service Law in 1971, and an Arbitration Law in 1983.

Syria

The legal system of Syria is basically Islamic, relying upon the Shariah of the Hanafi school. That is supplemented by a constitution (with socialist principles) and modern legal codes. Customary rules of law are still applied locally. Syria adopted a Labor Code in 1959, and added many other labor laws (Appendix).

United Arab Emirates

Islamic law is the principal source of UAE law. Adaptations to an oil and commerce economy have been made through codes and non-religious civil courts. An Abu Dhabi Labor Code was succeeded by a Federal Labor Code in 1980. Added were laws on Permits for Foreign Workers (1980), and a National Employment Service (1980).

Yemen Arab Republic

The Shariah is the basic law of the YAR; however, traditional rules and customs of Yemeni tribes, not contrary to the Shariah, are honored. Major statues have been patterned after Acts in other Arab states, including a labor code that was adopted in 1970.

People's Democratic Republic of Yemen

Deeply rooted customary and religious practices dictate the law for most personal relationships of Muslims, Hindus, Jews and Parsees; however the PDRY constitution and new legislation, including a 1978 Labor Code, bespeak socialist commitments, declared to be within the spirit of the Islamic Shariah. Other labor laws are listed in the Appendix.

After the manuscript for this book was sent to the printer, the Yemen Arab Republic and the People's Democratic Republic of Yemen announced that they were to consummate a merger of their governments. I held up the presses until I could obtain more information. It appears that on May 21, 1990 a new constitution for the Republic of Yemen was drafted to be submitted to a public referendum prior to November 1990. The draft preserves existing laws in both states unless nullified or amended by newly established Councils. I have retained my former findings and comments without alteration; but they must be read with the reservation that new enactments will be forthcoming.

The Persian State

Iran

The 1979 constitution of Iran declares that the Shi'a school of Islamic law is the primary source of the country's law; and all secular legislation in conflict with Islamic norms are unenforceable. An Iranian Code of Labor Law (1959), a Worker's Social Insurance Act (1960), a Fair Labor Standards Act (1965), a Profit Sharing Act (1970), a Social Security Law (1975), a Holiday and Leave Law for Agricultural Workers (1977) and a Settlement of Disputes Act (1977) have been reviewed by a Council of Guardians and found basically consistent with Islamic principles.

The Hebrew State

Israel

Israel has a common law legal system with the preservation of Hebraic and Islamic law for Jews and Arabs respectively in so far as they pertain to domestic relationships and inheritance. Numerous labor statutes have been adopted (listed in the Appendix), but a constitution has been held in abeyance.

The Occupied Territories

The legal system now prevailing in the Occupied Territories consists of military regulations, issued by Commanding Officers, enforced by armed personnel, and interpreted by military courts subject to review in the appellate courts of Israel. There is an acceptance of the provisions of the Hague and Geneva Conventions on military occupation. Substantive civilian law is that of Jordan, with remnants of British and Ottoman law.

States Without Constitutions

Israel, Oman and Saudi Arabia have not adopted formal constitutions. Various official pronouncements, however, are regarded as fundamental to their legal systems.

Israel

Israel set aside the writing of a constitution and adopted a series of Basic Acts, unfinished after years of jurisprudential discussion.[1] The UN General Assembly resolution that created the State of Israel declared that a constitution "shall be adopted by the Elected Constituent Assembly not later than the 1st October, 1948." The elections to the Constituent Assembly "which shall be conducted along democratic lines," were delayed by hostilities and organic problems until past that time. The Israeli Provisional Council abandoned the plan to formulate a constitution. Prime Minister Ben Gurion found it posed political issues too

[1] Amos Shapiro. Status of Fundamental Individual Rights in the Absence of a Written Constitution. Is.L.R. 1974, Vol.9, pp. 497-511; Meir Shamgar. On the Written Constitution. Is.L.R. 1974, Vol.9, pp. 467-476; Claude Klein. A New Era in Israeli Constitutional Law. Is.L.R. 1971, Vol.6, pp. 377-397; Eliahu Likhovski. Can the Knesseth Adopt a New Constitution. Is.L.R. 1969, Vol.4, pp. 61-69; Benjamin Akzin. The Place of the Constitution in the Modern State. Is.L.R. 1967, Vol.2, pp. 1-15; Shlomo Guberman. Israel's Super-Constitution. Is.L.R. 1967, Vol.2, pp. 455-460.

Guberman discusses Yoredor v Chairman, Central Election Committee for the 6th Knesseth (1965, III, 19 P.D. 365) in which the Supreme Court held that a law specifying only citizenship and age as prerequisites for candidacy to the Knesseth could not authorize a list of candidates who opposed the integrity of the State of Israel and its very existence. Claude Klein, supra., discusses the Bergman case (1969, I, 23 P.D. 693), in which the Supreme Court ruled on whether the Financing Law to the Knesseth Elections contradicted the Basic Law. The Bergman case was deemed by Klein to be a "turning point" towards the adoption of a constitution. Amos Shapiro, supra., quotes several decisions in which the Supreme Court referred to its normative sources for defending the fundamental rights of individuals (other than acts of the Knesseth), such as "tenets of liberty," "basic principles of equality, liberty and justice," "extrastatutory legal norms, standing not only above an ordinary law but also above the Constitution," "constitutional principles underlying all Israeli legislation," and "natural law." See also, Melville B. Nimmer, The Uses of Judicial Review in Israel's Quest for a Constitution (1970), 70 Columbia L.R. 1217.

difficult to resolve. A Transition Law transferred the authority of the Constituent Assembly to the First Knesseth. That passed the Harari Resolution (1950) which charged its Constitutional, Legislative, and Judicial Committee to prepare a constitution of several chapters, each to be submitted to the Knesseth as the Committee completed its work. The resolution stated, "and all the chapters together shall form the State Constitution." The "chapter-by-chapter" scheme has resulted in the adoption of five Basic Acts (devoted to the Knesseth (1958), Israel Lands (1960), the President (1964), the Government (1968), the State Economy (1975)). A proposal for a sixth Basic Law on Civil Rights reached its first and last legislative reading in 1974.

The enacted Basic Laws do not specify any labor rights, except for participation in the election of government officials. The proposed basic law on civil rights contained sections on personal freedom, searches, travel, occupation, contract, property—essentially banning government intrusions, "except by law" or "by authority of law" which was not defined. Labor statutes (sometimes referred to by labor law writers as the labor code of Israel) have been adopted cumulatively and will be mentioned below.

There has been much scholarly discussion of the need for, or the value of, a formal, written Israeli constitution. Decisions of the Supreme Court have been noted for their statements of reliance on principles of law higher than acts of the Knesseth, and comparisons have been drawn between them and a judicial power to hold statutes unconstitutional. To date, however, there has been no unequivocal, governmental pronouncement on such matters, and what is germane to this study is that there are no labor provisions of a special constitutional stature in Israel.

Oman

The government of Oman is an absolute monarchy, which only after 1970 has assumed some Western structural forms and functions. The Sultan rules by decrees, with a State Consultative Council and Ministers appointed by him. He has asserted subservience to Islamic law and his secular decrees co-exist with the

Shariah. A Labor Law authorizes an arbitration board to "apply the laws and decisions which have been made and to uphold legal practice and judicial principles in accordance with the economic and social conditions prevailing." Provincial and municipal governmental agencies are still maintained by traditional sheiks and qadis; but their jurisdiction does not extend to the subjects specified in national laws. Public statements of the Sultan have declared that it will be possible to create a democracy when a majority of the people are in a position to elect their deputies freely, but he said Oman needs more time to reach that stage.

Saudi Arabia

Officials of Saudi Arabia have said its constitution is the Koran. At various times, however, other fundamental pronouncements have been made. In 1960, the then Prime Minister Faisal announced a ten point program called the Basic Law. He declared, "I will set forth the fundamental principles of government and the relationship between the government and the governed in order to provide for the basic rights of the citizen." He proposed a consultative council with legislative authority, an independent judicial council immune from political pressure and regional and local governments with a measure of autonomy. Though Faisal later became King, the Basic Law was only partially fulfilled. In 1964, his father, King Saud, was deposed by a religio-legal decision (a Fatwa), signed by a Council of Islamic Clergy, 68 members of the Royal Family, some Ministers, and several tribal chiefs. The family members remained the primary ministers under the new King. Upon the death of Faisal (1975), the Prime Minister announced, "His Majesty, the late King Faisal, was anxious to introduce in his country a system of government emanating from the Koran and the Islamic religion . . . based on a consultative council entrusted with this role. . .[He] initiated the steps toward the execution of this plan but, unfortunately, he passed away before realizing his wish. Our Government, therefore, feels bound to complete what His Majesty King Faisal had started." In 1980, King Fahd succeeded to the throne and the constitutional plan is still unfinished.

* * * * *

The legal systems designated above all manifest some accommodation to modern labor conditions.

The Muslim countries pay tribute to the immutability of the revealed words of Allah as found in the Koran, the unimpeachability of the Sunna, and the primacy of the Shariah. Nonetheless, Islam has expanded its legal horizons. Its great scholars reached a consensus on the Ijma, and founded schools of approved law with few disagreements. Despite the closing of the gates of Ijtihad, many by-passes have been adopted. Particularly in the field of labor law, codes have experimented with norms for human conduct. The jurisdiction of the religious courts has been confined and secular courts have come to the fore.

The recent application of Hebraic law in Israel has also exhibited adaptation to labor needs. Religious rules have been restricted to personal relations such as marriage and divorce, for Jews and Muslims separately. Labor laws (except for immigration and citizenship affecting employment, and for the observance of the Sabbath) have been designed to deal with secular practices. Orthodox religious parties have played a minority role.

The legal system prevailing in each Middle East country has had spiritual, philosophic and cultural aspects of great concern to the government, and to the governed; but their peculiarities have not resulted in a wide diversity of labor laws.

THE OIL-CASH FLOW

The discovery of oil (in Iraq 1927, Bahrain 1932, Kuwait and Saudi Arabia 1938, Qatar 1939, United Arab Emirates 1958, and Oman 1964) and its exploitation following World War II caused great transformations in Middle East labor relations.

Wealth has flowed copiously, though unevenly among the nations.[2] In the year 1977, Saudi Arabia and Iran received 37 and 23 billion dollars in oil revenue respectively; Iraq, Kuwait,

[2] OPEC Annual Statistical Bulletin, Secretariat, OPEC, Vienna, Austria; OPEC Member Country Profiles, Vienna, 1983.

and the United Arab Republic, 8 to 9 billion each, and Qatar about 2 billion. Bahrain and Oman received less, but still substantial sums. With annual variations, like revenues continued, differentiating these countries only as "Oil Rich" and "Quasi Oil Rich." All experienced a relatively sudden and fabulously burgeoning of wealth. From an historical perspective, countries regarded as among the world's poor, were catapulted into the ranks of the very rich within just a few years.

Average per capita GNP in 1981 was $20,899 to $27,719 in Kuwait, United Arab Emirates and Qatar; $6,310 to $13,900 in Saudi Arabia, Oman, Bahrain, and Iraq. By comparison, the average GNP in the United States was $12,820, in Europe $10,599, in Latin America $1,760, in Africa $822, and in Asia $1,341.[3]

The impact of Middle East oil riches upon workers in the region came through their governments. Shortly after the discovery of oil and the development of refineries, the Middle East governments took over those properties. Even when exploitation was continued under joint ventures with foreign corporations, the domestic income came primarily to the governments. That enabled oil producing governments to engage in social welfare programs, subsidies, employment preferences, housing, and education in unprecedented proportions. Such benefits were limited primarily to nationals and were not spread among all of them.

The economic prosperity or hardship of workers in the Middle East can be seen more in the levels of personal and family incomes than in per capita GNP. Income distribution among the population has been widely divergent. Statistics are not fully available; but figures (reported by the World Bank in 1985, as of 1975) for five of the countries may be illustrative.[4] Contrasting the income enjoyed by the wealthiest 5% of the households with the lowest 20% of the households it appears that in Iran the

[3] World Bank, World Tables, Vol. 1, Economic Data, Table II, Geneva, 1984 pp.560-564.

[4] The World Bank, World Tables, Vol.II, Social Data, Washington, D.C., 1985.

wealthy 5% received approximately 28% of the nation's income and the poorest 20% got only about 4% of the total income; in Iraq, the respective shares of national income were 35% and 2%; in Israel, 13% and 8%; in Lebanon, 26% and 4%, and in Syria, 25% and 6%. Except for a general increase in earnings in the oil, construction and some service industries, and in public employment, there has not been a direct flow of oil revenues to workers. The large agricultural populace has prospered little, if at all. Nor has the seepage of oil wealth through the economic and social structures satisfied all basic human needs. The effects of oil wealth upon labor legislation, however, have beeen generally beneficial, as will become apparent

LABOR FORCE DISTRIBUTION

The discovery of oil in the beige sands of a desert not only upset the landscape, but also caused a disturbing rearrangement of native and neighboring workers. In lands where Bedouins were ever moving their sheep in search of sparse vegetation, where farmers cultivated dates as their staple crop, and along coastlines where fishermen brought in the food of a day or dived for pearls, men are now drilling for oil, storing the outpouring, flying in airplanes and helicopters, refining crude petroleum, laying down pipelines, filling tankers, constructing housing complexes, hotels and office skyscrapers, establishing schools and hospitals, and staffing a myriad of government agencies. From a few towns and oases linked by camels, there have appeared metropolises, traffic jams of motor vehicles and helter-skelter excitement. Skilled workmen practically unknown theretofore—geologists, tool and die men, medical specialists, accountants and teachers—were brought in; and as activities proliferated, manual workers, too, were imported. How the new workers are utilized today is the crux of labor problems in the Middle East.

How workers fit into the slots of production is everywhere a jigsaw puzzle. The challenge of finding and placing the proper person into the most suitable opening is made the more perplexing in the Middle East because the people are being transported while the pieces of the puzzle are being located.

The nature of the dispersal of workers in the Middle East is not easily portrayed. Statistics have not been compiled uniformly; most nations have been quite dilatory in adopting standards for labor statistics, such as proposed by the International Labour Office. Census taking has been erratic and terms of classification have been loosely defined. Still, researchers have brought together what appear to be reliable estimates. They demonstrate meaningful similarities and dissimilarities among the countries and they are sufficiently dependable for over-all comparisons.

The magnitudes of persons involved may be seen from the following table of populations and employed workers (as recently estimated).

TABLE 1. POPULATION AND LABOR FORCE[5]

	Population		Labor Force		
Country	Millions Mid-1987	% by age 15-64 years	% in Agriculture	% in Industry	% in Services
Bahrain	.5	41	5	85	5
Iran	45.6	53	36	33	31
Iraq	16.5	50	30	22	48
Israel	4.3	60	6	32	62
Jordan	3.6	49	10	26	64
Kuwait	1.8	58	2	32	67
Lebanon	3.3	51	N.A.	N.A.	N.A.
Oman	1.3	50	50	22	28
Qatar	.4	N.A.	10	N.A.	N.A.
S.Arabia	12.054	48	14	37	
Syria	10.8	48	32	32	36
U.A.E.	1.4	67	5	38	57
Y.A.R.	8.2	51	69	9	22
PDRY	2.2	51	41	1.8	41

The distribution of workers among the commonly recognized

[5] The World Bank, World Development Report, 1988, Tables 1, 32) Oxford Univ. Press, Oxford and New York, 1988.

sectors of the economy reflects the different stages of economic development in the various countries.

The Agricultural Sector

The countries of the Middle East fall into two groups with respect to the prominence of agricultural workers - 1. those with approximately one-third or more of their working population engaged in agriculture, and 2. those with only 2 to 10% of their workers in agriculture. In the former group, in declining order, are the Yemen Arab Republic with about 69% in agriculture, Oman 50%, Saudi Arabia 48%, PDRY 41%, Iran 36%, Iraq 30%, Syria 32%, Lebanon 28%. Among the more commercialized countries, Kuwait has only about 2% of its work force employed in agriculture, Bahrain 5%, United Arab Emirates 5%, Israel 6%, and Jordan 10%. The number of workers in agriculture has been diminishing; but such workers are still significantly numerous.

The Services Sector

The trend of employment in the services sector has been upward. It has ranged from one-third to two-thirds of the working population. The percentages in services has been lowest in Bahrain, the Yemen Arab Republic, and Oman; higher in Iran, Saudi Arabia, Syria, Qatar, PDRY, and Iraq; and highest in the United Arab Emirates, Israel, Jordan, and Kuwait.

The Industrial Sector

In the Middle East, employment in industrial enterprises has varied considerably. It accounts for relatively few workers in both the Yemens (9% in YAR and 18% in PDRY) and in Saudi Arabia only 14%. The largest proportion of industrialization is in Bahrain, 85% and in the United Arab Emirates 38%. The remaining countries range from 25% to 33 1/3 % of their working populations in industry. Notwithstanding the dramatic expansion of oil production, the growth of the proportion of workers in industry has been slight.[6]

The contrast between what was the traditional sector of employment and what is becoming a modern sector has been quite distinct. Traditional enterprise such as fishing, boat building, pearling, weaving, and date culture have been overshadowed. The animal husbandry of Bedouins is being curtailed and they are being sedentarized through government-encouraged and subsidized settlement. At the same time new industries, not only oil drilling and refining, but all kinds of construction, commerce, and communication have mushroomed.

The Public Sector

Government employment has undergone a tremendous increase. With the taking over of oil fields, there has been a great inflow of public revenue and consequential governmental activity. That instigated public employment of all kinds for exploratory, extractive, and processing workers. With more public wealth, there followed regulatory and planning agencies, social welfare programs and an insatiable demand for administrative, accounting and clerical personnel. Even in the non-oil states, governments have assumed new goals for which novel jobs have became necessary.

The Informal Sector

In the friction of societal change and the inability of many persons to find secure places, there has arisen an Informal Sector. Individuals who left old ties and were unable to grasp and hold positions in the evolving job structures have set up quasi-independent enterprises such as peddling, personal services, small repairs, shoe shining, hair cutting and similar pursuits. Their number has been growing in urban centers and in some rural areas.

The kinds of work required in the Middle East have altered the opportunities available to workers. More skill and new skills have become requisites for employment. Daily tasks and job

[6] Ibid.

environments have demanded strange adjustments. For multitudes of workers, their way of life has changed radically.

MIGRANT LABOR

The traditional Middle East migrations of shepherds, traders, and marauders have been dwarfed by the uprooting and replanting of workers with each discovery of oil. Historic exodi may be recalled, but they are small reminders of the possibilities of change. Several thousand Hebrews, it is said, took over twenty years to reach "the promised land." In 722 B.C., Sargon was reputed to have deported 27,900 persons from Palestine to Mesopotamia. In 586 B.C. Nebuchadnezzar captured Jerusalem and massacred or drove off 4600 persons. Muhammed and his followers were forced to flee to Mecca; and the successor Umayyet Caliphs (661-750) pushed multitudes of adversaries from the Indus Valley to the Lower Tigris. In 786 to 809 A.D., approximately five thousand persons moved from frontier lands to northern Syria. In 1401, Timurlane besieged Damascus and it was reported that he took all skilled artisans to Samarkand. Within only a few recent years, several million workers from neighboring countries and far off Asia have flocked to the Middle East. That movement of workers across national boundaries in the Middle East has been a physical upheaval of immense proportions and has transformed the composition of labor forces as never before.

Labor force statistics in the Middle East are rather fragmentary; yet the available censuses and estimates clearly indicate vast transformations, not an undifferentiated multitude of workers, rather a great variety of persons moving in defined directions and performing a prodigious number of tasks. The relative magnitudes have been enormous and very meaningful. Conditions of work and life have been, and are being, seriously refashioned.

The nationalities of the working population in each country have been literally turned upside down. The percentage of foreigners in the labor force has been reported to have risen at times as high as 90% in the United Arab Emirates, 89% in Qatar, 80% in Kuwait, 75% in Saudi Arabia and 57% in Bahrain. The percentage of native workers who left the Yemens has been estimated as high as 32% in the Yemen Arab Republic and 33% in the People's Democratic Republic of Yemen.[7] Lebanon, Jordan and Syria have experienced lesser emigrations, but also an influx of many thousands of Palestinian.

Refugees in the Middle East have amounted to substantial numbers. In Lebanon, they have numbered approximately 288,176; in Jordan, 870,490; in Syria, 265,221; in the West Bank, 385,634; and in Gaza, 459,074.[8]

Israel, under other motivations and influences, has encouraged an in-migration of several million Jews annually, however since 1985 it has had an out-migration of similar numbers. Before the *intifada*, it also facilitated the daily migration, in and out of Israel, of approximately 51,000 Arab workers from the West Bank and 43,000 from the Gaza Strip.

The workers who have recently moved into and out of countries in the Middle East have had diverse characteristics. They have consisted of single persons, families, or work crews, voluntary applicants, coerced recruits, reluctant refugees, and workers seeking temporary or permanent residence. They have been propelled largely by a desire for employment and higher earnings, an opportunity to remit savings to family members at home, an escape from adversity in their own countries, or a fear of persecution where they have lived. They have been enticed by invitations to enter, or have been confronted with regulations and controls restricting their rights, or both. In the turn of events, special places have been occupied by native nomads and war refugees.

Although there have been immigrants and emigrants in practically every country of the Middle East, some countries have been primarily "receiving" or "host" countries and others "sending" countries. Bahrain, Israel, Kuwait, Oman, Qatar, Saudi Arabia, and the United Arab Emirates have been predominantly host

[7] U.S. Central Intelligence Agency, the World Factbook, 1989, Washington, D.C., 1989.

[8] U.N.R.W.A. Summary Report, 1988. United Nations, New York.

countries; Lebanon, Syria, and PDRY sending countries. Jordan and the Yemen Arab Republic have been called "replacement migration countries" since masses of their men who left for the higher wages paid in the oil countries were replaced by immigrants from other countries. All countries have experienced some reverse movement.

Though the initial migratory workers have come from Arab countries, the need was not completely satisfied and many more workers have been brought in from Pakistan, India, South Korea and Indonesia. Foreign workers in Kuwait come from 68 different countries. As will be noted below, legal preferences and concessions have been made for Arab workers, but the Asians have come without such inducements.

Most migrant workers have been unskilled, or were willing to accept manual work because of the higher wages paid in the oil producing countries. Some of these workers acquired new skills, and others came with semi skills. Professionals and technically skilled workers were also caught up in the migration to improve earnings, so that countries such as the Yemens have complained of a brain drain. The enhanced economies of the Middle East have all improved their educational facilities, lowering illiteracy and raising the scholastic levels of foreign as well as native workers.

Migrants have been regarded as both a benefit and a problem. Most of them have supplied indispensable labor; they have increased productivity and wealth in the host country; they have supported themselves; and they have aided those to whom they have sent remittances. At the same time, they have been aliens or foreigners, injecting strange languages and customs into traditionally homogeneous societies, constantly raising suspicions that they may be taking jobs away from natives, and on occasion posing complaints and political issues. In the Iranian revolts 1978-79, the migrant poor were participants. Recent Iranian migrants to Lebanon have joined warring factions. In Israel the immigration of many Sephardic Jews has definitely influenced political alignments.

Insufficient interest has been displayed concerning the conditions of work and living of migrant laborers. Employment for up to 12 hours a day, housing in unwholesome wooden barracks, and the separation of men from their families for months and years at a time have been accepted as commonplace (though the emergence and persistence of a submerged stratum of poor society has been recognized as a social problem in some of the countries). Personal or familial deprivations became too onerous and many foreign workers left, but large numbers have returned after home visits. Substanital projects manned by foreign crews have been completed; and the workers have been sent home. Recruiters and middle men have made the replenishment of work forces with more migrants a profitable enterprise. The public decision of some host countries to supplant foreigners with newly trained native workers has elicited educational programs but scant replacement. The manpower needs, particularly in the countries seeking to broaden their industrial base and to achieve the material life styles of Western civilization, have not so far abated the dependence upon migrant labor.[9]

RELIGIOUS AND CULTURAL STRIFE

The Judeo-Christian-Muslim religions profess to believe all men are children of the one God; yet they have not induced most of their adherents to treat each other as brothers. Instead, there has been continuous divisiveness, distrust and disruption in the Middle East among Jews, Christians, and Muslims; and within sects of the same faith. Theological disputation has generally

[9] Shafeeq Ghabra, Palestinians in Kuwait, Westview Press, Boulder & London, 1987; Ragaei El Mallakh, The Economic Development of the Yemen Arab Republic, Croom Helm, London, 1986; G. Swamy, Population and International Migration, World Bank, Washington, D.C., 1985; Eliyahu Kanousky, Migration from the Poor to the Rich Arab Countries, Dayan Center for Middle Eastern and African Studies, Tel Aviv Univ., Tel Aviv, 1984; Ismail Serageldin, Manpower and International Labor Migration in the Middle East and North Africa, Oxford Univ. Press, New York & Oxford, 1983; A. Al-Miosa, K. McLachlan, Immigrant Labor in Kuwait, Croom Helm, London, 1984; S. Y Alessa, The Manpower Problem in Kuwait, Kegan Paul Int'l., London, 1981; J. S. Birks, Arab Manpower: The Crisis of Development, St. Martins Press, New York, 1980; Jon Swanson, Emigration and Economic Development in the Yemen Arab Republic, Westview Press, Boulder, Colo., 1979.

been tempered by a theoretical acceptance of human kinship. In politics and personal interaction, however, there has been a clear segregation along religious lines.

In the Arab states, Sunni and Shi'a Muslims have found impermissible heresy in each other's practices. In Israel, orthodox and non-orthodox Jews have clashed over ritual and work habits. Most Jewish-Arab relations have been emotionally charged with disparate desires for national identification. In Lebanon, where intermingling between Christians and Muslims have been most pronounced (or perhaps where the majority of workers have been of a religious faith without commensurate political power), the efforts to compromise their differences in a division of government offices have resulted only in brief periods of stability. Religious and cultural conflicts have insinuated themselves into labor relations in every Middle East country. Within each religious or cultural community, passionate devotion to distinguishing characteristics has perpetuated strife.

The religious distribution of people within the several Middle East countries is indicated in this tabulation.

TABLE 2. RELIGIOUS AFFILIATIONS[10]

(*Percent of Population*)

Country	Sunni	Muslim Shi'ite	Others	Christian	Jewish	Hindu
Bahrain	30	70	0	0	0	0
Iran	5	93	0	0	02	
Iraq	37	60	0	3	0	0
Israel	12.6	0.5	1.6a	2.3	83	0
Jordan	95	0	0	5	0	0
Kuwait	45	30	10	8	0	7
Lebanon	NA	b	b	25	0	0
Oman	20	4	75c	0	0	1
Qatar	d	d	d	0	0	5
S. Arabia	85	15	0	0	0	0
Syria	74	0	16e	10	0	0
U.A.E.	80	16	0	1	0	3

[10] Central Intelligence Agency, The World Factbook, 1989, op. cit.

Y.A.R.	NA	f	f	0	0	0
P.D.R.Y.	NA	g	g	g	g	g

a. Druzes
b. Total Muslims 75%
c. Ibadhi Muslims
d. Mainly Sunni and Wahhabi sects
e. Alawites, Druzes and other Muslim sects
f. Total Muslims 100%
g. Mainly Sunni and some Christians and Hindus

There are many individuals who earnestly seek harmony and labor cooperation throughout the region. In all faiths, there have been some learned theologians who, while attesting to a divine inerrancy in their own creeds, have preached tolerance toward other beliefs. Unfortunately, they have not swayed the multitudes. Religious suspicion and hostility have persisted as a virus undermining good labor relations in most Middle East communities.

THE DISRUPTION OF WAR

For several decades, the states of the Middle East have been plagued by wars, some small but others large and all disruptive to normal work. In one sense, all the states were born out of war. World War II brought the collapse of the Ottoman Empire and temporary mandates for Britain and France, from which and with the prompting of armed forces and revolutions, the separate Middle East states were formed. We tend to recall those convolutions of war as mere historical facts. Our attention shifts to subsequent developments of civil concern. The precondition of war, however, has left a legacy, a reliance upon further war as a means to new objectives.

The enactment of labor laws as an expression of the new sovereignties, arose within the background and atmosphere of war. For it, war meant and continues to mean not just an historical datum, but the death of workers, the interruption or diversion of work, and the disablement of manpower for the progress of nations.

In Lebanon a civil war erupted in 1958; stopped momentarily (with the aid of American troops), it broke out again in 1975 and continued with recurrent episodes of slaughter until 1985.

Amidst the turmoil and tension among feuding Christians, Muslims and Palestinians, Syrians were brought in to preserve peace, but violence continued and overlapped into Israel; and in 1982, Israel invaded Lebanon. Its efforts to dislodge the PLO added further chaos for the civilian population. An American attempt, with the cooperation of France and Italy, to stabilize conditions failed, and the country continued through the decade of the 80's to be marked by warring militias. The death toll mounts; urban employment has been immobilized; large numbers of workers have been obliged to emigrate or to subsist on remittances from relatives abroad.

Armed outbursts drove Britain to relinquish its mandate over Israel, and the establishment of that state in 1948 immediately prompted a full scale war of all the Arab states against Israel. A truce led to guerilla attacks and retributive assaults. In 1967, Israel launched a pre-emptive onslaught and defeated the combined forces of Egypt, Syria, and Jordan. She acquired the West Bank and Gaza; and later East Jerusalem. Sporadic incidents of killing by and against Palestinians continued a state of hostility. War broke out again in 1973 without a definitive conclusion. In 1977, peace was initiated by Egypt's Sadat; and an Egyptian-Israeli peace treaty was signed two years later.

A so-called "twilight war" between PLO activists and Israeli defense forces continued; and in 1982 Israel invaded Lebanon with considerable destruction and loss of life. PLO leaders were dislodged from Lebanon, but a Palestinian uprising beginning in 1987 and not over at this writing in 1990, opened a war of another nature. Stones, gasoline cocktails, commercial strikes and boycotts were met with tear gas, rubber bullets, bone breaking, arrests and the detention of thousands in the occupied territories of Gaza and the West Bank. Mass Arab defiance spilled over into East Jerusalem, involving permanent Arab residents. Deaths, though too numerous, have been relatively few; still the disruption of employment and the perpetuation of fear and antagonism has become as pervasive as in the more violent wars.

Iraq and Iran engaged in classic warfare for over 8 years from 1980 to 1989. Approximately a million human beings were killed; many more injured; still more pulled from their normal occupations and thrown into combat. The demolition of oil installations and the bombing of cities destroyed jobs as well as lives. (Ironically, such crises create more work, and normal biological impulses replenish the population.) Sectarian beliefs and political rivalries remain unsated.

The propensity for war in both Iraq and Iran had asserted itself in 1962-66 in attempts to counteract the efforts of dissident Kurds who sought tribal independence; and when in 1984 the Kurds interfered with the war against Iran, the Iraqis resorted to poison gas to annihilate the dissenters. Hundreds of thousands of Kurds fled from their homes; many remain refugees.

In addition to these major devastations, some Middle East countries have experienced war dislocations starting with struggles against colonial British and French troops, and followed by civil disorder in the new nations from time to time thereafter. PDRY faced Omani attacks from 1972 to 1976, and border conflicts with the Yemen Arab Republic in 1972 and 1979 to 1982. It also suffered a rebellion in 1968 and coups in 1970, 1978, and 1980. The Yemen Arab Republic experienced a civil war in 1967, and a coup in 1974. Syria sustained a succession of coups, some bloodless but others quite disruptive, in 1949, 1951, 1954, 1962, 1963, 1966, and 1970. No reliable records report the extent of turmoil and distress endured by civilian workers in these military actions, but it is obvious that the toll was, and still is, great.

Efforts to obtain peace in the Middle East have involved the Superpowers and until recently the United Nations, with little success. Unfortunately, foreign governments have been motivated by interests of their own and have relied upon the intrusion of arms more than persuasion.

Resort to war in the Middle East has become an addiction.

DEVELOPMENT AND PLANNING

In less time than the span of one life, the people of the Middle East have been whirled about from traditional labors to new and strange activities. Independence and the discovery of oil have swept through the lands with hustle and hurrah. All the countries, not alone those anointed by oil, have been transformed. People who lived by the sea or among date palms have found themselves lured into cities and manufacturies. Many have moved from their homelands to unfamiliar places. All have been urged to answer new callings. Amidst the uncertainties, obstacles, fears, promises, and choices, the nations have sought to sound their bearings and to chart their future courses. Development has become the popular watchword and planning for development has been seen as a necessary and felicitous tool.

The process of planning has been practically standardized. It has become a recurrent program of government, generally in five year stages. Planning commonly starts with an identification of a country's needs and opportunities. In the Middle East, the range of needs and opportunities has gone from simple food, clothing and shelter to a balancing of industry and infrastructure, and from heedless urbanization back to a restoration of agricultural self-sufficiency. Planners have noted and attempted to measure the amount of arable land, the erratic flow of water, the inhospitable climate, the lack of roads, housing and health care; they have tabulated the migration of workers, population growth and the advancement of education. With their data and their "guesses," they determine a set of social priorities. The planning then proceeds to the formulation of public policies and the selection of projects that appear to be essential to the satisfaction of the acknowledged needs. To complete the plan, there is a budgetary calculation—an estimate of the sources of funds, such as government surpluses, taxes, foreign assistance and user fees, and an estimate of planned expenditures. When the plan is published, there are still many tasks of execution and possible revision and adaptation because of unforeseen circumstances.

Most development plans stress economic factors and are oriented toward an increase in material products, goods or services. The beneficiaries of the projects may or may not be specified. It is assumed that the public welfare will be served. (More or less it is.) Safeguards against mistakes, corruption and waste have been difficult to devise. Whatever the outcome, the interests of workers in the community are deeply affected by the development plans of every nation. Significantly, the process of development planning is now a public strategy the must be taken into account in an appraisal of all Middle East aspirations and accomplishments, including labor law.

REFERENCES TO PUBLICATIONS

Elias H. Tuma, Economic and Political Change in the Middle East, Pacific Books, Palo Alto, CA 1987.

S. H. Amin, Middle East Legal Systems, Royston Ltd., 1985.

Kenneth Redden, gen.ed., Modern Legal Systems Cyclopedia, Vol.5, Wm. Hein & Co., Buffalo, N.Y., 1985.

Anwar M. Shabon, The Political, Economic and Labor Climate in the Countries of the Arabian Peninsula, Univ. of Pennsylvania Press, Philadelphia, 1981.

Eliyahu Kanowsky, Migration from the Poor to the Rich Arab Countries, Tel Aviv Univ., Tel Aviv, 1984.

Ismail Serageldin, Manpower and International Labor Migration in the Middle East and North Africa, Oxford Univ. Press, New York & Oxford, 1983.

J. S. Birks and C. S. Sinclair, Arab Manpower, Croom Helm, London, 1980.

Safouh Akhrass, Revolutionary Change and Modernization in the Arab World, Atlas, Damascus, 1972.

Norman Jacobs, The Sociology of Development, Praeger Publ., 1966.

REFERENCES BY COUNTRY

Bahrain

Emile A. Nakhleh, Bahrain, Lexington Books, N.Y., 1976.

Fuad I. Khuri, Tribe and State in Bahrain, Univ. of Chicago Press, Chicago & London, 1980.

Iran

Y. Noori, Legal and Political Structure of an Islamic State, Royston Ltd., Glasgow, 1986.

Razavi Hossein, Political Environment of Economic Planning in Iran: 1971-1983, Westview Press, Boulder, Colo., 1984.

Eric Hooglund, Land and Revolution in Iran, 1960-80, Univ. of Texas Press, Austin, TX, 1982.

Fred Holliday, Iran: Dictatorship of Development, Penguin Press, New York, 1980.

Iraq

Frederick Axelgard, ed., Iraq in Transition: Political, Economic and Strategic Perspective, Westview Press, Boulder, Colo., 1986.

Israel

Menachem Goldberg, Labour Law in Israel, Sadan, Tel Aviv, 1982.

S. M. Katz, H. Ludmer, Regional Organization and Management of Development, Settlement Study Centre Publications, Rehovat, 1982.

John Vidergar, Israel Social and Economic Development, Vance Bibliographies, Montecello, Ill., 1978.

Meir Heth, The Legal Framework of Economic Activity in Israel, Praeger, New York, 1967.

Don Lavoie, National Economic Planning, Ballenger Pub. Co., New York, 1985.

Izhak Englard, "Religious law in the Israel Legal System", Hebrew Univ. of Jerusalem, 1975.

Daniel Schorsch, "The Legal System of Israel", Modern Legal Systems Cyclopedia, Kenneth Redden, ed., Vol.5, Wm. Hein & Co., Buffalo, N.Y., 1985.

Jordan

B. Khader and A. Badran, The Economic Development of Jordan, Croom Helm, London, 1987.

Clinton Bailey, Jordan's Palestinian Challenge, 1948-1983, Westview Press, Boulder, Colo. 1984.

Peter Gubser, Jordan: Crossroads of Middle Eastern Events, Westview Press, Boulder, Colo. 1983.

Kuwait

A. Al-Moosa and K. McLachlan, Immigrant Labour in Kuwait, Croom Helm, London, 1985.

Jacqueline S. Ismael, Kuwait, Syracuse Univ. Press, N.Y. 1982.

Shamlan Y. Alessa, The Manpower Problem in Kuwait, Kegan Paul Int'l., London & Boston, 1981.

Youssef S. F. Al-Sabah, The Oil Economy of Kuwait, Kegan-Paul Int'l, London & Boston, 1980.

Lebanon

A. El-Gemayel, The Lebanese Legal System, International Law Institute, Washington, D.C. 1985.

Edward Azar, The Emergence of a New Lebanon, Praeger, N.Y. 1984.

David C. Gordon, The Republic of Lebanon-Nation in Jeopardy, Westview Press, Boulder, Colo. 1983.

Occupied Territories

Philippa Strum, Gaza and the West Bank, American-Israeli Civil Liberties Coalition, 1988.

Raja Shehadeh, The West Bank and the Rule of Law, Int'l. Commission of Jurists and Law in the Services of Man, Geneva, 1980.

Oman

Calvin Allen, Jr., Oman: The Modernization of the Sultanate, Westview Press, Boulder, Colo. 1987.

John Wilkinson, The Imamate Tradition of Oman, Cambridge Univ. Press, Cambridge, 1987.

B.R. Pridham, ed., Oman: Economic, Social and Strategic Developments, Croom Helm, London, 1987.

Qatar

Ragaei El Mallakh, Qatar: Energy & Development, Croom Helm, London, 1985.

Ragaei El Mallakh, Economic and Social Development in Qatar, Croom Helm, London, 1983.

Rosemarie Zahlan, The Creation of Qatar, Croom Helm, London, 1979.

Saudi Arabia

John Presley, Guide to the Saudi Arabian Economy, St. Martin's Press, New York, 1984.

Islami A. Reza, The Political Economy of Saudi Arabia, Univ. of Washington Press, Seattle, 1984.

John Shaw, Saudi Arabian Modernization—The Impact of Change on Stability, Praeger Publishers, New York, 1982.

Ragaei El Mallakh, Saudi Arabia, Croom Helm, London, 1982.

Syria

Raymond A. Hinnebusch, Peasant and Bureaucracy in Baathist Syria: The Political Economy of Rural Development, Westview Press, Boulder, CO, 1989.

Norman Lewis, Nomads and Settlers in Syria and Jordan, Cambridge Univ. Press, Cambridge, N.Y. 1987.

Yahya M. Sadowski, Political Power and Economic Organization in Syria, UCLA, Los Angeles, 1984.

Eliyahu Kanowsky, The Economic Development of Syria, Univ. Pub. Projects, Tel Aviv, 1977.

United Arab Emirates

A. O. Taryam, The Establishment of the United Arab Emirates 1950-85, Croom Helm, London, 1987.

Franke Heard-Bey, From Trucial States to United Arab Emirates, Longman Press, London, 1982.

Ragaei El Mallakh, The Economic Development of the United Arab Emirates, St. Martin's Press, N.Y., 1981.

Ali M. Khalifa, The United Arab Emirates: Unity in Fragmentation, Westview Press, Boulder, CO, 1979.

Yemen Arab Republic

Robert Burrowes, The Yemen Arab Republic: The Politics of Development, 1962-1968, Croom Helm, London, 1987.
Ragaei El Mallakh, The Economic Development of the Yemen Arab Republic, Croom Helm, London, 1986.
Richard Nyrop, ed., The Yemens—Country Studies, Foreign Area Studies, Washington, D.C., 1986.
Jon Swanson, Emigration and Economic Development in the Yemen Arab Republic, Westview Press, Boulder, CO., 1979.

People's Democratic Republic of Yemen

Richard Nyrop, ed., The Yemens—Country Studies—op. cit.
Helen Lackner, PDR Yemen: Outpost of Socialist Development in Arabia, Ithaca Press, London, 1985.
Joseph Kostiner, The Struggle for South Yemen, St. Martin's Press, N.Y., 1984.
Robin Birdwell-Longman, The Two Yemens, Westview Press, Boulder, CO, 1983.
Robert Stookey, South Yemen—A Marxist Republic in Arabia, Westview Press, Boulder, CO 1982.

II THE GAMUT OF LABOR LAW PROVISIONS

A modern labor law arises from the perception of a problem. It takes form in constitutional, statutory and treaty provisions; and in time its efficacy is seen in consequences and incidentals.

A presentation of labor law should, in my view, be as comprehensive as possible. Obviously, the commonplace topics of wages, hours and working conditions must be included. I believe also that, laws which define the status of workers within a society, which classify and differentiate certain classes of workers, which deal with collective as well as individual action, which confer or with-hold assistance against the risks inherent in the span of working life, or which offer civil rights for participants in the struggle for human betterment are labor laws. So are the administrative and fiscal regulations and international commitments that assure application and enforcement of the other labor laws.

There is a totality of laws, reinforcing or offsetting each other. The individual worker is benefited or neglected, protected or punished, helped or hindered by a welter of laws. What may satisfy some workers may be of little help or of no meaning to others (except in the broad embrace of the brotherhood of mankind). I have undertaken to scan whatever labor laws of the Middle East are available and to set them forth in a comparative arrangement. I shall observe in Chapters 3 through 16 the manner in which constitutions, codes, and treaties of Middle East countries deal with the following major topics.

1. The status of labor in the economic or social order
2. Special classes of labor
3. Remuneration
4. Hours of work and leisure
5. Occupational safety and healty
6. Employment

7. Collective action and dispute resolution
8. Labor's interest in social welfare programs
9. Labor's interest in civil rights

The scope of these topics is extremely broad and the details that could be listed are almost limitless. An anonymous philosopher once concluded that in order to determine the proper choice of things for him to say, it was first necessary for him to know the many choices he might have; he spent the rest of his life in silent meditation. To avoid that predicament, I have decided to be guided by a basic attitude toward labor law. That may be called a problem/solution approach. It seeks first to identify a labor problem, then to set forth the laws adopted to cope with that problem, and finally to assess how the problem is being overcome. Accordingly, for each of the topics in my exposition I shall follow these sub-headings, A—perceptions of the problem, B—constitutional provisions, C—labor code and statutory provisions, D—treaty provisions, and E—consequences and incidentals.

In pursuing this pattern with each topic of labor law, I shall first discuss aspects of the labor problem perceived to be perplexing serious-minded statesmen and workers in the Middle East. They may be immediate concerns or prospects for the future. They may concentrate on problems perceived by oil exploiters, food providers, preservers of tradition or pioneers of Westernization. Next I shall indicate the text of the laws devised to meet those problems. I shall confine myself to the words used in constitutions, labor codes, and treaties (relying upon translations from the Arabic or Hebrew as issued by official agencies). I shall group the provisions by subject matter; but I shall refrain from personal comment in that presentation. My evaluations are reserved for the last section of this book. Then I shall comment (albeit scantily) on publicly acknowledged consequences of the laws, and incidentally on the state of continuing problems.

To do that thoroughly would call for a social, economic and political history of each country. Since that lies beyond my capabilities (or the patience of most readers) I shall try to be rather painstakingly objective in the listing of the perceptions of the problem and the legal provisions. In touching upon consequences and incidentals I shall endeavor to be more sociological than journalistic. My biases and evaluations shall emerge later in concluding chapters.

Lay readers may choose to proceed to chapter 17 which summarizes the technical data in the preceeding chapters.

Chapter 3

THE STATUS OF LABOR IN THE ECONOMIC AND SOCIAL ORDER

A SPECIAL ROLE FOR LABOR

PERCEPTIONS OF THE PROBLEMS

In the persona dramatis of daily life in the Middle East, labor is customarily cast as an actor alongside government and management. Who the principals are and how they interrelate have set the plots for many fascinating plays on the human stage.

Most governments have been seen in leading roles. They include absolute kings, sultans and monarchial families, theocratic fundamentalists, religious ecumenists, secular democrats, free market entrepreneurs, and socialist planners—all with a commitment to national development and a desire to play a dignified role in a civilized world. They have adopted constitutions, enacted laws, signed treaties, adjudicated disputes and directed the behavior of their subjects with punishment or approval.

Management has been a group of doers with responsibility for bringing together, and balancing, men and materials so that income exceeds cost. Theirs has been the task of making and delivering goods and services. They have been directors of enterprise.

Labor has been the human ingredient in the economic endeavor. It has been a conglomerate of men and women who have made things individually or together, and whose needs have demanded satisfaction without end.

Government, management and labor have been seen from time to time as players caught up in a struggle of conflicting interests, or as social partners in a common striving. There have been leaders, followers, manipulators, exploiters, competitors or cooperators. Labor laws have set rules for the manner in which they were expected to play their varied roles.

The labor laws of the Middle East have painted workers with many brushes. With broad strokes, they have delineated some for separate treatment by occupation, residence, citizenship, or religion. At one extreme they have failed to differentiate workers from all persons in the nation, and at the other end of coverage, they have painted colorfully those who are expected to play a unique role in the transformation of society.

CONSTITUTIONAL PROVISIONS

All constitutions of Middle East countries contain pronouncements on the rights and responsibilities of labor. Most relate work to the need for economic development or personal dignity. Three constitutions, in countries with socialist objectives, pay special tribute to the role of workers in social change.

Linking work with property and capital as a fundamental constituent "of the social structure of the State and national wealth," some constitutions have declared work an "individual right with a social function, as regulated by law" (Bahrain, Kuwait, and Qatar). Others proclaim the protection of labor an express function of the state (Iraq, Jordan, UAE, and PDRY). Work is said to be a fundamental basis of development (the UAE and PDRY), and "Work shall be the duty of every citizen necessitated by personal dignity and the public good." (Bahrain, Kuwait).

Broader expressions of a revolutionary function of labor are found in the constitutions of Iraq, Syria and PDRY. Iraq announces the aim of "establishing the socialist system on scientific and revolutionary principles" for the Arab people. Syria proclaims the goal of socialism "to end all forms of exploitation" over "the Arab masses." PDRY committed itself to the "widest promulgation of the ideas of scientific socialism among the masses" and declared the working people are to exercise "all the political power; and the state is to express the "interests of the workers, the peasants, the intelligentsia, the petty bourgeoisie and all the working populace," "to deepen an alliance between peasants and the working class." (Omitted from draft of Unity States.)

Some constitutions also anticipate or authorize the enactment of laws recognizing the status of labor. Relations between employers and employees shall be regulated by law "on an economic basis, due regard being given to the principles of social justice" (Bahrain, Kuwait). "Labor relations" in the United Arab Emirates is made a federal matter; and work for all citizens shall be ensured "by providing legislation to protect the rights of the employees and to protect the interests of the employers." In the Peoples Democratic Republic of Yemen, the constitution adds to its proclamation of socialism a provision that "The basis of work relations shall be regulated by law."

LABOR CODE AND STATUTORY PROVISIONS

The above basic principles are further reflected in statutory enactments.

A common provision of Middle East labor codes commands an employer to respect his employees and to refrain from word or deed that may offend their dignity (Saudi Arabia, YAR, PDRY) or their religious beliefs (Saudi Arabia, YAR).

The Iraqi Code explains the underlying appreciation of work. "Work is a sacred duty dictated by the nobility of humankind and by the need to participate in the edification, progress and prosperity of society," and "the purpose of this Code is to involve labor in the process of building the national economy so as to achieve prosperity and improve living conditions."

TREATY PROVISIONS

The United Nations and the International Labour Office have promulgated Covenants and Conventions to induce all countries in the world to raise standards of life for workers, and most Middle East nations have signified their adherence to several of those treaties.

Although the UN Covenants embrace workers, without differentiation, as members of the human family, the ILO Conventions, as will be noted below, relate to specific labor topics and thereby define a special status for the workers involved.

The League of Arab States, in which the Muslim states are members, has reiterated the philosophical thesis, found in the ILO Philadelphia Declaration that "Labour is not a commodity."

The Arab Labor Organization (ALO) has also patterned labor Conventions along the lines of the ILO Conventions, but with a strong affirmation that they be in accord with Islamic principles. These too have been ratified by several Middle East countries and will be detailed further below.

CONSEQUENCES AND INCIDENTALS

The status of labor in the economic and social order of the Middle East has received mixed public attention. Traditionally, certain occupational groups have been the object of specific social status. Government and religious professions have enjoyed high status; "barbers, butchers, and bath workers" were, early on, despised and still remain in low esteem. Such social conditioning has resisted change. Nonetheless the improvement of the lives of workers has been kept alive by a traditional Islamic concern over the plight of the poor. In Arabic, the poor have often been referred to by the designation, "the weakened and the disinherited," and the Koran states that such persons are eligible for the highest rewards of the community. The preamble to the Iranian constitution proclaims the recent revolution as "a move towards complete victory of the poor over the powerful."

In Iraq, even with the constitutional laudation of workers and the socialist leadership role assigned to them, there has been a popular differentiation between "employees" and "workers" in which the latter appellation has carried a connotation of low-paid pariahs. In an effort to eliminate derogatory class distinctions, the General Federation of Labor Unions has undertaken to "convert" the term "workers" into "employees."[1]

Paradoxically, the wealthy and conservative country of Saudi

[1] JPRS-NEA-087-049-32. Interview with the President of the General Federation of

Arabia has found a need to exalt the idea of work. Having subsidized native Saudis and diminished the motivation to engage in business vocations, the government has looked ahead to the time when with the depletion of oil reserves it will want to substitute Saudi nationals for foreign workers, and it has embarked upon a publicity campaign importuning citizens to observe the social worth of work.[2]

In Israel, several labor groups have historically distinguished themselves and have been accorded high esteem. The early Jewish settlers assumed agricultural careers because the blossoming of the desert was their most pressing task. A European "Bund" movement brought in other pioneers as workers. In the 1920s, a Labor Battalion (Gedad Haavadah) tried to build a general commune of all Jewish workers. The Kibbutz was devised as a distinctive agricultural, and later industrial, form of a worker's society. The Histadruth expanded the role of workers from employees to promoters and owners of enterprises. Within the goals of Zionism, workers in Israel have been encouraged to constitute a primary and distinctive social force.[3]

The revolutionary role of socialist leadership assigned to workers in Iraq and Syria has not led to their transformation of society in those countries, but the philosophical concept is still preserved. In the PDRY, there is a persistent effort to utilize workers, through unions and cadres, as the predominant class in economic development.

Homage to labor may or may not give workers a distinct status. In the first May Day statement of the Ayatollah Khomeini, he spoke favorably of workers' power; however, on May Day of the year following, he said that "everyone" labors and "Labor Day is the day of all the people of Iran and not of a particular segment of the population."

Labor Unions: "Elimination of Class Differences Between Workers and Employees in Iraq," Baghdad. Al Dustur (in Arabic) 23 March 1987.

2 JPRS-NEA-086-023-80. "The Saudi Economy in its New Phase," Al-Iqtisad Wa Al-A'Mal, Dec.1985.

3 Abraham Daniel, Labor Enterprises in Israel: The Cooperative Economy, Vol. 1, Academic Press, Jerusalem, 1976.

The role of workers has been defined by tradition, social prejudices, and economic circumstances as well as by the fiat of government.

SLAVERY AND FORCED LABOR

PERCEPTIONS OF THE PROBLEM

In both Judaism and Islam, human bondage was originally regarded as an existing institution hopefully to be eliminated in time; and in time it was. Slavery is now anathema throughout the Middle East and reports of isolated vestiges are sternly abjured. Other forms of forced labor, however, have been viewed in a somewhat different light. Natural disasters and man made emergencies have left people in dire distress, and compulsory relief work has often appeared to be the lesser of two evils.

CONSTITUTIONAL PROVISIONS

Since all of the Middle East constitutions were adopted after the universal condemnation of slavery, an express prohibition of slavery was not a pressing concern. Only the constitution of the United Arab Emirates affirms the principle, "No man may be enslaved."

Forced labor, however, has been treated differently. The express outright prohibition in some constitutions is coupled with reservations.

Situations of unusual and extreme need have been singled out as exceptions to the interdiction - (a) national emergency (Bahrain, Kuwait),(b) a state of emergency (Jordan), (c) exceptional circumstances (United Arab Emirates). Less demanding conditions have led to exceptions for (d) public health or safety (Jordan), (e) a judicial decision (Bahrain, Jordan), (f) the public interest (United Arab Emirates, Yemen Arab Republic). These constitutions permitting forced labor in an emergency or in the public interest have required the specification of justifying circumstances in legislation; and generally forced labor under those circumstances must be paid a "just remuneration" or "appropriate wages."

The concept of forced labor is in some instances identified with "exploitation." In three constitutions, "exploitation" is banned. In the preamble to its constitution, Syria rejects the exploitation experienced during colonial conquest and calls for a return to an arena in which Syria, with other liberated countries, will surmount that reality and play its role in the construction of civilization and progress. The People's Democratic Republic of Yemen pronounces its aim to achieve "the complete abolition of the exploitation of man by man." (Not in the Unity draft.) Iran, in its constitutional profession of Islamic faith, asserts the exclusive sovereignty of God, the compassion of human beings, and their great worth, to be achieved through "the prohibition of all kinds of oppression, or acceptance of oppression." It determines to establish an economy on the principle that "no one shall be forced to have a job not of his choosing; no one shall exploit from the labor of others."

LABOR CODE AND STATUTORY PROVISIONS

Middle East labor codes have not used the term "forced labor".

Two codes do contain provisions prohibiting work "not agreed upon" (Bahrain, Oman). These laws still permit such work "to prevent an accident or to repair damage caused by an accident" or "in cases of force majeure" (Bahrain) or when "it is of an essential nature" (Oman). Both require such work to be temporary.

In Israel, statutes provide for involuntary services in prisons and in labor training programs. The Penal Law Revision requires every prisoner to work within a State institution unless granted an exemption. The Emergency Labor Service Law, 1967, provides for the calling up of persons for labor training by order of the Minister of Labor; and penalties may be imposed upon persons who fail to respond.

TREATY PROVISIONS

Treaty commitments, signed by Middle East countries, against slavery and forced labor go back to the League of Nations and on to the United Nations, the ILO, and the ALO.

Seven Middle East countries (Iran, Iraq, Israel, Jordan, Kuwait, Saudi Arabia, Syria) have ratified the League of Nations Convention on Abolition of Slave Trade and Institutional Practices Similar to Slavery. The Convention extends the definition of slavery to include debt bondage, the sale of women into marriage and any sham adoption of minors.

All of the nations of the Middle East except Oman and Qatar have ratified the ILO Convention No. 29 which calls for legislation prohibiting forced or compulsory labor. That Convention allows exceptions to be made for work of a purely military character, for services carrying out the normal civic obligations of citizens, for work exacted by a court after a criminal conviction, for emergency services in time of war, fire, flood, famine, earthquake, epidemic and circumstances endangering the existence or well being of the community, as well as for minor communal services after community consultation.

The ALO Convention 8, on Trade Union Rights and Freedoms, ratified by Iraq and Palestine, contains provisions on human rights, including protection against forced labor.

CONSEQUENCES AND INCIDENTALS

Slavery or the continuation of forced labor by former slaves and their descendants seems to have lasted in the Middle East for many years.[4] Under the aegis of Great Britain (which abolished slavery in 1838), Arab rulers of Middle Eastern territories signed treaties restricting and ultimately prohibiting slave trade. In 1838-39, the rulers of the Trucial States (now the UAE) granted the British the right to detain and search ships suspected of carrying slaves; and later treaties reinforced that agreement. Still, kidnappings and the sale of slaves in the Trucial States were recounted as late as the 1950s.

An early treaty between Britain and Dubai forbad the importa-

[4] W. Arafat. The Attitude of Islam to Slavery. Islamic Quarterly, Vol.10, pp.12-18, 1966.

tion of slaves into the sheikdom. Still, internal sales of slaves continued. As late as the 1930s the British government encouraged manumission and in one year, 50 slaves, used on pearling boats, applied to its Agency in Sharjah for their manumission.[5]

In the YAR, descendants of African slaves were used by land owners to cultivate farms and perform despised occupations. They lived in segregated areas. Not until 1967, five years after the republic was established, was slavery formally abolished in that country.[6]

The UN commitment to stamp out recurrent semblances of slavery in the whole world is seen in the name change given its Working Group on Slavery, now called the Working Group on Contemporary Forms of Slavery. It reports on the sale of children, the exploitations of child labor, prostitution, apartheid and colonialism.[7]

Forced labor, apart from slavery, has also been observed in parts of the Middle East. In Bahrain, it was practiced intermittently for specific tasks such as ditch digging, procuring water, transporting commodities and other low skilled tasks. Agents of any sheikh rounded up adult men and directed them to work for one or two days. In time, such acts were considered trespasses upon the rights of other sheiks who required the services of the same men, and when one sheikh thus took advantage of another it was regarded as a personal insult. In 1904, a quarrel of that nature erupted between a representative of a German firm and the nephew of a ruler. The British officials intervened and the sheikh abolished forced labor for foreigners.[8]

The use of soldiers on civil projects and the employment of

[5] Franke Heard-Bez, From Trucial States to the UAE, Longman, London, 1982.

[6] B. R. Pridham, ed., Economy, Society and Culture in Contemporary Yemen, Croom Helm, London, 1985.

[7] U.N. Economic and Social Council. Commission on Human Rights. Report of the Working Group on Contemporary Forms of Slavery. E/CN.4/Sub.2/ 1988/32. 22 Aug. 1988.

[8] Fuad I. Khuri, Tribe and State in Bahrain, Univ. of Chicago Press, Chicago & London, 1980.

civilians on unwanted work, brought on by crises of war, partake of the nature of forced labor. There have been many reports of such forced labor, but the extent to which that has occurred in the Middle East has not been documented by disinterested persons. Possible debt bondage among impoverished sharecroppers in the Middle East has been referred to as probably existent (due to the exorbitant interest rates charged by private money lenders).[9]

The moral and spiritual commandments to eliminate slavery, under Hebraic and Islamic law, have ultimately come to fruition. Yet the curtailment of forced labor has been limited by the persistence of war and natural calamities.

RIGHT AND DUTY TO WORK

PERCEPTIONS OF THE PROBLEM

Countries in the Middle East, experiencing new statehood and the discovery of oil, quickly recognized their need for innovation. Tribal patterns of work, in all aspects of life, were obviously inadequate. Nations had become newly responsible for their own destinies and they chose to acclaim the right to do anything necessary. Common to all their plans for development was an ingredient of work. They needed work and they were willing to work. Therefore work was asserted as a right, and where further assurance was desired, work was made a duty.

It was palpably clear that employment was indispensable and that work benefitted both the individual worker and his community. It was not evident how the individual right to work could be asserted or enforced; that did not deter its acclaim. While it was also known that more work was required to sustain development, no one intended the duty to work to deprive workers of their freedom. For want of answers to such matters, however, the right to work and the duty to work were left undefined.

[9] Judith Ennew. Debt Bondage—a Survey. Anti-Slavery Society. London. 1981.

STATUS OF LABOR IN ECONOMIC AND SOCIAL ORDER

CONSTITUTIONAL PROVISIONS

In their constitutions, Bahrain, Iraq, Kuwait, Syria and PDRY establish both the right and duty to work; and Jordan, Qatar and YAR proclaim the right alone. In Iraq, work is also declared an honor and a sacred duty.

The constitutions, however, prescribe that the right to work is to be (a) in accord with public order and moral standards (Bahrain), (b) within the limits of the law (United Arab Emirates, Yemen Arab Republic), (c) not contrary to the principles of Islam, the public interest and the rights of others (Iran), or (d) in accordance with one's ability, qualifications and the social interest (PDRY). (Omitted from the draft constitution.)

LABOR CODE AND STATUTORY PROVISIONS

Several labor codes reiterate the right to work and speak of it as inherent in citizens or nationals, thereby leaving the rights of aliens or immigrants to other treatment (Iraq, Saudi Arabia, UAE, YAR, PDRY).

TREATY PROVISIONS

The right to work, but not a duty to work, has been mentioned in treaties.

The UN Covenant on Economic, Social and Cultural Rights, signed by Iran, Iraq, Israel, Jordan, Lebanon, Syria, and the PDRY, provides "The States Parties to the present Covenant recognize the right to work, which includes the right of everyone to the opportunity to gain his living by work which he freely chooses or accepts, and will take appropriate steps to safeguard this right." The steps to be taken include "technical and vocational guidance and training programmes, policies and techniques to achieve steady economic, social and cultural development and full and productive employment."

CONSEQUENCES AND INCIDENTALS

The right to work has been a common catchword in public discussions of current labor problems. Editorial comments in

PDRY newspapers have equated the right to work with employment opportunities and nondiscrimination for women.[10] It has been one of the demands of organized labor in Bahrain.[11] In Saudi Arabia, as well as in other states hosting immigrant labor, the right to work has been stressed for citizens as differentiated from alien workers.[12]

FREE CHOICE OF OCCUPATION

PERCEPTIONS OF THE PROBLEM

Choosing a vocation may be an introductory baptism into the uncertainties of life, or it may be a ceremonial proposal of lifelong marriage. It is a beginning with exciting possibilities.

Freedom of occupational choice is cherished, particularly when external circumstances constrict alternatives. Rarely are job opportunities unlimited; and the existence of a choice or a right of refusal nourishes the possibility of improvement and a hope of fulfillment.

Laws proclaiming a freedom of choice in occupation have opened vistas of anticipation in the Middle East. Without assuring employment or the reality of accomplishment, they have signalled that traditional tribal roles may be left behind, that unskilled workers may acquire skills, that a vast assortment of commercial and industrial jobs may repose in a grab bag, and that workers may aspire to something better than what they or their parents have had.

CONSTITUTIONAL PROVISIONS

Several Middle East constitutions provide for free choice of occupation.

Every citizen shall have the right "to choose his type of work"

[10] JPRS-NEA-086-094, Article by Dr. Muhammad Salah, "Labor Law on Employment of Women". Aden. Sawt Al-Ummal (Arabic), 1986.

[11] JPRS-NEA-086-022. Abdallah Khalifaha, Interview of Chairman, General Committee Workers of of Bahrain. Al-Shauqah Al-Khalif (Arabic). March 18, 1986, p.14.

[12] JPRS-NEA-086-057-038. Interview with Minister of Labor and Social Affairs. Riyadh. Al-Yamamah (Arabic), Jan. 15, 1986, p.26.

(Bahrain, Kuwait), "to choose the profession he wishes" (Iran), "to choose his occupation, trade or profession" (United Arab Emirates), "to undertake work chosen by him" (Yemen Arab Republic). He shall not be "hindered from practising his profession, job or work" (PDRY).

Some constitutions provide that the freedom may be qualified by the limits of law (United Arab Emirates, Yemen Arab Republic), the public order and moral standards (Bahrain), the public interest, the principles of Islam and the rights of others (Iran).

LABOR CODE AND STATUTORY PROVISIONS

Lebanon, Qatar, and PDRY have unusual statutory provisions against restrictions upon occupational choice.

"No person may commit himself by the terms of any agreement to remain in a given employment for the whole of his lifetime or not at any time in his life to take employment in a given occupation " (Lebanon). After providing that the employer shall "direct, distribute and place the workers in occupations that shall suit their educational qualifications, experience and abilities", PDRY prescribes, "It shall not be permissible to change the occupation of the worker except with his consent, or if the public interest so warrants." In Qatar, a worker may not contract to "restrain himself for life from practising, after leaving the employer's service, any trade or profession he may be able to practise."

TREATY PROVISIONS

The ILO Convention No. 122, on Employment Policy, requires signatory nations to establish a policy of freedom of choice of employment. That has been ratified by Iran, Iraq, Israel, Jordan, and Lebanon.

Without specifying free choice of occupation, the Convention on Labour Norms of the Arab Labor Organization does require a written contract for employment. That Convention has been ratified by Iraq, Jordan, Lebanon, Palestine, and Syria.

CONSEQUENCES AND INCIDENTALS

Freedom of occupational choice has meant different things under varying social and economic conditions.

Choice of employment by women in the Middle East has been severely restricted by custom. Their participation in the industrial sector has been confined to positions deemed clean and environmentally safe, often set apart from male workers.[13] Conservative Shi'ites, particularly in Iran, have invoked religious scruples inhibiting women's occupational outreach.[14] In Saudi Arabia and other countries, seeking to expand the economic activities of native personnel, particularly in skilled positions filled by foreign workers, women have been encouraged to obtain education for such work. Alien workers, brought in for specific tasks, have not been accorded freedom to choose other occupations.

Middle East pearling workers, whose industry had been practically eliminated by pearl culture in other lands, and Bedouins, whose tribal migration had been restricted, were reluctant to leave their customary occupations; but many have taken advantage of a freedom to do so. Unemployed workers in the countries without oil, not only in the poorer Yemens, but also in the more developed Syria and in war-torn Lebanon, have necessarily been dependent upon the freedom to seek other employment.

WORKERS' PARTICIPATION IN MANAGEMENT

PERCEPTIONS OF THE PROBLEM

The promotion of workers' participation in management, a relatively recent aspect of labor law in industrialized countries, has been seen from varying points of view in the Middle East.

Some Islamic precepts have been pertinent. All persons, employers and employees, are regarded as equal in the sight of Allah; consultation with wise or learned men in the community was practiced by the Prophet, and was prescribed for all rulers.

[13] JPRS-NEA-086-087-52. Interview with Dr. Hekmat Al-Urabi, Head of Women's Section at Ministry of Planning. Riyadh, Al-Riyad (in Arabic), 18 April 1986, p.4.

[14] JPRS-NEA-086-97-81, London, Keyhan (in Persian) 26 Jan.1986, p.6.

Labor law in early Islam stressed other relationships; and personnel adjustments in response to evolving industrial interests in modern Islamic countries have asserted themselves slowly. Islamic critics of both capitalism and communism have seen a consultative relationship between management and labor as their distinctive contribution to a moral future.[15] As qualities of social welfare states have emerged in the Middle East, an increasing interest in labor-management consensus has been manifested.

Pioneer Jews viewed the establishment of a homeland in Israel as a communal effort, originally without sharp differentiation between management and labor. In the building of a viable economy, during the last few decades, Israel has emphasized the distinction and has espoused the policy of worker participation in management. Its fundamental query has been how to balance productive efficiency with social equity. In a succession of experiments, Israel has wrestled with the problems of how to interest workers in the tasks of management, how to train workers for effective managerial participation, how to develop an acceptance of worker partnership in the role of management, and how to inspire enthusiasm for the program.[16]

CONSTITUTIONAL PROVISIONS

There are no explicit provisions in Middle East constitutions for workers' participation in management.

LABOR CODE AND STATUTORY PROVISIONS

The Labor Codes of Bahrain, Iraq, Qatar and the PDRY provide for collaboration between management and labor, in these words,

> (a) "Labor relations shall be based upon social solidarity between the various parties concerned and thus presuppose their collaboration and assumption of responsibilities" (Iraq).

15 Khalid M. Ishaq. Islam and Law in the Twenty-First Century. Islamic and Compartive Law Quart., Vol.5, No.3-4, Sept.-Dec. 1985.

16 I. Barak and N. Ork, Worker's Participation in Decisions Within Undertakings, National Report, Israel; C. Crouch, ed., Organizational Democracy and Political Processes, Chap.22, John Wiley & Sons Ltd., 1983.

> (b) "Employers and workers of any establishment may form amongst themselves joint committees for cooperation in the . . . increasing of productivity and in any other matters of mutual interest to the two parties" (Bahrain).
>
> (c) "The employer shall be obliged . . . to let the worker participate, through periodic meetings, called and presided over by the head of the establishment, assisted by the trade union committee . . ." to improve the work system and increase production. Also, management "shall facilitate the participation of the workers in administering production and shall discuss, without delay, the worker's views and proposals that aim at correcting the negative aspect and developing the work for the better" (PDRY).
>
> (d) "Joint consultative committees composed of representatives of employer and worker may be formed in any establishment . . . [and] may consider and make proposals on matters connected with raising the standard of work and workers" (Bahrain, Qatar).

Not having adopted a labor code, as such, Israel has enacted separate laws and issued regulations promoting worker participation in management. Although much voluntary experimentation with labor-management joint action was undertaken under the Cooperative Societies Ordinance of 1933 and the Collective Agreements Law of 1957, the government enacted the Government Companies Law in 1975 dealing with the appointment of worker representatives to the directorship of companies in which the State held more than half of the voting power.

TREATY PROVISIONS

Although the ILO Convention 135 on Protection and Facilities for Worker Representatives does not mention the participation of such representatives in managerial functions, it does protect trade union representatives from prejudicial treatment and offers them facilities to carry out their functions promptly and efficiently (whatever their functions may happen to be). The Convention has been ratified by Iraq, Jordan, Syria, and the Yemen Arab Republic. Also the ALO Convention 11 on Collective Bargaining, ratified by Iraq and Jordan, contains language on the participation of employers and employees in the solving of their respective problems.

CONSEQUENCES AND INCIDENTALS

The Israeli experience with workers' participation in management, proclaimed as an effort to achieve industrial democracy and social justice, has been a pragmatic experiment in enterprises designed to make a profit.[17] The process has been scrutinized, criticized, manipulated and adjusted to attain effective labor participation in managerial functions - with a concomitant of profit sharing. The peculiar development of the Histadruth as a General Federation of Labor, that has owned and operated manufacturing, construction and service businesses, has given rise to conflicting considerations and difficulties inherent in the attempt to carve a managerial role for labor. A primary concern for more wages and a lack of interest or skills in accounting, distribution, and industrial innovation, have led some worker-turned-managers and politically oriented committeemen at times to derail the process. Special training programs have been instituted to qualify workers to serve both roles, their labor role and representative role in management.

In farming, labor and management have not been as differentiated as in factories or large-scale enterprise, and the Israeli agricultural enterprises (Kibbutzim, Moshavim, and Cooperatives) have found it necessary to pay special attention to aspects of workers' participation in farm management. In all the Israeli economy, workers' participation in management is an ongoing and experimental endeavor.

The announced socialistic objectives of Iraq, Syria, and PDRY have stimulated a few projects in which unions and management have undertaken forms of concerted activity in those countries.

[17] Abraham Daniel, Labor Enterprises in Israel, Vol.II: The Institutional Economy, Academic Press, Jerusalem, 1976.

DISCRIMINATION

PERCEPTIONS OF THE PROBLEM

All the countries of the Middle East have experienced the humiliation of subject peoples under colonial powers; and even after independence they have endured the disdain of the "more developed nations" or the prejudice of narrow religionists. They have had sufficient cultural reason to dislike discrimination (unless there is a perversity in man that seeks to assert superiority through the creation of inferiors). No Middle East government has defended discrimination among its own workers.

Notwithstanding the truth of such generalizations, differences among individuals have been unmistakable, and the extent to which they appear to warrant discriminatory treatment has become the subject of much debate. For the purposes of employment most characteristics, other than skill and ability, have been unacceptable; yet the list of grounds given for discrimination has been very long. The adventitious circumstances that may justify exceptions (or serve as excuses for the concealment of acknowledged wrongs) have been even more perplexing. In reflecting popular attitudes on discrimination among workers, laws have been comprehensive or selective, binding or wishful.

CONSTITUTIONAL PROVISIONS

All constitutions of Middle East countries provide for equality before the law; and the states guarantee their citizens equal opportunities.

In Iran, even "The Leader or members of the Council of Leaders and all other citizens of the country are equal before the law."

Discrimination is explicity prohibited when based on (a) *religion* (Bahrain, Iraq, Kuwait, Jordan, Qatar, United Arab Emirates, PDRY), (b)*race* (Bahrain, Iran, Iraq, Kuwait, Jordan, Qatar, United Arab Emirates), (c) *color* (Iran, Yemen Arab Republic), (d) *origin* (Bahrain, Iran, Iraq, Kuwait, Yemen Arab Republic, PDRY), (e) *nationality* (United Arab Emirates), (f) *language* (Bahrain, Iran, Iraq, Kuwait, Jordan, Yemen Arab Republic, PDRY, (g) *sex* (Iran, Qatar, Yemen Arab Republic,

PDRY (omitted from new draft)), (h) *tribes* (Iran), (i) *education* (PDRY, also not in new draft), (j) *profession* (Yemen Arab Republic), (k) *social position or status* (Iran, United Arab Emirates, PDRY).

Constitutional provisions for a state religion usually affirm the freedom to practice other creeds as well.

LABOR CODE AND STATUTORY PROVISIONS

A few labor codes have deemed it necessary to reaffirm the constitutional provisions on nondiscrimination.

Iraq, Saudi Arabia, Syria, YAR, and PDRY have such general statutes.

Several labor codes have special provisions banning discrimination against women. Iraq guarantees the right to work under equal conditions and with equal opportunity . . . to all citizens . . . without any discrimination on the basis of sex." Syria provides female workers "shall be subject to all the stipulations governing the employment of male workers without discrimination in the same job." PDRY states it shall endeavor "to create conditions that enable women to combine participation in productive and social work with their role within the framework of family life." Also it guarantees Yemeni women the right to work and to equal employment opportunities and it requires the Ministry of Labor and Civil Service to achieve full equality in remuneration and employment opportunities. However it bans women labor that will harm a woman's health or that will expose women to industrial poisons known to affect female organs. The Israeli Equal Opportunities Law forbids the denial of employment by reason of sex, marriage or parenthood; and a Women's Equal Rights Law gives women equal status in any legal proceeding, without derogation of their rights under any law "protecting women as women."

Labor codes which refer to "citizens" in their sections on nondiscrimination (Iraq, Saudi Arabia, PDRY) leave undeclared the rights of noncitizens. They are usually covered by laws specifically dealing with immigration or citizenship.

TREATY PROVISIONS

All ILO and ALO Conventions call for labor standards without distinction among workers except where reservations are specified; so that the ratification of these Conventions by any Middle East country involves some commitment to nondiscrimination. A few Conventions deal directly with nondiscrimination.

The principal ILO convention on nondiscrimination, No. 111, seeks the elimination of all discrimination based on race, color, sex, religion, political opinion, national extraction or social origin which impairs equality of opportunity or treatment in employment or occupation. It has been ratified by Iran, Iraq, Israel, Jordan, Kuwait, Lebanon, Qatar, Saudi Arabia, Syria and the Yemen Arab Republic.

Equal Remuneration for Men and Women engaged in work of equal value is the subject of Convention 100; and that has been ratified by Iran, Iraq, Israel, Jordan, Lebanon, Saudi Arabia, Syria, and the Yemen Arab Republic.

Convention 117, concerning Basic Aims and Standards of Social Policy declares that policies of subscribing governments shall be directed primarily to the well-being and development of the population, particularly with respect to improvement of standards of living. To that end, it promotes measures for the equal protection of migrant workers and underpaid workers, and for the abolition of discrimination on grounds of race, color, sex, belief, tribal association, or trade union affiliation. That has been ratified by Israel, Jordan, Kuwait, and Syria.

Other Conventions, limited in scope or relating to other subjects, also provide for nondiscrimination and have been ratified by Middle East countries. Convention 19 on National and Foreign Workers has been signed by Iran, Iraq, Israel, Lebanon, Syria, and PDRY. Convention 107 concerning the protection and integration of Indigenous, Tribal and Semi-Tribal Populations calls for legislation giving equal opportunities for "less advanced" workers to acquire land ownership, employment, vocational training, social security, health, and education. It has been signed by Iraq and Syria.

Each of the mentioned signatory nations is required to report to the ILO the steps taken by it to carry out the intent of its signed conventions, and the reports are reviewed for advice and assistance by the Special Committee of the ILO on the Enforcement of Conventions.

ALO Convention 5 on Women at Work, ratified by Iraq and Palestine, provides for the equality of male and female workers in placement, remuneration, and working conditions.

CONSEQUENCES AND INCIDENTALS

Smoldering prejudices of ancient origin appear to be rekindled again and again, threatening to make a mockery of the laws against discrimination. Persistent cultural conflicts, accentuated by war, have created fears and antagonisms that have expressed themselves in employment discrimination. Although the ILO has obtained commitments to the contrary and an enlightened element in every country has spoken out against discriminatory practices, they have often been ignored.

The *Arab-Zionist* embitterment has had insidious effects. In Arab states, governments have forbidden the entrance of Jews to engage in trade or to represent companies that refused to boycott Israel. In Israel, many employers have confined the employment of Arabs to manual work or low-paid jobs. Back and forth recriminations have not ended the claims of "illegal" discrimination.[18]

The treatment of *women workers* has been more subtly discriminatory. Islamic fundamentalists have imposed patterns of proper behavior that have restricted the work of women. In 1988, the ILO directed the attention of the Iranian government to Article 163(1) of its constitution which bars women from serving as judges. Custom in all Middle East countries has assigned

[18] One of the many accusations of discrimination was raised by an Arab worker who became Chairman of a radical, left wing party and was dismissed from his employment for lack of work in a department of the Histadrut. The National Labor Court ruled that there was convincing evidence that his dismissal was caused by a lack of work and extraneous or background motive did not affect the validity of the dismissal. Saliman v. Histadrut, Int'l. Labor Law Rpts. Vol. 2, p.156.

women to certain traditional types of work, generally in nonexecutive and lower paid positions. A rising feminist movement has proceeded unevenly with promised reforms.[19]

Iran has been accused of perpetrating special forms of discrimination. Flagrant acts against members of the Bahai faith have not been denied; the government has sought to justify them.[20] The Secretary General of the United Nations reported to its Commission on Human Rights that countless Bahai civil servants had been arbitrarily dismissed and denied back-pay or pensions, that many Bahai students had been expelled from their positions, including some in their final year of professional training, that Bahai nurses who had completed their education had been denied diplomas; that official pressure had been put upon Islamic employers to dismiss their Bahai employees and that a large number had complied. A directive from the Minister of Labor, approved by the Iranian Parliament on 27 September 1981 was quoted as providing that any member of the "misguided" Bahai group was to be dismissed for life from goverment service. These charges were submitted by the ILO Committee of Experts on the Observance of ILO Conventions to the Government of Iran in 1983 and it has been repeated annually thereafter. The only replies from Iran were that Bahai was not a religion; it was an organization of heretics to Islam and of spies for external enemies. Similar charges that Iran was discriminating against Freemasons were countered with the claim that their Masonic membership implied allegiance to atheism.

Israel has been inspected for job discrimination, and has been found not living up to the standards of the ILO. Ever since 1978, with the consent of the Israeli government, the ILO has conducted on-site investigations and issued annual reports on the situation of Arab workers in the occupied territories of Palestine. The latest report, 1988, took into account the recent and continu-

[19] Farah Azari, ed., Women of Iran, Ithaca Press, London, 1983; G. Nashat, Women and Revolution in Iran, Westview Press, Boulder, Colo., 1983.

[20] "Religious Persecution of the Bahai's in Iran," Hearing before the Subcommittee on Human Rights of the Committee of Foreign Affairs, HR, 98th Congress, 2nd Session, May 2, 1984.

ing uprising of the Arab population.[21]

In that and earlier reports, the ILO recommended 1 - the application of employment policies promoting productive activities in the territories (and lifting restrictions on trade); 2 - the extension of vocational training and development of job opportunities for young Arab graduates; 3 - equal treatment for Arab workers employed in Israel, particularly in view of the impact of the work permit system on job security; 4 - combatting irregular employment in Israel; 5 - improvement of working and living conditions and health infrastructure; 6 - eliminating unequal opportunity and treatment resulting from Israeli settlements in occupied territories; 7 - eliminating unequal treatment in social security for workers from the territories employed in Israel; and 8 - effective exercise of trade union rights by Arab workers from the territories, both in Israel and in the territories. The ILO offered technical assistance to overcome some of these difficulties, with financial assistance from the U.N. Development Program. Some assistance, particularly in vocational, entrepreneurial, and trade union training, was accepted.

Out of a population of approximately 1-1/2 million in the occupied territories (383,00 in the East Bank, 545,000 in Gaza, 15,000 in the Golan Heights, and 140,000 in East Jerusalem as of 1986), it is estimated that around 761,000 Palestinians are economically active—and they have limited prospects of employment. Half of those are employed in the building sector of Israel; and about half of them are hired outside the official channels of the Israeli Employment Service. That constitutes for Palestinians a high rate of dependence upon uncertain Israeli employment. Beyond these economic stringencies, there is also a "psychological dimension" of oppression, expressed by the 1988 uprising.

[21] ILO. Report of the Director-General. International Conference. 75th Session, 1988. Appendices (Vol.2). Geneva, ILO. Same for 73rd Session. Geneva 1987. U.S. Department of State: Country Reports on Human Rights Practices for 1987. Washington, 1988. ILO. Committee on Freedom of Association. Official Bull. Vol. LXX, 1987, ser.B, No.2 approved by the Governing Body, 236th Session. May 1987, par.215-229.

Among the pressing labor problems of Palestinian workers from the territories, the ILO has pointed to the difficulties inherent in a monthly work permit system, the requirement of travel back each night, and irregular employment in circumvention of the official Employment Service. Personal hardships have resulted in absenteeism (as high as 50%). Pervasive discrimination has occurred in the relegation of Arab workers to manual or unskilled jobs at minimum wages, with a shortage of training centers and instructors. The recent violent confrontations, curfews, school closings, and work stoppages have aggravated all of these long-standing problems.

Special labor law inequities have been charged with respect to the prevailing social security system. Nonresident Arab workers are handled through separate funds. They do not qualify for any social security benefit in the Gaza Strip, and receive limited insurance against sickness, invalidity and occupational accidents if employed in the West Bank. Insurance schemes do not provide nonresidents the coverage received by residents for old age, unemployment and occupational disease. Israeli law requires uniform contributions from workers; and nonresident contributors are not entitled to tax credit points given resident workers.

More critical labor law questions have arisen with respect to trade union rights. Arab workers from the occupied territories are assessed 1% of wages for dues to the Histadrut, which, many of them believe, does not care for their needs. Arab trade unions have not been given official registration since 1979 and many employers refuse to bargain with them. Security cautions have on ocasions led the military authorities to incarcerate Arab union leaders, to ban union meetings or the election of union officers, and to exile active trade unionists. Strikes in a "civil disobedience campaign" have been met by arrests, jail sentences and deportation. ILO formal determination that Israel violated the normal rights of trade unionists in specific instances has not yet altered the official Israeli opposition to many forms of Arab union activity.

Much of the labor difficulty in agriculture, in the occupied territories, has been attributed to the settlement policies of Israel. Since 1967, more than 52% of the land in the West Bank and over 40% of the Gaza Strip have been taken by the government on the ground of public necessity; much of it has been assigned by military authorities to the building of settlement houses for Israelis (3000 dwellings scheduled for 1988); water quotas for Arab farms have been reduced; electricity formerly supplied to East Jerusalem Arabs has been shifted to Israeli settlers; and year after year the situation of Arab farmers has deteriorated.

The conflict of interest between some religious Israelis determined to acquire dominion over all the land of historic Judea and Samaria and those Arabs who have dug their livelihood into the soil has produced or aggrevated the above series of labor problems. These are now in a limbo of political crisis.

Discrimination among workers has been outlawed in the Middle East by constitutions, statutes, and treaties; yet it is a common heartache.

DEVELOPMENT AND PLANNING

PERCEPTIONS OF THE PROBLEM

All countries of the Middle East see development as a high, if not their highest, priority. Many rulers have had faith in historical progress and have proceeded on the assumption that with the inflow of oil revenue, there would inevitably follow substantial improvement in the welfare of their citizens. In time, multiple, new problems and the uneven development of their economies have caused them to seek means for diversifying or increasing the overall benefits showered upon them by oilwell gushers. Even nonoil bearing neighbors, upset by the sudden dislocation of their peoples, have sought to control their activities. Every Middle East government has determined to plan its development; and has been confronted by the question of how to convert its plans into realities.

Development and planning have been viewed from the standpoint of general economic progress or from the perspective of benefits to the workers (or other special groups) involved. The two have always been interrelated. Specific projects though designed primarily for national purposes such as resource conservation and exploitation, or military strength, or for individual enterprises such as roads, dams, schools, houses, have had by-product effects. Much of the time, the fallout effects have become more significant than the completion of the projects. One test of the success of planning or any specific measure undertaken has been the extent to which the working population has been benefitted by it.

Planning for development has become a formalized procedure, with government agencies, investigations, budgeting, five-year goals, and evaluations. The consideration of demographic factors involving the workers of a country has been accepted as indispensable to sound planning. Workers have been seen as ultimate beneficiaries of development.

CONSTITUTIONAL PROVISIONS

All constitutions of Middle East countries contain provisions relating to development and planning.

They declare their choice of a market or socialized economy and add terms indicating how they desire the system to progress. (a) *Private enterprise* is established in most countries with specific references to its social purpose. That is denoted as "fair cooperation between public and private sectors" (Iraq, Qatar), "sincere cooperation between public and private activity" (United Arab Emirates), "provided it does not violate the interests of the society" (Yemen Arab Republic). (b) *Socialism* is the declared goal in Iraq and the PDRY. The former country also guarantees private ownership and individual economic freedom that "will not contradict or be detrimental to general economic planning." The latter also supports "the productive activity of the private and combined enterprises." (c) Iran decries a "materialistic" school of thought and regards its economy as "a means" to its *Islamic ends*. Its constitution speaks of a "cooperative system . . . providing interest-free loans and . . . other legitimate means which will result in neither the concentration of wealth . . . nor its use by particular individuals or groups, nor the transformation of the government into a monopolistic employer."

The constitutions provide for economic development under these systems with express or implied reference to planning. The ends sought are to produce "social justice" (Bahrain, Kuwait, United Arab Emirates, Yemen Arab Republic), to "fulfill the needs of mankind" (Iran, PDRY), to improve production and raise the standards of living (Jordan, Kuwait, United Arab Emirates, PDRY, Yemen Arab Republic), to result in "economic self sufficiency" and to forbid "speculation, usury, profiteering" (Iran), to achieve Arab unity (Iraq). Planning is referred to in the PDRY as "democratic centralization" which combines state planning and administration with initiative in local organs. Its plans are to be "executed with the effective participation of the workers and the toiling masses on the basis of scientific studies and statistics." (Stated more generally in the draft constitution.)

Related to planning is a prohibition of monopolies (in Iran, Yemen Arab Republic), with such exceptions as may be provided by law, for a limited period (Bahrain, Kuwait, Lebanon).

LABOR CODE AND STATUTORY PROVISIONS

The broad development goals expressed in constitutions have needed little repetition in labor codes, but implementing statutes have been quite numerous.

The Labor Code of PDRY provides that the state "shall guarantee the right of work through an increasing and progressive planning to develop the natural economy in all fields." The other labor codes as such do not specify planning; however other statutes have created executive or administrative agencies of government with the express function of planning economic development, and their plans have dealt with labor problems and objectives. Even when plan documents have not mentioned manpower needs, their provisions have clearly been designed to affect the nature and conditions of work in the countries.

TREATY PROVISIONS

UN covenants as well as ILO and ALO conventions calling for development and planning have been signed by Middle East governments. Although the conventions are usually confined to a single occupation or labor relationship, many of them propose the adoption of policies promoting general economic development.

The UN Covenant on Economic, Social and Cultural Rights, ratified by Iran, Iraq, Israel, Jordan, Lebanon, Syria, and PDRY obligates those countries to take steps including "policies on techniques to achieve steady economic, social and cultural development."

Planning and development are mentioned in ILO Convention No. 117 on Social Policy (Basic Aims and Standards). That states "All practicable measures shall be taken in the planning of economic development to harmonize such development with the healthy evolution of the communities concerned." That convention has been ratified by Israel, Jordan, Kuwait. Convention 122, concerning Employment Policy, provides that each signatory shall "by such methods and to such extent as may be appropriate under national conditions" take steps, including "the establishment of programmes" for employment. That Convention has been ratified by Iran, Iraq, Israel, Jordan, and Lebanon.

ALO Convention II on Collective Bargaining, ratified by Iraq and Jordan, encourages workers, or their representatives, to work with national labor administrations on social and economic development.

Such legal measures reinforce what all the countries of the Middle East have earnestly desired to do.

CONSEQUENCES AND INCIDENTALS

The economic details of currently announced plans in the Middle East show where, if not precisely how, labor gains are anticipated.

The "oil rich" countries—Saudi Arabia, Iran, Iraq, Kuwait and the UAE, as well as the "quasi oil rich" Bahrain, Oman, and

Qatar, now look primarily to a diversification of their industries. (a) *Saudi Arabia's* fourth five-year plan (1986-90) has recalled the investment of about 80 billion dollars in two hydrocarbon industrial complexes, at Jambu and Jubail, and it now seeks to develop additional industries that utilize natural gas and crude petroleum and that increase production of food, chemicals, and metallic goods. It has offered incentives and financial aid to private enterprise, and has required that foreign companies re-invest 35% of the value of their technical works in joint ventures with Saudis. Considerable emphasis is given to the reduction of expatriate labor and the expansion of health services.[22] (b) *Kuwait* and the *UAE*, plan to expand their commerical and banking activities. The largest of the United Arab Emirates, Abu Dhabi, Dubai and Shrjah, have continued to derive their principal income from oil, but the three Emirates that have no oil have been recipients of aid and have planned to improve their agriculture, fishing, and tourism.[23] (c) *Iran* and *Iraq*, locked in 8 years of war, have planned to repair their damaged oil facilities and to strengthen their agriculture and domestic support industries. Iran has announced plans (revised in 1986) to step up investment in agriculture, to create self-sufficiency in food, and to shift public consumption away from imported luxury products. It has also announced the objectives of securing the interests of the "deprived or downtrodden people" and the expansion of education and culture.[24] Iraq has focused on investment in the government sector, the infrastructure and social services, as well as the balancing of national and local economic activities.[25] (d) *Bahrain* has sought new economic outlets such as the erection of an aluminum plant and the construction of a causeway (carrying traders and tourists

[22] JPRS-NEA-086-023-80, "The Saudi Economy in its New Phase", Al-Iqtisad Wa Al-A'Mal, Dec., 1985.

[23] JPRS-NEA-086-071-16, Interview with Fu'ad Mulla Husayn, Deputy Minister of Planning, A-Tadamun (in Arabic), p.19-25, April, 1986; Ragaei El Mallakah, The Economic Development of the UAE, St. Martin's Press, N.Y., 1986.

[24] JPRS-NEA-086-100-85, Vahe Petrossian, "Iran Plans for Self-Sufficiency," London, 1 MEED, The Middle East's Business Weekly (in English), 19 Jul.86, pp.4-5.

[25] JPRS-NEA-086-016-45, Adnan Salah, "The War and the Brilliant Horizons of the Course of Economic Development in Iraq," October, 1985.

back and forth) to Saudi Arabia.[26] (e) *Oman*. In its third plan, 1986-90, Oman has stressed interest free loans to small and medium sized industrial units, and assistance to farmers and fishermen in the form of pest spraying, veterinary clinics, equipment repairs, seed laboratories, and training for the growth of new crops.[27] (f) *Qatar* (with a 1973 development plan designed for the following 20 years), has relied upon oil and gas resources, and has proposed to enhance its infrastructure by building a hospital, an airport, a university, electricity and desalinization plants, government offices, and civilian housing, also by tying into a road system leading all the way to the English Channel.[28]

The non-oil producing countries, Israel, Jordan, Lebanon, Syria and the Yemens, have planned along lines peculiar to each: (a) *Israel* has planned to build a viable Westernized economy. With a substantial infusion of foreign financial aid, it has announced goals of (1) population growth and dispersal, (2) new industries and expanded trade, (3) improved income and employment, (4) adequate social services (housing, education, and health) (5) ethnic survival, and (6) military security.[29] (b) *Jordan's* 1986-90 plan has called for the optimal utilization of its natural resources (phosphate and oil shale), the improvement of its logging, mining and construction, the development of small industries and crafts and the attainment of food sufficiency. It has forecast that as many as 100,000 jobs will be created. The plan also seeks the replacement of foreign workers by citizens. The planners have held in abeyance adjustments for the anticipated settlement of the Israeli-Palestinian dispute.[30] (c) *Occupied Pal-*

[26] JPRS-NEA-086-064-32, Interview with Planning and Economy Minister Yusef Al-Shirwai, London, Al-Majallah (in Arabic), April 1986, p. 36,37.

[27] Calvin H. Allen, Jr., Oman: The Modernization of the Sultanate, Boulder, Westview Press, 1987; JPRS-NEA-086-008-93, Development in Agriculture and Fishing, Abu Dhabi, Al-Ithihad (in Arabic), Nov. 3, 1985.

[28] Zuhair A. Nafi, Economic and Social Development in Qatar, F. Printer, Dover, N.H., 1986.

[29] Israel Rashut, Basic points of a Plan for the Public Economy, 1977-81, Ministry of Finance, Econ. Planning Authority, Jerusale, 1981; Israel, Rashut, The Economic Plan, 1974-1978, Ministry of Finance, Econ. Planning Authority, Jerusalem, 1977.

[30] B. Khader & A. Badran, The Economic Development of Jordan, Croom-Helm, London, 1987.

estine. In 1986, Jordan prepared a development plan for the territories occupied by Israel. It had planned to invest Jordanian money in West Bank and Gaza projects to create 20,000 jobs in four years, thereby reducing emigration to Jordan and Israel. The USA offered to contribute 4.5 million dollars to the development schemes. Due to increased hositilities in the occupied areas, King Hussein abruptly terminated much of his assistance, and the Intifada has brought formal planning to a standstill.[31] (d) *Lebanon*. Apart from emergency plans for the relief of the dislocated and the unemployed, there have been a few efforts to maintain or restore the historic functions of Lebanon as a center of international finance and education. Current plans are to normalize food production as much as possible.[32] (e) *Syria's* sixth development plan, 1986-90, has sought to cut imports and to reduce military spending and at the same time to increase investment in agriculture and domestic industries.[33] (f) *Yemen Arab Republic*. Its third 5 year plan (1987-91), as its earlier plans, has been devoted to the guidance of agriculture. It continues to wrestle with irrigation schemes to store water in the mountain catchment basin and to save it in the run-off low lands. It aims to achieve self-sufficiency in plant and animal products; and it now concentrates on the improvement of drought resistance crops, fodder crops, and sugar, vegetables, and grapes for export. More cotton growth and the revitalization of a Chinese built cotton mill are also expected to increase exports. The discovery of some oil in 1984 has led to cautious planning for the possibility of a balanced economic growth.[34] (g) *People's Democratic Republic of Yemen*. Pursuant to its philosophy of socialization, PDRY has a fourth 5 year plan (1986-91), calling for the expansion of

[31] JPRS-NEA-086-001-156, "Strategy of Jordan's 1986-1990 Economic Development Plan," Al-Iqtisad Wa Al-A'Mal (in Arabic), Beirut, Sept. 1986, pp. 52-54.

[32] JPRS-NEA-087-082-34, "The Year of Economic Reckoning in Lebanon" by I. Awaydah, London, Al-Tadamun (in Arabic), May, 1987, p. 45.

[33] JPRS-NEA-086-033-53, "Work Begins on 5-Year Plan to Boost Agriculture," Middle Eastern Economic Review (in English), London, Jan. 25, 1986, p. 32.

[34] Robert Burrowes, Yemen Arab Republic: The Politics of Development, 1962-1986, Westview Press, Boulder, Colo., 1987; JPRS-NEA-087-094-70, "Third 5-Year Economic Plan Approved" (in Arabic), Sana'a, Al-Thawra, 17 July 1987.

state farms with irrigation networks, mechanized farming, technical cadres, and worker training. In addition to seeking increased operation of its oil refinery (working for Kuwait, Iran, and the USSR), it has planned publicly owned manufacturies such as a flour mill and fish canneries.[35] Both the Yemens have experienced a surplus of unskilled labor and a shortage of capable managers; and they (as Jordan and Syria) have planned to use remittances from emigrant workers as well as grants from oil producing Arab countries in their domestic planning.

The extent to which Middle East countries have met some of the goals of their development plans may be gleaned from the concluding chapters of this book; however, some effects of their planning efforts on the living standards of workers may be noted here. Whenever there has been an improvement in the economy of a country, it is probably safe to infer that there has been some advance in the well being of workers. That is not to say that the successful completion of every planned project has benefitted workers or the nation as a whole. All too frequently, new projects have enriched only the members of ruling families, and the trickle of income to lower strata has been insignificant. Some plans designed to yield revenue or greater production have primarily increased the public debt. Nevertheless, the social out-fall of development planning has been an important factor in the lives of workers.

A few general observations may be made differentiating the improvement of life for workers through planning in agriculture and in industry.

Agrarian reform as an element of development planning has had a special impact upon workers. In all Middle East countries (except Bahrain, Israel, Kuwait, the UAE), one third or more of the labor force is still engaged in agriculture. Plans for agrarian reform, though described as measures for the benefit of land owners, have had considerable impact upon agricultural workers. A wide variety of reforms, including the redistribution or granting

[35] JPRS-NEA-086-070-25. Interview with 'Abd-al-Qadin, Head of the State Farm Sector, by F. 'Ali Mubarak, Aden 14, Ubtubar (in Arabic), 30 March 86.

of land to families, the encouragement of cooperatives, the protection of share-cropper interests, and the reduction of allowable rental payments, have generally resulted in improving the lot of those who work the land. In addition, there have been plans for increasing worker productivity through new patterns of cultivation, which have included worker training and the improvement of personal skills. More mechanization has presented difficult choices between the use of labor saving devices against a greater utilization of family members. Yet, the desire for farm machinery has been practically ubiquitous, and development plans have included provision for rental agencies and low interest loans to facilitate the use of such equipment. All of these efforts have produced mixed results, many of benefit to agricultural workers. Rather than relying entirely upon market forces, develop-ment plans for agrarian reform have introduced the possibility of rational accommodation to the needs of changing economies and to the welfare of workers.[36]

Planning for industrialization has involved other objectives and modalities; but they also have had significant consequences for Middle East workers. Oil producing country plans have stressed the need to round out emerging economies. That has meant not only the attainment of an adequate and stable labor force for current operations, but also planning for the time when oil resources will be depleted or substantially reduced. The in-migration of large numbers of alien workers from Arab countries nearby and from distant Asian and Pacific areas has called for many arrangements and rearrangements. As will be observed below, foreign workers have been drawn in by many advantages not available to them in their native lands and though development plans have not expected most of them to remain permanently, they have remained for years and their labor problems have continued. The relatively sudden and tremendous increase in industrial activity has also required the development of admin-

[36] A. Beaumont, Agricultural Development in the Middle East, Chichester (Sussex), New York, Wiley, 1985; J.A. Mollett, Planning for Agricultural Development, Croom Helm, London, 1984; A. Uthoff and E.M. Pernia, An Introduction to Human Resource Planning in Developing Countries, ILO, Geneva, 1986.

istrative and professional skills among persons traditionally untrained for such work.

There are many economic and philosphical questions left unanswered with respect to the accomplishments of development planning in the Middle East. The control of population growth, the education and retraining of the population, and the participation of women in economic activity remain uncertain factors. Nonetheless the incipient industrialization of the Middle East has meant an enormous reorientation in the lives of many persons. It is an ongoing and ever shifting process, raising new labor problems and requiring new planning, directed at both general economic progress and specific labor standards.

Chapter 4

SPECIAL CLASSES OF LABOR

CHILD LABOR

PERCEPTIONS OF THE PROBLEM

When the activities of children turn from a process of learning to a pursuit of earning, dangers and deprivations abound. Children, leaving the caring environment of a home, walk unguarded in a field beset with strangers struggling for selfish advantage. Child workers may bring in money sorely needed at home; but they remain the lowest-paid workers — prey to many predators. Exceptional individuals may hone their native talents and outwit those who would abuse them; but for many youths, child labor is bondage for pay and stultifies the mind and spirit before they reach their human potential. For all too many, it also stunts the body. Poor countries accept the continuation of child labor, almost as an unavoidable plague. Prosperous countries, or those committed to social welfare programs, often regard the problems of child labor as matters which will disappear with the general improvement of socio-economic conditions. In time, that may come to pass. In the present, however, no Middle East country has developed to that state, and persistent adversities cry out for attention. No nation looks forward to its progress without hoping for the ultimate elimination of child labor.

The most perplexing questions are what should be done to raise the minimum age for admission to the labor market, to protect the immature worker from excessive hours of work and hazardous conditions, and to insure child workers a fulfilling education. These needs call for several kinds of social legislation.

CONSTITUTIONAL PROVISIONS

The constitutions of Middle East countries provide for the protection of children, without specifically setting standards for child labor.

The Jordanian constitution does provide that "Special conditions shall be made for the employment [of] juveniles"; and a few other constitutions call for laws that shall defend the young "against exploitation" (Bahrain, Kuwait, Qatar).

Several constitutions declare that the State shall provide care for children (Bahrain, Iraq, Kuwait, Qatar, Syria, Yemen Arab Republic, PDRY), and particularly to care for their physical, mental and moral growth (Bahrain, Kuwait, Yemen Arab Republic, PDRY).

LABOR CODE AND STATUTORY PROVISIONS

Restrictions upon child labor and personal safeguards are covered by statutes as follows.

(a) *Minimum age*. Child labor is prohibited under the age of: 8 (Lebanon, except on machinery), 12 (Iran, Qatar, Syria, YAR), 13 (Jordan, Lebanon , on machinery, Oman, Saudi Arabia), 14 (Bahrain, Kuwait), and 15 (Iraq, Israel, UAE). Work "unsuited to age" is forbidden in Oman and Syria. PDRY provides that "no minor shall be employed unless they have completed the first stage of education. . .or by a special resolution issued by the Minister of Labor." In Qatar, "no minor shall be employed without the special permission of the Director of Labor granted with the approveal of the Minister of Education."

(b) *Night work*. Night work is forbidden for children under the age of: 15 (Israel, Syria, YAR), 16 (Bahrain, Jordan, Lebanon, Oman, UAE), 17 (Iraq, Qatar), 18 (Iran, Kuwait, Saudi Arabia). Administrative exemptions, however, are permitted.

(c) *Maximum hours*. The work day for minors is limited to 6 hours (Bahrain, Jordan, Kuwait, Qatar, Saudi Arabia, UAE, YAR), 7 hours (Iraq, Lebanon, Syria), 8 hours per day, 40 per week (Israel). Qatar also provides that during Ramadhan, the work day for minors shall not exceed 4 per day, 24 per week.

(d) *Overtime* for child workers is prohibited (Bahrain, Iran, Iraq (under 17), Oman, Qatar, Syria, UAE, YAR).

(e) *Arduous or hazardous work* is prohibited (Bahrain, Iran, Iraq, Israel, Jordan, Kuwait, Lebanon, Oman, Saudi Arabia, UAE). The Minister of Social Affairs and Labor (in Oman and Syria) is given the power, within his discretion, to prohibit child employment in unspecified industries. A medical examination of a minor is required before work is commenced and periodically thereafter (Bahrain, Iraq, Israel, Jordan, Kuwait, Lebanon, Oman, Qatar, Saudi Arabia, Syria, United Arab Emirates).

(f) *Wages.* Bahrain provides "wages of juveniles shall not be fixed on the basis of piece work or productivity." Wages due a minor "may be paid to his guardian . . . provided his guardian submits to the employer a written request to that effect" (Qatar).

(g) *Exemptions.* Employment "within a family where only members of the same family work together" is exempted in Iraq, Qatar, and Syria. All agricultural work is exempted in Oman and Syria.

TREATY PROVISIONS

Both ILO conventions and UN covenants with provisions on child labor have been signed by Middle East countries.

ILO conventions have obligated signatory nations to deal with minimum age for child workers (Conv.57,110,123,138), medical examinations of youth (Conv.16,77,78,124) and prohibition of night work (Conv.79,90). One or more of these treaties has been ratified by Iraq, Jordan, Israel, Lebanon, Saudi Arabia, Syria.

The UN Covenant on Economic, Social and Cultural Rights as well as the Covenant on Civil and Political rights have been signed by Iran, Iraq, Israel, Jordan, Lebanon, Syria, and PDRY. The former provides, "Special measures of protection and assistance should be taken on behalf of all children and young persons without any discrimination for reasons of parentage or other conditions. Children and young persons should be protected from economic and social exploitation. Their employment in work harmful to their morals or health or dangerous to life or likely to hamper their normal development should be punishable by law. States should also set age limits below which the paid employment of child labour should be prohibited and punishable by law." The Civil and Political Covenant calls for "such measures of protection as are required by his status as a minor."

CONSEQUENCES AND INCIDENTALS

The countries of the Middle East which have substantial portions of their populations engaged in farming have a considerable amount of child labor. Most of that is confined to family work; but in peak seasons of planting and harvest, many children do work out for wages. Wages are low, hours are many, and the tasks are extremely arduous. Education of rural youngsters is postponed or sacrificed.

Service trades have also utilized child labor. Little "street merchants" are a common sight in urban centers.

Child labor in industry has been unabated particularly in countries experiencing a labor shortage or a state of war. The YAR Highway Authority has been reported as employing many road workers between the ages of 11 and 15.[1] During the war, Iran and Iraq have pressed young workers into shops calling them patriots.[2] Some Lebanese authorities have lamented unemployment among adolescents. It is apparent that those Middle East nations which suffer privations of many kinds find child labor a lesser problem. The enforcement of child labor laws in the Middle East has not become a major priority in any country.

WOMEN LABOR

PERCEPTIONS OF THE PROBLEM

The stereotype of a woman in the Middle East as a person hidden within a black robe and a head veil is an obfuscation or a deception. A small minority wear the veil, most perform work, and an increasing number are engaged in public occupations.

[1] JPRS-NEA-88-094-070, Dr. Muhammad Salah, Labor Law on Employment of Women and Children Discussed, Aden, Sawt Al-'Ummal (in Arabic), 6/15/86.

[2] JPRS-NEA-88-002-47, 27 October Report, Stockholm, Nameh-ye Mardom (in Persian), 27 Oct. 87, pp.4-5.

They encounter problems not unlike those of working women in other lands — set in different dress and circumstance.

Modern women workers most everywhere seem to be confronted with three difficulties: 1 - unequal access to employment, training and education; 2 - concentration in certain occupations; 3 - unequal pay; and at least two redemptive factors, 1 - a biological function worthy of special protection, and 2 - an awakening feminism that is being heard around the world.

In the Middle East, as elsewhere, there has been a common conception of "female industries" — textiles, clothing, food, health care; and "female occupations" — clerks, secretaries, assemblers, work requiring dexterous hands. Other positions have been closed to them, except when necessity has dictated otherwise. In some areas, religion has been interpreted to keep women and men apart. Even in industries in which both genders are employed, women have been relegated to lower skilled jobs because of limitations in education as well as traditional male dominance. In agriculture, women have been especially devoted to small animal production and to the processing, storing and marketing of produce.

The question of equality in remuneration for male and female workers has been even more baffling. Controversies have not been resolved by a mere banning of discrimination. Efforts to narrow the issues have led to the formulation of criteria, such as equal pay for "the same work," "substantially similar work" or "work of equal value." The available statistics (and they are quite meager in the Middle East) demonstrate a considerable disparity exists in the pay received by men and women workers. In addition, the working woman usually has additional household chores for which she receives no monetary compensation.

Many laws seeking to ameliorate conditions of work do not cover the activities in which women are employed. Common exclusionary clauses in labor legislation exempt agricultural, domestic and family work. Those, unfortunately, are areas of women's work; so women are deprived of the protective provisions of such laws.

The approach to a correction of the difficulties of women workers in the industrialized West has been to grant women special legislative protection on the ground of their biological needs and their bargaining weaknesses, an approach somewhat abandoned recently by a feminist desire to acquire greater employment opportunity which it is believed is thwarted by the costs of protective measures on hours and conditions of work. That belief has not been completely shared in the Middle East. Protection of women workers is not regarded as a serious inhibition to further employment; nor is it considered as unwelcome male patronizing by most women leaders in Middle East countries. The women (and cooperative men) who are advocating measures for the improvement of labor conditions for women of the Middle East have sought a balance between employment and protective laws, without sacrifice of the latter.

CONSTITUTIONAL PROVISIONS

Constitutions in the Middle East contain general provisions for the equality and protection of women; only a few refer specifically to their working conditions. Apart from implying equal treatment in the assertion of most rights, the basic constitutional documents stress a concern for the social and religious relationships of working women.

Middle East constitutions declare the *family* a "cornerstone of society" (Bahrain, Kuwait, Qatar), "the basic social unit" (Iran, Syria), "the nucleus of society" (Iraq), and the object of State support (PDRY).

In PDRY, the state is enjoined to work for the creation of circumstances that will enable a woman to combine participation in "productive and social work and her role within the family sphere." Similar provisions are found in Iran and Syria. An article of the PDRY constitution is devoted to the General Union of Yemen Women which "shall work for the widest participation of the Yemen woman in economic, social and political life and raise their vocational standards." The preamble to the Iranian constitution pays tribute to the contributions of women to the revolution and guarantees them "the restoration of their material and spiritual rights."

Some constitutional references are made to *Islamic standards* for women. In Iran, personal rights "guarantee the rights of women in all areas," "the creation of an environment favorable to the personal growth of women and to the restoration of their material and spiritual rights" and "the establishment of a special insurance for widows and elderly and destitute women." In the Yemen Arab Republic, women are said to be "the sisters of men." "They have their mandatory rights and obligations as stipulated in the Shariah and in accordance with the law." . . . "The Shariah and the law guarantee the means for their protection."

Only in Jordan and PDRY do the constitutions provide broadly that "Special conditions shall be made for the employment of women."

(The draft constitution of the Yemens omits the above references to women.)

LABOR CODE AND STATUTORY PROVISIONS

Details concerning the protection of women workers are spelled out in labor codes and other statutes. They are directed primarily toward dangerous and socially unacceptable work.

(a) *Arduous or hazardous work.* Such work by women is prohibited (Bahrain, Iran, Iraq, Jordan, Kuwait, Oman, Saudi Arabia, Syria, UAE, Yemen Arab Republic, PDRY). The same is said for work harmful to the health of women (Bahrain, Iran, Iraq, Israel, Kuwait, Oman, Syria, UAE, PDRY) or to the health of an unborn child (Bahrain, Iraq).

An article in the labor codes of Lebanon and Oman states more generally that the Minister of Labor may declare woman labor unlawful in trades or occupations that he may specify.

(b) *Work harmful to morals.* Such work by women is prohibited in Oman, Syria, UAE, PDRY.

(c) *Night work.* Night work by women is prohibited, with some exceptions. It is forbidden generally in Bahrain, Iran, Iraq, Israel, Jordan, Kuwait, Oman, Saudi Arabia, Syria, UAE,

Yemen Arab Republic, and "in work of a mechanical or manual nature" in Lebanon. Exemptions are permitted for jobs specified by the Minister of Labor (Bahrain, Kuwait, Oman, Syria, UAE, Yemen Arab Republic) and for work in infirmaries (Bahrain, UAE), private medical clinics (Kuwait), health or recreation services (Iraq), administrative or technical work (Iraq, UAE), and in transport or communication services (Iraq). Iraq additonally allows night work if "required by the necessity of preventing a loss of raw materials or perishable products."

(d) *Comfortable facilities.* Employers are required to provide comfortable facilities during working hours, particularly "seating arrangements in accordance with the nature and conditions of work" (Iraq, Saudi Arabia, Syria).

(e) *Pregnancy leave.* Work by a pregnant woman is forbidden for 6 weeks before confinement (Bahrain, Iran, Israel) and may not be resumed after confinement for 6 weeks (Israel, Saudi Arabia), 4 weeks (Bahrain, Iran), 40 days (Syria), 30 days (Lebanon). In Iraq, a woman may begin her maternity leave 30 days before confinement and may take the remaining 32 days after confinement. Female workers may not be terminated during such periods. Overtime, or work over 7 hours a day is also prohibited for pregnant workers.

(f) *Commingling with men.* The Code of Saudi Arabia provides: "In no case may men and women commingle in the place of employment, in the accessory facilities or other appurtenances thereto."

(g) *Exemptions.* The provisions restricting employment of women are made expressly not applicable to agricultural workers (Oman, Syria), family workers (Iraq, Syria), or to workers in charitable institutions (Saudi Arabia, UAE), vocational training institutions (Saudi Arabia, UAE), in restaurants, hotels, pet care centers, newspapers, and executive posts (Israel).

TREATY PROVISIONS

Numerous treaty provisions for the equality of the sexes and special protection of women have been adopted by Middle East governments.

The UN Covenant on Economic, Social and Cultural Rights, ratified by Iran, Iraq, Israel, Jordan, Lebanon, Syria, and PDRY, provides that signatory states "undertake to ensure the equal right of men and women to the enjoyment of all economic, social, and cultural rights set forth" in that covenant, subject "only to such limitations as are determined by law, only in so far as this may be compatible with the nature of these rights and solely for the purpose of promoting the general welfare in a democratic society."

Commitments to the protection of women workers have been made by the ratification of ILO Conventions, No.45, on underground work (in Lebanon, Saudi Arabia, and Syria); No.89 on night work in industry (in Bahrain, Iraq, Kuwait, Lebanon, Syria, and the United Arab Emirates), and No.127 on weight lifting (in Lebanon).

ILO Conventions prohibiting or limiting night work for women and minors (Nos. 4,20,41,79,89,90) have undergone modification. The early Convention 20 on Night Work for Women was ratified by Israel and the later Convention 41 was ratified by Iraq. The more recent Convention 89 relating to female night work has been ratified by Iraq, Kuwait, Lebanon, Saudi Arabia, Syria, and the United Arab Emirates. Convention 90 dealing with night work by minors has been ratified by Israel and Saudi Arabia. Though with the spread of the feminist movement restraints upon night work are being reviewed, the obligations incumbent upon past ratifications are still receiving serious attention.

The ALO Convention 5 on Women at Work, ratified by Iraq, and Palestine, contains a preamble that explains the discrimination experienced by women in Arab countries, and the text sets standards to assure women the same job opportunities and remuneration afforded men as well as protection against arduous and hazardous work.

CONSEQUENCES OR INCIDENTALS

A variety of observers and commentators on the status of working women in the Middle East have reported different rates of progress in overcoming traditional difficulties — and some advance in most countries.

(a) *Iran*, under the Shi'ite regime, has been described as a bastion of Islamic conservatism, and the current plight of its working women is seen as involving a retreat in employment opportunities. In the 1960s, women were granted the franchise and a Family Protection Law. The Iranian Labour Act of 1965 contained provisions protecting women workers. In the 1970s, female employment expanded, many women entered the labor market, and some established professional careers in medicine, engineering, law, and government. Following the Khomeini revolution, Islam was interpreted as assigning women to the home, requiring the wearing of a robe and veil, and shielding women from men in their occupations. Women's participation in the commercial and industrial world was discouraged; segregated education was directed to other fields; and nondomestic employment declined. The depletion of the male labor force by the Iraq-Iran war imposed new burdens upon Iranian women. The few female members of Parliament, steadfast in their loyalty to the Ayatollah and to Islam, have cried out for more recognition of the contributions and needs of Iranian working women; but their pleas have found little acceptance in the political uncertainties of the country.[3]

(b) *Saudi Arabia* has been approaching work by women from the standpoint of motivating its citizenry to play a greater role in its economy, so that some day it can send away or reduce the overwhelming number of foreign workers it now harbors. With the financial subsidies it has been bestowing on its natives for housing and other amenities of life, there has been less economic pressure to induce Saudi women to seek employment. Alien labor has supplied all the manual effort required, and many

[3] G. Nashat, Women and Revolution In Iran, Boulder, Colo., Westview Press, 1983; Farah Azari, ed., Women of Iran, Ithaca Press, London, 1983.

forms of work have become socially unacceptable to Saudis. The government, however, has been urging its people to assume occupational responsibilities. Education is publicly funded and the government has tried to encourage women, who have preferred the arts and literature, to undertake training in business and professional skills such as accounting, personnel management, and law. Little concern has been expressed over the economic acitivities of alien women, though most emigrant workers are men who have left their wives at home (presumably cared for by cash remittances).[4]

(c) *Oman*, also seeking to preserve traditional Islamic practices in the home, in public garb, and in the segregation of the sexes, has nevertheless opened up some employment possibilities for women. They are now found in administrative, government positions, sometimes supervising male employees. As customs inspectors at airports, Omani women workers are quite visible.[5]

(d) *The Yemens*. The Yemen Arab Republic and the People's Democratic Republic of Yemen, similar in culture and resources, present interesting likenesses and differences in the problems of working women. Both countries have been basically agricultural (though some oil has been discovered in the YAR in 1984 and in PDRY in 1987). Both have had a surplus of labor and a large out-migration of male workers. Both have Muslim populations with traditions, patrilineal authority, and emphasis upon woman's place in the home. In the YAR, committed to a private, market economy, women workers have retained most of their customary roles — confined to home keeping and children rearing, and assigned farm duties such as the care and feeding of small animals and the picking of cotton or other crops. With the shortage of male workers, women in industry have increased, to

[4] JPRS-NEA-086-087-52, Interview, Dr. Hiskmat al-Urabi, Head of Women's Section, Ministry of Planning, Riyadh Al-Riyad (Arabic), April 18, 1986, p.4.

[5] C. Eickelman, Woman and Community in Oman, Westview Press, Boulder, Colo., 1984; B. R. Pridham, ed., Oman: Economic, Social and Strategic Developments, Croom Helm, London, 1987.

about one-third of the industrial labor force in the 1980s.[6] In the PDRY, committed to a centrally directed economy with socialist intentions, women workers have adapted to economic changes but still bear old burdens. Household chores are women's work. Many women labor on state owned farms and in cooperatives where tasks still observe gender classifications; yet more women are given managerial functions. The veil has practically disappeared. There is an affirmative encouragement of women's participation in all necessary work (and all forms of labor are needed in this poor country). Factory and service trade jobs have been opened to women with social approval.[7]

(e) *Bahrain*. In Bahrain, 13% of all working Bahrainis are women working outside the home; and a large portion of government jobs and administrative positions are filled by women. Vocational training for women is also stressed.[8]

Women workers in some Muslim countries have been affected by the enactment of Family Protection Laws. These have dealt primarily with divorce and the custody of children; but they have also altered property rights between husband and wife. Such statutes were adopted in Iran in 1967 and in the Yemens in 1974. They established a minimum age of the bride at 18 in Iran, and 16 in the Yemens; they restricted polygamy to exceptional circumstances of barrenness or disease; and they increased the rights of the wife in a divorce. In Iran, a court might award her alimony and child support. In the PDRY, the law has stipulated that both spouses shall "share in bearing the costs of their married life." Such provisions have modified traditional Islamic precepts in ways that have improved the status of working women.

(f) *Israel*. Conditions of work are at times prescribed by collective agreements instead of in laws. Such an agreement for

[6] Ragaei El Mallakh, The Economic Development of the YAR, Croom Helm, London, 1986.

[7] Maxine Molyneux, State Policies and the Position of Women Workers in the PDR Yemen, ILO, Geneva, 1982; JPRS-NEA-086-094-070, op. cit. at footnote 31.

[8] JPRS-NEA-087-011-036, A Study of Bahraini Women by the Ministry of Labor and Social Affairs, London, Al-Majallah (in Arabic), 24 Sept. 86, p.48,49.

public employees (executed by the Histadrut and the Treasury) provides that a working mother can leave work at least 30 minutes before the 4pm regular quitting time to pick up her children from a day care center, as long as she makes up the time in other ways.[9]

AGRICULTURAL WORKERS

PERCEPTIONS OF THE PROBLEM

Farm work has been romanticized in literature, with a touch of national pride. Farm chores are often portrayed as a vigorous communion with nature. On small farms, work is shared by all able bodied members, and the produce or income is enjoyed by all. Peak demands in seasonal planting and harvesting are likewise partaken by the larger community. Conviviality and compassion abound. The back-breaking toil, sun-up to sun-down, is submerged in recollections of holiday festivals. Even those workers who have escaped from the harsh realities often tend to think that those who work the farms are nurtured in the bosom of the family and protected from the advance of hostile industry and commerce.

The lure of city lights has led many surplus farm workers to a better life; but it has also crowded many into an unproviding and impersonal environment. The opening of new opportunities, moreover, has diverted attention from the condition of those who have remained behind.

Some of the difficulties encountered by agricultural workers in the Middle East have been dictated by the terrain in which they have lived. Deserts have obliged sheep herders to roam as Bedouins in search of sparse vegetation. Sands have restricted sustenance in some places to a diet of dates. Rocky soil has yielded little grain in return for arduous labor. Hilly regions have required intricate schemes of irrigation. These natural limitations have been mitigated, not overcome, by more work and by various agrarian reforms.

[9] JPRS-NEA-89-36-13. Public Sector Agreement. The Jerusalem Post (in English), Jerusalem. Apr.30, 1989 p.8.

The flow of events in the Middle East has brought social conditions less favorable to the life of agricultural workers. The emigration of men to oil countries and new cities has left women stranded with tasks formerly performed by their husbands, in addition to the responsibilities of home care. Price controls have often favored the urban population at the expense of farmers. Cultivation of crops has been set by custom with infrequent adjustment for market changes. The payment of hired farm help has often failed to take account of inflationary prices for domestic staples. Farm workers, unorganized and bound by tradition, have been squeezed by many developments beyond their control.

Overlaying all these factors has been the attitude that agricultural workers are land owners or share croppers — rarely wage earners — and what needs to be done for their welfare is primarily to improve productivity. Development has been viewed in terms of the preservation of the family farm and the promotion of its efficiency. Official policies and plans have been couched in terms of agrarian reform rather than in the improvement of the lives of agricultural workers; and in the process of seeking plentiful produce, little thought has been directed toward the enhancement of the qualities of life for agricultural workers.

CONSTITUTIONAL PROVISIONS

Although agricultural workers are specifically designated in only a few contexts, several Middle East constitutions deal with agriculture in ways that clearly affect farm workers.

The concentration of land ownership is treated apprehensively in Bahrain, Iraq, and Syria. In Iraq, excess land is regarded as the property of the people. Syria provides that "The law defines the maximum limit of agricultural ownership in a manner that will guarantee the protection of the farmer or the agricultural worker against exploitation." In Bahrain, "The law shall specify the means whereby assistance and ownership of land are granted to small farmers."

Agricultural organizations, including workers, receive special recognition in Iran and the PDRY. The Iranian constitution establishes councils of representatives of workers, farmers and other employees and managers "to safeguard Islamic justice in the preparation of programs and in the coordination of progress in agricultural production units." The PDRY constitution provides the Democratic Yemen Union of Peasants "shall work for deepening the alliance betwen the peasant and the working class" and shall direct all peasants for "active contribution in executing . . . the tasks of the national democratic revolution." (Omitted from the draft constitution.)

More general articles provide that the State shall "emphasize agricultural and livestock production" (Iran), "ensure the productive use of arable land," and "raise the standard of farmers" (Bahrain), "work for the expansion of reforming the agricultural lands. . .and increase of the livestock and fish wealth sources" (PDRY), and protect "agricultural and animal wealth" (United Arab Emirates). Iran expressly pledges to achieve self-sufficiency in agriculture as in other areas of activity.

LABOR CODE AND STATUTORY PROVISIONS

Labor codes adopted by Middle East countries contemplate primarily nonagricultural workers.

Some codes contain express exclusions that make their protective clauses inapplicable to agricultural workers (Bahrain, Iran, Jordan, Lebanon, Oman, Saudi Arabia, UAE, YAR). A few of these save out of the exclusion "workers who operate or repair agricultural establishments which process or market their products" (Bahrain, Saudi Arabia, UAE) or workers who are employed in agricultural enterprises on a permanent basis (YAR). Lebanon, however, excludes "all agricultural corporations having no connection with commerce or industry." Agricultural workers are also exempted in Oman from code provisions on "employment of children, juveniles and women." Qatar exempts "persons employed on casual labor for a period less than 4 weeks."

The Iraqi labor code alone embraces agricultural workers (albeit by implication). It states it "shall apply to all workers employed in the private, mixed and cooperative sectors . . . The provisions of this Code apply to . . . workplaces in which one or more workers are employed." Although a large number of workers in many of the other countries are engaged in agriculture, they are rarely singled out for special protective legislation.

TREATY PROVISIONS

The well-being of agricultural workers has been pinpointed in only a few treaties.

The UN Covenant on Economic, Social and Cultural Rights, signed by Iran, Iraq, Israel, Jordan, Lebanon, Syria, PDRY, provides that parties to it "recognizing the fundamental right of everyone to be free from hunger, shall take, individually and through international cooperation, the measures, incuding specific programmes, which are needed . . . by developing or reforming agrarian systems in such a way as to achieve the most efficient development and utilization of natural resources."

Only three Middle East countries (Iraq, Israel and Syria) have ratified an ILO Convention on standards for agricultural workers. The early Convention 10, on minimum age of farm workers and Convention 12, on workmen's compensation in agriculture were adopted by Iraq. Convention 101, on holidays in agriculture and Convention 141, on the organization of rural workers and their role in economic and social development were ratified by Israel. Convention 11, on rights of association and combination of agricultural workers, Convention 99, on minimum wage fixing machinery in agriculture, Convention 101, on holidays, and Convention 129, on labor inspection in agriculture were ratified by Syria.

The ALO Convention 12, issued in 1980, pertains to Agricultural Workers, but to date it has not been ratified by any Middle East nation.

CONSEQUENCES AND INCIDENTALS

Agricultural workers, consisting of farmers, share croppers and hired hands, have been dealt with more often through general economic measures than through legislation specifically directed at them. It has been assumed that whatever is done to improve the gross national product or the returns from agriculture would increase the income of such workers. That has often not been so. Even the improvement of soil fertility, the development of new seeds or the breeding of better livestock has not always resulted in more or better food for rural workers. Every advance in agriculture has contained the potential for elevating standards of living; but seemingly extraneous factors such as changes in population size or in the balance of prices between exports and imports have often offset the anticipated benefits. Agricultural workers in the Middle East have been and remain at the bottom of the social ladder.

Some direct aid to farm workers has been forthcoming. Educational programs have improved personal skills that have enabled some farm workers to command better paying jobs. Price policies have at times been tailored to augment farm earnings. The most pronounced relief has come from wage remittances sent home by family members who emigrated to oil producing countries. In the latter countries, some of the oil wealth has trickled down through public welfare services to native agricultural workers

Many distressed agricultural workers have found avenues of escape. Their emigration to oil countries has been encouraged and facilitated. Their wage remittances have helped those who remain at home. Some countries, however, have urged even underemployed farm workers to stay at home in order to preserve domestic farms and to spare those who remain the hardships they would endure in overcrowded urban centers. A few countries have attempted to stimulate rural industries and service trades to supplement the income of agricultural workers.[10]

Efforts to increase the size of small farms have been numerous,

[10] P. Beaumont and K. McLachlan, Agricultural Development of the Middle East, John Wiley & Sons, Ltd., London, 1985; Ismail Serageldin, Manpower and International Labor Migration in the Middle East and North Africa, Oxford Univ. Press, New York & Oxford, 1983; J. S. Birks and C. S. Sinclair, Arab Manpower, Croom Helm, London, 1980.

but all too frequently they have been frustrated by under-financing or political favoritism and corruption. The break-up of large landholdings and the public distribution of adequate plots have fallen far short of plans and expectations. Even in Syria and Iraq where egalitarian principles and land redistribution have been proclaimed as constitutional commitments, the landless have received rather tiny plots in comparison with the average farm, which has been fifty times as large.[11] In Jordan, one half of the farms are only 3 hectares or less in size. In the Yemens, and elsewhere throughout the Middle East, the limited arable soil severely restricts the land available for growing populations. In addition, the traditional Islamic laws of inheritance have divided estates equally among all sons of the deceased (and half shares to daughters) causing the size of family farms to decline. The Israeli program to settle in-migrant Jews on farms, even on improved desert soils, has also experienced a need for more land. Natural factors have not been propitious for Middle East agricultural workers, and government assistance, even though inadequate, has been indispensable.[12]

The need for more improvement in rural living conditions has been recognized in development plans.[13] Oman has adopted programs for clinics on pest spraying and veterinary care; it has provided free repair of fishermen's equipment, and it has made available new seed laboratories.[14] Bahrain, suffering from a scar-

[11] Farhat Ziadeh, "Land Law and Economic Development in Arab Countries", American Journal of Comparative Law, Vol. 33, pp 93-106,1985; Ziad Kalany, "Land Reform in Syria", Middle Eastern Studies, Vol.16, Frank Cass & Co., Ltd., London, pp.209-224, 1981.

[12] Bichara Khader and Adnan Badran, The Economic Development of Jordan, Croom-Helm, London, 1987; H. Bowen-Jones and Roderic Dutton, "Agricultural Production and/or Rural Development, The Arab Gulf Journal, Vol.4, No.1, pp.51-64, 1984; John Vidergar, Israel Social and Economic Development, Vance Inc. Monticello, Ill., 1978.

[13] Farhat Ziadeh, "Land Law and Economic Development in Arab Countries", American Journal of Comparative Law, Vol.33, p.93-106, 1985; Jon C. Swanson, "Emigrant Remittances and Local Development in the Economic Development of the YAR, by Ragaei El Mallakh, Croom-Helm, London, 1986.

[14] JPRS-NEA-086-008-93, Development in Agriculture, Abu Dhabi, Al-Ittihad (in Arabic), Special Supplement, pp. 53-54, Nov. 3, 1985.

city of farm labor, has with the aid of the United Nations FAO developed plastic greenhouses, thereby saving water and fertilizers.[15] PDRY employs a substantial portion of its population on state farms, with plans to train management engineers and to increase farm worker wages.[16] Israel's program to settle inmigrant Jews has involved initially complete support of the workers, re-education in language and farming techniques, and a guided introduction to all phases of a new life. Saudi Arabia, and other oil-rich nations, have devoted large portions of their oil revenues to subsidize farmers — in land grants, interest free loans for machinery, incentives for growing export crops, and training in modern methods, as well as for general agricultural projects such as dam construction, desalinization plants and other farm aids.[17] All of these endeavors acknowledge the needs of agricultural workers; but most of them deal with the problems of labor only as incidental portions of larger economic plans.

FOREIGN OR MIGRANT WORKERS

PERCEPTIONS OF THE PROBLEM

Workers who come from across a nation's borders to perform needed services have been seen as special guests or as alien visitors. How they are treated may depend upon which questions are asked at any moment. Are the talents of migrants indispensable or replaceable? Do they seek to earn more money, to escape from home unemployment, or to partake of new freedoms? Do they desire temporary residence or permanent settlement? Do they bring with them a kindred tongue, a friendly religion, familiar holidays and compatible mores, or frightening practices? Are they so numerous as to appear overwhelming? As circumstances

[15] JPRS-NEA-086-102-16. Hafiz Imam, "Why Doesn't Bahrain Move to the Next Stages in Protected Agriculture?", Manamah Al-Adiva (in Arabic), p.16, Jan. 28, 1986.

[16] NEA-086-070-29, 'Ali Muhammad 'Abdallah, "Improvements Planned for State Farms", Aden, 14 Uktubar (in Arabic), p.4, 2 April 1986.

[17] JPRS-NEA-087-001-74, "The Growth Rate of Saudi Agricultural Production", Al-Mustaqbal (in Arabic) 8 Nov.1986; JPRS-NEA-086-084-51, Dr. Walid A. Hashem, "Interview with Minister of Agriculture", Jeddah, Arab News (in English) p.9, 28 May 1986.

change, migrant workers in the Middle East have been seen in new lights, most of which have disclosed more problems then solutions.

The benefits and the difficulties accompanying migratory labor have been magnified by the enormity of the influx or the outflow in every country. Nowhere has there been enough time to adjust to all the changes. Expectations have run ahead of realization. Planning has never been sufficiently accurate to produce an equilibrium; and experiences have not taken on the semblance of normalcy. Legal controls have been patterned after the techniques utilized elsewhere to deal with immigration and citizenship; but they are still experimental.

CONSTITUTIONAL PROVISIONS

At the time of the drafting of the Middle East constitutions, the explosion of the labor market was not foreseen hence the constitutions do not refer to the influx of foreign workers that occurred later.

LABOR CODE AND STATUTORY PROVISIONS

Labor codes have offered many adjustments to problems and worries concerning in-migrant workers.

(a) *Legal entry*. Most commonly, it is required that a worker enter the country legally (Bahrain, Kuwait, Oman, Qatar, Saudi Arabia, UAE). He must have a valid passport or residence permit (Bahrain, Kuwait, Qatar), or he must have complied with residence regulations (Oman, Saudi Arabia, UAE, YAR). Israel has a Law of Return under which every Jew has a right to come to the country and to receive automatic citizenship (subject to orthodox religious rules defining a Jew); and military regulations restrict the entry of non-Jews deemed to endanger public security.

(b) *Personal qualifications*. The foreign worker is required to be of good reputation and conduct (Bahrain, Kuwait, Qatar, YAR), and be physically fit for employment and free from infectious diseases (Bahrain), and of sound morality (YAR). He must possess the vocational skills and educational qualifications which the country has been found to need (Oman, Saudi Arabia, UAE). In Oman, the Minister of Labor is empowered to decide if it is permissible to have foreign unskilled labor.

(c) *Contract guarantees.* In Saudi Arabia and Oman, the foreign worker must be under contract with an employer who guarantees compliance with the law.

(d) *Work permits.* Employers are forbidden to hire workers without a work permit (Bahrain, Iraq, Kuwait, Qatar, Oman, Saudi Arabia, Syria, UAE, YAR, PDRY). Registry and clearance by the Minister of Labor or the labor department is required (Kuwait, Oman, Saudi Arabia, UAE, YAR, PDRY). In Syria, the Ministry of Labor may waive the need for a work permit. Work permits are valid for only 1 year (Bahrain, YAR) or 2 years (Kuwait, Qatar); and they may be cancelled in case (a) the worker fails to comply with any condition stated in the permit, (b) the worker becomes unemployed for 1 to 3 months (Bahrain, Kuwait, UAE) or for a period exceeding 3 months (Qatar), or (c) continued employment competes with the employment of a national able and willing to perform the work (Kuwait).

(e) *Work priorities.* Citizens are given first priority for employment (Bahrain, Kuwait, Oman, Qatar, UAE, YAR). Arabs are given second priority (Bahrain, Kuwait, UAE, YAR). Release from employment is to be in reverse order (Bahrain, Qatar). In Oman, the Labor Minister may decree the proportion of Omani to non-Omani workers that may be employed by any one employer. In Saudi Arabia, the number of Saudis employed by an employer shall be no less than 75% of the total employees, and at wages no less than 51% of the total wages, unless the Minister of Labor finds that technical or educational qualifications are not available in the native population. Foreign workers in the Yemen Arab Republic shall not account for more than 10% of the total workforce at any workplace. In PDRY, the Code provides employers shall appoint Yemeni workers to assist foreign employees and receive training in their field with a view to replacing them on the expiry of their work permits.

These legal provisions are obviously different for oil producing countries with a current need for outside workers and an expectation that the need will diminsh or disappear; they differ also for countries with a surplus of native workers. In addition, the clash between Israeli desires for a Jewish state and Arab opposing interests has been a potent factor in determining manpower policies and labor laws in the Middle East.

TREATY PROVISIONS

Treaty commitments to equal or fair treatment of migrant workers have been few.

The ILO has a multifaceted Convention No. 117, many provisions of which affect migrant workers. The Convention, ratified by Israel, Jordan, Kuwait, and Syria, urges planning for the healthy evolution of communities, including efforts to avoid the disruption of family life, especially through close study of migratory movements and appropriate action. It provides also that account be taken of the normal family needs of migrant workers, and that agreements be reached whereby the migrant shall enjoy protection and advantages not less than those enjoyed by resident workers, and shall have facilities for a transfer of part of his wages to his home. Where workers and their families move from low-cost to higher-cost areas, account should be taken of the increased cost of living.

Israel, alone among the Middle East countries, has ratified ILO Convention 97 concerning Migration for Employment. It commits signatories to provide free services and accurate information to migrants and to treat them without discrimination, in so far as adminstrative regulations govern, with respect to remuneration, union membership, accommodations, social security, and employment taxes. The convention, however, does not apply to frontier workers, certain short-term professionals, and seamen. It annexes a complex list of terms for recruitment, placing, and conditions of employment.

Convention 118 an Quality of Treatment of Nationals and Non-nationals in Social Security has been ratified by Iraq, Israel,

Jordan, and Syria. It seeks to promote reciprocity among signatory states.

The UN Covenant on Economic, Social and Cultural Rights, after providing for nondiscrimination on the ground of national or social origin, adds a reservation: "Developing countries, with due regard to human rights and their national economy, may determine to what extent they would guarantee the economic rights recognized in the present Covenant to non-nationals."

Two ALO Conventions provide for the relationship between migrant workers and nationals. Convention 2 on Migrant Policy has been ratified by Iraq, Jordan, and Syria. Convention 4 on Emigrant Workers has been ratified by Iraq, Jordan, and Palestine. They are limited to workers from Arab countries.

CONSEQUENCES AND INCIDENTALS

No country in the Middle East (or in the world) has a labor force composed entirely of its nationals. Oil producing countries (Saudi Arabia, Kuwait, and Oman) have shared the unique distinction of having experienced a labor force in which a majority of their workers have been foreigners. Some have had the same preponderance of expatriates in their entire population. The overwhelming presence of foreign workers continues in all technical and skilled categories as well as in the mass of service laborers. Typically, in Bahrain, which has a balanced domestic/foreign population, there have been more expatriate workers than native workers in professional and managerial positions, and in such industries as hotels, and insurance; further, it has generally as many foreigners as natives in transport, retail trade, and even in public administration and cultural services. Laws have been directed to offset the influx of these foreign workers without appreciable effect.[18]

[18] E. Kaczorowska, Legal Aspects and Policies of Migration in the Middle East, Geneva, Nov. 1988; Eliyahu Kanovsky, Migration from the Poor to the Rich Arab Countries, Tel Aviv Univ., Tel Aviv, 1984; ILO, Employment & Manpower Problems and Policy Issues in Arab Countries, ILO, Regional Symposium Geneva, 1983; Naiem A. Sherbing, "Expatriate Labor Flows to the Arab Oil Countries in the 1980's", The Middle East Journal, Vol. 38, No. 4, 1984, p 643; J. S. Birks, Arab Manpower, op. cit.

The ubiquitous laws requiring work permits and native sponsorship for expatriate workers have been enforced laxly. Original statutes, mandating that those workers leave the country immediately or within a few weeks of the termination of their jobs have been amended to facilitate the transfer of a sponsorship for such reasons as failure to pay wages and the death or bankruptcy or prolonged absence of a sponsor (Oman, UAE). Amnesty from criminal prosecution for workers illegally in Kuwait, who would leave voluntarily, resulted in some exodus in 1982; but it is estimated that half of them have returned since then, still illegally. Work permits are issued gingerly; but recruiters of foreign workers maintain profitable businesses, and the passing of recruits from one importer of labor to another and to a second, for further profits (Bahrain) has been reported.

Naturalization laws have strictly limited the granting of citizenship (which assures permanent residence) to foreign workers desiring it. In Kuwait, there is a requirement of 10 years residence by Arabs and 15 years by non-Arabs. That law also restricts the number of new citizens to 50 in any one year, and subjects the number to the discretion of the Minister of the Interior, who may be guided by the law's statement that it is revocable in the supreme interest of the State or for national security.[19]

The deliberate effort to reconstitute a labor force from foreign to native has been expressed in popular terms such as Saudization, Kuwaitization, Bahrainization. They have articulated a policy to inculcate in all citizens a patriotic desire to contribute their personal services in all occupations found in short supply, and particularly to replace the foreigners who are furnishing professional and administrative skills. Educational programs at all levels, including universities, have been promoted with considerable success; but the need for foreigners has remained. Five-year plans have provided inducements for the nativization of work forces through repatriation grants to foreigners and improvement

[19] A. Al-Moosa and K. McLachlan, Immigrant Labour in Kuwait, Croom Helm, London, 1985; JPRS-086-097-14, "Means Proposed to Balance Kuwaiti and Expatriate Population", Kuwait Arab Times (in English) p.4, 2 July, 1986.

grants to citizens. Notwithstanding such measures, the dependency of oil producing countries upon foreign workers seems unabated.[20]

The in and out movement of workers in most countries, especially the non-oil producing nationals in Jordan and the Yemens, has involved incessant readjustment. The countries of emigration to other Middle East countries have tried various ways to staunch their loss or replenish their farm and service workers. The PDRY, having been abandoned by needed agricultural workers, legally banned emigration in 1974. Few leavers were apprehended, and in 1979 those who had left unlawfully were offered amnesty if they returned. In 1980, a congress was held in Aden to integrate migrants into the Yemen society. Investment laws of 1969 and 1981 offered tax and customs concessions to emigrants who were willing to trade with their homeland. The government also raised the salaries of its doctors and technicians, and increased their material perquisites. These efforts, like the remittance of earnings from abroad, did more to improve the home economy than to correct the outflow of labor.[21]

The sources of foreign workers have been undergoing changes, not readily controlled by law. The early migration from Arab State to Arab State has diminished, and new workers have come from India, Pakistan, the Philippines, South Korea, Thailand, Sri Lanka and China.[22] Korean contractors have systematized their methods of operation, building temporary housing for their workers and transporting them home on completion of their

[20] JPRS-NEA-086-008-21, "Recommendations for Reducing Expatriate Labor Force in Bahrain", Abu Dhabi, Al-Ittihad (in Arabic), p.4, 29 Nov. 1986; JPRS-NEA-086-071-19, M. Al-Shubnan, Deputy Minister of Labor and Social Affair of Kuwait, "Reduction of Foreign Labor Force; JPRS-NEA-086-057-38, Interview with Saudi Arabia Minister of Labor and Social Affairs, Riyadh, Al-Yamamah (in Arabic), 15 Jan. 86.

[21] Ahmed Ali Abdulsadiq, "Problems of Development Planning in PDR Yemen," in Economy, Society and Culture in Contemporary Yemen, by B.R. Pridham, ed., Croom Helm, London, 1985; J.S. Birks, C. Sinclair, "Aspects of Labour Migration from North yemen", Middle Eastern Studies, Vol. 17, 1981, p 49.

[22] E. Kaczorowska, Effects of Temporary Contract Migration from Southeast Asia and Other Asian Countries on the Labour Market of the Receiving Countries of the Gulf Area, Geneva, Nov. 1988.

projects. Workers from the other Asian countries have come and lingered for the wages, hjgher than they could receive at home, regardless of their greater insecurity.

The living standards of foreign workers have varied. Well paid professionals have been known to move from Kuwait to Saudi Arabia in order to earn more; and they have lived well. The crews brought in by contractors, who have supplied housing and have provided other facilities, have been able to save money for remittances to home; but they have accepted overcrowding and even deprived themselves of ordinary necessities in order to increase their savings. Most foreign workers, however, have lived in urban centers and have subsisted at the community's lowest levels. The host governments' refusal to permit families to accompany or follow them have added to their social misery. Brief annual visits home, or longer visits during the month of Ramahdan, have lessened their plight. On the other hand, some emigration from rural areas, as in the YAR, has been an escape route for unemployed or underemployed workers or for workers traditionally cast in occupations socially despised.[23]

Israel has been trying to enlarge its labor force from abroad as part of its aliyah program — the in-calling of all Jews from the Diaspora. It has assumed the burdens entailed thereby with the aid of supporters throughout the world. When the West Bank and Gaza with their large Arab populations were occupied, many Israelis had misgivings. Fear was expressed over the possible inundation of its labor market by non-Jews. Their experience that the occupation solved a domestic manpower shortage was heralded as "a miracle", and the foreign workers came to be regarded as a benefit. Other special conditions for Palestinian workers in the occupied territories developed. Most of them have been obliged to come and return as daily immigrants; and

[23] Ahmed Al-Kasir, "The Impact of Emigration on the Social Structure in the YAR", and Gunter Meyer, "Labor Emigration and Internal Migration in the YAR", in the Economic Development of the YAR by R. E. Mallakh, Croom Helm, London, 1986. John Show, Saudi Arabian Modernization: The Impact of Change on Stability, Praeger Publishers, New York, 1982. A. Al-Moosa, Immigrant Labor in Kuwait, op.cit.

the violence accompanying, and in response to, the intifada has created a zone in which normal labor laws do not prevail.

Even more particular is the status of persons in the refugee camps in the West Bank and in Lebanon. Housing, rations, schooling and some welfare services have been provided by the UN — except in periods of military massacre and destruction. No responsibility has been assumed for the employment of the refugees; and unproductivity has become a way of life for most residents in the camps.[24]

In a real and unfortunate sense, all Middle East foreign workers lack legal rights enjoyed by native workers. They dare not antagonize employers who may terminate their employment and lead to their expulsion or exile They generally haven't the means needed to hire lawyers. In the UAE, a statute has expressly given foreign workers recourse to the civil courts for the satisfaction of grievances. However, the federal statutes (on passports and work permits) have often not been heeded in the rural emirates.[25]

The labor laws pertaining to foreign workers in the Middle East have hardly disposed of the social policies raised. Manpower needs have dictated practices, and the administration of laws has followed along. National aspirations for the accumulation and distribution of wealth have vied with a desire for political stability. A preference for the welfare of native citizens and a fear of dependence upon a restless populace of foreigners have been constant concerns. In seeking to shape the labor force as desired, laws have been tools often ineffective.

TRIBAL OR ETHNIC WORKERS

PERCEPTIONS OF THE PROBLEM

Tribes which once were the unit of communal life and law

[24] JPRS-NEA-087-053-32, "Arab Workers in Israel" London, Al-Majallah (in Arabic) p.33, 24 Feb. 1987; UNRWA, Palestine Refugees in the West Bank and the Gaza Strip, U.N. Relief and Works Agency, New York, 1988. Luis Turiansky, "Social and Economic Picture of an Occupied Country", World Trade Union movement, No. 3, 1989, p 15.

[25] Kenneth Redden, ed., Modern Legal Systems Cyclopedia, Vol. 5, Wm Hein & Co., Buffalo, N.Y., 1985.

throughout the Middle East set patterns for work and government. They determined who performed the tasks essential for subsistence. They established customary work relationships, embedded in generation after generation of kinfolk. When colonial powers took over, changes were made slowly. With the advent of independence and world commerce, political forces subordinated many tribes and transformed many of their practices.

Still, tribal identification has persisted. (Notably the Kurds, Lurs, Turkmen, Baluchi, Shahsavan, Hawala in Iran; the Kurds, Baluchi and Assyrians in Iraq; the Baluchi, the Bani Riyem, the Ghafiri and Hinawi in Oman; the Al-Khalifa in Bahrain; the Hashed and Bakil in YAR.) After numerous struggles for supremacy, many assertive tribes have stood out as ethnic minorities in new nationalities. Their traditional work patterns were distorted by shifts in the emerging economies and by conflicting community attitudes. In the countries experiencing economic upheaval, minority tribes were often regarded with concern, suspicion, accusation, fear or hostility. Some old enmities were rekindled.

These conditions gave rise to stereotypes of tribal inferiority or incompetence that perpetuated employment discrimination. Paradoxically, the exclusion of minority tribes from main-stream activities led in some instances to their defensive specialization in certain endeavors (trade, finance, absentee land ownership, learned professions) which the prejudiced, less successful, members of the majority population regarded as exploitive or fraudulent and as an excuse for persecution. The denial of education in tribal languages thwarted occupational growth and reinforced the low status of the unskilled tribal workers. The threat, real or imagined, of tribal political dissent nourished further resistance to any tribal expression.

The reactions of tribesmen to such conditions were usually rebellious and militant. Blame for hardships of every kind became reciprocal, and at times that led to violence and war. The fate of the Kurds, in Iraq and Iran particularly, has been characterized by bloodshed.[26] Even where peaceful coexistence has prevailed, the employment relationships between dominant employers and subordinate tribal workers have frequently been unsympathetic and inhospitable.

Biological continuities, linguistic ties and religious sectarianism have kept many tribes intact even under adversity. Land ownership, personal pride and inertia, as well as more aggressive political rivalry, have sustained some small and some large tribes regardless of the problems they have faced.

A special set of labor problems has been posed by nomadic tribes — pastoral groups moving with the seasons to grass lands or resting places, indifferent to national boundaries and resentful of taxes. It has been thought by some Middle East rulers that such migratory Bedouins could be sedentarized through financial subsidies, housing and schools for their children. Age-old patterns of occupation or life style, however, have remained obdurate.

Another set of special problems with tribal aspects has been associated with religion. Christians and Jews in the Arab world have been distinct ethnic groups in the Arab world. Although the Copts have been Christian Arabs and other Christians have adopted Arabic as their language of worship, they have been a minority in the over-all Arab population. Jews in even smaller numbers have been a community apart. Both Christians and Jews have been recognized by Muslims as "people of the Book"; but that has not eliminated the distinctions. Sectarian groups within and without the major religions have in many respects been regarded as tribal entities.

CONSTITUTIONAL PROVISIONS

Near East constitutions recognize minority cultures in several ways. Iraq states it is formed of two nationalities, the Arab and the Kurdish, and its constitution affirms "the national rights of

[26] Forced relocation of Kurds has moved over 1/2 million from Iraq to Iran. NEA-89-43-66. London Keyhan (in Persian) April 20, 1989 p.9. Also NEA-89-33-77. Keyhan International (in English). Tehran, Mar. 7, 1989 p2.

the Kurdish people and the legitimate rights of all minorities within the unity of Iraq." It prohibits conduct "undermining the national unity of the masses of the people, provoking racial or sectarian or regional bigotry." The United Arab Emirates declares "The people of the Union shall be a single people, and shall be part of the Arab Nation". The PDRY states it shall "emanicipate the society from . . . reactionary tribal and clannish inclinations," and every citizen must "strive against the tribal separatist, regional and clannish traditions, ideologies and customs which conflict with the aims of the national democratic revolution." (Not repeated in the draft constitution.)

Other constitutions resolve to perpetuate Islam and Arabic unity even with the preservation of separate languages. Iran declares its official and common language is Persian; at the same time, it requires education in Arabic, the language of the Koran, and it expressly allows the use of local and ethnic languages in the press and mass media. Iraq names Arabic as its official language and declares Kurdish as an official language in the Kurdish region.

LABOR CODE AND STATUTORY PROVISIONS

The Middle East labor codes do not mention tribal workers, and such other statutes as may deal with tribal workers have not been indexed.

TREATY PROVISIONS

Treaties concerning tribal workers have sought to improve their standards of life and to prevent discrimination in their terms and conditions of work.

ILO conventions referring to tribal workers are No. 107, entitled Protection and Integration of Indigenous and Other Tribal and Semi-Tribal Populations, and No. 117 which deals more generally with basic Aims and Standards of Social Policy.

Convention 107, ratified by Iraq and Syria, provides that the integration of tribal populations is to be accomplished by "promoting the social, economic and cultural development of these populations and raising their standard of living." This is to be done through special measures for "the protection of the institutions, persons, property and labour of these populations," taking due account of their cultural and religious values and customary laws.

Convention 117, ratified by Israel, Jordan, Kuwait, and Syria states, "It shall be an aim of policy to abolish all discrimination among workers on grounds of . . . tribal association" in labor legislation, admission to public or private employment, vocational training, conditions of work, wage rates, discipline and promotion.

At its International Labor Conferences in 1988 and 1989, the ILO considered a partial revision of the Convention 107. It stressed consultation with tribal representatives and their participation at all levels of decision making in matters of human rights and freedoms. It provided for the recognition of the traditional rights of ownership and possession of land, the protection of recruitment and conditions of employment, vocational training in handicrafts and rural industries, and the progressive extension of social security and health legislation to tribal workers. The proposed revisions have been submitted to all Middle East countries, and the new text will be voted on in succeeding years.

The UN Covenant on Civil and Political Rights, ratified by Iran, Iraq, Jordan, Lebanon, Syria, and PDRY, provides that "In those States in which ethnic . . . minorities exist, persons belonging to such minorities shall not be denied the right . . . to enjoy their own culture . . ."

CONSEQUENCES AND INCIDENTALS

The desire for political unity has led most Middle East countries to announce policies of acceptance and cooperation toward workers identified with tribes.[27] In so far as the workers have

[27] Jorg Janzen, Nomads in the Sultanate of Oman, Westview Press, Boulder Colo., 1986; Richard Tapper, The Conflict of Tribe and State in Iran and Afghanistan, St. Martin's Press, N.Y., 1983; Akbar Aghajanian, "Ethnic Inequality in Iran: An Overview", International Journal of Middle East Studies, Vol. 13, Cambridge Univ. Press, 1983; Fuad I. Khuri, Tribe and State in Bahrain, Univ. of Chicago Press, Chicago, 1980; J.

participated in traditional allocations of function and forms of remuneration or support, there has been little occasion for government interference. A tendency on the part of some urbanized and educated officials to regard tribal customs as backward and inferior to modernized practices has aggravated problems; or the magnitude of economic adjustments has probably been beyond the talents and resources of administrators. In general, tribal workers have received some assistance with job opportunities and have benefited from whatever prosperity, if any, their country has acquired.

A 1983 study of ethnic inequality in Iran analyzed the economic and social standards found in the several provinces of Iran; and observing the preponderance of certain tribes in the population of each province, the researchers concluded that the Kurd, Baluchi, and Turkomen tribesmen had less urbanization (and lower income from agriculture) than other Iranians, also less literacy, lower mortality, less diversity in occupational skills; their homes had less availabilty of electricity and piped water; their household budgets were lower and they suffered a higher degree of poverty. In general, the tribal population lived in the less affluent provinces and assimilation into Iranian society had not reversed the ethnic inequality.[28]

With respect to the nomad populations in all Middle East countries, the efforts to induce them to settle on farms or to enter into other occupations have had very limited success. Some of the programs of sedentarization in Saudi Arabia and Israel have resulted in improvement of living standards. Expectations for education and personal comforts have convinced some Bedouins to alter some of their traditional occupational relationships.[29] The government of Oman, following violent confrontations with

E. Peterson, "Tribes and Politics in Eastern Arabia", Middle East Journal, Vol.31, pp.297-311, 1977; Philip Salzman, "National Integration of the Tribes in Modern Iran", The Middle East Journal, Vol.25, pp.3254-336, 1971; Shirley Kay, The Bedouins, Crane, Russack & Co., New York, 1978.

[28] Richard Tapper, The Conflict of Tribe and State in Iran and Afghanistan, St. Martin's Press, New York, 1983.

[29] Shirley Kay, The Bedouins, Crane, Russack & Co., New York, 1978.

the nomads of southern Dhofar, undertook various means to assure loyalty to the nation, including repair and supply of water wells, grant of building land on an equal footing with others, and the offer of public employment with a constant flow of cash income. These measures improved standards of living among tribal workers as well as among those who changed their occupations.

Nomadic tribal work still remains for significant numbers of Middle East workers. In Iran, religious and linguistic differences and varying degrees of adversity, have minimized the response to resettlement plans. Even the opening of more lucrative employment, such as that of night watchmen in the United Arab Emirates or as supervisors over oil drillers in Oman, has not been sufficiently attractive to cause an appreciable number of nomads to leave their tribal occupations. The alternatives available to provide a secure and reliable livelihood for nomadic tribal workers are few and are still uncertain.[30]

GOVERNMENT WORKERS

PERCEPTIONS OF THE PROBLEM

Every government in the Middle East has faced the urgent problem of how to marshall a staff of public employees to do things they have never done before. The sudden appearance of oil and money scurried people off in many directions, on new economic endeavors that required some societal direction and support. Governments stepped in regulating, designing, constructing, and administering, in rapidly changing economies. British investors were eager to help exploit the oil; but eventually the profit led to the taking over of that enterprise by the Middle East governments themselves. Novel terms came into usage, "infrastructure" and "suprastructure". Infrastructure was a catch-all word for all of the facilities and services required to sup-

[30] Jorg Janzen, Nomads in the Sultanate of Oman, Westview Press, Boulder, Colo., 1986; JPRS-NEA-086-076-051, Aslam Abdullah, Interview with Meir Hassain Masaru, Prime Minister, Iran, The Islamic World Review (in English), No. 57, May, 1986.

port the major economic activities (the supply of materials and equipment, transportation, communication, and finance); and "suprastructure" referred to the government agencies that observed, planned and regulated not only the economy; but also the needs and social services of the people (housing, education, health services, financial assistance). How to cope with the multitude and magnitude of the new responsibilities and tasks of government fell upon ill-prepared public servants.

Some experienced help could be imported from abroad. Training and basic education of native persons seemed a more desirable alternative, but all these measures took time and complicated social adjustments. Funds for solutions were available in the oil producing countries, but not in countries which suffered a net loss of migrant workers. Where wealth was new found, there still were problems of adequate compensation. Greater inducements from other countries frequently disrupted top level personnel, and the mass of government workers who were not skilled worked at wage levels traditionally low and lacking in design needed to motivate productivity. Moonlighting became a problem. Corruption also reared its devouring head. Efficiency and under-utilization often became endemic. How to overcome such evils or shortcomings or "normal problems" in civil service has been an ongoing concern of Middle East governments.

CONSTITUTIONAL PROVISIONS

Middle East constitutions set numerous standards for public employees — their qualification, performance, discipline or dismissal, and work restrictions.

Appointment. Most constitutions repose the power of appointing civil servants in the executive head of the State (Iraq, Kuwait, Lebanon, Qatar, Syria, United Arab Emirates, Yemen Arab Republic). All of these (except Kuwait and including Bahrain and Jordan) add the qualification that appointments are to be under conditions prescribed by law.

Qualifications. Constitutions require public employees to possess (a) merit (Jordan, Lebanon), (b) competence (Iran, Lebanon), (c) citizenship (Bahrain, Israel, Kuwait, Lebanon, United Arab Emirates).

Equal opportunity for public employment is provided by Bahrain, Iraq, the United Arab Emirates. Lebanon amended its constitution in 1947, to declare "as a provisional measure and for the sake of justice and amity, the sects shall be equitably represented in public employment." However, Islamic religion is a prerequisite for public employment in Iran. The Iranian preamble quotes scripture: "The earth will be inherited by the virtuous servants", and it follows with "Thus precise and profound supervision by experts in Islam, the just, ascetics and dedicated people [the just clergy] is necessary and useful." The administration of affairs should be in the hands of those who know God — who are faithful in doing what he has commanded and refraining from doing what he has forbidden."

Standards of Performance. Public employees are called upon to exercise their duties in the public interest (Bahrain, Iraq, Kuwait, Qatar, United Arab Emirates, PDRY). Public office is said to be (a) a national service (Bahrain, Kuwait, Qatar, United Arab Emirates), (b) a noble obligation and honor (Yemen Arab Republic, PDRY), (c) a social service and a sacred trust (Iraq).

Discipline and Discharge. The Executive is authorized to supervise civil servants (Qatar); and dismissals may be made by the Executive in accordance with law (Kuwait, Lebanon, Syria, United Arab Emirates, Yemen Arab Republic).

Restrictions. In Iran, government employees other than teachers shall not hold more than one government job. In Syria, state workers may nominate themselves for membership in the Assembly and those elected are given leave with a reservation of their civil jobs.

LABOR CODE AND STATUTORY PROVISIONS

Several of the labor codes in the Middle East are designed to deal only with private employment and expressly exclude public employees from their coverage (Bahrain, Iran, Jordan, Kuwait,

Lebanon, Oman, Qatar, Syria, United Arab Emirates, YAR). Other public service statutes supplement the codes.

In the absence of a constitution or a comprehensive labor code, Israel has enacted a few basic laws on public employment. State employees are required to be Israeli nationals, and must declare their property, debts and sources of income. Appointments to public service (except in religious courts, the military, police, prison, security and temporary posts) are to be made on competitive, merit examinations. A special Court of Discipline for State Employees is empowered to hear charges of conduct "infringing on the discipline of the State Service" or "likely to impair the image or good name of the Service" or "an offense involving ignominy." Subject to an appeal to the Supreme Court, it may impose penalties ranging from loss of pay to personal disqualification for State service. Other laws provide for retirement benefits of 20% to 70% of salary, and prohibit representation of outside conflicting interests within 2 years of retirement.

TREATY PROVISIONS

Two Middle East countries, Israel and Syria, have ratified the ILO Convention 94 concerning Labor Clauses in Public Contracts. That convention requires public employment contracts to provide wages, hours of work and other conditions of labor no less favorable than such terms in trade or industry where the work is carried on, as set by collective agreements, arbitration awards, or national regulations.

CONSEQUENCES AND INCIDENTALS

Middle East laws governing employment relations in the civil service have incorporated principles approved generally throughout the world. Some governmental idiosyncracies and social responses have been obstacles to fulfillment of the stated objectives.

In countries ruled by sultans and members of their extended families (Saudi Arabia, Bahrain, Oman) there has been a tendency to concentrate responsibility on selected, trusted persons even though they may have been indisposed or unwilling to give personal attention to many of the routine problems of public employment. In Bahrain, one adviser to the ruler was reputed to have organized revenues, headed the state police, sat on the benches of a Higher Court and a Lower Court, inspected public education and supervised all public departments. Inevitably, many personnel problems failed to receive attention.[31]

In the republic of Iran, other concentrations of governmental authority and political difficulties also caused a subordination of civil service needs. The supreme Ayatollah established priorities in accordance with service to God and a holy war. Manpower was drained away from public employment and needed woman power was denied or restricted. Brutal suppression of the expression of disatisfaction with government policies delayed or prevented improvement of obvious civil service deficiencies. Insufficient pay, procrastination on the job, and corruption were openly condemned, but no decisive measures were undertaken to put an end to such practices.[32]

In Kuwait, oil revenue has been ample so that in addition to various social welfare grants, citizens desiring employment have been practically guaranteed work as civil servants. Unfortunately they have not been motivated sufficiently to improve their skills, and instead of following a career path based on personal qualifications, many government workers have received priorities on a ranking of mere length of service. The realities that Kuwaitis in public employment are paid substantially more than non-Kuwaitis in the same or comparable positions and that only Kuwaities are assured of permanent employment have also depressed morale and productivity in the public work force. A two-year study of the civil service by a Supreme Committee for Modernization of the Administrative System, completed in

[31] S. H. Amin, Legal Systems of the Middle East, Royston Ltd., Glasgow, 1985; Emile A. Nakhleh, Bahrain, Lexington Books, N.Y., 1976.

[32] JPRS-NEA-086-031-127, Interview with Deputy Prime Minister and Secretary General of the National Administration and Employment Organization, Teheran, Keyhan (in Persian) 12/04/85; Forhad Kazemi, Poverty and Revolution in Iran, N.Y. Univ. Press, New York, 1980.

December 1986, recommended the shifting of some government programs from national to regional levels and the reclassification and consolidation of numerous positions; but the slowness of change in education, and apathy, have prevented the revitalization of the government work force.[33]

The relative quiet of labor relations in the civil service of oil producing countries has not been mirrored in Israeli public work. Government employees in Israel are organized in the Histadrut, and Israeli courts have generally applied wage and other labor laws to them just as to workers in the private sector. In 1986-87, a critical wage dispute in goverment employment was settled on terms not desired by private employers; and in 1987, negotiations for a 5-day week and the extension of cost-of-living increases for goverment workers brought forth public opposition by the Association of Private Manufacturers.[34]

The Yemenis, as labor-exporting, agricultural countries, also have had some differences. North Yemen or the Yemen Arab Republic, dedicated to the promotion of private enterprise, has developed its public employment slowly, but still at an increasing rate of about 7% a year. South Yemen or the People's Democratic Republic of Yemen, has sought a socialistic or communist transformation, but in addition to socialized agriculture and a few manufacturing mills, it has endorsed joint ventures with private capital and a number of cooperatives. Both countries have suffered from low levels of education and a shortage of skilled administrators, technicians, and professionals. Similarly they have experienced moon-lighting and some corruption of official workers.[35]

[33] American Embassy, Foreign Labor Trends-Kuwait, U.S. Dept. of Labor, Bureau of International Labor Affairs, Washington, D.C., 1987; Jacqueline S. Ismail, Kuwait, Syracuse Univ. Press, 1982.

[34] American Embassy (Tel Aviv), Foreign Labor Trends-Israel, U.S. Department of Labor, Bureau of International Labor Affairs, Washington, D.C., 1987; C. Crouch and F. Heller, eds., Organizational and Political Processes, John Wiley & Sons, Ltd., London, 1983.

[35] Richard Myrop, ed., The Yemens: Country Studies, Foreign Area Studies (U.S. Army) Washington, D.C. 1986; Robert W. Stookey, South Yemen, Westview Press, Boulder, Colo. 1982.

The Middle East countries have been keenly aware of deficiencies in their public services and they are trying to correct those situations.

APPRENTICES

PERCEPTIONS OF THE PROBLEM

Artisans throughout the ages were known to have been trained by their fathers, and those who didn't have or want that opportunity, served an apprenticeship in the home of a mastercraftsman. They worked as household servants while they learned their craft at the will or whim of their masters. That conception of apprentices still lingers in the Middle East. The more impersonal aspects of formal education have been brought in from the Western world.

CONSTITUTIONAL PROVISIONS

There is no mention of apprenticeship in the Middle East constitutions.

LABOR CODE AND STATUTORY PROVISIONS

The recent insatiable demand for skilled workers has led to a considerable detailing of the terms and conditions of apprenticeship in Middle East labor codes.

(a) *Apprenticeship contracts.* Formal written contracts of apprenticeship are required (Bahrain, Iraq, Israel, Jordan, Lebanon, Qatar, Saudi Arabia, Syria, UAE, YAR); however, oral agreements are acceptable in Lebanon. They shall state the term of the apprenticeship, its successive stages (Iraq), the graduated wage for each phase (Bahrain, Lebanon, Qatar, Saudi Arabia, Syria, UAE), and the rights and duties of the trainee (Iraq). The contracts must be in Arabic (Bahrain, Iraq, Lebanon, Qatar, Saudi Arabia, UAE) but may be translated into a foreign language if the worker is unfamiliar with Arabic (Lebanon, Qatar). In Iraq, the Kurdish language "shall be used for the same purposes as Arabic in the autonomous region of Kurdistan." The contract is required to be filed with an appropriate labor office (Bahrain, Israel, Jordan, Saudi Arabia, UAE).

(b) *Wages*. Lebanon provides for one third of the ordinary remuneration in the first apprenticeship period, one half in the second period, two thirds in the third period. Other countries provide that wages in the final phase of the apprenticeship "shall be not less than the minimum wage fixed for similar work" (Bahrain, Israel, Saudi Arabia, Syria, UAE, YAR). Nor shall the wages be fixed on a "piece rate", or a "productivity" or "output" basis (Bahrain, Saudi Arabia, UAE).

(c) *Employer qualifications*. The employer of an apprentice must have a "good reputation" and "adequate skills and experience" (Saudi Arabia, UAE) and must be a least 21 years of age (Jordan, Lebanon, Saudi Arabia). He must not have been convicted of crime (Jordan, Lebanon). No unmarried employer may engage a female apprentice (Jordan); and no employer "unmarried, widowed, separated or divorced shall give lodging in his or her home to a minor" apprentice (Lebanon).

(d) *Training*. An apprentice shall be trained "systematically" (Jordan), "progressively and exhaustively" (Lebanon), "methodically" (Saudi Arabia). In Qatar, the period of training varies according to the age of the worker and the requirements of the trade or profession. The employer shall insure the apprentice "suitable guidance and a work method calculated to impart the trade" (Israel), "work with him" (Syria), treat him "as would a good father, guiding him and supervising his conduct" (Saudi Arabia), and provide full vocational training consistent with the principles of the occupation" (UAE). No apprentice shall be required "to perform any work which is not in accordance with his curriculum of studies" (Bahrain, Israel, Saudi Arabia). In the PDRY, the employer is obliged "to train cadres that are required for the execution of the work plans." The employer shall inform the apprentice's guardian of serious errors, unexcused absence, illness, and moral or tempermental aberrations" (Bahrain, Saudi Arabia).

(e) *Termination*. An apprenticeship may be terminated for

failure to perform contractual duties or inability to learn (Bahrain, Israel, YAR), inaptitude (Iraq, Syria), incompetence (YAR), or because of the apprentice's conduct during training (Iraq).

(f) *Post apprenticeship employment.* Neither the employer nor the apprentice has the right to retain an employment relationship after the completion of an apprenticeship, unless otherwise provided in the apprenticeship contract (Saudi Arabia, UAE). In Iraq, neither party "may claim compensation from the other party" as a result of the termination of the training contract.

TREATY PROVISIONS

ILO Convention 117 on Social Policy (Basic Aims and Standards), ratified by Israel, Jordan, Kuwait and Syria, calls for "the progressive development of broad systems of education, vocational training and apprenticeship." Convention 97 on Migration for Employment, ratified only by Israel, provides for nondiscriminatory treatment of immigrants with respect to "apprenticeship and training."

CONSEQUENCES AND INCIDENTALS

The introduction of prescribed standards for the training and work of apprentices in the Middle East has been slow; and apprenticeship training proceeds mostly in traditional ways.

WORKERS IN COOPERATIVES

PERCEPTIONS OF THE PROBLEM

The concept of cooperatives has always been a philosophical dream as well as a series of experiments in real cooperative endeavors. For tribal Arabs, well defined groups working together without individual differentiation by land ownership were traditional. With the inroads of industrialization and Western ideas, there were modifications toward formal cooperatives to satisfy needs, primarily for water, housing and marketing. The early Israeli settlers came with ideologies in which cooperative goals loomed large. They sought to build a new economy in which workers controlled enterprise in a communal effort.

With the changes brought about by Middle East oil and the possibilities of economic expansion and prosperity, attitudes toward cooperatives have shifted. Capitalistic enterprise and employment for wages have offered many persons greater attractions than the existing cooperatives. The hiring of nonmember employees by cooperatives has also increased. Cooperatives have become regarded as auxiliaries to other forms of economic acitivity more than as alternatives.

CONSTITUTIONAL PROVISIONS

Provisions in a few Middle East constitutions promote cooperatives with only isolated references to their working conditions.

The constitutions "encourage . . . cooperative activities" (Kuwait), "ensure, promote and support all kinds of cooperation in production, distribution and consumption" (Iraq), guarantee cooperatives "protection and support" (Syria), sponsor "various cooperative establishments" (Yemen Arab Republic).

The constitution of Iran designates three sectors of its economy — governmental, cooperative, and private. "The cooperative sector shall include cooperative corporations and means of production and distribution which shall be formed . . . in accordance with Islamic principles" as "determined by law."

Syria refers to protecting and supporting "collective ownership" including property of cooperatives.

The PDRY also refers to "collective property" of the state and of cooperatives and mass organizations, which "may not be employed for personal purposes." The state shall support the cooperative movement and encourage voluntary affiliation with the aim of increasing production and "improving the standard of living of the cooperative peasants." Cooperatives are identified as societies of peasants, fishermen, craftsmen and "the working people," and the state grants them "permanent and free usufruct over the lands." It shall convince the peasants, by means of presenting the positive example, that the economy is best organized on the basis of co-operative collectivism." (Not in the draft constitution.)

LABOR CODE AND STATUTORY PROVISIONS

The labor codes in the Middle East countries have not singled out workers in cooperatives. Special statutes for the promotion of cooperatives, creating specific projects or entities for credit and mechanization, have been numerous; but since they have affected standards for employment only inferentially, I have not detailed them.

TREATY PROVISIONS

ILO Convention No. 117 concerning Basic Aims and Standards of Social Policy calls for "the reduction of production and distribution costs by all practicable means and in particular by forming, encouraging and assisting producers' and consumers' co-operatives." This Convention has been ratified by Israel, Jordan, Kuwait and Syria.

CONSEQUENCES AND INCIDENTALS

Some Middle East countries have concerned themswelves with cooperatives much more than others.

Both the YAR and the PDRY have had extensive cooperative programs. The YAR made them a major emphasis in its second 5-year plan. In addition to provision for aid to agricultural cooperatives and the construction of access roads, the government assisted fishing cooperatives through funds for boat repair and the purchase of new equipment. The levy of taxes on cooperatives has raised questions concerning the handling of administrative funds and the number of co-ops has grown slowly.[36] In the PDRY attention has been divided between cooperatives and collective farms. Progress has been restrained by lack of capital; but as many as half of the agricultural workers in 1980 had been working within the cooperative system. Bedouins, in tribal coop-

[36] Ragaei El Mallakh, The Economic Development of the YAR, Croom Helm, London, 1986.

erative groups, have supplied a large portion of the livestock in the country. Fishing co-ops have also been active. The government has collected land taxes and additional charges for its management and marketing services. It has subsidized seeds, fertilizers and machinery, has built cold storage facilities, and has provided wholesaling services for cooperatives. Government price setting for the farmer and the consumer has had mixed results, dissention and no clear policy formulation. Workers in the cooperatives have been paid wages, and at times the agricultural workers have received less than salaried staff, with consequent grievances.[37] Both the YAR and the PDRY have suffered from a low gross national product, but cooperatives have been a vital portion of their economies.

Jordan has extended much-needed credit to cooperatives. It has also made available machinery, supplies, and technical services.[38]

Cooperatives and their workers in Israel have had a unique status in several ways. Jewish settlers, long before the establishment of an Israeli state, created producer and consumer cooperatives they called kibbutzim (on collectively owned land, with equally shared income and common living arrangements) and moshavim (on individually owned farms and households, with cooperative marketing and village management). Their Arab neighbors set up some separate cooperatives. The development of the State of Israel has relied upon old cooperatives, and has grown with private industrial and institutional enterprises — as well as with the extensive economic ventures of the Histadrut, an organization democratically operated by its members. Formal cooperatives and cooperative endeavors of the people have penetrated into almost every aspect of civilian life in Israel.[39]

[37] Robert W. Stookey, South Yemen, Westview Press, Boulder, Colo., 1982.

[38] Peter Gubser, Jordan, Westview Press, Boulder, Colo., 1983.

[39] Abraham Daniel, Labour Enterprises in Israel, Chapter VII, Jerusalem Academic Press, 1974.

SPECIAL CLASSES OF LABOR

EXCLUDED WORKERS

PERCEPTIONS OF THE PROBLEM

The thoughts and motivations of legislators are not all set forth in their debates or public utterances. So for a variety of unspecified reasons, the labor codes and statutes of the Middle East exclude some segments of the working population without explanation. The difficulties of administering labor laws in widely dispersed places of employment or in very numerous small shops are quite obvious. At times, it may seem desirable to postpone the coverage of some workers until more experience is gained. Less apparent are the pressures of special employer groups who desire to avoid regulation. Whatever the reasons or excuses, it has often been decided not to extend the benefits of certain labor laws to some workers.

LABOR CODE AND STATUTORY PROVISIONS

The following exclusions have been made in the Middle East Labor Codes. (a) All employees in establishments hiring *fewer than 6 workers* (Qatar); or *fewer than 10 workers* (Iran, Kuwait, Oman, Saudi Arabia, UAE); (b) *family workers* (Iran, Lebanon, Oman, Qatar, Saudi Arabia, UAE); (c) *temporary workers* (Bahrain, Iran, Kuwait, UAE, YAR); (d) *domestic servants* (Bahrain, Iran, Kuwait, Lebanon, Oman, Qatar, Saudi Arabia, UAE, YAR); (e) *casual workers* (Bahrain, Iran, Qatar); (f) *fishermen* (Iran); (g) *dock workers* (Iran); (h) *military personnel* (Bahrain, Oman, UAE); (i) *members of the Public Security Force* (Qatar). The exclusion of *agricultural workers*, who constitute a large portion of the labor force in most Middle East countries, is particularly significant (Bahrain, Iran, Jordan, Lebanon, Oman, Saudi Arabia, UAE, YAR).

By contrast, the Iraqi labor code expressly includes all employees in establishments hiring one or more.

Among the several separate labor laws in Israel, there are excluded (a) from the Hours of Work and Rest law, miscellaneous public employees and employees whose hours it is "impossible" for the employer to control; (b) from the Annual Leave law, sharecroppers and casual workers; (c) from the Employment of Women law, all employees in specified industries; (d) from the State Service (Appointment) law, employees in non-Jewish religious courts, the police and others in public positions.

TREATY PROVISIONS

The ILO has found it unavoidable, or pragmatic, to make allowance in most of its Conventions for signatory countries to exclude those workers they deem inappropriate to cover under conditions peculiar to national circumstances. Often this is coupled with a proposal that the exclusion be treated as temporary.

CONSEQUENCES AND INCIDENTALS

The workers expressly excluded from the coverage of labor laws in the Middle East have lacked unionization or aggressive spokesmen to champion their interests. Although the ILO conventions have often permitted the exclusions, the ILO has on occasion attempted to have a signatory nation eliminate an exclusion or restrict its scope. In reviewing compliance with the convention on the right to organize, the ILO has criticized the YAR for excluding civil servants and agricultural workers. and denying the right to groups of less than 50 workers. On the same convention, it has taken Kuwait and Syria to task for excluding foreign workers with less than a specified period of residence in the country from union membership. As laudable as such efforts may be, they have not been sufficient to avoid the many exclusions of unorganized and voiceless workers from protective labor laws.

Chapter 5

REMUNERATION

PERCEPTION OF THE PROBLEM

One of the oldest forms of magic — common to all cultures — is the transformation of what workers get paid into food, clothing and shelter. Participants in that sleight of hand have many divergent interests. Not the least of which is seeking agreement upon the needs that should be satisfied and the quantity of wages required to fulfill those needs. Labor laws establish rules to assist them in arriving at a reasonable and just resolution of those dilemmas.

Such laws frequently define minimum living standards, procedures for wage setting, and safeguards of payment. The choices are very many. They rest upon difficult questions like what is the unacceptable level of poverty; should a base wage suffice for a family as well as a worker; should wages differ for occupations and regions of the country; may there be deductions or withholdings and if so what kinds; must remuneration be paid in cash or in kind and must it be paid at regular times and not in certain places. The laws may authorize governmental agencies to answer those questions or may relegate the matter to individual or collective agreements.

In the Middle East (outside of the oil producing states), there are a large number of workers whose earnings are below what is regarded in their communities as a living wage. All countries deplore the situation; yet custom and inertia tend to perpetuate much poverty. Even in some well-to-do states, there remain a substratum of underpaid workers and a widespread sense of insecurity. The awareness of such conditions promotes wage legislation.

In the countries that have experienced an out-migration of workers to the oil countries, wage remittances have been regarded as a countervailing boon, to be encouraged as much as possible.

CONSTITUTIONAL PROVISIONS

The constitutions of the Middle East make a commitment to economic development and the improvement of life in various forms; but only half speak of work remuneration directly and they provide wage standards only in general terms.

The Iranian constitution asserts the principle of planning to the end that every individual will have sufficient means to improve himself and his skills "and to increase his initiatives." Iraq undertakes to "promote standards of living" and to "provide the means of enjoying the achievements of modern civilization for the masses of the people." Qatar seeks to "realize such prosperity in the country as will ensure an honorable life for its citizens." PDRY promises to work for "raising the standard of the under-developed areas with the aim of gradually obliterating the differences in the standards of living between the various parts of the Republic." (Not in the draft constitution.)

A few constitutions contain more specific wage clauses. Jordan calls for legislation on the principle that "every workman shall receive wages commensurate with the quantity and quality of his work." Syria guarantees every citizen "the right to earn his wage according to the nature and yield of work." PDRY affirms "the absolute application of the principle from each according to his ability and for each according to his work"; "Remuneration shall be determined according to the quantity and type of work"; trade unions shall participate in determining wages; and the general principles of remuneration shall be regulated by law. (Not in the draft.)

LABOR CODE AND STATUTORY PROVISIONS

Labor statutes (in Iran, Iraq, Israel, Jordan, Lebanon, Oman, Qatar, Saudi Arabia, United Arab Emirates, YAR, PDRY) go beyond constitutional provisions by providing for minimum wages and for conditions of wage payment, withholdings, preferences, and attachments.

Minimum wages

The standards set for a minimum wage are generally what suffices to cover the essential needs of a worker. The employee's family is included by Lebanon, Iraq, and Iran, the latter of which designates the family as consisting of a man, his wife and two children. In Qatar, the minimum basic pay is that which "His Highness the Ruler may deem fit to determine."

Other factors to be considered are fluctuations in the cost of living (Syria, United Arab Emirates, YAR), the general economic situation (Lebanon, Oman, Saudi Arabia), national production growth (Iraq), currency devaluation (Syria), economic crisis (Syria), and employment conditions (Jordan).

Minimum wages are to be determined for industry, occupation, or area (Iran, Jordan, Saudi Arabia, Syria, United Arab Emirates, PDRY), for the country as a whole (Saudi Arabia, United Arab Emirates, PDRY) or "for an unskilled worker" (Iraq).

The frequency of wage setting is set for once a year (Syria, YAR), every two years (Iran), at regular intervals (Iraq), and whenever the government chooses (Lebanon, Oman, Saudi Arabia).

The wage setting authority is generally a Minister of Labor or a Council of Ministers. Boards involving employers and worker representatives are also utilized (Iran, Iraq, Jordan, Lebanon, Syria, United Arab Emirates, YAR, PDRY). Wages in Qatar are determined by the Amir.

Premium Pay

Extra compensation is provided for *overtime* (Bahrain, Iran, Iraq, Israel, Kuwait, Lebanon, Oman, Qatar, Saudi Arabia, Syria, United Arab Emirates, YAR, PDRY), *night work* (Bahrain, Iran, Iraq, Qatar, Syria, United Arab Emirates, PDRY), *holidays* (Bahrain, Iran, Iraq, Kuwait, Oman, Qatar,

Saudi Arabia, Syria, United Arab Emirates, YAR, PDR Yemen), *day of rest* (all of the latter except Oman), and *shift work* (Iran, Qatar PDRY).

Equal Pay for Equal Work

Labor codes provide that men and women shall be paid an equal wage for the same or equal work (Iran, Iraq, Kuwait, United Arab Emirates). Israel provides equal pay for the same or substantially the same work.

Concerning the respective wages paid citizens and aliens, the foreign worker shall not be paid more (Bahrain, Oman, Saudi Arabia).

Severance Pay

Nearly all Labor Codes provide for some termination pay. The amounts generally range from 15 days' pay for each of the first 3 or 5 years of employment to one month's pay for each succeeding year (Bahrain, Iran, Lebanon, Oman, Saudi Arabia, Syria, YAR). Qatar provides 3 weeks' pay plus a cost of living allowance for each of the first 5 years of continuous service and up to six weeks' pay for each year of continuous service over twenty years. Lesser amounts may be paid to piece workers (Jordan, Kuwait), retirees (UAE), workers who resign (Bahrain, Saudi Arabia). PDRY provides that at the end of the worker's service, the employer shall pay a gratuity to the worker either in a lump sum or as a monthly pension or both. In Israel, salaried employees have a right to severance pay of one month, and non-salaried employees, two weeks, for each year of continuous service.

General provisions for severance pay are tied to pension or social security payments in Iraq and Qatar. Saudi Arabia also sets a policy of taking into account the terminated employee's age, family responsibilities, degree of arbitrariness in the dismissal, and rules of equity and generally accepted practice.

Wage Payment and Collection

Labor codes require wages to be paid at the place of employment (Bahrain, Iran, Iraq, Israel, Oman, Lebanon, Qatar, Saudi Arabia, Syria, United Arab Emirates, YAR, PDRY), and to be paid in legal tender (Bahrain, Lebanon, Syria) or in legal currency (Kuwait, Oman, Saudi Arabia, YAR, PDRY), "official currency" (Qatar, United Arab Emirates), "national currency" or in cash or check (Israel), or specifically in "Iraqi currency" since payment in other currencies "shall not release the employer from his obligations to the worker" (Iraq).

Bahrain, Iran, Israel, and Lebanon permit some payment in kind. Jordan allows it if the kind consists of essential commodities supplied at agreed upon prices; and Oman provides that land used for cultivation or other similar benefits may constitute payment.

Wage Remittances

The encouragement of wage remittances has resulted in the enactment of laws that provide income tax exemptions for earnings remitted, special government bond issues for domestic development, and the waiver of import duties on goods sent home (Jordan, YAR, PDRY).

Wage Withholdings

Employer deductions from the earnings of workers are frequently restricted to certain obligations and in certain amounts.

For loans extended by the employer or payment of debts due him, no more than 10% of the wage may be deducted, and no interest may be charged on the loan (Bahrain, Kuwait, Oman, Qatar, Saudi Arabia, Syria, United Arab Emirates). In Qatar, the indebted worker can agree in writing that deductions shall not exceed 35% of the workers wage; but no deduction in any one month shall exceed five days pay. In Israel one fourth of the wage may be so deducted; and in Iran the worker may request withholding of no more than one fourth of his wages when the debt was incurred through the purchase of essential goods from a cooperative society. In Iraq, wages "may not be subject to deductions other than those provided by law."

Specific deductions are permitted (a) for social insurance premiums, savings, home construction, not to exceed one fourth or one half of the wages (Saudi Arabia); (b) for social security, income tax, court judgments, housing and services provided by the employer (Jordan, United Arab Emirates); (c) for housing or transport facilities, trade union dues, or for savings (YAR); (d) for damage to tools or products (3 to 5 days' pay in Bahrain, Saudi Arabia, Syria, UAE, PDRY); (e) for violation of shop rules, approved by the government (Jordan); or (f) for specified fines (Saudi Arabia, UAE).

In Israel, withholdings are permitted if consented to in writing.

Attachments

The amount of an employee's wage that may be seized by court attachment is limited to 25% of the wage (Bahrain, Iran, Kuwait, Saudi Arabia, Syria, YAR), 20% in Iraq, 35% in Qatar. Attachments for alimony are given priority in Bahrain, Jordan, Kuwait, Qatar, Saudi Arabia, Syria, and the UAE. In Israel, attachments are imposed after the deduction of income tax; and a number of pounds in respect of the employee and additional amounts in respect of his wife and each child. PDRY provides that wages shall not be attached except by court order.

Wage Preferences

Wages are made a prior claim over other debts of the employer in Bahrain, Iran, Iraq, Lebanon, Qatar, Saudi Arabia, United Arab Emirates, YAR, PDRY. That is after the claims of court costs, taxes and expenses of conserving the employer's property (Bahrain), after Treasury claims, judicial costs and compulsory mortgages (Lebanon). Elsewhere, the wage preference comes before taxes (Iran, YAR, PDRY); and for one month's pay before even bankruptcy and liquidation costs (Saudi Arabia). In case of insolvency, workers shall be paid in full without being subject to rules concerning distribution among creditors (PDRY).

Profit Sharing

In 1963, Iran enacted a Profit Sharing Law, and in 1975 it adopted a Divestiture Law which provided that in establishments hiring more than 10 employees, profits up to 20% were to be received by the workers (and additional percentages were to be divested to public ownership).

TREATY PROVISIONS

The ILO, the UN and the ALO have all promulgated Conventions or Covenants on the remuneration of workers.

ILO Convention 26 on the Creation of Minimum Wage-Fixing Machinery (1928) was ratified by Iraq, Lebanon, and Syria. That was followed, in 1951 ,by Convention 99 on the same topic, relating to Agriculture, which has been ratified only by Syria. Convention 131 on Minimum Wage Fixing, with Special Reference to Developing Countries (1970) has been ratified by Iraq, Lebanon, Syria, and the Yemen Arab Republic. These undertakings significantly have been of benefit to workers engaged in economic activities other than the exploitation of oil.

A general Convention 95, concerning the Protection of Wages provides that wages shall be paid only in legal tender and prohibits payment in the form of promissory notes, vouchers or coupons. Payment by cheque or money order is allowed when customary, when stipulated by a collective agreement or arbitration award, or when consented to by the worker concerned. That convention has been ratified by Iraq, Iran, Israel, Lebanon, Syria, and PDRY.

Convention No. 100 concerning Equal Remuneration for Men and Women Workers for Work of Equal Value (1951) has also been ratified by Iran, Iraq, Israel, Jordan, Saudi Arabia, and the Yemen Arab Republic.

The UN Covenant on Economic, Social and Cultural Rights, ratified by Iran, Iraq, Israel, Jordan, Lebanon, Syria and PDRY, provides that parties to the Covenant "recognize the right of everyone to the enjoyment of just and favorable conditions of work which ensure, in particular: (a) Remuneration which provides all workers, as a minimum, with fair wages and equal remuneration for work of equal value without distinction of any kind . . ., (b) a decent living for themselves and their families . . ., (c) equal opportunity for everyone to be promoted in his employment to an appropriate higher level, subject to no considerations other than those of seniority and competence."

The ALO Convention 1 on Labor Norms (revised by Convention 6), has committed its signatories, Iraq, Jordan, Lebanon, Palestine, and Syria, to protect worker's remuneration against an employer's creditors and against employer deductions. It also calls for indemnities on cessation of employment. In 1982, a draft of a Convention on Minimum Wages was prepared; but it has not yet been approved by the ALO or issued for ratification.

CONSEQUENCES AND INCIDENTALS

Reports appearing in the native press frequently highlight public concerns over special wage issues and laws pertaining to worker remuneration. A few examples may illustrate recent crises or recurrent events.

In Iran, the payment of public employees became a subject of much debate and a new law was presented to the Council of Ministers in 1985. It provided (a) for comparable pay with that received by private employees; (b) for classifications of pay, adjustable as much as 30% on the quality of the work done; (c) for public awards (Service to the Oppressed Award, Islamic Republic Presentation, Merit and Initiative Award) and noncash prizes such as 30 day vacations and trips to the Holy Shrine; (d) for minimums, maximums and cost-of-living adjustments; and (e) for health care, dependent allowances, housing and other welfare assistance.[1]

[1] JPRS-NEA-086-031-127, Interview with Deputy Prime Minister and Secretary General of the National Administration and Employment Organization, Teheran (in Arabic) Keyhan, Dec. 4, 1985.

In Israel, the redetermination of minimum wages became a controverted issue in 1986. Private employers bitterly opposed the fixing of minimum wages as a percentage of the average wage in the marketplace; and offered specified increases instead. The Histadrut disagreed; and a compromise on scheduled increases in the minimum wages was reached.[2]

In Kuwait, the social problems presented by expatriate unskilled workers gave rise to a perception that lower paid expatriates had become a troublesome lower social class. That led to a discussion of the illegal entry of more Asian Workers.[3]

The amount of remittances that expatriate workers have mailed to relatives left at home or taken back on their return has been quite significant. Surveys in Jordan have indicated as many as two-thirds of its emigrants have made remittances, from 5% to 50% of their earnings. The total rose throughout the 1970's to more than the nation's imports. Most of the remittances have gone into consumer goods, but some into investments and savings.[4] Wage remittances in the Yemens have resulted in home construction and farm improvements.

In Bahrain, The Director of Labor was reported as saying he refused to set a minimum wage because it would benefit foreign workers at the expense of Bahraini employers' profits, whereas the benefit to Bahraini workers would be extremely limited.[5]

Issues of worker remuneration, perhaps the most basic of all labor problems, have been dealt with by numerous labor laws,

[2] JPRS-NEA-086-149-5a. Y. Winkler and T. Zaharis, "An Attempt to Find a Compromise on the Minimum Wage Issue (in Hebrew). Tel Aviv, Ha'aretz, 7/28/86. JPRS-NEA-086-022-47, "Minimum Wage Increased", Tel Aviv (In Hebrew) Ma'ariv, 12/24/85.

[3] JPRS-NEA-086-102-28, "Study Shows Expatriates Contribute to Social Disparity", Kuwait Arab Times, 7/23/86. A. Al-Moosa & K. McLachlan, "Wage Patterns Among the Foreign Labour Force in Kuwait", The Arab Gulf Journal, Vol. 2, No. 2, Oct. 1982, p 55.

[4] M.A.J. Share. The Use of Jordanian Workers Remittances. Ch 3 in Bichara Khader, ed. The Economic Development of Jordan. Croom Helm. London. 1987.

[5] JPRS-NEA-89-42-27, Interview with Abd al Rahman S. Al Zayani, in Ministry of Labor and Social Affairs. Sada al Usbu (in Arabic), Mar. 7, 1989, pp. 8-10

many of them benign and well crafted. Still, the aspirations and ingenuity of workers pose unending challenges.

Chapter 6

HOURS OF WORK

PERCEPTIONS OF THE PROBLEM

Hours of work have been generally viewed as the time a worker is required or willing to work. Since most production, whether on a farm, in an office, or in a factory can be performed over an indefinite period — taxing the comfort or endurance of workers — some limitations have customarily been imposed. In traditional Middle East farming, the work day has lasted from sun up to sun down; and legal restraints were seen as necessary only to ease the burden of children and women in the fields. In the burgeoning commerce and industry, Middle East employers sought to push activity to completion, without restriction; and the lure of cash income led many workers to be eager to work as many paid hours as possible. Rapidly changing developments in oil producing countries spurred employers to require more and more hours of work and ultimately induced the fatigued to seek relief. Notions of the desirability of shorter days and periods of rest came from abroad with the immigrant workers. Health and family considerations for an optimal work day were too sophisticated for popular articulation. Yet in some areas, worker unrest took such political expression. The International Labour Office supplied standards for laws on daily and weekly hours, rest breaks and vacations. Religious sects demanded time off for prayer, holidays, and pilgrimages. The scene was set for the adaptation of onerous work schedules to personal and social needs; laws seemed essential and unavoidable.

CONSTITUTIONAL PROVISIONS

Most constitutions of the new Middle East states were adopted prior to the oil activity, and only few provided for the regulation of work hours or rest.

Syria declared, "The State fixes worker hours." Jordan stated, "The number of hours of work per week shall be limited." The PDRY provided that the State shall ensure the right to rest" by means of "regulating the working hours according to the law."

Other provisions designated "a right to rest" and indicated that further steps were to be taken to give effect to that right. Syria stated both "rest and leave rights" were to be regulated. The PDRY spelled out that the State shall prepare "adequate circumstances to enable the workers to enjoy their right to rest by means of expanding and regulating the public recreation places and the workers' rest house and encouraging the mass organizations to play a greater role in this field." Iraq proclaimed, "The State shall endeavor to organize the programme and ensure the necessary means which enable working citizens to spend their leaves in an atmosphere that helps them to improve." Implementing features reflected the socialist or social welfare commitments of those constitutions. (Hours and rest are not mentioned in the new Yemeni draft constitution.)

LABOR CODE AND STATUTORY PROVISIONS

Legislation throughout the Middle East has limited hours of work, set periods for rest, and provided for paid vacations; in pursuit of economic development, however, numerous exceptions have been legalized.

Hours of work per day

The basic regulation in all Middle East countries prohibits work in excess of 8 hours per day.

A reduction to 7 hours has been set for night work (Iraq), 6 hours for days in the month of Ramadhan (Bahrain, Oman, Qatar, Saudi Arabia, United Arab Emirates, YAR), and for shifts preceding the weekly rest period or religious festival days (Israel).

On the other hand, the normal 8 hour day has been extended to 9 hours for hotels and restaurants (Jordan, Saudi Arabia, YAR) and to 10 hours for hospitals, guard duties, old age homes, child care centers, pharmacies, nonindustrial and publicly essential state services (Israel). Unspecified increases or open exemptions have been provided for hotels and restaurants (Israel, Kuwait), for cafes (Lebanon, United Arab Emirates), hospitals (Kuwait), for guard duties (Kuwait, Saudi Arabia, United Arab Emirates), for transport or dock work (Jordan), for seasonal work (Israel), for cinemas (Jordan), for stock taking, preparation of annual balance sheets, and repair of accidents (Israel), and for the prevention of a serious loss or a dangerous event or to repair the effects of such loss or event (Qatar). Still broader administrative exemptions have been allowed by decrees of Ministers of Social Affairs and Labor for any category of worker, type of work, or branch of production in Syria; in Bahrain if "the circumstances and the nature of work so require," and in Oman if the application of the hours law "is not practicable." In Iraq, the Code provisions on hours of work do not apply to agricultural workers, domestic workers and watchmen.

Hours of work per week

The maximum hours of work per week has been set at 48 in the Arab states and 47 in Israel, with a large number of exceptions or further restraints.

The maximum may be reduced under circumstances deemed harmful to workers, namely, when found to be "*arduous or injurious*", "*hazardous*", "*harmful to health*", or "*dangerous*" (Iran, Iraq, Kuwait, Lebanon, Saudi Arabia, United Arab Emirates, YAR). In Kuwait, this applies also to work found "oppressive" or "performed under harsh climatic conditions".

Limitations on weekly hours of work are said not to apply in many specified situations: (1) agricultural corporate employment (Lebanon); (2) annual stock-taking, liquidation, preparation for commencement of a season (Bahrain, Iraq, Jordan on accounts, Saudi Arabia, Syria, YAR); (3) prevention of dangerous incidents (Bahrain, Iraq, Jordan, Kuwait, Saudi Arabia, Syria, YAR); (4) repair of damage (Bahrain, Iran, Iraq, Jordan, Saudi Arabia, Syria); (5) avoidance of loss of perishable materials

(Bahrain, Iraq, Jordan, Kuwait, Saudi Arabia, Syria, YAR); (6) unusual pressure of work (Bahrain, Iraq-technical reasons, Jordan, Saudi Arabia, Syria, YAR); (7) seasonal work for feasts, seasons, public holidays (Bahrain, Iraq, Israel-bakeries, Saudi Arabia, Syria, YAR); (8) force majeure (Iran, Jordan-national catastrophes); (9) manpower shortage (Jordan); (10) work of an extraordinary nature (Kuwait); (11) work necessarily intermittent (Bahrain, Iran, Jordan, Saudi Arabia, Syria); (12) prospect drilling in remote areas (Saudi Arabia); (13) caretaking, cleaning (Syria); (14) work beyond employer control (Israel).

Exemptions have been granted also for certain persons: (1) supervisory or managerial employees (Jordan, Qatar, United Arab Emirates); (2) legal representatives of employers (Syria); (3) confidential employees (Israel, Jordan); (4) seaman (Iran, Israel, Qatar, United Arab Emirates); (5) airport and aircraft personnel (Iran, Israel); (6) fishermen (Iran, Israel); (7) professional or technical employees (Qatar).

Periods for rest

Labor codes and other statutes in the Middle East provide for intervals of rest within each work day and for time off each week.

Continuous hours of work are limited to 5 (in Iraq, Jordan, Kuwait, Qatar, Saudi Arabia, Syria, United Arab Emirates, PDRY) and 6 (in Bahrain, Jordan, Lebanon, Oman); with an interval for rest — 1/2 hour (in Bahrain, Jordan, PDRY), 1 hour (in Jordan, Kuwait, Lebanon, Syria, United Arab Emirates), 1/2 to 1 hour (in Iraq and Oman), 1 hour (YAR), and 1/2 to 1-1/2 hours total (Saudi Arabia). In Bahrain and Syria, however, the Minister of Labor may waive the rest period for technical reasons or circumstances requiring continuity of work.

The work week is also circumscribed by provisions for time off. In several Arab countries, Friday is declared a day of rest (PDRY), and with pay (Bahrain, Iran, Jordan, Oman, Qatar, Saudi Arabia, United Arab Emirates, YAR). In Israel, Saturday is observed as a day of rest, with the right of non-Jews to choose their own Sabbath. In Iraq, "the employer shall schedule the weekly day of rest on the same day for all staff, or shall grant (it) on a rotating basis, as long as each worker can take his or her day of weekly rest on a predetermined day."

In Syria, time off applies only to commercial establishments; in Kuwait, payment is not required. In Lebanon, the weekly uninterrupted rest period must be not less than 36 hours.

Saudi Arabia requires every employer of 50 or more to provide, at his expense, suitable rest and recreational facilities for his employees.

Holidays

In all Middle East countries, certain official holidays are designated as paid days of rest. These number 7 in Kuwait, Syria, United Arab Emirates, 8 in Bahrain, Israel, and 10 in Iran, Qatar, Saudi Arabia, YAR. The laws refer to all holidays and feast days, without specification, in Iraq, Jordan, Oman, and PDRY.

Vacations

Annual vacations with pay are commonly prescribed by Middle East laws. The minimum length of vacation varies: 12 days (Iran); 14 (Israel, Kuwait, Qatar, Syria); 15 (Lebanon, Oman, Saudi Arabia); 20 (Iraq — except 30 days for workers in jobs which are arduous or harmful to health); 21 (Bahrain, Jordan, YAR — except 30 days for employees whose work is primarily administrative or intellectual); 24 (United Arab Emirates, PDRY). The period is increased after a specified number of years of service: after 1 year, to 30 days in United Arab Emirates; by not less than 2 days per year for every 5 years of service in Iraq and PDRY; after 3 years, to 30 days in Oman; after 5 years, to 28 days in Bahrain, to 21 days in Kuwait , to 30 days in Qatar; after 10 years, to 21 days in Saudi Arabia and Syria.

Upon the termination of an employee within a year, his vacation time is prorated (Bahrain, Iran, Jordan, Oman, Saudi Arabia, United Arab Emirates).

To preserve the health and efficiency benefits of vacations, some laws provide the annual leave may not be waived or renounced (Bahrain, Iran, Iraq, Saudi Arabia, Syria), or must be taken at least once in two consecutive years (Oman, United Arab Emirates). Bahrain prohibits the payment of money in lieu of annual leave. Several countries forbid the employment of a worker by any employer during the vacation period (Bahrain, Iraq, Saudi Arabia, Syria, United Arab Emirates). In Israel, taking other employment during the leave period may result in a loss of the leave pay and the Minister of Labor may prescribe a longer period of leave or prohibit the accumulation of leave when an employee's health or other circumstances require it. The Israeli leave law does not apply to agricultural workers who receive their entire remuneration in the form of a share of the produce or in services, nor to employees paid entirely in a share of profits, nor to casual employees.

Pilgrimage Leave

In a few Muslim countries, members of the faith are entitled to a leave of absence to perform their lifetime pilgrimage obligation. The time allowed is 2 weeks in Bahrain, 15 days in Oman, and up to 30 days in Qatar and the United Arab Emirates.

TREATY PROVISIONS

The ILO, the UN, and the ALO have drafted and recommended the adoption of treaties on hours of work.

The International Labour Office promulgated its first convention in 1919, on the subject of an 8-hour day and a 48-hour week. That was in time ratified by Bahrain, Iraq, Israel, Lebanon, Kuwait, Saudi Arabia, Syria, the United Arab Emriates. At frequent intervals thereafter, the ILO formulated new conventions on hours of work, rest periods and vacations.

Convention 14 on the Application of Weekly Rest in Industrial Undertakings has been signed by Bahrain, Iran, Iraq, Israel, Lebanon, Saudi Arabia, Syria, Yemen Arab Republic. The same countries (except for Bahrain and the Yemen Arab Republic) have ratified Convention 30 on Hours of Work in Commerce and

Offices and Convention 106 on Weekly Rest in Commerce and Offices. Kuwait did likewise.

A number of other ILO conventions on hours of work relate to specific occupations not especially prominent in the Middle East; however, Iraq has ratified specialized conventions on hours of seamen (No. 109) and road transporters (No. 153).

Standards for Holidays with Pay have also been drafted by the ILO. A holiday convention for a 6-day annual vacation in manufacturing and construction (No. 52) has been ratified by Iraq, Israel, Kuwait, Lebanon, Syria; and a revised version for a paid vacation of at least 3 work weeks, covering all employees except seaman, (No. 132) has been signed by Iraq and Yemen Arab Republic. A paid holiday convention for agriculture, leaving the details of length of time and manner of payment to each signatory nation, (No. 101) was signed by Israel and Syria.

These conventions constituting treaty obligations allowed ratifying countries considerable latitude in the framing of implementing legislation; but they stimulated a broad acceptance of the basic principles limiting hours of work. They also directed special attention to the desirability of not permitting waivers of time off for rest and recreation as well as protecting women and child workers.

The UN Covenant on Economic, Social and Cultural Rights, ratified by Iran, Iraq, Israel, Jordan, Lebanon, Syria, and PDRY, provides that parties to that Covenant shall recognize the right of everyone to "Rest, leisure, and reasonable limitation of working hours and periodic holidays with pay, as well as remuneration for public holidays."

The ALO Convention 1, revised by 6, on Labor Norms, ratified by Iraq, Jordan, Lebanon, Palestine, and Syria also contains articles prescribing the length of work periods.

CONSEQUENCES AND INCIDENTALS

Several aspects of the regulation of working hours in the Middle East merit specific comment.

In Iran, there has been a long history of concern with hours of work. In 1910, the Social Democratic Party campaigned for an 8-hour day, and not until 40 years later, with aborted intervening efforts, were hours laws enacted. In 1923, the Prime Minister issued a directive to a Governor to limit hours of work in carpet making, which was not effectuated. In 1927, the Persian Communist Party demanded an 8-hour day. In 1943, the Prime Minister directed the Minister of Commerce and Labor to reduce hours of women and children in factories, without effect. In 1946, the Prime Minister agreed to decree a 48-hour week and a paid holiday every Friday. The Anglo-Persian Oil Company, an employer of 50,000, pressured by strikes and labor needs, instituted a 49 1/2-hour week. Eventually, in 1949, the Government adopted a law for an 8-hour day and a 6-day work week.[1]

In Saudi Arabia, the Labor Code of 1969 ordained the same daily and weekly maxima, with 6 hour days in the month of Ramadhan, a 15-day vacation at the close of the first year of work, increasing annually to 21 days after the tenth year, and 10 paid holidays a year. That applied to employers of 50 or more; at the time, the very large employers had a shorter work week (40 hours) and more paid holidays.

In Israel, efforts to attract young people to industrial jobs met with limited success because wages were lower and working conditions less attractive in industry than in service trades. The Ministry of Labor proposed to offset the disadvantages by reducing the work week in industry to five days.[2]

A large number of the Yemenis who have emigrated to work in the oil producing countries have increased their holiday leaves by coming home for days before Ramadhan and festival times. In the PDRY, the need for more production to meet targets set by the state led to a public exhortation with the slogan, "Eight hours of work, not eight hours at work."[3]

[1] H. Ladjevardi, Labor Unions and Autocracy in Iran, Syracuse Univ. Press, 1985.

[2] JPRS-NEA-086-088-39. Article by Avraham Dishon, Ministry of Labor Proposes A New Plan to Attract Workers to Industry, Tel Aviv, Yedi'at Aharonot (in Hebrew) 2 June 86, p.22.

[3] JPRS-NEA-086-094. Article by M.M. Salah, "Labor Law on Employment of Women". Aden, Sawt al'Ummal (in Arabic), 6/15/86, p.6.

In following up on its ratified conventions, the ILO has induced signatory nations to improve some hours legislation. In Syria, an early law permitted workers to be present at places of employment up to 11 hours a day, and under ILO urging, it was amended to require presence only during authorized hours of work. Also office workers were granted compensation for work on the weekly day of rest. In Iraq, permission of overtime for developmental purposes was limited to exceptional cases. In Kuwait, the coverage of an hours statute was extended to temporary workers and to employees in small undertakings; overtime was limited to 2 hours and then only in exceptional situations.

Absent from the public forums of the Middle East have been discussions of some policy issues that have emerged in the industrialized West and Europe, such as the staggering of work hours to avoid traffic jams, the rescheduling of three 10-hour days to provide a longer weekend, the reduction of hours to 35 a week to offset unemployment, and the deregulation of all hours to accommodate home computer work. Middle Eastern countries have been primarily concerned with how to prevent onerous or stifling hours of work.

Chapter 7

OCCUPATIONAL SAFETY AND HEALTH

PERCEPTIONS OF THE PROBLEM

Of all labor law topics, the least controversial, yet probably the most evasive, is the subject of occupational safety and health. Everyone deplores accidental injuries and occupational illness; still, those plights are ubiquitous, and seemingly unavoidable. Health experts have difficulty keeping abreast of new poisonous compounds and environmental hazards; but they know far more about prevention than most governments, employers, and employees are able or prepared to accept. All Middle East governments have endorsed the underlying principles; all have directed that steps be taken to protect the vitality of workers. But the allocation of adequate revenues for inspection, education, and regulation enforcement has been lacking everywhere. There are many hidden dangers in machine operation, and the negligence of short sighted workers is imponderable. Traps and mistakes are inherent in old as well as new forms of work. Overcoming them is a breathless race.

CONSTITUTIONAL PROVISIONS

Two Middle East constitutions take explicit notice of safety and health.

The PDRY has declared occupational safety and health a constitutional "right". "Workers have the right to . . . vocational safety and health." It also provides that "medical care is the right of all citizens," and the State shall aim for "preventive" medicine, health and safety. To that end, it seeks "the propagation of medical consciousness among the citizens with the effective participation of the mass organizations." (Not in draft constitution.)

Jordan's constitution also specifies that "Factories and workshops shall be subject to health rules," and special compensation shall be given to workmen in "emergencies arising out of the nature of their work."

LABOR CODE AND STATUTORY PROVISIONS

Occupational safety and health laws in the Middle East spell out responsibilities of the employer, the employee and the government.

Allocation of Responsibilities

Employers are required by all countries to take precautions to protect their employees from the hazards of their work. Detailed measures are prescribed to insure safety in the use of certain machines, inflammable or poisonous materials, and electric currents. Specific regulations are authorized with respect to lighting, ventilation, potable water, toilet facilities, and first aid.

Employers are also required to inform their workers, prior to the commencement of their work, of the dangers involved in the work and of the safeguards to be assumed by them (Bahrain, Iraq, Iran, Israel, Oman, Qatar, UAE, YAR, PDRY).

Employee responsibilities are likewise itemized. They call primarily for obedience to safety and health orders and job instruction. They also require the use of safety methods and equipment and prohibit the misuse or damage of protective equipment (Bahrain, Iraq, Oman, Qatar, Saudi Arabia, Syria, UAE).

Safety Committees composed of an equal number of employer and employee representatives are required by Israel in establishments employing 25 or more workers. In small shops, the Minister of Labor may establish safety committees.

Occupational safety laws usually provide for regulatory and overseer functions by the government. A Minister of Labor and Social Affairs is directed to issue necessary orders and to see to their enforcement (Bahrain, Iraq, Israel, Jordan, Kuwait, Oman, Qatar, Syria, UAE, YAR, PDRY). Labor inspectors are empowered with exceptional authority. They are authorized to enter a workplace (Iran, Iraq, Israel, Oman, Saudi Arabia, Syria, UAE,

YAR). They are given the right to inspect work performed, records and documents (Iran, Iraq, Israel, YAR), to question any person necessary (Bahrain, Iraq, Israel, Oman, Saudi Arabia, Syria, UAE), and to take samples of materials handled (Iraq, Israel, Saudi Arabia, UAE). If labor inspectors find conditions of great or imminent danger, they are further invested with the power to stop work or to evacuate a workplace (Iraq, Israel, Oman, Saudi Arabia, UAE, PDRY) or to request a local magistrate to order a closure (Iran). Internal security forces shall assist inspectors when so requested (Iraq).

Most labor codes, or other statutes, also provide for employer compensation to workers who sustain work related injuries or occupational diseases. (These shall be referred to below in conjunction with social welfare legislation.)

TREATY PROVISIONS

The undertakings of Middle East countries to abide by Conventions on Safety and Health have been several.

The most widely ratified has been ILO Convention 81 on Labor Inspection in Industry and Commerce (signed by Iraq, Israel, Jordan, Kuwait, Lebanon, Qatar, Saudi Arabia, Syria, UAE, YAR). It requires signatory nations to maintain a system of labor inspection to secure the enforcement of many labor laws, in addition to safety and health (wages, hours child and women labor laws), to supply information and advice to employers and workers, and to notify competent authorities of abuses or defects. Labor inspectors are to be public officials with proper credentials to take the steps indicated above. They are to be prohibited from having any interest in the enterprises under their supervision and are to be charged with the duty to inspect as often as necessary, to treat sources of complaint confidentially, and to safeguard all secret work processes that come to their attention. Reports of their services are to be made annually.

Other ILO conventions commit signatories to enact laws for:

(a) Medical Examination of Young Persons in Industry (Convention No.77) and Non Industrial Occupation (Convention

No.78) ratified by Iraq, Israel, Lebanon, and a similar Convention 124 for Young Persons in Underground Work ratified by Jordan and Syria;

(b) The Guarding of Machinery (Convention 119) ratified by Jordan, Kuwait, Syria. This is to prohibit the sale, hire, transfer, use or exhibition of power driven machinery without appropriate guards. Dangerous projecting and moving parts are to be itemized and safety devices and controls are to be designed;

(c) Hygiene in Commerce and Offices (Convention No. 120) ratified by Jordan, Lebanon and Syria. Statutes are required embodying the principles of cleanliness, sufficient lighting (as far as possible, natural), fresh or purified air, comfortable and steady temperature (as circumstances permit), wholesome drinking water, washing facilities, sanitary conveniences, suitable seats and reasonable opportunities to use them, facilities to change into dry clothing not worn at work, practical measures to reduce harmful noise and vibrations. Every workplace, according to size or risk, shall maintain a dispensary, or a first-aid post, or have one or more first-aid cupboards or kits.

(d) Dangerous chemicals have been identified for special protection, and two of those Conventions have been ratified. Benzene (No.136) signed by Iraq, Israel, Kuwait, Syria, and Carcinogenic Substances (No. 139) signed by Iraq.

(e) Single countries have ratified Conventions concerning Maximum Weight (No.127) Lebanon; Prevention of Accidents (No.134) Israel; Air Pollution, Noise and Vibration (No.148) Iraq; Safety and Health in Dock Work (No.152) Iraq.

The UN Covenant on Economic, Social and Cultural Rights, ratified by Iran, Iraq, Israel, Jordan, Lebanon, Syria and PDRY, commits its signatories to ensuring "safe and healthy working conditions" and "industrial hygiene" as part of the many steps to be taken for the health of the community.

The ALO has promulgated three Conventions on Safety and Health, No.7 on Hygiene and Industrial Safety, No. 13 on the Working Environment, and No.5 on Women at Work — as well as a Recommendation on the general subject. These run the usual course of the publication of standards, research on new hazards, inspection of plants, and safety education. Convention 7 has been ratified by Iraq, Palestine, and Syria; No. 5 by Iraq and Palestine; and No. 13 not yet by any country.

CONSEQUENCES AND INCIDENTALS

Laws promoting occupational safety and health are probably the most common labor laws in the Middle East. They engender no controversy, just pleas for more effective administration. When enforcement funds are not made available, the explanation is one of deep regret. Considerable assistance has been offered by the ILO and other UN Agencies, and advantage has been taken of such help.

Progress in safety and health can perhaps be measured by the degree of public awareness or recognition given to the subject. A few notable instances might be mentioned. In the Yemen Arab Republic, one of the poorest Middle East states, the labor code, adopted in 1970, served as the stimulus for extensive government health care services in 1985-86, which spread throughout rural areas reaching an estimated 90% of the country's population.[1] The Israeli Factory Ordinance of 1946 was applied in a very sensitive and empathetic manner by the Israeli Supreme Court in a case posing the extent of an employer's responsibility for the safety of his employees.[2] The employer had supplied a safety guard for a machine, the type of guard commonly used; but it did not prevent an injury and the court held the employer had an absolute duty to secure the safety of the employee.

The social philosophy reflected on these occasions has been matched by the devotion of scientists and engineers to the maintenance of occupational safety and health. Still the rate of industrial accidents and occupational disease in Middle Eastern countries — in agriculture as well as in industry — has not been declining.

[1] JPRS-NEA-086-100-41. "One Year's Growth of Services — Developing Process". Ta'izz al-Sumhuriyah, 13 June 1986.

[2] Atia v. Rosenbaum, CA 176/53.

Chapter 8

EMPLOYMENT

PERCEPTIONS OF THE PROBLEM

Employment is so indispensable to obtaining the means of subsistence that most persons in the Middle East (or in the world at large) think primarily of employment, any employment, as an end in itself. Few policy makers have explored the nature of the potentials as well as the deficiencies of employment.

Due to the recent and rapid transformations in Middle Eastern economies, most attention has been given to the shortages of industrial skills, to the international migration of labor forces, to education and training, to the eventual replacement of foreign workers by nationals, and to possible manpower controls. There is a recognition that basic censuses and uniform statistics of population growth, age, sex, nationality and job distribution are missing or lacking in comparability. Still there is widespread probing and an acceptance of the need for developmental planning to secure more or better employment. Most governments have had faith in progress; the countries not endowed with oil have felt restricted in growth of employment by limited funds, mounting public debt, marginal natural resources, and some hostile climatic conditions; all have envisioned expanding job opportunities if only they had more revenue and if external forces didn't disrupt their plans.

Since agriculture is an essential component of all Middle East economies, and the major utilizer of labor even in oil states (Oman, Saudi Arabia, Iran, and Iraq), their rural employment problems have been especially significant. Migration to urban areas has appeared to create pockets of unemployment in overcrowded towns, and more burdensome work responsibilities for women on the farms. At the same time, seasonal inactivity has caused underemployment.

Underemployment has also been a quixotic condition in countries with ample cash inflow as they have attempted to avoid unemployment by employing inadequately trained nationals. Over-staffing of public agencies has been a common dilemma.

A sober analysis of employment needs and goals has led government planners to evaluate many demographic factors. Population growth in some countries has been seen to outrun economic growth. Illiteracy rates have signaled the inherent sluggishness of native labor forces. These social characteristics have stimulated educational programs; and have prompted the commencement of family planning in new perspectives on the problems of employment.

The niceties of employment, such as the selection of the best job for the individual's potential or the designing of job conditions so that work becomes enjoyable, have been appreciated by some Middle East leaders, but they have not become public priorities.

Affirmative programs of job creation, vocational training and manpower placement have been seen as the most pressing requirements to meet Middle East employment needs.

CONSTITUTIONAL PROVISIONS

Several constitutions of Middle East countries contain provisions concerning employment. Most commonly, the state undertakes to insure that work is made available to its citizens (Bahrain, Iran, Iraq, Jordan, Kuwait, UAE). In Iran, "full employment" for "everyone" is declared a principle upon which the economy is based. Jordan makes its commitment "within the limits of its possibilities" and Iraq undertakes to provide work for "every citizen capable of it."

The terms of work are to be "equitable" (Bahrain, Kuwait), in accordance with the need of society for various occupations (Iran) and are to be improved (Iraq). In PDRY, the constitution spells out the basic services for state ownership and enterprise, and provides that mass organizations shall participate in "creating and developing work conditions." (Not in draft constitution.)

The regulation of the legal profession is prescribed by the constitutions of Bahrain and PDRY.

LABOR CODE AND STATUTORY PROVISIONS

In view of the insatiable demands for workers in the oil countries, there has been no Middle East legislation just to create jobs. The labor codes and supplementary laws have stressed the stability and preservation of employment. Placement services, registration and certification of workers, and measures to restrict dismissals are common, with qualifications indicative of national characteristics.

Placement Services

All Middle East states have laws to facilitate the work of public labor exchanges.

(1) The services of the employment agencies are gratuitous (Iran, Iraq, Jordan, Qatar, Saudi Arabia, Syria, UAE, YAR, PDRY). Bahrain, Iraq and Kuwait prohibit private for-profit employment agencies.

(2) Guidance to the unemployed taking into account the economic state of the country is called for in Lebanon.

(3) Organizing the placement of workers "in relation to available jobs and in such a way as to achieve equity and equality between workers" is specified in Iraq.

Priorities

In the placement of workers by employment agencies, certain priorities are prescribed.

(1) Preference is given persons residing in the area in which employment is available (Iraq).

(2) First, Yemenis, second, other Arabs, and then foreigners not to exceed 10% of the employees at any work place (YAR).

(3) Those injured in defending the homeland and sons of martyrs, persons who completed compulsory military service, qualified professionals, and those rendered unemployed by redundancy, in that order (PDRY).

(4) Citizens are given priority to fill vacant jobs (Oman).

Registration and Certification

Employees are required to register and obtain certifications or job assignments from employment agencies.

(1) No person shall be employed unless he possesses a certificate of registration — as well as a work card issued by the Ministry of Labor and Social Affairs — (Bahrain, Iran, Kuwait, Syria).

(2) In Iraq, unemployed persons wishing to work "may register with the unemployment office in his or her region."

(3) Israel prohibits employment in specified trades and occupations unless the employee has been sent by the labor exchange (except during a strike or a lockout). The trades specified for referral embrace nearly all employment, with exceptions for positions requiring higher education or a special measure of personal trustworthiness, and for managers, foremen and household workers.

(4) In Oman and Saudi Arabia, discretion to require employment through an employment office is reposed in the Minister of Labor.

(5) In Qatar "any unemployed person and worker seeking new employment may . . . register at an employment office and obtain a certificate of registration."

Job Security

Employers are required to give notice of termination a designated number of days in advance of dismissal or to pay the full wage for that period.

(1) The time varies with the type of employment — one month for monthly workers and one or two weeks for shorter term workers (Iraq, Lebanon, Oman, Qatar, Saudi Arabia, UAE). It is 15 days in Iran.

(2) Bahrain and Kuwait refer generally to custom.

(3) PDRY and YAR require notice for a period equal to the wage period.

Cause for Dismissal

An employee may be dismissed without notice and without compensation for the following reasons:

(1) Failure to perform essential duties (Bahrain, Kuwait) or basic contractual obligations (Qatar, YAR).

(2) Repeated disobedience of instructions (Kuwait) or the contravention of rules and regulations three times in a year (Lebanon).

(3) Causing serious material damage or heavy losses to employer (Bahrain, Iraq, Jordan, Kuwait, Qatar, Saudi Arabia, YAR), provided the employer so informs the Ministry of Labor within 24 hours (Bahrain, Qatar, Saudi Arabia) or within 3 days (Lebanon).

(4) Failure to comply with safety instructions after given written warning (Bahrain, Iraq, Jordan, Oman, Qatar, Saudi Arabia).

(5) Absence (a) for 15 days in a year (Lebanon), 20 days (Bahrain, Saudi Arabia, YAR), 30 days (Iraq); (b) for consecutive days absence, 10 days (Bahrain, Oman, Saudi Arabia, YAR), 8 days (Iraq), 7 days (Jordan, Kuwait, Lebanon, Oman); (c) absence without a lawful excuse (PDRY); (d) absence without reasonable cause for more than 10 days in a year (Oman).

(6) Disclosure of company's secrets (Bahrain, Iraq, Jordan, Kuwait, Oman, Qatar, Saudi Arabia, YAR).

(7) Conviction for crime (Iraq) involving dishonesty or immorality (Bahrain, Jordan, Kuwait, Qatar, Saudi Arabia, YAR). Also public immorality (Kuwait) or commission of misdemeanor at the workplace (Iraq, Lebanon, Oman).

(8) Falsehood, forgery or fraud to obtain work (Bahrain, Iraq, Jordan, Kuwait, Lebanon, Oman, Qatar, Saudi Arabia, YAR).

(9) Working under the influence of alcohol or drugs (Bahrain, Iraq, Jordan, Qatar, UAE, YAR).

(10) Assault at the workplace (Bahrain, Iraq, Jordan, Kuwait, Lebanon, Oman, Qatar, Saudi Arabia, UAE, YAR).

(11) Probationary status (Iraq, Jordan, Lebanon, Saudi Arabia, UAE, YAR).

(12) Conduct which is incompatible with respect for work (Iraq).

Adjudication of Wrongful Dismissal

Employees claiming discharge without proper cause may file grievances before designated tribunals.

(1) To the Minister of Labor and Social Affairs and if he doesn't settle the dispute, to a civil court (Bahrain); to a Disputes Board (Iran); to the Director of Labor (Oman and Saudi Arabia); to the highest Administrative Authority (Iraq and Syria); or to a civil court (Jordan, Qatar, UAE).

(2) If the complaint is sustained, the appropriate agency is authorized to award damages for wages lost (Bahrain, Syria), or compensation (Qatar) not to exceed 2 months pay (Jordan), or 3 months'pay (UAE).

(3) In several countries, the authority may reinstate the employee to his position (Iran, Iraq, Oman, Qatar, Saudi Arabia).

TREATY PROVISIONS

Treaties committing states parties to certain employment policies, and the Middle East signatories, are the following:

The UN Covenant on Economic, Social and Cultural Rights, ratified by Iran, Iraq, Israel, Jordan, Lebanon, Syria, and PDRY, calls for policies and techniques to achieve "full and productive employment". The UN Civil and Political Covenant, signed by the same governments, provides that every citizen shall have access, on general terms of equality, to public service in his country.

The ILO Convention 122, on policies to overcome unemployment and underemployment, was signed by Iran, Iraq, Israel, Jordan, and Lebanon. Two other conventions sought the prohibition of discrimination in employment (No. 111 signed by Iran, Iraq, Israel, Jordan, Kuwait, Lebanon, Qatar, Saudi Arabia, Syria and YAR; and No. 122 signed by Iran, Iraq, Israel, Jordan,

Lebanon). Separate employment conventions for special occupations, seamen, and nursing personnel, were signed by Iraq.

Convention No.96 on fee charging employment agencies was ratified by Israel and Syria. A separate one to establish facilities for finding employment for seamen was signed by Israel.

No Middle East government has yet signed the ILO Convention 151 on conditions of employment in the public service, or No. 158 on termination of employment at the initiative of the employer.

The ALO Conventions on Employment deal with various aspects of migrant workers. Convention 2 on Migratory Policy has been ratified by Iraq, Jordan, and Syria; and Convention 4 on Emigrant Workers has been ratified by Iraq, Jordan, and Palestine. They propose a preference for the hiring of workers from Arab countries and provide for the Arab Labour Bureau to do further research and planning on employment.

CONSEQUENCES AND INCIDENTALS

If the countries of the Middle East are likened to sailboats on uncertain seas, employment may be seen in their sails — some blown taut and others flapping, all shifting from time to time, all being manipulated to catch new winds. Full employment and the tugging of additional workers have been experienced by most oil producing countries. Labor exporting countries have experienced sagging employment and episodes requiring the replenishing of manpower. Governments attentive to employment have been beset with an alternating pulsing of fulfillment and frustration. They have enacted labor laws to steer a course or to win a race, rarely attainable.

The great surge of oil exploitation in the Middle East, it would seem, should have taken care of the primary problem of employment, namely, unemployment. It did in certain places; but it also augmented several other employment problems there and elsewhere throughout the region and in far-off places. New enterprises and their movement of workers have involved some temporary displacement or "frictional unemployment". They have also spawned a flock of social adjustment problems. These employment opportunities and difficulties have presented unending challenges to policy makers and labor law administrators.[1]

Initial responses to the "oil revolution" have been modified from time to time and the employment/unemployment situation has responded accordingly. Recent reports from the American embassies in the Middle East highlight differences in over-all employment figures. Unemployment leveled off to a minimum in Kuwait, at 1.8% of the labor force in 1980 and 1.5% in 1985. Irreducible "frictional unemployment" has become characteristic of the oil exploiting countries (with some variation at the time of a slump in oil prices).[2] In Israel, however, unemployment was estimated at 6% of the civilian labor force in 1985, 7.1% in 1986, 5.7% in 1987 and 8.2% in 1989. Other relatively thriving Middle East economies are still confronted with what they consider unacceptable amounts of unemployment. Jordan reported a 10% unemployment in its national work force in 1989.[3] An Iranian census, 1986-87, reported 14.1% unemployment. Bahrain estimated its unemployment in 1989 at 8-10%[4] War-torn Iran, Iraq, and Lebanon have experienced explosions of unemployment. The poorly endowed Yemen countries also have had idiosyncratic employment problems.

All of the countries, in their separate ways, have sought to deal with their employment problems through development planning. They have just begun to appreciate the need for scientific surveys of their situations if they are to locate, quantify and deal effectively with their employment needs; however, they are proceeding to formulate policies and plans based on the observations of knowledgeable individuals and a few professionals. Their findings and proposals are promising. But nowhere is there an ade-

[1] ILO, Employment and Manpower Problems and Policy Issues in Arab Countries, ILO, Geneva, 1984.

[2] American Embassy-Kuwait, Foreign Labor Trends, 1987, U.S. Dept. of Labor, Washington, D.C., 1987; American Embassy-Tel Aviv, Foreign Labor Trends: Israel, 1985-1987, U.S. Dept. of Labor, 1987.

[3] JPRS-NEA-89-055-51. Jordan Times (in English) Amman, June 28, 1989, p.3.

[4] JPRS-NEA-89-38, Ettela'at (in Persian) Tehran, Mar. 25, 1989, p.4; JPRS-NEA-89-42-27, Sada al Usbu (in Arabic) Mar. 7, 1989.

quate integration of economic growth and human employment needs. Public concerns and budget allocations are directed toward individual projects and nationalistic goals that do not take into account the personal and social needs of large numbers of workers.[5]

Probably the most publicized employment aim of Middle East countries has been to obtain a predominance of nationals in their labor force. That was to create job security for their own people, also the elimination or minimization of competition from expatriate workers. Since not enough natives have been skilled or experienced in the work required, education and training programs with special inducements have been made available to them. Saudi Arabia has offered to finance higher education for its citizens at any universities of their choice. No Middle East country, however, has yet succeeded in elevating the qualifications of its nationals sufficiently to meet its manpower needs.[6] The eagerness to achieve self-sufficiency of nationals in the field of skilled labor has also detracted from proper consideration of employment opportunities for foreign workers. Not that the latter haven't received employment and more pay than they could receive at home. But social treatment as second class people and the denial of civil rights to those who might object to the terms of their employment have been ubiquitous irritants as well as obstacles to social progress.[7]

In agriculture, animal husbandry, and fishing, which loom large in Middle Eastern economies, family relationships traditionally determined who and how members shall work; but the

[5] Karl Wohlmuth, Employment Creation in Developing Countries, particularly Ch.13 "The Social Meaning of Unemployment" by E.D. Schwefel; and Ch.2, "Political Economy of Employment Creation" by W. Kersten and K. Wohlmuth. Praeger Publ., N.Y., 1974.

[6] *Bahrain*, JPRS-NEA-89-062-23, "Government Dictating Bahrainization", Gulf Daily News (in English), July 12, 1989, p.1. JPRS-NEA-89-33-35, "Government's New 5-Year Job Plan, Al-Hayah Al-Tijarab (in Arabic and English), Manama, Feb. 1989, p.7. *Kuwait*, JPRS-NEA-89-032-20, T. Al-Hamad, Labor Regulation Decree, Al-Muhjtama (in Arabic), Kuwait, Jan 14, 1989, p 10-11. *Oman*, JPRS-NEA-89-060-62, Times of Oman (in English), Aug. 3, 1989.

[7] Jean Mayer, ed., Bringing Jobs to People: Employment Promotion at Regional and Local Levels, ILO, Geneva, 1988.

fruits thereof are now at the mercy of government policies and laws. There has been a common effort to prevent or to slow down the draining away of workers from rural to urban areas. Assistance has usually been directed toward increasing output and income rather than taking advantage of new jobs. Agricultural reforms — making more arable land available, better irrigation, soil and seed improvement, new machines, and advance of credit — have ordinarily enhanced productivity without nationally increasing rural employment opportunities. Controls over exports and domestic prices have been administered with various effects upon the incomes of farm owners, sharecroppers and farm workers. More educational, health and recreational facilities have been found necessary for the stabilization of rural employment. Still, the drive to Westernize or to acquire what appear to be the glamorous, material attractions of industrialized countries has shunted off public expenditures in other directions and has left traditional Middle East farming, herding, and fishing relatively unattended. A precarious dependency upon imported foodstuffs has led some countries to plan for a greater devotion of manpower to domestic foods. Employment in the basic nonmanufacturing productive sector throughout the Middle East has required many forms of adjustment.[8]

The optimum utilization of women and the self-employed has also posed special problems. Islamic fundamentalism has relegated women to homes and segregated employment, or to limited types of farm work, with a denial of personal potential. Admittedly, no country in the world has provided a proper evaluation of women's work in the home and family; but the Middle Eastern countries have faced special difficulties peculiar to their economic and social conditions. The oil rich have subsidized female inactivity though some are struggling to interest native, university educated women to concentrate on managerial and commercial skills, whereas the less anointed nations have resigned themselves to the employment of housewives and mothers to meet rising expectations for a better existence.

[8] A.S. Oberai, Changes in the Structure of Employment with Economic Development, ILO, Geneva, 1981.

In the informal sector of Middle Eastern economies, there has been a fairly numerous population of individuals who have been unable to find employment in urban centers and who subsist from ventures of their own. These have sometimes created large-scale services, as with taxi cabs and mechanical repair shops; but most have been impecunious, individual endeavors at the bottom of the social scale. They pose outstanding and seemingly intractable employment problems in every Middle East country.[9]

The measures undertaken by Middle East governments to cope with these employment problems have been primarily aimed at the over-all economic growth of each country. Implicit has been the anticipation that with the expansion of economic activity or the increase of productivity the employment situation would be adjusted satisfactorily through normal market transactions. Development plans, however, have at times singled out certain employment difficulties for special relief. They have attempted to enable employees and employers to take advantage of national economic gains or national employment policies. Fortunately, the wealth of oil exploitation, foreign aid, emigrant remittances and world trade have favored Middle East countries; kept some at the top of the world GNP index and none in the range of those countries deemed unable to extricate themselves from their distress. Fear of the eventual exhaustion of oil and imagined dangers to current administrations have resulted in a miscellany of labor laws and regulations to preserve a preferred status for native workers; and these have ignored employment hardships imposed on expatriates. More serious and extensive has been the inadequate attention to the private, personal and social aspects of employment. Except for the provision of education and vocational training, the potential benefits of employment to the individual worker have hardly been recognized.[10]

[9] ILO, Employment and Manpower Problems and Policy Issues in Arab Countries, ILO, Geneva, 1984.

[10] J.S. Birks and C.A. Sinclair, "Employment and Development in Six Poor Arab States", Int'l Journal of Middle East Studies, Vol.14, Cambridge Univ. Press, 1982, pp.35-51.

Chapter 9

UNIONIZATION

PERCEPTIONS OF THE PROBLEM

In labor relations, an individual employee has practically always been weaker than his employer, and when circumstances have stirred him to strive to better his lot he has welcomed the support of fellow workers. Many Middle East workers have at various times deemed their living conditions intolerable and they have chosen to come together and to act in concert. Such collective action, even when it has failed to achieve an immediate goal, has remained as a well-spring for the future. Human aspirations are unlimited; the grievances of workers cry out constantly; and disputes, whether violent or peaceful, need resolution. To deal with these ever changing aspects of collective action, labor laws have established guide lines.

The attitudes among governing officials towards unionization in the Middle East have varied widely. Older states, Iran, Iraq, Jordan, Lebanon, Syria, have had years of experience with unions as a vehicle of social protest; they have grown to expect more unions to emerge and they have thought of them in terms of the specific issues raised by the different organizations at different times. In so far as socialistic parties have been dominant in governments, they have expressed a reliance upon the organization of workers. Israel in its mission to create a Jewish homeland has been outstanding in its devotion to and dependence upon unions.

Other governments have been testing the waters and evolving their policies and administrative techniques. Kuwait has found unions in the affluent oil related enterprises and in its civil service to be manageable, but it has decided to limit unionization of non-Kuwaiti workers. The ruling elites of Bahrain, Oman, and Saudi Arabia, have generally been hostile to any organizations that might challenge their supremacy or authority in a hierarchical society. YAR has tolerated and hoped to control unions, whereas the PDRY has ideologically embraced unions as an essential builder of a new social order. Each country has been aware of an ongoing and volatile relationship with unions.

The attitudes of workers in the several countries toward worker organization have also displayed sharp distinctions. The content and the lethargic workers in most countries have been numerous; and seemingly they have resigned themselves to accept their lot, even when suffering. But a desire to ameliorate oppressive conditions has been universal. Leaders have sprung up and made converts willing to assert themselves through unions (some initially through general welfare organizations with tribal or cultural ties). The struggle for a right to form trade unions and the development of labor demands and strategies still perplex large segments of workers in the Middle East. Unionization, however, is seen generally as an available social process.

CONSTITUTIONAL PROVISIONS

Unionization is recognized, sanctioned, or restrained in the founding documents of half the Middle East countries. Their constitutions proclaim

(a) the "freedom" to form unions "in accordance with the conditions and procedures prescribed by law" (Bahrain, Iraq, Kuwait, Syria, YAR, PDRY); however, Bahrain and Kuwait provide that no one shall be compelled to join any union.

(b) Unions are required to have "lawful objectives" (Bahrain), and to be "peaceful" (Bahrain, Kuwait).

The constitutions of Syria and the People's Democratic Republic of Yemen manifest their socialist or collectivist philosophies by elaborating on the purposes and functions of unions.

(a) Syria provides that "popular organizations" shall work to realize (1) building the socialist Arab society and defending the system; (2) planning and guiding the socialist economy; (3) developing work conditions, safety, health, culture, and all other affairs pertaining to the lives of the organization members; (4)

achieving scientific and technical progress and the development of the means of production.

(b) The PDRY guarantees "the right of congregation in the mass organizations which serve the aims of the Constitution." At the forefront of those organizations are noted, the General Confederation of Trade Unions of the Republic's Workers, the Yemeni Socialist Youth Union, The General Union of the Yemeni Women, and the Democratic Yemeni Union of Peasants. Trade unions are referred to as "class organizations" to "organize the activity of the workers and officials and protect their interests." They shall regulate "the participation of the toiling masses in the administration of production affairs and its control and in planning work and production. They shall exercise mass control over the work and living conditions of the workers. They shall further participate in the implementation of the labor and social security laws, in determining wages and developing the forms of material and spiritual incentives." (Not in the draft constitution.)

LABOR CODE AND STATUTORY PROVISIONS

Legislation has been designed to amplify the basic policies declared in the constitutions and to deal with the process of unionization. Codes and supplemental statutes have attempted to clarify the rights of workers (and employers) to form associations for the promotion of their interests, to create administrative oversight agencies, and to specify the types of union activity that are to be considered lawful.

Right or Freedom to Form Unions.

(1) This is announced forthrightly by some countries (Iran, Israel, Kuwait, YAR, PDRY). It is "guaranteed" in Kuwait.

(2) In other countries, workers are told they may join unions (Jordan, Lebanon, Syria). Lebanon uses the term "industrial association", Syria refers to "general trade unions".

(3) The size of the work place or occupation (50 or more in Iraq; 20 or more in Jordan) is also specified.

(4) The worker may join or refrain from joining a union (Lebanon, YAR).

(5) Coercion, force or threats to induce or prevent membership is forbidden (Iran). No employer shall make employment subject to joining or withdrawing from a union (Jordan, Kuwait).

(6) Foreign workers, over age 18, with good reputation and conduct and a work card may join a union but may not hold office or participate in elections (Kuwait, Lebanon).

The Purposes of Trade Unions

Some countries have enacted laws spelling out the following purposes of trade unions:

(1) To defend the rights and interests of members (Iran, Iraq, Jordan, Lebanon, Syria, YAR, PDRY).

(2) To represent workers in all matters concerned with labor affairs (Kuwait), in all matters of their concern (YAR).

(3) To conclude collective agreements (Iran, Jordan).

(4) To better the financial and social standing of members (Kuwait).

(5) To safeguard workers interests as regards wages "as well as other matters likely to secure the raising of their financial, cultural and social standard" (Jordan).

(6) To stimulate progress from an economic, industrial or commercial point of view (Lebanon).

(7) To work for improvement in material and social circumstances (Syria).

(8) To develop the workers' personalities and talents (Iraq).

Other purposes indicating a more active participation in public affairs are mentioned in some countries.

(1) Iran itemizes, "The aim of the trade union shall be to organize the labor struggle in a free, open-minded, progressive and methodical manner, for the protection of the sacred nature of work and its noble human values . . . and in pursuing the aims of the Arab peoples for unity, freedom and socialism" and promote "prosperity and abundance among the ranks of the working class."

(2) YAR has detailed the promotion of "a spirit of cooperation and collective work," "the establishment of cooperative associations, the utilization of spare time . . . the provision of all such services as may contribute to the improvement of . . . the welfare of the members and their families, the increase and qualitative improvement of production."

(3) PDRY has also listed union "participation in inspection and supervision of the application of labor laws," "in formulating and implementing national economic development plans," and "in organizing social security and rendering general services to the workers."

Restrictions on Union Activities

Unions are forbidden by law:

(1) to deal in matters of politics (Kuwait, Jordan, Syria);

(2) to "engage in any political activity or participate in any gathering or demonstration of a political character" (Lebanon);

(3) to "interfere in political affairs provided that they may, for the purpose of safeguarding their occupational and economic interests, show preferences towards, or cooperate with political parties" (Iran);

(4) to become involved in religious matters (Jordan, Kuwait, Syria);

(5) to engage their property in financial speculation (Kuwait, Syria) in financial or commercial competition (Jordan);

(6) to accept gifts and legacies except with the permission of the Ministry of Social Affairs and Labor (Kuwait, Syria);

(7) to construct or purchase a building without a decision of members in a general meeting (Syria).

Union Registration

In a number of countries, unions are required to be registered with government authorities in order to obtain legality.

(1) On being formed, founding documents must be deposited with the Ministry of Labor (Kuwait, Syria). Union rules must be registered in Iran and Jordan. In YAR, a union is required to

send a list of its members, their addresses, occupations and places of work to the Labor Administration.

(2) The PDRY, however, expressly provides that unions "shall not be subjected to registration in government organs."

(3) A union is recognized as having a legal or juridical personality (Jordan, YAR); and it is not to be deemed unlawful on the ground that any of its objects is alleged to be in restraint of trade (Jordan). In Israel, although cartels are prohibited, a union arrangement which restrains employment conditions is not to be held a cartel.

Dissolution of Trade Unions

Several laws or regulations provide for the dissolution of a union on a judicial finding that it has been guilty of unlawful activity.

(1) If it commits "an act deemed incompatible with any of the laws in force for the maintenance of public order (Jordan).

(2) If it violates the Labor Code (YAR) or carries on business deemed in violation of the Labor Code or ordinances relating to public order and morals (Kuwait).

(3) If it incites subversion, hatred or contempt of the established system of government; if it advocates doctrines aimed at changing fundamental principles of the constitution or fundamental institutions of society; if it incites hatred or contempt of one or more classes of persons; if it abandons or deliberately refuses to perform public functions or work to fulfill a public need; if it uses force, violence or intimidation to infringe on the right of any third party to work or employ any person (Syria).

(4) If it oversteps the limits of its objectives or uses funds for purposes other than those provided in its internal regulations (YAR).

Formation of Joint Committees

Several labor codes provide for joint labor/management committees instead of or in addition to unions.

(1) In Oman, "In order to maintain good relations between

workers and employers, an employer with more than 50 workers must submit to the Minister proposals for creating a joint representative body. . . . Employers must make no distinction between workers who belong and those who do not belong to such a body as far as rights and duties are concerned."

(2) In Bahrain, "employers and workers may form, joint committees for cooperation in the settlement of disputes, securing improvements to the workers' social standards, organizing social services, fixing wages, increasing productivity and in any other matters of mutual interest." Kuwait provides similarly.

(3) In Iraq, "In every work project where the number of workers exceeds 30, a joint committee shall be established to organize the work. . . . The committee shall endeavor to achieve optimum cooperation. . . . in all matters pertaining to the advancement and benefit of the project . . . the workers, output and organization of the work."

(4) In Qatar, employers and workers may form "joint consultative committees" to develop "cooperation between employer and workers" and which "may consider and make proposals on matters connected with . . . work organization and productivity, conditions of employment, training of workers, safety measures and measures for improving the general culture of workers."

Employers Associations

Lebanon provides every employer "shall be free to join or not to join an industrial association." The Kuwait statute states "Employers shall have the right to form employer unions with the purpose of organizing and protecting their interests."

TREATY PROVISIONS

UN Covenants and several ILO Conventions have stressed the right of workers to join unions. The ALO has sought to do likewise.

The ILO has regarded unionization as elemental to the consideration and advocacy of labor standards. Its tripartite composition demands representation of employees through delegates chosen by the dominant union in each member country, and the formulation of standards for unionization came early in its existence.

At its third session (1921), the ILO adopted Convention No. 11 on Rights of Association in Agriculture. It pledged governments to secure to all those engaged in agriculture the same right of association and combination as to industrial workers. That was ratified by Iraq and Syria.

ILO Convention No. 87, entitled Freedom of Association and Protection of the Right to Organize, adopted in 1948, committed signatory nations to establish the right of workers to join organizations of their own choosing without previous authorization, and the protection of union members against any act prejudicial to them including dismissal based on their status or activities. That Convention was ratified by Israel, Kuwait, Syria, and the YAR. It was followed soon by Convention No. 98, Concerning the Application of the Principles of the Right to Organize and Bargain Collectively. That affirmed the principle that workers shall enjoy adequate protection against acts of anti-union discrimination; it also recognized the right of workers and employers to organize and provided that they "shall enjoy adequate protection against any acts of interference by each other." It has been ratified by Iraq, Israel, Jordan, Lebanon, Syria, YAR, PDRY.

Although rural workers were not excluded from the earlier Conventions 11, 87, and 98, the ILO and the UN Food and Agricultural Organization gave further attention to the persistent scarcity of food products in various regions of the world and to the massive underutilization of land and labor. Both agencies concluded that land reform in the developing countries was essential to the improvement of the conditions of work and life of rural workers, and that it was imperative to encourage organizations of rural workers, capable of protecting and furthering the interests of their members. They joined in the formulation of the ILO Convention No. 141, Concerning Organizations of Rural Workers and Their Role in Economic and Social Development.

It relates to all persons engaged in agriculture, handicrafts or related occupations in a rural area whether as a wage earner or a tenant, sharecropper or small owner-occupier who derives his main income from agriculture, who works the land himself, with the help only of family or occasional outside labor. It commits signatories to establish freedom of association for such workers without discrimination, to eliminate legal obstacles or impairments to such organization, and to promote the widest possible understanding of the need for the development of rural workers' organizations. To date, this Convention has been ratified in the Middle East only by Israel.

Both UN Covenants on Economic, Social and Cultural Rights and on Civil and Political Rights, ratified by Iran, Iraq, Israel, Jordan, Lebanon, Syria and PDRY, have provisions on unionization. The former declares "The right of everyone to form trade unions and to join the trade union of his choice, subject only to the rules of the organization concerned, for the promotion and protection of his economic and social interests." This right and the right to form national and international federations of unions are to be unrestricted except as prescribed by law and as "are necessary in a democratic society in the interests of national security or public order or for the protection of the rights and freedoms of others." The Political and Civil Covenant provides, "Everyone shall have the right to freedom of association with others, including the right to form and join trade unions for the protection of his interests."

The ALO Convention 8 on Trade Union Rights and Freedoms, ratified by Iraq and Palestine, guarantees workers and employers the right to create associations of their own choice and to join them without prior authorization. Unionization is also implicit in the ALO Convention 11 on Collective Bargaining, ratified by Iraq and Jordan.

CONSEQUENCES AND INCIDENTALS

The unionization of Middle East workers has grown very unevenly. At one extreme is Israel, whose early settlers joined farm collectives, the kibbutzim, and others in 1920 (decades prior to independence), formed the Histadrut, an organization of workers seeking to promote all aspects of a viable economy. It is estimated that currently in Israel 75 to 90% of the labor force is unionized, the largest percentage of organization in the world. The workers are primarily members of the Histadrut, and a small number are in a second federation, The National Federation of Labor. At the other end of the spectrum, there appear to be no unions in Oman, Qatar and Saudi Arabia. Unverified statistics report 33% of the labor force in PDRY is unionized; 24% in Lebanon; 20% in Jordan; 5% in Kuwait.[1] These extremes in unionization appear also to be poles apart in sophistication and function.

In Israel

The Histadrut has played a central role in building the Jewish State. Prime Ministers David Ben Gurion and Golda Meir were members. Its Trade Union Department negotiates collective agreements in the public as well as private sectors, nationally and locally. It has a strike fund, it coordinates the strikes of its members, and it casts the final vote in breaking impasses. To fulfill its mission of promoting the entire economy, it has established numerous enterprises (industrial manufacturies, banks, agricultural cooperatives and marketing firms, insurance funds, hospitals and clinics, recreational homes, etc.) which it owns and operates; it administers a pension system, conducts vocational training networks, and manages a myriad of its own welfare agencies, cultural and recreational organizations. It is a democratic organization, with a Council and Executive Committee elected by its dues paying members, and with workers committees in each plant or enterprise, which committees are affiliated to local councils and national unions.[2]

[1] F. John Harper, Ed. Trade Unions of the World. Gales Research Co. Longman Group. Harlow Essex. 1987.

[2] Abraham Daniel, Labour Enterprises in Israel, Vol.II, Int'l Centre of Research and Information, Jerusalem Academic Press, Jerusalem, 1976. The President of the Federation of Palestinian Workers has complained that the Histadrut deducts 20% of

Other countries also have had unions which have dealt variously with political and economic crises and have persisted in some representation of workers.

In Iran

What may have been the Middle East's first union, a printer's union, was organized in Iran in 1906. A few unions followed and their political demands brought on legal bans. In the 1920s, numerous unions, under communist leadership in the International Confederation of Free Trade Unions, conducted strikes for political as well as economic goals, and they were repressed. Leaders were arrested, some shot, and autonomous unions disappeared. A Labor Law of 1959 provided for the registration of unions and 50 syndicates were registered, others waited for approval which was not granted. The Shah published a book stating he believed in free trade unions as an instrument of democracy; but his Minister of Labor and the National Security Police, SAVAK, acted otherwise. No unions were permitted in the oil fields. By 1972, approximately 519 syndicates were registered and factory councils were established; however, many existed on paper only and the authorities confiscated the assets of aggressive unions.[3]

After the revolution that overthrew the Shah, there followed periods of shifting public policies. Until September 1979, unions were generally regarded as obstacles to the government; leftist and independent leaders were attacked; headquarters were ransacked and newspapers banned. From late 1979 to mid 1981, the administration found ways to manage supporting unions and the Minister of Labor prevented the formation of other organiza-

the wages of Palestinian workers as taxes even though they are denied vacation, termination, health and other benefits. JPRS-NEA-89-017-05. Hayder Ibrahim, Yaha al Juju, al-Dustur (in Arabic), Amman, Jan. 9, 1989, p. 6.

[3] H. Ladjevardi, Labor Unions and Autocracy in Iran, Syracuse Univ. Press, 1985. Valentine M. Moghadam, Industrialization Strategy and Labour's Response. Ch.7 in Roger Southall, Trade Unions and the New Industrialization of the Third World. Univ. Ottawa Press. 1988; H. Nazari, "The Social and Economic Situation After the Cease Fire", World Trade Union Movement", No. 5, 1989, pp. 17-18.

tions. Factory councils were permitted only a consultative role. From 1984 on, the clergy tightened its control over labor relations. Opposition by the Tudeh Party led to its elimination, and its leaders were executed as spies of the USSR. Only unions that have expressed loyalty to the Muslim rulers and that have refrained from participating in elections and from making annoying demands have continued to exist.[4]

At various times, Works Councils were established in Iranian factories and they functioned as spokesmen for worker grievances. The Shah's secret police infiltrated and controlled many of them. In the turmoil that eventually dislodged the Shah, more councils were formed in plants where managers had fled or were ousted, and in a number of places the Works Councils managed and carried on the affairs of the factories. The ruling clergy created Islamic Councils in the same establishments, initially for religious instruction and oversight. However, the authorities increasingly undertook to undermine independent and aggressive Works Councils; they arrested activist leaders, executed some; and by 1989 the Councils were held under government control.

In Bahrain

While Bahrain was under a British political agent, there were mass meetings and sporadic organization of a few unions. They obliged the government, in 1954-56, to set up a tripartite committee to draft a labor ordinance acknowledging a right to form unions. After independence, the Bahrain government continued that affirmation, but managed to keep union activity at a minimum.[5]

In Lebanon

Notwithstanding the cultural fragmentation of the population, there has been a trade union movement in Lebanon of remarka-

[4] Ibid.

[5] JPRS-NEA-086-085-22, Interview with 'Ali al Hammadi, Chairman of the General Committee of the Workers of Bahrain by 'Abdallah Khalifah. Al-Shariqah, Al-Khalis (in Arabic), 18 Mar.1986.

ble stability. The union membership grew from 14,000 in 1950 to around 55,000 in 1980; and then comprised approximately 24% of the country's workforce. There were 165 separate trade unions and 18 trade union federations. An excellent sociological survey of the economic levels, religious allegiances, and political orientations among union members found that Islamic Sunnis, Shi'ites, and Druzes, and Christian Maronites, Greek Orthodox and Greek Catholics were members of the same unions, with overlapping cultural ties and political cleavages.[6] Though certain individual unions were characterized as Left or Right in their outlook and demands, their members were "consociational." Their solidarity, however, did not prevent the devastation of war in the 1980s; nor did the violent conflict destroy the trade union movement.

In PDRY

The PDRY with its socialist ideology, has affirmatively sponsored the formation of trade unions. It is estimated that over one third of the labor force is organized in unions of petroleum workers, banks, trading and insurance workers, building, services and light industry workers, agricultural workers, public employees, farmers, and journalists. In addition to participating in government functions such as development planning, safety inspection, social security administration, they provide social and cultural facilities for workers. The General Confederation of the Republic Workers' Trade Unions embraces all of the unions, and is affiliated with the International Confederation of Arab Trade Unions and the World Trade Union.

Foreign Affiliations

Middle East workers who organized or considered the possibility of concerted action were confronted with inducements held out by unions and governments abroad which sought to acquire

[6] Theodor Hanf, Homo Oeconomicus-Homo Communitaris: Crosscutting Loyalties in a Deeply Divided Society. Ch.10 in M.J. Esman and Itamar Rabinovitch, Ethnicity, Pluralism and State in the Middle East. Ithaca. Cornell Univ. Press. 1988.

influence in the region. The United States government helped finance the AFL-CIO efforts to build the International Confederation of Free Trade Unions as a bulwark against the spread of communism. The USSR supported the outreach of the World Federation of Trade Unions to embrace all organizations of workers aligned with or sympathetic to it. The Organization of Arab States, with objectives of its own, set up an International Confederation of Arab Trade Unions. All the while, the ILO continued to accept as participants in its deliberative and policy forming bodies any representatives of labor who were recognized by the governments of their countries, regardless of their affiliation with a world federation.

The only Middle East country in which the trade unions have affiliated with the International Confederation of Trade Unions is Israel. All the Arab countries, except Bahrain, Iran, Oman, and Qatar, have had unions affiliated with the International Confederation of Arab Trade Unions. Countries with unions affiliated with the World Federation of Trade Unions are Iraq, Jordan, Kuwait, Lebanon, YAR and PDRY. Unions reportedly part of the WFTU, but unrecognized in their own countries, are a Union of Workers of Bahrain and the Workers Union of Saudi Arabia, with offices in Syria; and an Omani workers organization with an office in the PDRY. All Middle East countries, but Oman, have been members of the ILO. The effects of such affiliations have been varied.

(a) The International Confederation of Free Trade Unions has maintained secretariats for the coordination of the economic goals of unions within areas of industrial competition; and Israel has participated in their interchange of information and opinions.

(b) The World Federation of Trade Unions has held world congresses attended by some Middle East unions. Their resolutions have offered solidarity in economic struggles, but they have dealt primarily with political issues posed by US/USSR relations.

(c) The International Confederation of Arab Trade Unions (ICATU) was formally established in 1956. Though Egyptians were the primary moving force, and Arab unions in Africa became members, unions from Iraq, Jordan, Lebanon, and Saudi Arabia were among the charter members, and the government of Syria assisted the first Congress of the Confederation, held in Damascus. Other affiliates came later from Kuwait, Palestine, Syria, UAE, YAR, PDRY. The constitution and resolutions of the ICATU have committed its members to Pan-Arab Unity and opposition to Israel, as well as to "liberation from imperialist exploitation and economic, political and social retrogression." Among the economic goals, they specify better living conditions for Arab workers, higher vocational and educational standards, and the development of trade union consciousness. The Confederation established secretariats for unions in metals and chemicals, transport, agriculture, weavers, food industry, postal, telephone and telegraph, construction, commerce, bank, insurance and finance, engineering and electronics. Following the Camp David Accord, the Egyptians were expelled and the Confederation headquarters were transferred from Cairo to Damascus. The Confederation has been affiliated with the leftist World Federation of Trade Unions. Though it seeks economic gains for member unions, the primary activities of the ICATU have remained political.

(d) Since certain Middle East countries have ratified the ILO Convention No. 87 on Freedom of Association and the Right to Organize, they have had the benefit and prodding of the ILO oversight committee on compliance. That committee, the ILO Committee of Experts, has targeted the shortcomings of labor laws in signatory nations and it has followed through in annual correspondence with Kuwait, Syria, and the Yemen Arab Republic concerning their laws affecting unionization.[7]

The Committee called *Kuwait's* attention to twelve defects in its Labor Law, including: (a) the requirement of at least 100 workers (of whom 15 must be Kuwaitis and all foreign workers must have 5 years residence in Kuwait to establish a union); (b) requiring the approval of the Minister of Labor for a new trade

[7] ILO, Reports of the Committee of Experts on the Application of Conventions and Recommendations, Geneva, 1984-1987.

union; (c) requiring a certificate of good reputation for each member; (d) limiting unions to one in any establishment or to representation of similar occupations; (e) confining affiliation to one general confederation; (f) giving authorities supervisory powers over union records and ownership of the assets of dissolved unions; and (g) prohibiting unions from engaging in political or religious activity. A draft of amendments to the law was found wanting, particularly in its continuation of monopoly positions for unions, and in its governmental controls. In 1986, the ILO Committee resubmitted its request for amendments to the items mentioned above. It acknowledged the government's statement that it desired not to fragment the trade union movement, but the ILO replied its standards required that that should be left to the workers to decide. In 1987, the Committee noted assurances received from Kuwait that the ILO convention would be given effect, but the same breaches were listed again, with an elaboration of the analysis made by the Committee. The exchange of courteous criticism continues.

The ILO Committee of Experts has had a similar running discourse with the government of *Syria.* On the question of trade union unity, the Committee insisted, without endorsing pluralism or unity, that the ILO expected that to be a matter of the workers' choice. With respect to the unionization of foreign workers, it objected to requirement of a one year residence and it rejected the notion that reciprocity between nations could be made a condition to membership in unions. Concerning union finances, it disapproved the conditioning of gifts to unions on the approval of the Minister or the General Federation, which it regarded as interference by public authorities, that should not extend beyond requiring financial reports periodically. As to a requirement that a candidate for union office have 6 months "experience in an occupation", the Committee accepted the idea of requiring competence, but held that it was for the unions themselves to decide conditions for eligibility to their offices. The Committee, in its usual fashion, requested the government to keep it informed of developments; and in 1988 the Committee expressed its regret that it had received no report from Syria.

To the *Yemen Arab Republic,* the Committee, in 1984, called attention to laws that appeared inconsistent with Conventions ratified by that government. It noted particularly: (a) the exclusion of civil servants and certain agricultural workers from the right to establish unions; (b) the requirement of a minimum number (50) of members for a union; (c) the provision for administrative verification that applicants for unionization be persons who had not been accused of jeopardizing the security of the state or sentenced for acts contrary to honor; (d) the power of the Council of Ministers to dissolve a union under certain circumstances, without provision for a judicial review. The government responded, stating there were only a few unions involved and the complaints were only of an administrative nature. The Committee, undeterred, asked for a further report on the taking of corrective measures. It noted further, (a) that the YAR Labor Code prohibited union political activity and subjected union financial activities to administrative authorization, and (b) that a Ministerial Decree empowered the Ministry to dissolve a union when the claims of workers reached a certain level of importance. The Committee asked what precise criteria were set for the exercise of the Minister's discretion. In 1987, the Committee acknowledged receipt of another report from the government and commented that certain divergences from its Conventions had not been addressed. Further, it observed that among the new unions formed in the YAR there was none for civil service or agricultural workers; also the government restricted the number of unions to one per undertaking or one general union per town or economic activity. That deprived workers of their own choosing. The government had reported that the Ministry of Labor and Social Affairs reviewed union applications and rules and provided model rules just to see that they conformed to law; but the Committee replied that under the ILO Convention the union should be free to draw up its own rules subject only to the verification of formal questions. The Committee trusted the Government would re-examine its legislation and keep the Committee informed.

Chapter 10

COLLECTIVE BARGAINING

PERCEPTION OF THE PROBLEM

Collective bargaining came to the modern Middle East as a foreign practice, demanded though untried by fledgling unions, mistrusted and rejected by tradition-bound employers. It came backed by years of reassuring experience abroad and with the firm recommendation of the ILO and other world agencies. In time, it was seen as an alternative to mass demonstrations and political rebellion. As unions multiplied, it was tried cautiously. It was a technique to be mastered and, in time, capable persons learned to manage it.

In social theory, collective bargaining has been presented as the application of reason and the balancing of opposing interests in a peaceful manner. Or it has been expounded as a process of extending the benefits of industrialization to workers at a pace that can be absorbed by capital. On the other hand, recalcitrant entrepreneurs and autocratic rulers have regarded it as an invasion of their initiative and prerogative by radical leaders exploiting false dogmas for their personal gain. All of these views have vied for acceptance as collective bargaining has been spreading in the Middle East.

CONSTITUTIONAL PROVISIONS

The Middle East constitutions do not mention collective bargaining.

LABOR CODE AND STATUTORY PROVISIONS

Formal Requirements

The right to conclude collective agreements is mentioned in

statutes of Iran, Iraq, Israel, Jordan, Syria, YAR, and PDRY. Laws in the newer, oil producing States are silent on the subject.

The following requirements are specified for collective agreements:

(1) *Written document* (YAR, PDRY, Israel)

(2) *Registration* with the Minister of Labor (in the YAR, and within 3 months of execution in Israel)

(3) *Special terms* Provisions are invalid, (a) if prejudicial to public safety (Syria); (b) if likely to constitute a breach of security (YAR); (c) if likely to damage the country's economic interests (Syria, YAR); (d) if in contradiction to existing laws and regulations (Syria); (e) if in contradiction to the interests of public order (Syria, YAR).

(4) *Transfer* On sale or amalgamation of an enterprise, the new employer is bound by the collective agreement (Israel).

Status of Individual Agreements

Individual employment contracts are common, and possible conflicts between them and collective agreements or Labor Codes are recognized.

(1) *Contravening collective terms.* Terms in an individual employment contract that contravene a collective agreement are invalid unless more advantageous (YAR). Personal provisions in collective agreements (rights of employment and personal obligations) may not be waived by an employee (Israel).

(2) *Less favorable than codes.* Employment contracts less favorable to the worker than Labor Code provisions are null and void (Bahrain, Iran, Iraq, Jordan, Kuwait, Oman, Syria, U.A.E., PDRY). The same holds true for less favorable terms of collective agreements in Iran.

Extension of Collective Agreements

The terms of collective agreements may be extended to workers and employers not mentioned therein, in Israel and Jordan.

The Israeli Minister of Labor may extend the scope of application of any provision of a general collective agreement if, in his opinion, it is right to do so, having regard to the number of employees and employers covered and to the importance of the agreement in regulating labor relations and conditions in the labor market. There will be no extension order if the collective provisions are repugnant to an international labor convention ratified by Israel or if such provision impairs the right to employment by reason of union membership or nonmembership.[1]

The Jordanian statute provides that when a collective agreement covers the majority of the employers and workers in a particular area or in a trade or calling, the Director of the Department of Labor may, at the request of both parties, make all or certain provisions of the agreement applicable to all employers and workers in such area or trade or calling.

TREATY PROVISIONS

ILO Convention No. 98, entitled Concerning the Application of the Principles of the Right to Organize and to Bargain Collectively, obligates signatories to take "Measures appropriate to national conditions . . . where necessary, to encourage and promote the full development and utilization of machinery for voluntary negotiations between employer' organizations and workers' organizations, with a view to the regulation of terms and conditions of employment by means of collective agreements." That Convention has been ratified by Iraq, Israel, Jordan, Lebanon, Syria, YAR, PDRY.

In 1981, the ILO promulgated a new Convention No. 154 on Collective Bargaining, designed to elicit greater efforts to achieve free and voluntary collective bargaining. It extended the subject to "all branches of economic activity," recognized national practices with respect to armed forces and police, and specified that special modalities of application might be fixed for the public service. It also sought to clarify the intent that "workers' represent-

[1] Israeli extension orders have been issued in the rubber, wood, building, and agricultural industries; and for specific cost of living allowances and vacation premiums. An extension order in agriculture was replaced by a new, signed collective agreement. Jewish Natl. Fund v. Abraham Sultan, Intl. Labor Law Rpts., Vol. 6, p. 282.

atives" not be used to undermine the positions of workers' organizations. This has not yet been ratified by any Middle East country.

The UN Covenant on Economic, Social and Cultural Rights does not mention collective bargaining; but does require signatories to ensure "The right of trade unions to function freely."

The ALO followed its initial Convention 1 containing articles on collective bargaining with a later Convention 11 that obliged unions and employers' associations to recognize the right to bargain collectively, to promote negotiation, and to train responsible officers to take charge of negotiation at factory, industry, and national levels. That Convention has been ratified by Iraq and Jordan.

CONSEQUENCES AND INCIDENTALS

The ILO's Committee of Experts, which has monitored the labor laws enacted by the countries that have ratified ILO Conventions, has communicated with several signatories on matters affecting collective bargaining.[2]

With respect to Jordan, over several years the Committee called the Government's attention to the absence of any specific law that protects workers' organizations against interference by employers. Finally, in 1988, the Government replied that there was no need to adopt legislation since there had never been acts of such direct or indirect interference at any time during the history of industrial relations in the country. The Committee's rejoinder was that was insufficient, since the Convention on Freedom of Association and Collective Bargaining imposed an obligation on its ratifiers to take specific action, particularly through legislative means to ensure respect for the guarantees laid down in the Convention. The Committee requested the Government to reconsider the situation. The Committee also noted the Government's proposal of a new law that would grant certain domestic and agricultural workers, who had been excluded from full pro-

[2] ILO, Reports of the Committee of Experts on the Application of Conventions and Recommendations, Geneva, 1987-1988.

tection under its Labor Code, recourse to the courts; and the Committee asked the Government to indicate how the draft would enable those workers to negotiate their terms and conditions of employment.

As to collective bargaining in the Yemen Arab Republic, the Committee observed, in 1987, that there was no collective agreement in force in that country, and it emphasized the obligation of the Government to establish machinery encouraging discussion between employers and workers with a view to the conclusion of an agreement freely entered into. Furthermore, the YAR Labor Code provided for advance registration of collective agreements, with the administration's power to cancel an agreement on the ground of prejudice to the country's security or economic interests or on incompatibility with public order; and the Committee declared it considered such measures in conflict with the ILO Convention 98. It acknowledged that a system could be established in which a collective agreement would be held up for a reasonable period following its deposit, and if clauses were deemed unacceptable from an economic point of view the problem could be submitted to a body of employer and worker representatives; however, the final decision whether or not to amend the agreement must remain with the parties to the agreement.

That matter is still unsettled, as are many other questions of policy and practice in Middle East collective bargaining.

Chapter 11

STRIKES

PERCEPTIONS OF THE PROBLEM

The flight of the Hebrews from Egypt might have been seen as a strike of workers on the pyramids; but that version of the event has not been shared by historians of the Middle East. In modern thought, some strikes may appear as upsetting as the Biblical Exodus and the intervention of God has been prayed for, but He apparently has preferred to let man fumble and find solutions himself.

A strike may be seen as the outcome of a labor problem; it is also a problem in itself. Usually when it succeeds, it involves a costly solution, and when it fails it is often an unfinished episode. All Middle East governments seek to avoid strikes. Their only concerns have been how to minimize their number, how to limit their violence or destruction, and how to settle the differences between the parties. There has been little consensus on how to dispose of these questions, and the laws of the Middle East relating to strikes have been cast in controversy or indecision.

CONSTITUTIONAL PROVISIONS

There is no mention of strikes in the Middle East constitutions.

LABOR CODE AND STATUTORY PROVISIONS

There are very few statutory enactments concerning strikes or lockouts.

(1) *A right to strike* is recognized in Iraq, Israel, Jordan, Syria. In the PDRY, the Trades Union Confederation "shall have the right to call a general strike."

(2) *Permissible strike action*. In Iraq, the law states that if an employer refuses to comply with a settlement judgment of a

court, the workers "shall have the right to stop work with the period of the work stoppage considered as a period of service for the purpose of rights guaranteed them by law." In addition, any employer "who has refused to implement the decision shall be subject to a penalty." Striking workers in Qatar "shall not commit any aggression against their employer, his agent or any other workers who are willing to continue with their work."

(3) *Strike prohibition.* In Oman, "It is absolutely forbidden to provoke a strike for any reason." Strikes have also been banned by decree in Saudi Arabia and the UAE. In Syria, Jordan, and Qatar, a strike or work stoppage is unlawful if an application has been made to, or is being examined by, a conciliation or arbitration board. In Israel, a court may prescribe that public service employees engaged in an "unprotected strike" not a complete work stoppage, are entitled to only a partial wage for work they actually did during the strike.[1] An anomalous Syrian Labor Code of 1958 prohibited strikes in the agricultural sector; but in response to a 1987 complaint from the ILO Committee of Experts, the government drafted an amendment to repeal that provision.

(4) *Lockouts.* In Oman, it is forbidden for an employer to close places of work, put off work or refuse to continue the employment of any worker because of a dispute about terms or conditions of work. In Syria, it is unlawful for an employer to declare a lockout "unless he is compelled to do so for serious reasons and has obtained the consent of the Ministry of Social Affairs and Labor." He may lockout if the Ministry fails to reach a decision within 30 days. In Jordan and Qatar, lockouts are unlawful pending proceedings before an industrial tribunal or conciliation board, or while a settlement or award is in effect (Jordan).

TREATY PROVISIONS

Freedom to strike was founded in the philosophy of human

[1] A strike in a public service company was declared unprotected because no prior notice was given and it was not approved by the Histadrut. Damages were assessed by the Labor Court. Workers Committee v. Eilat-Ashkilon Pipe Line, 3 Intl. Labor Law Rpts. p. 282.

freedoms and became a treaty-based right.[2]

The United Nations Covenant on Economic, Social and Cultural Rights, ratified by Iran, Iraq, Israel, Jordan, Lebanon, Syria, YAR and PDRY, provides, "The States parties to the present covenant undertake to ensure the right to strike provided that it is exercised in conformity with the laws of the particular country. This article shall not prevent the imposition of lawful restrictions on the exercise of these rights by members of the armed forces, or of the police, or of the administration of the State."

The ILO Convention No. 87 on Freedom of Association, ratified by Israel, Kuwait, Syria, and YAR, has been interpreted as protecting lawful strikes, even though the Convention does not use the term "strike." That Convention has not been ratified by Bahrain, Oman, Qatar, Saudi Arabia, and UAE.

The term "strike" is used in Convention 105 (ratified by Iran, Iraq, Israel, Jordan, Kuwait, Lebanon, Saudi Arabia, Syria, and PDRY) which relates to the Abolition of Forced Labor, and it prescribes that signatories shall not use any form of forced or compulsory labor as punishment for having participated in a strike. "Strike" is also coupled with "lockout" in ILO Recommendation No. 92 on Voluntary Conciliation and Arbitration (which is not a binding Convention); but that Recommendation states it is not to be interpreted as limiting in any way whatsoever the right to strike. The Convention 151 deals with settlement of "disputes". That Convention adopted by the ILO in 1978 has not yet been ratified by any Middle Eastern country.

The ALO Conventions on Labor Norms and Trade Union Rights and Freedoms refer to social harmony and the conciliation and arbitration of labor disputes; but they do not mention a right to strike.

CONSEQUENCES AND INCIDENTALS

The laws governing strikes (or how to govern strikes) have

[2] Ruth Ben Israel. The Case of Freedom to Strike. Kluwer Law and Taxation Publishers. Deventer. 1987.

rained on windows of the Middle East, asking to come inside. Sometimes, they have been denied admittance; sometimes they have cleared the atmosphere of fears. A few incidents may be enlightening.

Iran

The history of modern Iran records the persistence of dire economic circumstances for large portions of the working population, and upheavals in the government were interspersed with sporadic strikes. Few concessions were made to the workers, and strike leaders were repeatedly imprisoned or executed. In the background, there moved foreign and Iranian investors in oil with power to exert diplomatic pressures for government intervention. A cold war between communist and anticommunist activists was constantly played out in Iranian affairs. Headquarters were smashed, newspapers silenced, radicals exiled or sent underground; but new challengers arose time and again. Poverty was never eliminated. Strikes were disturbing to the employers dominant in society, and they found allies in nearly all administrations. Laws for the peaceful settlement of industrial disputes were hard won, and were frequently emasculated by administrative regulation or overridden by the force of police and troops.

A few, quite random, details of strikes in Iran may convey the vicissitudes and difficulties involved.[3] In 1922, the school teachers of Tehran, who had not been paid for 6 months, walked out and the country's Cabinet fell. Oil workers employed by the Anglo Persian Oil Co. in Abadan went on strike for a 100% wage increase; British troops broke up their demonstrations; their communist leader was arrested and 2000 workers from India were forcibly repatriated. When striking printers threatened to call a general strike, their leaders were released from jail and the suspension of 14 newspapers was lifted. In 1925, a May Day celebration was made a political offense and leftist unions went underground. In 1929, they celebrated May

[3] H. Ladjevardi, Labor Unions and Autocracy in Iran, supra. Valentine M. Moghadam. Industrialization Strategy and Labour's Response. supra.

Day. Also 9000 oil workers struck (for a 15% wage increase, a 7-hour day for workers under age 18, and for worker participation in hiring and firing); troops attacked them; 200 workers were arrested; many were confined for over 2 years.

In 1943, Iran declared war on Germany and the left wing Tudeh Party denounced all strikes in war industries. In 1946, a law supported by unions recognized the right to organize and required the registration of agreements. The Ministry's High Labor Council issued a regulation which declared strikes would be lawful only when called after an Arbitration Board failed to settle the dispute within 20 days and a Board of Settlement failed for another 20 days to decide the issues. In Abadan, oil workers inspired a general strike, which was crushed with 50 deaths and 165 casualties (British colonels were blamed for instigating the violence).

In 1953 under the Pahlevi state, leaders of the the Tudeh Party were arrested, some executed, and strikers were met with a declaration of martial law. In 1957, wage demands brought strikes in oil refineries, brick yards, textile mills, and a lead mine.

During the Iraq-Iran war, under the need for increased production, wages were increased and workers were moved by patriotism and religious zeal; yet protests were raised in several factories for higher wages, more profit sharing and child care centers. The Revolution of 1978-79 involved massive street demonstrations and strikes of organized oil workers, bank employees, railroad and electrical workers. The protest escalated into a general strike of many thousands of industrial workers in large plants throughout the country. Economic demands were coupled with political demands. A number of plants were taken over and managed by Works Councils of employees. Islamic Councils, originally coexistent with Works Councils, were promoted by the Khomeini regime and the government made concessions on wages, social benefits, and bonuses. A law proposed by the Minister of Labor in 1983, seeking to prescribe religious qualifications for Works Councils and to restrict strikes, was not adopted.

Israel

In Israel, where the right to strike has been clearly established, there has been a record of many situations in which that right has been exercised. They have occurred in the government sector of the economy (including enterprises in which the Government has an ownership of 50% or more), a private sector (largely in manufacturing) and an Histadrut sector (in which the labor organization is both entrepreneur and worker representative). Economic and political demands have been interwoven; a shift in government from the Labor Party (supported primarily by the Histadrut) to the Likud (conservative) Party has altered trade union influences; and the pent-up grievances due to war and inflation have complicated the picture further. Studies of the relative importance of these factors have produced only tentative findings and little evaluation of the qualitative social factors (such as a striving for full employment and the balancing of temporary losses against long-term income stability.[4]

An example of the disposal of a tense strike situation in Israel occurred in 1985. A flurry of strikes were brought on by inflation and demands for cost of living adjustments. In despair, a state of emergency was declared and enforced until a compromise was reached in an Histadrut agreement acceptable to the Government.

The outstanding difference between the record of strikes in Israel as compared with strikes in other Middle East countries is that strikes in Israel have been a mature and sophisticated process of adjustment to the wage and working conditions problems of that country.[5] They have demonstrated the possibility of democratic techniques in dealing with the intricate complexities of a Westernized society.

[4] Yonatan Reshef and Brian Bemmels. Political and Economic Determinants of Strikes in Israel, in Rudolf Madner, ed. Economic and Industrial Democracy. Sage Publications. London. 1989.

[5] Illustrative is the decision of the National Labor Court which held that strikers, entitled to take annual leave, may not be placed on annual leave against their will. Ginstler v. State of Israel, Intl. Labor Law Rpts. Vol. 4, p.290.

Other Middle East Countries

Work stoppages have occurred in other Middle East countries too, but they have not been well documented: (a) In Bahrain, before independence in 1938, there were oil field strikes against foreign domination and for a right to strike. Independence brought the curtailment of British interests, but not the right to strike. More strikes arose in 1972 and 1974. (b) In Saudi Arabia, oil industry strikes of 1945 and 47 resulted in a ban upon all strikes; but more strikes occurred in 1983 and 1985, with the imprisonment of the unsuccessful strike leaders. (c) In Lebanon, there have been many public demonstrations for and against the political actions of sectarian, religious leaders, with occasional involvement of trade union strikers. In 1972-73, there were strikes of tobacco growers, confectionery factory workers, and teachers in various regions of the country. Police killing of pickets in Beirut led to a one day general strike in November, 1972; and continued repression produced another general strike in August, 1973. Student demonstrations against US Arab-Israeli proposals were joined by workers, and in January, 1974, Beirut firemen and watchmen struck for more pay, and later bank employees struck for higher wages and bonuses. These public disturbances were not particularly outstanding amidst the repeated outbreak of confessional, civil war.[6] (d) In Oman and the Yemens, early strikes were also associated with political protests and violence. Further industrialization in these countries will come with little strike experience.

[6] Michael Johnson. Class and Client in Beirut. Ithaca Press. London. 1986.

Chapter 12

SETTLEMENT TECHNIQUES AND AGENCIES

PERCEPTIONS OF THE PROBLEM

There is an old Arab legend illustrating the value of arbitration. It tells how a dispute among three heirs of a sheik was settled. Their father wrote in his will, "I give to my sons as recompense for their services to me, all my camels to be divided as follows. To my eldest son, I give half of the camels I own, to my next born, I give half of the number received by his older brother, and to my third son I give half of the number given to the second." Regrettably when the father passed away, he owned just seven, equally fine camels. As the sons quarreled over the division of the camels, the eldest saw a lone camel and rider coming over the horizon. He proposed the brothers consult the stranger. When the rider approached their tent, they invited him to share their food; and when he had rested they told him of their problem of distributing seven live camels in their declining half shares. The wise stranger pondered for quite a while and then spoke. "I will add my camel to your father's. You now have eight camels. Half, or 4, I give to the first son; half of that, or 2, I give to the second son and half of that, or 1, I give to the last son. 4, 2 and 1 are seven. That leaves one camel, which I will take as my compensation for arbitrating your dispute." He mounted his camel and rode off into the setting sun, leaving the three heirs satisfied.

Perhaps the lesson has not been learned widely enough in the modern Middle East because industrial disputes have been feared more as dangers or disasters than as dilemmas seeking solutions. To an extent, arbitration as well as conciliation has been offered in an effort to pre-empt strikes. Also labor courts have been created to dispose of grievances in accord with rules of law. The thought that unions and their collective bargaining, backed by occasional strikes, might be the best way to ameliorate poverty or to achieve justice in the distribution of oil wealth has been held by only a few persons in a few places. Strike prevention and strike bashing as well as conciliation and arbitration and court adjudication have all been seen as ways to settle disputes in the Middle East.

CONSTITUTIONAL PROVISIONS

Arbitration is referred to in the constitutions of Iran and PDRY as a desired technique.

In Iran it is mentioned as integral to the powers of all judges, who are given the power of "interpreting the law in pursuance of their duties as arbitrators." In the PDRY, "statal arbitration panels shall, within the limits of their powers (specified by law) determine the economic disputes between the ministries, organizations and corporations." (Arbitration not in draft constitution.)

LABOR CODE AND STATUTORY PROVISIONS

Further Bargaining

Labor laws recognize that the first step in the settlement of labor disputes is to continue conversations and negotiations between the parties in disagreement.

(a) The Labor Code of Iran directs that in the event of a collective dispute the local labor department shall first call a meeting of representatives of the workers and the employer.

(b) In Iraq, the Minister of Labor and the Confederation of Trade Unions are to consult regularly and have meetings with the parties to a dispute.

(c) Oman provides that a resolution of collective grievances must first be attempted through "the grievance procedure laid down by the employer". Other codes refer to or assume that an impasse has been reached and proceed to call for settlement measures.

Conciliation and Arbitration

All countries in the Middle East provide for some form of conciliation or arbitration by one or more government agencies. Normally the Minister of Labor and Social Affairs is made responsible for appropriate action. If one agency fails to settle the dispute, another may or must be utilized.

(a) In *Bahrain*, the Minister of Labor and Social Affairs assigns disputes to conciliators or arbitrators. (b) In *Iran*, the parties go from a Disputes Board to the Minister of Labor. (c) In *Iraq*, the settlement path goes from the Minister to the Labor Court to the Court of Cassation. (d) In *Israel*, conciliation is undertaken by a Chief Labor Relations Officer unless the Minister takes over; and arbitration follows as provided in written agreements. (e) In *Jordan*, unsettled disputes go from a conciliation board to an industrial tribunal. (f) In *Kuwait*, labor disputes go from the Ministry to a Labor Arbitration Board. (g) In *Lebanon*, labor disputes may go to Boards of Arbitration or to a Labor Arbitration Council. (h) In *Oman*, on failure of the Department of Labor to conciliate, the Director of Labor may refer the dispute to a binding arbitrator or to another conciliator. (i) In *Qatar*, on failure of the Department of Labor to conciliate, the Director of Labor shall refer the dispute to the Conciliation Board for binding arbitration provided the parties agree they are prepared to accept the Board's decision. Otherwise, the Board's decision is treated as a recommendation to the parties. (j) In *Saudi Arabia*, disputes may be sent to a primary labor disputes board or the Supreme Labor Disputes Board, or on agreement by the parties, to an arbitrator. (k) In *Syria*, disputes go to a local administrative authority and if its conciliation fails, to an arbitration board. (l) In the *United Arab Republic*, parties go to the Labor Department for mediation; if that fails, to a competent conciliation board; and decisions of that board may be appealed to the Supreme Arbitration Board, all within the Ministry of Labor. (m) In the *YAR*, parties go to a Board of Arbitration or on mutual agreement to a single arbitrator; and appeals lie to the High Board of Arbitrators. (n) In the *PDRY*, parties to a dispute may request assistance from the General Trade Union; if that fails, they go to an Arbitration Committee (composed of representatives of the Ministry of Labor, the Trade Union Confederation, and an equal number of representatives of each party); if that is unsuccessful, they go to a Divisional Magistrates Court.

Several countries specify that the following principles or laws shall be applied in the settlement efforts.

(a) *law generally* (Bahrain, Oman, Saudi Arabia, Syria, UAE); (b) *regulations or orders* (Bahrain, Syria); (c) *custom* (Bahrain, Saudi Arabia, UAE, YAR); (d) *equity* (Bahrain, Saudi Arabia, Syria, UAE, YAR); (e) *judicial principle or precedent* (Oman, Saudi Arabia, YAR); (f) *Islamic doctrine or law*, (UAE, YAR); (g) *natural law* (UAE); (h) *justice* (Saudi Arabia, YAR); (i) *collective agreement* or trade practices, and if they offer no solution, *justice and fairness* (Israel); (j) in accordance with *economic and social circumstances* (Bahrain, Oman, Syria).

Some labor codes have indicated the finality or enforceability of arbitration awards in their countries. The terms used are the following:

(a) *final* (Bahrain, Iraq, Jordan, Kuwait, Saudi Arabia, UAE); (b) *binding* (Iran, Iraq, Kuwait, Oman, Qatar); (c) *enforceable* (Saudi Arabia); (d) *enforceable* through the courts (Iran); (e) *no appeal* "save by way of an objection lodged in accordance with ordinary procedure" (Lebanon); (f) parties have the *right to appeal* against the award on a point of law (Syria).

Labor Courts

Special labor courts have been established in Iraq and Israel. They consist of regional courts and a Supreme or national court. Their composition, jurisdiction and enforcement powers are detailed as follows:

(a) *Members of the labor court.* In Iraq, the court is composed of a sole judge named by the Minister of Justice on the recommendation of the presiding judge of the Court of Appeal. In Israel, the court consists of a judge and "representatives of the public"; the latter are appointed by the Ministers of Justice and

Labor after consultation with employers' and employees' organizations.

(b) *Jurisdiction* of the labor court. In Iraq, labor courts "have jurisdiction of matters and disputes referred to in the Labor Code, and the law on pensions and social security." In Israel, the regional labor courts have jurisdiction over specified actions, (1) between an employee and an employer arising out of the employer-employee relationship (but not including the illegal breach of a contractual or statutory obligation); (2) collective disputes; (3) suits relating to benefit funds; (4) disputes connected with union membership or activity; (5) disputes as to the obligatory referral of the labor exchange; (6) suits under safety orders; (7) criminal matters regulated by labor laws; (8) incidental questions which must be resolved to clarify labor matters. The National Labor Court has appellate jurisdiction, and original jurisdiction over disputes between unions or between employer associations.[1]

(c) *Powers* of the court. In Israel, the independence of a labor court is sought by the provision that the public representative on a labor court is to act in accordance with his conscience and not to "regard himself as owing allegiance to the organization in consultation with which he was appointed or to the section of the public which he represents." Also, except in criminal hearings, the court is not bound by the rules of evidence.

TREATY PROVISIONS

None of the Middle East States has ratified the ILO Conventions that refer explicitly to conciliation or arbitration; however, Convention No.87 on Freedom of Association and the Right to

[1] Decisions of the National Labor Court and decisions of the High Court of Justice on labor matters have been published in the International Labor Law Reports, Martinus Niejhoff, Geneva. A selection of questions decided follow. May collective agreements set different retirement dates for men and women? Nevo v. Jewish Agency, Vol. 7, p. 243. Is dismissal compensation due upon the death of an employer? Haddad v. Est. of A. Manes, Vol. 4, p. 148. May work on a day of rest be offset by rest on another day? Nat'l Aircraft Employers v. Israel Aircraft Industries, Vol. 3, P. 113. Is an employee disciplined by demotion, entitled to severance pay. Mekoroth v. Malkowitz, Vol. 1, p. 219.

Organize has been applied, as will be seen below, in ways that affect the settlement of labor disputes.

The ALO Convention 11 on Collective Bargaining encourages Arab States to adopt mechanisms of conciliation and arbitration. It has been ratified by Iraq and Jordan.

CONSEQUENCES AND INCIDENTALS

There has been frequent resort in the Middle East to conciliation and arbitration for the settlement of threatened or active strikes.

The ILO in monitoring its member nations has sought to improve dispute settlement laws. The Kuwaiti Labor Code provisions on the arbitration of labor disputes was interpreted by the ILO Committee of Experts as amounting to compulsory arbitration, and the grievant was advised that that jeopardized the application of Convention No. 87, which guarantees the right of unions to further and defend the interests of their members. A Ministerial Decree of 1975 in the YAR gave the Ministry of Labor power to end a labor dispute when it decided the claims of the workers were too important for economic action; consequently the ILO Committee of Experts requested the government in 1987 to state whether that power could be exercised at the discretion of the Ministry or whether precise criteria were to be applied. The Committee felt the latter should be prescribed so the degree of importance of the dispute could be judged under legal standards.

The Arab Labor Organization, largely through the Arab Labor Bureau, has arranged for several symposia of Arab scholars, and appointed a tripartite Commission for the investigation and conciliation of trade union issues. In 1981, the Commission considered a complaint filed by the International Confederation of Arab Workers' Trade Unions against the Yemen Arab Republic, and made formal findings and recommendations thereon. The Commission also submitted a report on the situation of trade union freedoms in the Arab world, in which it indicated the existence of widespread agreement on the need for such freedoms even for unions not well established.[2]

Early Persian kings asserted their responsibility, under Islam, to administer justice even to the point of subjecting themselves to public hearing of grievances against them.[3] They accepted the rule of law. That tradition, it appears, is being carried out today by the Saudi Arabian Board of Governors which hears complaints against the government and its agents.[4] As part of its rather extensive jurisdiction, it considers grievances against administrative decisions, and it rules on pensions, job appointments, promotions and disciplines. The President of the Board, appointed by the King, has cabinet rank.

[2] Arab Labour Conference. Director-General's Report. Benghazi. Mar. 1981.

[3] Nizam Al Mulk, The Book of Government or Rule for Kings, London, Utledge & Kegan Paul, 1960, pp. 44-45.

[4] David E. Long, "The Board of Grievances in Saudi Arabia", The Middle East Journal, Vol.16, 1983, pp. 71-75.

Chapter 13

SOCIAL SECURITY

PERCEPTIONS OF THE PROBLEM

Prophets in the Middle East promised eternal blessings for those who care for the poor, and it appeared to them that the poor they would always have with them. The complexities of modern industry have assured those who are sensitive to the suffering of man that ever new forms of need cry out for help. Private charity, the time honored balm of Gilead, seems not sufficient. Not alone for the impoverished; those maimed by machines or infused with chemicals or pushed aside in business cycles or strange technologies, and the old who with science stay alive longer, have also become the needy. Individual earnings or savings have not kept pace with the cost of "new necessities". Public assistance is therefore seen as an essential element in the development of the Middle East.

The oil wealthy countries have waivered in their conception of how many foreign workers they must secure against the risks of transplanted lives, and they remain unsure as to their future social requirements. The less affluent countries have been caught up in such perturbation too. All have acknowledged a desire to acquire social security, but the constraints of budgets affect every one of them.

CONSTITUTIONAL PROVISIONS

Nearly every Middle East country has a constitutional provision for some form of social security.

A generalized commitment to social security or social insurance is found in the constitutions of Bahrain, Iran, Kuwait, Syria, UAE, YAR, PDRY. These take the form of a statement of a right, a government guarantee or assurance.

"Social insurance or aid in other forms . . . is a public right"

(Iran). "Workers have the right to social security" (PDRY). "The hungry, the naked, the wounded and the sick have the right to be cared for" (YAR). "The State shall undertake to provide wider social insurances for all citizens" (Iraq). "The State shall adopt a social security plan that will assure assistance to citizens" (Qatar). "The State guarantees social security" (Syria). "The State shall insure the accomplishment of social security" (Bahrain, Kuwait). "Society shall protect minors and others unable to look after themselves" (UAE).

Separate forms of social protection are covered in constitutions as follows:

Old age benefits. These are called for in Bahrain, Iran, Iraq, Jordan, Kuwait, Qatar, Syria, UAE, YAR, PDRY.

Sickness benefits. The State shall provide "medical care" (Bahrain, Kuwait); "free medical care" (PDRY); "means for the care of the health of its citizens" (Qatar, Syria); "hospitals" and "medical facilities" (Bahrain, UAE, YAR); "the protection and improvement of the environment, the care for preventive medicine and vocational health and safety, and the development of all types of hospitals, health institutions and the people's clinics" (PDRY); "medical services, treatment and care" (Iran).

Maternity benefits. The State shall protect "mothers, especially during pregnancy and the child rearing periods" (Iran); it shall protect "motherhood" (Bahrain, YAR); "motherhood and childhood" (Kuwait, Syria, UAE). The State "shall foster maternity and childhood" (Iraq); and "shall provide the means for fostering motherhood and child care" (Qatar).

Family assistance. The family is to be protected as a basic unit of society (Bahrain, Iran, Iraq, Jordan, Kuwait, Qatar, Syria, UAE, YAR, PDRY).

Unemployment compensation. The government shall provide aid for the unemployed (Bahrain, Iran, Iraq, Jordan, UAE).

(The draft Yemeni constitution does not itemize the above programs.)

LABOR CODE AND STATUTORY PROVISIONS

The constitutionally proclaimed social welfare programs have been detailed in numerous statutory provisions. Under circumstances peculiar to the enacting country, the terms and conditions of each plan take on special meanings; however, several outstanding features common to most of the plans may suffice to supply an overall comparative view.

Old Age or Retirement Provisions.

Social security retirement systems ordinarily set an age for qualification to receive benefits and tie that to the amount of contribution made to the plan by the beneficiary. They also specify the amount of money that will be paid qualified persons. Since spouses and dependents may share in the benefits, the old age or retirement plans also provide for those who may survive the principal beneficiary.

(1) *Qualifying ages and contributions.* (a) The earliest retirement age is that in Kuwait, 50 years with 15 years of contributions, or under-50 retirement with 20 years of contributions; (b) The most common qualifications are age 60 for men and 55 for women (Bahrain, Iran, Iraq, Jordan, PDRY), after 15 and 10 years of contributions, respectively, in Bahrain and Jordan, and 20-25 years in Iran and Iraq; (c) 60 is the retirement age for men and women in Saudi Arabia after 10 years of contributions, with 3 years of coverage in the last 5 years; (d) 60 with 10 years of contributions or 55 with 20 years of contributions in Syria; (e) In Israel, the ages are 65 for men or 60 for women with 5 years of coverage in the last 10 or 12 years. A 1987 amendment sought to eliminate the gender difference except as provided in collectively bargained agreements.

(2) *Benefit amounts.* Monthly pensions are usually calculated on average earnings, with a stated minimum and maximum. (I shall round out the native currency in U.S. dollars.) In Bahrain the monthly pension is set at the higher of 40% of the average earnings or a number of dinars, amounting to approximately $148. In Iran, it is 50% of the average earnings. In PDRY, it is

50% of the beneficiary's earnings. In Iraq, the amount is a minimum of $97 and a maximum of $129. In Jordan, Saudi Arabia and Kuwait, there is a minimum of 2% the average earnings times the years of contributions, with a maximum of 75% of the average monthly wage (95% for civilians and 100% for military in Kuwait). In Syria, the pension is 2.2% of average earnings with a minimum of $11 and a maximum of $13. In Lebanon, a pension is paid equal to the higher of the final month's earnings or the average of 20 years earnings plus 1 1/2 of a month's earnings per year of service beyond 20 years. In Israel, a base pension of 16% of the average earnings is increased by 2% for each year worked beyond 10, and by 5% for each year retirement is postponed.

(3) *Early retirement.* Reduced pensions are paid on earlier retirement in all of the above countries.

(4) *Survivor benefits.* A percentage of the insured's pension is paid to a surviving spouse. In Bahrain, the spouse receives 37.5% of the pension; in Iran, 50%; in Iraq, 60%, and in Israel, 12-16% and a widow, under 40 years of age, gets a lump sum payment equal to 3 years pension; in Jordan 50%, in Kuwait 33 1/3% to 100%; in Lebanon 50% if widow is over 60; in Syria 37 1/2% to 75%.

For dependents other than a spouse, Bahrain pays 50% of the deceased's pension, divided equally among children under 22 (26 if a student), 12 1/2% among dependent parents, brothers and sisters; Iran pays 25% of the pension to children and 20% to each aged parent; Iraq pays 40% to each son and each unmarried daughter under 17 (27 if a student), and 40% to the dependent mother, invalid father, unmarried sister and brother under age 16; Israel pays 7 1/2% of the deceased's average wage to each of the first two children (10% to a full orphan); Jordan distributes the full pension among the widow, children, unmarried daughters, dependent parents, brothers and sisters. Kuwait pays 33 1/3 to 100% of the deceased's earnings, divided by schedule among the widows, children, parents, brothers, sister's and son's children; Lebanon divides 50% of the deceased's benefits equally among children and parents, or if none survive, among brothers and sisters under age 16; Saudi Arabia pays 25% of the pension to each dependent son under 20 (under 25 if a student) to each unmarried daughter and dependent parent; Syria gives 25% of the pension to an orphan and 37 1/2% to a "full orphan", 12 1/ 2% to each parent.

(5) *Coverage and exclusions*. The pension plans cover (a) all employees (Kuwait, Lebanon, Syria); (b) employees in establishments hiring more than a specified number of employees (Bahrain 10, Iraq 15, Jordan 20, over 16 years of age, Saudi Arabia 20); (c) employees in specific occupations or areas (Iran); (d) residents over 18 years of age or under 60 (Israel).

They exclude (a) domestic servants (Bahrain, Iraq, Jordan, Saudi Arabia, Syria); (b) self-employed (Bahrain, Jordan); (c) family laborers (Iraq, Jordan, Saudi Arabia, Syria); (d) temporary workers (Bahrain, Iraq, Syria); (e) noncitizens (Bahrain, Saudi Arabia, Jordan as specified, Lebanon from nonreciprocal countries); (f) casual workers (Bahrain, Saudi Arabia, if less than 3 months service, Syria); (g) agricultural workers (Lebanon, Syria).

Special pension systems are provided for public employees (Bahrain, Iran, Iraq, Kuwait, Lebanon, Saudi Arabia, Syria).

(6) *Source of funds*. Contributions to the pension funds are required from insured employees, their employers and the government in the following percentages. (Iran, 77% of earnings from employees, 20% of payroll from employers and 3% of payroll from the government; Israel, 1.9% from employees, 3/4% from employers, 15% of both from the government, with other amounts for invalidity and long term care; Jordan and Saudi Arabia, 5% employees, 8% employers, balance from government; Kuwait, 5% employees, 10% employers and government, Bahrain, 5% employees, 7% employers, government none; Iraq, 5% employees, 12% employers or 25% from oil field employers, none from the government, Lebanon 8 1/2% from employees, none from employers or government.

(7) *Administrative organization*. The pension plans are admin-

istered by a special agency, a General Organization for Social Insurance (Bahrain, Iran, Jordan, a corporation, Saudi Arabia); a Social Security Institute (Iraq); a National Insurance Institute (Israel); a Social Insurance Institute (Syria). All are under the general supervision of a Ministry of the government.

Disability Benefits

For persons unable to work because of a disability, the above countries provide a cash disability benefit. In cases of 100% disability, the payments approximate the sums paid to old age pensioners; for partial disability, the sums are reduced generally in proportion to the degree of disability.

(1) *Sick leave pay.* There is an annual allowance of days each year for absence from work due to illness, during which earnings must be continued at full or part pay. The periods and amounts vary: full pay only (Iran 8 days; PDRY 60 days; full pay and half pay (Bahrain 15 and 15 days); Iraq, escalated by years of seniority, 30-180 days; Lebanon 30-75 days; Qatar, 15 and 30 days full pay and 3/4 pay; (Saudi Arabia, 30 and 60 days; UAE 15 and 30 days). Other periods and calculations are set at 90 days with 90% pay plus 90 days at 70% pay (YAR); 6 days at full, 6 more at 3/4, 6 more at 1/2, 6 more at 1/4 and 6 days without pay (Kuwait); and 2 weeks at full, 2 more at 3/4, 2 more at 1/2 and 4 more at 1/4 (Oman).

Medical certification of illness is required in Bahrain, Iraq, Kuwait, Lebanon, Oman, Qatar, UAE, YAR, PDRY. Illness beyond the period for sick leave may be compensated and deducted from annual leave (Bahrain, Lebanon). No paid sick leave is granted if the illness is caused by misconduct (as certified by a government doctor in Oman; or as resulting from alcohol or drugs in the UAE). Incurable or malignant disease carries 6 months' more sick leave pay, extendable to 2 years (Iraq). In Qatar, a worker may be terminated at the end of the 12th week of sick leave if certified as medically unfit to resume his work at that time.

(2) *Medical and hospital care.* Every country in the Middle

East provides some medical and hospital assistance to its residents, limited by the development of its facilities and available funds.

(3) *Free services*, including general and specialist physician care, laboratory work, medicines, hospitalization and rehabilitation are offered, in Iran, through medical facilities belonging to the Ministry of Hygiene, Health and Medical Education; in Iraq, through government health centers and hospitals supported by the Social Security Institute; in Israel at hospitals owned and operated by or under contract with the Social Insurance fund; in Jordan at government clinics and hospitals; in Kuwait through government payments; in Lebanon through reimbursement by the National Social Security Fund (70% generally, 100% for maternity care, kidney dialysis and cancer treatment).

(4) *Coverage and exclusions.* Sickness benefits are conferred upon all employees in firms with 5 or more employees (Iraq); employees in industry, commerce, agriculture, education and civil service (Lebanon); all workers insured for medical care (Israel); and insured civil servants (Jordan).

Free medical services as available are offered the general population in all Middle East countries.[1] Excluded are agricultural workers, domestic servants, temporary workers and family labor (Iraq), and agricultural workers and aliens from countries without reciprocity (Lebanon).

(5) *Sources of funds.* Generally contributions to sickness and medical care programs are the same as those for old age pensions.

(6) *Administrative organizations.* In most instances cash benefits are paid through a Social Security Organization, and medical services are provided by local health authorities under the supervision of the Ministry of Hygiene and Health or the Ministry of Labor and Social Affairs.

[1] Recently enacted laws in Bahrain, Iran and Qatar have extended the same medical treatment given citizens to nationals from the Arab Gulf Corporation Council countries. JPRS-NEA-89-45-4A, Gulf Daily News (in English) Manama, April 18, 1989, p. 4. JPRS-NEA-89-52-62A, Kayhan International (in English), Tehran, June 25, 1989, p. 6. JPRS-NEA-89-040-37, Muscat Times of Oman (in English) April 27, 1989, p. 17.

Maternity Benefits

Women workers who become pregnant are assisted by laws requiring their employers to compensate them, at full or part pay, before and after childbirth, and in some instances to provide nurseries and rest periods for nursing.

Maternity leave. The period of paid maternity leave varies — 62 days (Iraq); 40 days (Lebanon); 15 days (UAE); 50 days (Syria); 60 days (PDRY, with 20 more for hard delivery or twin births); 70 days (YAR); 30 days before and 40 days after (Kuwait); 3 weeks before and 3 weeks after (Jordan); 4 weeks before and 6 weeks after (Saudi Arabia); 6 weeks (Oman); 6 weeks before and 6 weeks after (Israel); 12 weeks in all (Iran).

Pay during the leave period is required in full (Iraq, Lebanon); 75% of earnings and cost of hospital and layette (Israel); 66 2/3% of average earnings (Iran); 50% (Jordan, and Saudi Arabia if the mother has been employed for three years). In Iraq, maternity leave may be extended up to nine months "in the case of a difficult childbirth or the birth of more than one child." Such extended leave is unpaid "unless the woman is subject to the law on pensions and social security." Dismissal during medical leave is prohibited (Bahrain, Iran, Israel, Lebanon, Oman, Saudi Arabia, Syria). If the mother voluntarily leaves her employment, Iraq gives her a lump-sum payment of 1 month's benefit for each year of her contribution.

Workplace nurseries. In Jordan, an employer of over 30 women shall provide a suitable room for their children under age 6. In Iran a workplace where there are more than 10 nursing children shall set aside premises for a creche. In Iraq, employers of women shall provide a kindergarten or contract with a children's home to do so. In Saudi Arabia, an employer of 50 or more employees shall provide suitable premises entrusted to a female nurse to care for the employee's children under 6. In Syria, every employer of 100 or more women shall provide a nursery, and the Ministry of Social Affairs and Labor shall regulate its construction and the workers contribution to operating expenses.

Rest periods for nursing. Mothers nursing their children shall be granted the following rest periods for that purpose. 1 hour each day (Bahrain, Iraq, Israel); 1/2 hour break after every 3 hours of work (Iran); not more than 1 hour a day (Saudi Arabia); 2 additional breaks, neither over 1/2 hour (UAE). All of these are to be in addition to rest periods granted other employees.

Family Allowances

To assist families with children, the laws of Iran, Israel, and Lebanon grant parents cash subsidies. The monthly allowance in Iran is set at three times the lowest daily wage of unskilled laborers, payable for each of the first two children. In Israel, 39 new shekles are paid for each of the first two children, 79 for the third, 148 for the fourth, 128 for the fifth, and 138 for the sixth. There is also a special allowance for the third and subsequent children if any member of the family has served or is serving in the armed forces. Lebanon pays 65 pounds a month for the mother and 35 pounds for each child up to a maximum of 175 pounds a month.

Family allowances are ordinarily given to families in need; but in the poorer or non-oil countries there is a general subsidy apparently to preserve or protect the family as a basic institution.

Funeral Grants

Single payments of a sum to cover funeral expenses are given in Bahrain, Iran, Israel, Kuwait, Saudi Arabia, and Syria.

Unemployment Benefits

There is an outstanding absence of provision for unemployment benefits in the Middle East except for the requirement of severance pay.

(1) *Amount of benefit*. (a) Israel is the only country that has a statutory unemployment payment plan. It calls for the payment of 40-80% of the wage earned during the last 75 work days of a qualifying period. A 5 day waiting period is imposed every four months of continuous unemployment; and a maximum is reached

after 138 days of compensation (175 for people over 45 or with 3 dependents) in any year. (b) Iraq authorizes its health and welfare fund to provide unemployment assistance. (c) In Kuwait, if the employment is terminated by sickness, the old age pension is paid.

(2) *Coverage and exclusions.* Israel's unemployment compensation plan covers all employees 18 years of age or over (or insured for pensions). It excludes the self-employed, members of cooperatives, and small-holders of settlements. In Iraq, the Health and Welfare Fund is authorized to provide unemployment assistance. In Kuwait, unemployment benefits are paid to those covered by the old age pension system, only when unemployment is caused by sickness. In Bahrain, the General Insurance Agency also pays unemployment benefits as covered by insurance.

(3) *Source and administration of funds.* In Israel, contributions for unemployment compensation are made by employees at 0.1% of earnings, by employers at 0.2% of payroll, and none by the government. The funds are administered by the National Insurance Institute.

Work Injury Compensation

Statutes pertaining to work related injuries commonly provide for medical and hospital care, the continuation of some earnings, in amounts differentiating permanent and temporary disabilities, the rehabilitation of the partially injured, and the payment of a death benefit to widows and dependents.

(1) *Permanent total disability.* The statutes provide for monthly payments of a cerain percentage of the average earnings of the worker sustaining a total and permanent disability as follows: (a) 82 1/2-86 1/4% (Bahrain); (b) 80% (Iraq), 75% (Israel, Jordan, Saudi Arabia, Syria); 66 2/3% (Lebanon); 50%(Iran).

(2) *Permanent partial disability.* Workers who sustain a permanent partial disability in a work related injury are given monthly payments if the disability exceeds a certain percentage

of their capacity to work, or a lump sum payment if the disability is rated at less than that percentage; monthly payments for 35% or more partial disability (Iraq, Syria); 33% (Iran); 30% (Jordan, Lebanon, Saudi Arabia); 20% (Israel). In a few countries, no payment is made after it is determined that the permanent disability is less than 10% (Iran, Saudi Arabia) or 5% (Israel).

(3) *Medical benefits.* Medical care, surgery, specialist care, hospitalization and prescribed medicines as well as rehabilitation assistance are also provided the disabled under the general medical and hospital systems of the country.

(4) *Grounds for denial of payment.* Injured workers are denied compensation if their injury has been caused by (a) gross negligence (Jordan, Qatar); (b) self infliction (Bahrain, Kuwait, Qatar, UAE); (c) premeditated misconduct (Kuwait); (d) serious or wilful misconduct (Bahrain); intentional violation of safety instructions or refusal to submit to a medical examination without cause (Qatar, UAE); work under the influence of narcotics or alcohol (Qatar).

(5) *Coverage and exclusions.* Compensation and medical benefits for work related injuries are given to all employees generally, within specified employment or with certain exclusions. Some inclusions are limited to firms of a designated size (5 or more employees in Iraq, 10 or more in Bahrain, 20 or more in Jordan). Exclusions are specified for domestics, family labor, agricultural workers (Bahrain, Iraq, Jordan); for self employed (Bahrain, Jordan); for temporary employees (Iraq); for seamen, fishermen (Jordan); and some foreign workers (Jordan).

(6) *Source and administration of funds.* Contributions to workmen compensation funds are ordinarily required from employers at a percentage of payroll (0.7% in Israel; 2% in Jordan and Lebanon; 1 to 3% in Bahrain; 12%, 25% in oil fields, in Iraq; 20% in Iran). The agencies charged with administering these funds, and making payments to the work injured, are the same as those used for old age pensions.

TREATY PROVISIONS

Social Security has been the subject of several treaties in the Middle East.

The UN Covenant on Economic, Social and Cultural Rights, ratified by Iran, Iraq, Israel, Jordan, Lebanon, Syria and PDRY provides that signatory states shall "recognize the right of every one to social security, including social insurance." It also calls for the recognition that "The widest possible protection and assistance should be accorded to the family" and "Special protection should be accorded to mothers during a reasonable period before and after child birth. During such period working mothers should be accorded paid leave or leave with adequate social security benefits." The steps to be taken by the parties to the Covenant shall include "The prevention, treatment and control of . . . occupational and other diseases." The UN Covenant on Civil and Political Rights also provides "The family is the natural and fundamental group unit of society and is entitled to protection."

The ILO Convention No 102 on Minimum Standards for Social Security has been ratified in the Middle East only by Israel. It sets benefit standards for (a) medical care, (b) sickeness, (c) unemployment, (d) old age, (e) employment injury, (f) family, (g) maternity, (h) invalidity and (i) survivors. In elaborate detail, it specifies formulae for the determination of the workers to be covered, the sums to be paid, and the services to be rendered them.

Early ILO Conventions were designed to achieve social equity in the application of established social security benefits, whatever their provisions. Convention No. 118 on Equality of Treatment of Nationals and Non-Nationals, ratified by Iraq, Israel, Jordan, and Syria, was to maintain equal treatment between nationals and non-nationals. Convention No. 107, on Protection of Indigenous and Tribal Populations, ratified by Iraq and Syria, was to protect indigenous and tribal populations. Convention No. 48 on Rights under Invalidity Insurance, ratified by Israel, was to establish an international scheme on invalidity, old age and widows and orphans insurance for workers who transfer their residence from one country to another. Convention No. 2, ratified by Syria, related to benefits for workers from another country, and No. 8, ratified by Iraq, dealt with the indemnification of sailors unemployed when their ships were lost or foundered at sea. All contain public policy comments on Social Security.

ALO Convention 3, ratified by Iraq, Palestine, and Syria, prescribes minimum norms for social security. It deals with standards to be followed in the eventuality of work related accidents, illness, maternity, disablement, death, unemployment and family need. Its primary objective is to provide these benefits through government supported plans.

ALO Convention 1, on Labor Norms, provides that every signatory shall make every effort to improve its system of social security to bring it up to the level recommended by the ILO Convention 102.

CONSEQUENCES AND INCIDENTALS

Social security programs in the Middle East are quite uneven. Certain benefits are not made available in several countries, and in every country there are special limitations upon the extent to which statutory provisions can be realized. Social security systems require years to acquire administrative expertise. Nearly all the Middle East programs have been introduced relatively recently (Bahrain, Oman, UAE in the late 1970s and the Yemens in the 1980s). All social security programs are costly. Low income countries have little capacity to contribute to insurance funds. Rural areas have been extremely difficult to service. Even in the oil wealthy countries, the massive influx of alien workers (continued despite policies to nationalize or nativize the labor force) has presented ever changing and more demanding administrative tasks. Still social security has been seen as a starting point for progressive development.

The primary emphasis of Middle Eastern social security has been upon health needs. Traditional caring for the ill and disabled, through the tribe and the extended family has been taken for granted. Government assistance has been looked upon in much the same vein.

Illustrative of the levels of medical care and their growth are the number of doctors and hospital beds available. In the Yemen Arab Republic's firt 10 years, hospitals increased from 3 to 30 and doctors from 2 to 179. In the People's Democratice Republic of Yemen, from 1978 to 1980, hospital beds almost tripled and doctors increased about five fold (including 25% from China and some 12% from Russia). In Oman, from 1970 to 1986, 1 hospital with 12 beds and 9 government health centers grew to 15 hospitals and 80 clinics with over 2500 beds. In Saudi Arabia, the ratio of doctors to population increased between 1975 and 1980 from 3.8% to 6.7%, and hospital beds doubled. The Third Development Plan (1980-85) added 36 new hospitals and 1050 additional beds. In the UAE, from 1975 to 1982, hospital beds increased from 1450 to 4240, and the ratio of doctors rose to 1 per 734 people.[2]

Similar expansion has occured in the number of old age pension beneficiaries. In Saudi Arabia the system covered slightly under three fourths of a million persons in 1980 and a million and a quarter in 1985. Such statistics have not been published by most Middle East countries; but all report progress.

The problem of unemployment in the Middle East has been obscured by the insatiable manpower demands of oil production. A high rate of turn-over among migrant workers, resulting in many cases of temporary unemployment, has not been seen as a disturbing social problem. At times, however, the number of unemployed workers in the permanent labor force has become significant. Currently there is a troubling amount of unemployment in Jordan and Syria, and even in war-torn Iraq and Iran, without any formal unemployment compensation system. In Israel, immigration has produced a critical absorption point and employment opportunities for highly educated and skilled work-

[2] ILO, Into the 21st Century; The Development of Social Security, Geneva, 1984; ILO, The Changing World of Work, Geneva, 1986.

ers have not been sufficient to keep many Israelis in their homeland even with unemployment compensation.

Compensation for worker related injuries has been tied to public medical and hospital care and has become widespread in the Middle East. Sickness leave and maternity leave have followed industrial employment.

The amount of social benefits paid has been relatively moderate or low. Family assistance or poverty relief are generally regarded as matters for private and religious charity. Social security programs have been very attractive and necessary, but a commitment to the redistribution of wealth, essential to their growth, has not been the prevailing public will. Social security systems in the Middle East have been born, but except for public health plans, they are incubating slowly.

Chapter 14

WORKER HOUSING

PERCEPTIONS OF THE PROBLEM

The universal desire of a man to have a roof over his head has been confounded in the Middle East by an unprecedented crowding in of foreign workers and a topsy-turvy migration of citizens from farm to city. Nowhere has there been enough housing, and the demand for new dwellings has far exceeded the supply. For low-income workers, the transition has been from sun baked mud huts or hand woven cloth tents to apartment units, or when rental housing has not been available, to scrap-board shacks. For skilled workers with ample income, there has often been no place for their families. The resultant public prospect has been a massive problem of under-housing and makeshift arrangements.

All countries have been aware of the over-all problem and the particular needs of their people, in certain localities. Private capital has found investment opportunities in soaring land prices and rents; and it has been generally more profitable to build for the well-to-do class than for poorer workers. Government subsidies, low interest loans, and public housing projects have been scheduled in development plans; however, those projects have always been limited by a balancing of budgets. Housing in the Middle East has caused a flurry of activity, not without human privation and suffering.

The Islamic countries have had a religious base for housing the working poor. The Koranic verses on Allah's concern for the weakened and disinherited have inspired repeated public appeals for housing to assist the impoverished as a matter of religious duty. In a somewhat similar spirit, Israel, in seeking to establish a homeland for Jews, has been motivated by its religion to house its inmigrants. Both groups have experienced difficulty in putting those faiths into practice.

CONSTITUTIONAL PROVISIONS

Middle East constitutions have promised housing.

Bahrain declares "The State shall strive to provide housing for citizens with limited income."

In Iran, the constitution states, "A suitable dwelling, according to need, is the right of every Iranian person and family. The Government is responsible for laying the groundwork to accomplish this, with first consideration given to those who are in need, in particular, villagers and laborers," and "the economy of the Islamic Republic of Iran shall be established upon the following principles: 1) to fulfill basic needs for housing. . . ."

In the PDRY, the constitution states, "The state-owned dwellings shall be distributed among the citizens according to the law." (The draft constitution doesn't refer to housing.)

The constitutions of Bahrain and Kuwait specify that landlord-tenant relations are to be regulated by law "with due regard being given to social justice".

LABOR CODE AND STATUTORY PROVISIONS

Legislation to provide the housing mentioned in constitutions or in constant public discourse has been included in some labor codes and other statutes.

Employers with workers in remote areas are obliged to provide them with "adequate living quarters" (Saudi Arabia, Syria, Qatar, PDRY) or with "suitable living accommodation" (Kuwait, Oman, Qatar). In Saudi Arabia, some quarters must be assigned for married workmen. The PDRY requires that "The employer shall make available accommodation and proper meals for the workers in remote places"; and Qatar provides that if transportation is not served by normal transport, it shall be done by the employer.

In Saudi Arabia, the provision for housing applies not only to remote areas, but also to workers "in mines, quarries, or oil prospection, extraction or exploitation sites."

The Minister of Labor shall specify the standard of accommodations to be provided by employers for their workers (Iraq,

Oman, Saudi Arabia, Syria). Kuwait provides the accommodations shall be "in conformity with the terms agreed upon by both parties". In PDRY, the Minister shall consult the Trades Union Confederation and then specify the remote places, the accommodation and "the share the worker pays of the cost."

TREATY PROVISIONS

The UN Covenant on Economic, Social and Cultural Rights, ratified by Iran, Iraq, Israel, Jordan, Lebanon, Syria, and PDRY provides that parties to it "recognize the right of everyone to an adequate standard of living, including . . . housing . . ."

CONSEQUENCES AND INCIDENTALS

The efforts to acquire enough housing for workers in the Middle East may be gleaned from a miscellany of reports, interviews and newspaper accounts.

In the oil rich Arab states, there has been a steady improvement in housing facilities and at the same time, a recognition that more must be accomplished. In Saudi Arabia, under the First Five-year Plan, 17,500 units were constructed each year, under the Second Plan, 40,000 units per year, and the Third Plan scheduled over 50,000 a year. It also provided for the servicing of about 15,000 plots for lower income families. High rentals, estimated to range from \$2,850 to \$8,600 per year for a single family home, made homes in Saudi Arabia accessible only when shared by 8 to 12 people.[1] The UAE, which had no state planning on housing, constructed several hundred thousand units, and 24,000 more in 1982.[2] Oman, by royal decree, announced a program for low-cost housing as early as 1977, and has had a substantial growth in urban construction.[3]

At the other extreme in national income, the Yemeni governments have wrestled with special housing needs in their charac-

[1] Raggaei El Mallakh, Saudi Arabia, Croom Helm, London, 1982; JPRS-NEA-087-003-94, "Urgent Major Public Housing Projects in Numerous Provinces", Al-Riyadh (in Arabic), Riyadh, 24 Aug. 86, p.3.

[2] Omran T. Abdullah, The Establishment of the UAE, Croom Helm, London, 1987.

[3] Popular Housing Law, Royal Decree 35/77, 0650 No. 126, June 1, 1977.

teristic ways. Both have built primarily apartment houses in their capitals. Both have relied heavily for home improvements upon remittances sent by their citizens who emigrated to other countries. The YAR experienced problems with escalating land prices. The PDRY nationalized housing except for owner-occupied dwellings. In both countries new construction has lagged behind announced goals.[4]

In Israel, the national dedication to an in-gathering of Jews from all over the world brought in tens of thousands of new settlers each year and a hectic placement of them in temporary housing until more lasting structures could be built. Even with the recent substantial out-flow of Israelis for employment elsewhere, the process of in-migration and the construction of new dwellings continues. Foreign aid and private investment are still insufficient to provide satisfying housing for many workers.[5] Political complications in the occupied territories of the West Bank and Gaza have created special housing problems which are discussed below.

In Iran, the Minister of Housing stated that 50% of the nation's population was living in residential units of less than 50 square meters, and there was no alternative but to build residences on a mass production basis.[6]

[4] Robin Birdwell-Longman, The Yemens, Westview Press, Boulder Colo., 1983; Ragaei El Mallakh, The Economic Development of the YAR, Croom Helm, London, 1986.

[5] Esther R. Cohen, Human Rights in the Israel-Occupied Territories, Manchester Univ. Press, 1985; Philippa Strum, Gaza and the West Bank, American-Israeli Civil Liberties Coalition, Inc. — Newsletter, Vol.VI, No.4, March, 1988.

[6] JPRS-NEA-89-55-63, Minister S. Kazerumi, London, Keyhan (in Persian), July 6, 1989, p 4.

Chapter 15

WORKER EDUCATION

PERCEPTIONS OF THE PROBLEM

No one questions education but the educated. They want more of it and the kind that serves their most cherished purposes. In the rececnt transformations of life in the Middle East, there have been multiple needs, and education has been given high priority in the discussions on how the needs can be met. Every country, awakened to the oil boom, has experienced a dearth of knowledgeable, skilled, trained, ready-and-able persons to undertake the novel tasks before it. The oil rich nations hastened to import talent; the more successful they were the more they felt overwhelmed, and the more they grew determined to educate their own nationals to take charge. The unfortunate, dry states found themselves being drained of professionals, semiskilled and even common labor, which they also needed; in turn, they felt obliged to educate and recruit replacements.

Relief was envisioned in tapping two reservoirs. One was the mass of unskilled workers, many of whom had to be made literate to qualify for industrial jobs and many others who required on-the-job training. The second human resource was the pond of women who had been confined by custom and some religious traditions to the home and the farm. Their potential was immense, but so was the resistance of the old attitudes toward change. Education to meet the challenges of the rapidly altering economies was seen as indispensable. The difficulties lay in deciding whom to educate and what to teach them.

CONSTITUTIONAL PROVISIONS

Constitutions commit Middle East governments to the education of their citizens in several ways.

General education. In some countries, education is broadly declared a constitutional right (Kuwait, Qatar, Syria, Yemen Arab Republic, PDRY). It is made compulsory for the primary grades (Bahrain, Iraq, Jordan, Kuwait, Syria, United Arab Emirates). It is to be free in primary schools (Bahrain, Jordan, Kuwait, Lebanon); through high school (Iran); through all levels of schooling (Iraq, Qatar, Syria, United Arab Emirates, PDRY omitted from draft). Private schools, moreover, have been authorized when established by religious communities (Bahrain, Jordan, Lebanon) or by others in accord with provisions of law (United Arab Emirates).

"Inviolability" of educational institutions has been guaranteed in Bahrain; and in the Yemen Arab Republic, they "cannot be violated except in cases necessitated by security requirements as described by law." The Yemeni constitution also declares, "Places of . . . education are revered."

Islamic values and economic objectives are joined in several constitutions. In Iraq, education is to create "a free, nationalist and progressive generation . . . which takes pride in its people . . . sympathizes with the rights of all its nationalities, and opposes the doctrines of capitalism, exploitation, reaction, Zionism and colonialism in order to achieve Arabic unity, freedom and socialism." Qatar places "the goal of education in the creation of a nation of citizens . . . believing in God, possessing good morals, proud of their Arab-Islamic heritage, enlightened with knowledge, aware of their responsibilities and mindful of their rights." The constitution of Syria aims to create "a socialist nationalist Arab generation which is scientifically minded and . . . proud of its heritage." Lebanon provides that education shall "not affect the dignity of any of the religions or creeds."

Vocational education. Vocational training is expressly mentioned in a few constitutions. In Iraq, it is said, "the State shall . . . expand vocational and technical education . . . and particularly promote evening education which enables the popular masses to correlate knowledge between science and labour." In Iran, "to train individuals in skills" is declared a fundamental principle. The PDRY proclaims it "shall raise the standard of vocational qualifications and expand the scope of vocational training and education"; "shall render special care to the vocational qualifying of the working woman." Omitted from draft constitution. The constitution of the United Arab Emirates provides it shall ensure that the citizens are prepared for work.

LABOR CODE AND STATUTORY PROVISIONS

Education of the general populace, ordinarily the province of a Ministry of Education, and vocational training, the responsibility of a Ministry of Labor, have both promoted the competence of workers and their employability. Since every Middle East country now offers education at the three levels — primary, secondary and university — the laws providing facilities and teachers for that entire range of general education have become too numerous to be detailed here. It may suffice to note the laws specifically relevant to vocational education.

Vocational training

Some labor codes have specified provision for vocational training. They have defined their objective as affording workers "the opportunity to develop their knowledge and skill so as to raise their productive efficiency and prepare them for particular occupations or to enable them to transfer from one occupation to another." (Bahrain); or providing "the workers in the various sectors of employment . . . with technical training with a view towards furnishing various sectors with the qualified workers they need . . . raising the technical skill level of trained workers and improving their occupational qualifications and productivity" (Iraq). More generally, statutes have delegated the responsibility for vocational education to a Minister of Labor, and have authorized him to maintain public training centers and to supervise private industry programs (Bahrain, Iraq, Oman, Saudi Arabia, Syria, UAE, YAR, PDRY).

An obligation to participate in vocational training has been placed upon employers. They have been required to comply with educational orders of the Minister of Labor (Bahrain, UAE,

YAR), to make all necessary facilities available in the workplaces (Iran, PDRY), to execute a training program agreed upon between the Ministry and the employers (Oman), or to offer an official curriculum, to hold tests and grant certificates of completion (Saudi Arabia, Syria, UAE).

A responsibility for vocational education has also been placed upon employees in the PDRY — "The worker shall be obliged to train and develop the skill of his colleagues efficiently."

Vocational Rehabilitation

Labor codes have also provided that rehabilitation services shall be furnished to a disabled worker "to recover his capacity to resume his original employment or to perform any other work suitable to his condition" (Bahrain, similarly, Oman, Saudi Arabia, Syria). The employment of rehabilitated workers, sent by the Labor Ministry, is required to the extent of 2% of the work force (Bahrain, Oman, Saudi Arabia, Syria).

TREATY PROVISIONS

Treaty commitments to provide vocational training, as set forth by the UN and the ILO and the ALO, have been signed by several Middle East states.

The UN International Covenant on Economic, Social and Cultural Rights, ratified by Iran, Iraq, Israel, Jordan, Lebanon, Syria, and PDR Yemen provides the following:

Right to education. The parties to the covenant "recognize the right of everyone to education," and primary education "shall be compulsory and available free to all"; "higher education shall be made equally accessible to all, on the basis of capacity, by every appropriate means and in particular by the progressive introduction of free education." Parents may undertake "to ensure the religious and moral education of their children in conformity with their own convictions" by enrolling their children in private schools which meet "such minimum educational standards as may be laid down or approved by the state."

Vocational education. The covenant also specifies steps to be taken by the parties to "achieve the full realization of the right to work." They "shall include technical and vocational guidance and training programs, policies and techniques." "Adequate provision shall be made to the maximum extent possible under local conditions for the progressive development of broad systems of education, vocational training and apprenticeship, with a view to the effective preparation of children and young persons of both sexes for a useful occupation. . . . In order to secure high productivity through the development of skilled labor, training in new techniques of production shall be provided in suitable cases."

Such training "shall be organized by or under the supervision of the competent authorities, in consultation with the employers' and workers' organizations of the country from which the trainees come and of the country of training."

The ALO Convention 9 on Professional Training and Advice, ratified by Iraq, Jordan, Palestine, and Syria, commits signatory countries to undertake education and vocational training throughout a worker's active life so that he might make adaptations to the needs of the Middle East labor market.

Tribal worker training. ILO Convention 107, concerning the protection and integration of indigenous and other tribal and semi-tribal populations (ratified by Iraq and Syria) provides that "persons belonging to the populations concerned shall enjoy the same opportunities as other citizens in respect of vocational training facilities." Also, whenever vocational training programs "do not meet the special needs of persons belonging to the populations concerned, governments shall provide special training facilities for such persons . . . they shall in particular, enable the persons concerned to receive the training necessary for occupations for which these populations have traditionally shown aptitude."

Disabled person training. ILO Convention 142 concerning vocational guidance and vocational training in the development of human resources (ratified by Iraq, Israel, Jordan) provides each member shall "adopt and develop comprehensive and coordinated policies and programmes of vocational guidance and training closely linked with employment, in particular through public employment services." Such programs "shall encourage and enable all persons, on an equal basis and without any discrimination whatsoever, to develop and use their capabilities for work in their own best interests and in accordance with their own aspirations, account being taken of the needs of society." Each state "shall gradually extend its systems of vocational guidance . . . to all children, young persons and adults, including appropriate programmes for all handicapped and disabled persons."

Paid educational leave. ILO Convention 140, concerning paid educational leave (signed by Iraq) provides each member "shall formulate and apply a policy designed to promote . . . the granting of paid education leave for the purpose of . . . (1) acquisition, improvement of occupational skills and the promotion of employment and job security in conditions of scientific and technological development; (2) promotion of appropriate continuing education and training, helping workers adjust to contemporary requirements; (3) to the human, social and cultural advancement of workers." ALO Convention 10, ratified by Iraq alone, also provides for paid educational leave.

CONSEQUENCES AND INCIDENTALS

For workers in the Middle East, in particular, education has meant literacy for masses, mobility for those mired in stagnant areas, more money for multitudes, and for the most talented, prosperous careers. Regrettably the number of persons just starting their education or shifting to new forms of work has exceeded the number who needed to be transformed to meet all the changes in Middle East economies. Under the urgency of the times, the quality of the education often has not received the personal and painstaking consideration it could have. Traditionally, the elite in the Middle East had been educated in arts and literature, whereas the needs of economic development have required science and engineering, administrators and managers. Societal custom denigrated industrial and commercial occupations and all manual effort as work to be performed by the lower classes. Re-education to overcome such prevailing social attitudes has lagged behind the creation of more facilities for vocational education.

The realities of education and vocational training in the Middle East can be seen in a miscellany of experiences.

Saudi Arabian educational facilities have been expanded constantly, at all academic levels, so that by 1980 it was estimated that all boys and 50% of the girls had completed elementary grades and 20% of the population were engaged in some government-organized education program. Several national agencies, like the Educational Development Center and the National Center for Adult Literacy, were supplemented with Regional Institutes of Education in an effort to eliminate all illiteracy. In the field of vocational guidance, both public and private efforts were enlisted. The government itself inaugurated an extensive training program for its employees in an Institute for Public Administration. An Interministerial Committee on Manpower prepared a master plan, balancing the distribution of students by disciplines or specialties critical to the country's development. Grants were given to university students who were willing to prepare for top managerial positions. Private employers were urged to undertake on-the-job training program and did so. An overarching motivation was to educate enough native Saudis so that they might supplant the skilled foreign workers at least in high government and corporate posts. The well-financed programs have still fallen far short of that goal.[1]

Kuwait has supplied free education, including free school uniforms and daily meals at the lower levels, and professional college education to its foreign expatriate population as well as to Kuwaitis. When in the early 1980s it retrenched somewhat, it decided to limit the enrollment of foreigners in schools unless one-fifth of the students there were its nationals. But it was said Kuwaitis "despised" technical professions and chose to be edu-

[1] JPRS-NEA-086-057-38, Interview with the Minister of Labor and Social Affairs, His Excellency Muhammad bin 'Ali Al Fa'iz, Riyadh, Al-Yamamah (in Arabic) 15 Jan.86, pp.26-31.

cated in the arts and theoretical subjects that qualified them only for white collar positions. The government policy of preferring Kuwaitis was shown in its placing a large percentage of Kuwaitis in civil service classifications and grading them for top salaries regardless of the degrees they had achieved. Government sponsored vocational training centers have suffered a discouraging dropout rate. The Kuwaiti Oil Company and other oil companies have maintained their own on-the-job training programs, and have even sent key employees to be educated in the United States and the United Kingdom. Kuwaiti educational programs have substantially reduced illiteracy (though not to the remaining nomads) and have advanced adult education; still the country is dependent upon foreign (largely Palestinian and Jordanian) workers.[2]

Iran's educational policies have changed with its recent rulers only in certain respects. The Shahs, Khomeini and his followers have all shared the Islamic devotion to the study of sacred literature. That priority has led them to regard a proficiency in the knowledge of the Koran as a qualification for all prominent public positions. It has also been accompanied by a denigration of physical labor. The Khomeini revolution accentuated Islamic fundamentalism. The Ulamma ordained public separation of the sexes and a ban on the teaching of girls by male instructors. Vocational education of men fell under the restraints of limited funds. When the ILO sponsored a Workers' Training Center in South Teheran, the required funds were not fully forthcoming. A society of Muslim Women Office Employees, and similar groups for Nurses and Teachers, won approval for their affirmation of loyalty to the political/religious regime, but little was done to educate more women for work, even in war ravaged industry.[3]

Other oil producing countries have had similar educational

[2] Shamlam Y. Alessa, The Manpower Problem in Kuwait, Kegan-Paul Int'l., London & Boston, 1981; American Embassy-Kuwait, Foreign Labor Trends, U.S. Dept. of Labor, 1987.

[3] H. Ladjervardi, Labor Unions and Autocracy in Iran, New York Univ. Press, 1985; Farah Azari, ed., Women of Iran, Ithaca Press, London, 1983.

experiences, notwithstanding their different situations. Public education has expanded, illiteracy has been diminished, vocational training has been recognized as a pressing need, and nationalistic concerns have encouraged and assisted citizens to acquire competencies pertinent to their country's development; but traditional values have favored education in religion, art and literature and the countries have not supplied enough vocational education to meet the technical requirements of industry or public administration.

The Middle East countries without oil production and enormous revenues have furthered education for workers in more modest or idiosyncratic ways. Jordan has promoted vocational training for low income groups, particularly for girls. Its successive five-year plans have allocated increasing funds to vocational education, including support for technical faculties at the university.[4] Syria has done likewise. In rural areas, the lower level of income and the persistence of traditional values have limited progress.[5] In the YAR, a shortage of teachers and funds has slowed the steady process of eliminating illiteracy and has left noticeable gaps in technical or scientific education.[6] PDRY has endeavored to advance its official ideology with a Higher School for Socialist Sciences and with special literacy and training institutes for women. Half of its medical school graduates have been women. Its College of Technology has received aid from UNESCO. Its boarding school for Bedouin children has not yet imparted modern learning to most of the nomads in its population.[7] Israel has had educational problems arising from its desire to unify a culture among Jews from all over the world. Traditional Hebrew has been a new language for a large proportion of immigrants, and many leaders have been agnostics or non-conforming reli-

[4] JPRS-NEA-86-001-156, "Strategy of Jordan's 1986-90 Economic Development Plan", Al-Iqtisad Wa Al-A'mal (in Arabic), Beirut, Sept., 1985. pp. 52-54.

[5] JPRS-087-096-21, "The Situation of Rural Women and The Progress Which Has Been Achieved", Al-Thawrah (in Arabic), Damascus, 8 Aug.87, p.5.

[6] JPRS-NEA-086-100-41, "One Year Growth of Services — Development in Process", Ta'izz Al-Jumhuriyah, 13 June 86.

[7] Maxine Molyneux, State Policies and the Position of Women Workers in the People's Democratic Republic of Yemen, ILO, Geneva, 1982.

gionists. There has been wide consensus, however, on working the soil and erecting new industries; so vocational training has been uninhibited.

Education for workers in the Middle East has been enshrined in constitutions, labor codes and official institutions. Its realization has become a progressive phenomenon circumscribed only by traditional inertia and lack of funds.

Chapter 16

LABOR'S INTERESTS IN HUMAN RIGHTS

PERCEPTION OF THE PROBLEM

Observance of human rights is seen in the Middle East as a principal qualification for admittance to the society of civilized nations. If a government is found violating human rights, it is certain to receive condemnation in other countries. Watchdog organizations like Amnesty International and the International Commission of Jurists, established by private devotees, ferret out violations; and there are governmental agencies like the UN Commission on Human Rights created to promote the ideals of the UN Declaration of Human Rights and to seek the enforcement of the UN Covenants which several Middle East nations have signed. It is a matter of national pride for each country to be recognized as a proponent and defender of human rights.

Heads of State have taken pains to identify their traditions with human rights. Precepts of Judaism, Christianity, and Islam have been quoted to demonstrate a commitment to the sanctity of human rights. Political pronouncements have been carefully crafted to display a devotion to those principles. Nonetheless, at one time or another almost every government has found it necessary to "justify" its challenged official activities. The victims of abuse have been accused of illegal anti-government conduct, from subversion to disturbance of the peace; and the need for the degree of severity employed in dealing with them has been at the heart of the dispute. The most common response to alleged inhuman practices in the Middle East has been that they were required to preserve national security. Just what dangers were encountered and how necessary were the actions taken to eliminate the risks have continued to be topics of endless debate. It has become commonplace for most countries to proclaim human rights and to insist that criticisms leveled at their own government were unwarranted.

Not all human rights are considered of equal importance. The UN Universal Declaration of Human Rights catalogues a large number of human rights — several hundred by count if one is not deterred by some overlapping. They impinge upon some cultures more than upon others, and with different implications.

In the Middle East, the right to practice one's religious beliefs has always had a high priority, not only to avoid repression but also to encourage the devout to strengthen their faith. In addition, there has been concern for many separate economic, social, and political rights. Economic rights have been clearly the substance of labor legislation. At the same time, throughout the cultural and civic areas of life there have been other personal rights which have been auxiliary to, and in reality indispensable to, the creation and enforcement of labor laws. The latter are the human rights to which this chapter is addressed.

Labor law is known to thrive or perish as these human rights are observed.

1. The right to organize and assemble;
2. The right to speak freely;
3. The right to print freely;
4. The right to practice one's religion;
5. The right to petition for redress of grievances;
6. The right to personal life and security;
7. The right to a fair trial;
8. The right to just punishment;
9. The right to free movement;
10. The right of suffrage.

These are the conditions of climate and weather under which the makers of labor law and their beneficiaries undertake their day-to-day endeavors.

CONSTITUTIONAL PROVISIONS

The Declaration of Worker Rights

In the constitutions of the Middle East, there are a great variety of human rights provisions. Some are stated absolutely; others with qualifications.

1. *The right to organize and assemble.* The right to form "associations and trade unions" is affirmed in the constitutions of Bahrain, Kuwait, and YAR. Similar provisions refer to "groups, political and professional associations" (Iran), "unions and societies" (Iraq), "societies" (Jordan), "association" (Lebanon), "assembly" (UAE), "mass organizations" (PDRY The draft constitution affirms the right to form national unions).

The protected unions are those formed by peaceful means "on a national basis" and "in accordance with the conditions and procedures prescribed by the law" (Bahrain, Kuwait, YAR). They must have "lawful objectives" and purposes and means "peaceful and not contrary to morals" (Bahrain, Kuwait). They must "not violate principles of independence, freedom, and national unity," nor be "contrary to the principles of Islam or the Islamic Republic" (Iran). They shall be "in accordance with the aims of the Constitution and within the limits of the law" (Iraq, Jordan, Syria).

"No one shall be compelled to join or remain in any association or union" (Bahrain, Kuwait, similarly Iran). In PDRY, however, "The State shall support the mass organizations with the aim of elevating their role and effectiveness in all the social activities, in developing democracy and organizing and mobilizing the workers, peasants, fishermen, youth and all the toiling masses. . ." (omitted from the draft constitution)

The "right of private assembly without permission or prior notification" is also provided (Bahrain, Kuwait, YAR not in the draft constitution). In Bahrain, "no member of the security forces may attend such private meetings."

2. *The right to speak freely.* Nearly all the constitutions in the Middle East guarantee freedom of speech, expression, or opinion within conditions and procedures specified by law (Bahrain, Iraq,

Jordan, Kuwait, Lebanon, Syria, United Arab Emirates, Yemen Arab Republic, PDRY).

Specific requirements for free speech are spelled out — "according to Islamic principles" (Iran); "in line with the nationalist and progressive line of the Revolution" (Iraq), and "in the manner that strengthens the national democratic regime and preserves the public ethics and the state security without prejudice to the freedom and dignity of the citizens" (PDRY). In Syria, every citizen is given the right "to participate in supervision and constructive criticism in a manner that will safeguard the soundness of the domestic and nationalist structure and will strengthen the socialist system."

Secrecy in postal, telegraphic and telephonic communication is guaranteed (Bahrain, Iran, Iraq, Jordan, Kuwait, Yemen Arab Republic, PDRY), except in situations of necessity prescribed by law (Bahrain, Iran, Iraq, Jordan, PDRY), or when forbidden for reasons of state security (Iraq, PDRY), or during a criminal trial (PDRY).

3. *The right to print freely.* The Middle East constitutions guarantee freedom to express opinions in writing, or freedom of the press, much as they do free speech. The same restrictions are specified for the press as for speech. Qatar, which does not refer to free speech, does provide for "freedom of publication and the press . . . in accordance with the law."

Iran declares the State "shall employ every possible means to achieve . . . raising the level of public awareness in all fields, by a correct use of the press, the mass media and other means." It adds that publications shall not be "detrimental to public rights," the details of which are to be provided by law.

4. *The right to practice one's religion.* The preambles to the constitutions of most Arab states contain an invocation to God, the All Merciful and the All Compassionate, and declare a faith in Allah or Islam. Subsequent articles elaborate on the practice of religion.

Islam is declared the State religion in seven Arab nations (Bahrain, Iran, Iraq, Jordan, Kuwait, Qatar, United Arab Emirates, PDRY). The Shariah is said to be "a main source of legislation" (Bahrain, Kuwait, Syria), "a fundamental source" (Qatar), the "principal source" (United Arab Emirates), or "the source of all laws" (Yemen Arab Republic).

The same constitutions proclaim freedom of religion. "Freedom of conscience (or belief) is absolute" (Bahrain, Iran, Iraq, Kuwait, Lebanon). Similarly "freedom of faith" is guaranteed (Syria, PDRY). "The State shall guarantee the inviolability of places of worship and the freedom to perform religious rites . . . processions and meetings in accordance with the customs observed in the country" (Bahrain).

In some constitutions, the guarantee of religious practice is conditioned, "provided that this freedom shall neither contradict the provisions of the Constitution and the law nor violate morality and public order" (Iraq, United Arab Emirates), nor "conflict with public policy or morals" (Kuwait), nor be "inconsistent with public order or decorum" (Jordan, Syria). In pluralistic Lebanon, the constitution guarantees "the personal status and religious interests of the population, to whatever religious sect they belong."

The constitution of Iran is quite explicit: "The official religion of Iran is Islam, and the sect followed is Jafari Shi'ism and this Article is unalterable. Other Islamic denominations such as Hanafi, Shafi'i, Maliki, Hanbali and Zaydi, shall enjoy complete respect . . . free to perform their religious rites . . . personal affairs such as marriage, divorce, inheritance, wills etc. In any region in which the followers of any of these denominations are in the majority, the local regulations . . . will be based on the religious laws governing that denomination." "The Iranian Zoroastrians, Jews and Christians are the only recognized minorities, who, within the limits of the law, are free to perform their own religious rights," personal affairs, and teachings; "the Islamic Republic of Iran and Moslems shall treat non-Moslems according to the dictates of virtue and Islamic justice and to honor their human rights," if they do not become involved in anti-Islamic or anti-Republic activities. "The interrogation of people regarding their beliefs is forbidden. No person shall be attacked for his beliefs." "Absolute sovereignty over the world and mankind is God's and He alone has determined the social destiny of human beings. No one shall take away this God-given right from another person or make use of it to serve his special personal or group interests."

Congregations have a right to establish and maintain their own schools provided they comply with the law (Bahrain, Jordan) and submit their "curriculum and tendency" to government control (Jordan). "The State shall endeavor to instill proper Islamic religious principles in society and to purify it from all manifestations of moral disintegration" (Qatar).

5. *The right to petition for redress of grievances.* Although freedom of speech and press may encompass pleas or protests to the government, a few Middle East constitutions provide explicitly for a right of petition and how it is to be exercised.

"Any individual can address the public authorities in writing and with his signature. Only duly constituted organizations and corporate bodies shall have the right to address the public authorities collectively" (Bahrain, Kuwait). Jordanians are entitled to address public authorities on personal matters or on public affairs in the manner and conditions prescribed by law.

Lodging complaints against the government is also given special attention. In Iran, "a complaint about the way in which the National Assembly, the Executive Power, or the Judicial Power operate" may be submitted to the Assembly which shall demand an investigation and obtain a satisfactory answer "and announce the results in due time"; if "related to the public, the result should be announced to the public." A Tribunal of Administrative Justice shall investigate complaints. In the United Arab Emirates, every person has "the right to submit complaints to competent authorities" concerning the abuse or infringement of rights and freedoms. In the PDRY, "every citizen has the right to lodge complaints to the state organs". . . "either directly or through his social organization."

Public demonstrations also are expressly authorized.

"Unarmed assemblies and marches are permitted provided they do not violate the principles of °Islam" (Iran). Freedom to demonstrate is proclaimed in various ways: In Iraq, "freedom of demonstration"; in Jordan, "public meetings, processions and gatherings"; in Kuwait, "to meet and to demonstrate"; in Syria, "to hold meetings"; in PDRY, "to assemble and demonstrate" not in the draft constitution; in UAE "freedom of assembly and to hold meetings"; and in the YAR, "public meetings and processions" — all within the limits set by law.

6. *The right to personal life and security.* All constitutions in the Middle East guarantee life and oblige the states to promote or protect numerous conditions deemed essential to a better life. Some refer to individuals, some to the community, and some to philosophical or religious aspects of life.

The terms used to express these objectives are (1) *freedom* (Bahrain, Jordan, Kuwait, Syria, United Arab Emirates, Yemen Arab Republic, PDRY); (2) *personal liberty* (Bahrain, Jordan, Kuwait, Lebanon, Syria, PDRY); (3) *justice* (Bahrain, Iran, Kuwait, Qatar, Yemen Arab Republic); (4) *equality* (Bahrain, Iran, Jordan, Kuwait, Qatar, United Arab Emirates, Yemen Arab Republic); (5) *peace and tranquility* (Bahrain, Kuwait, Qatar, Yemen Arab Republic, PDRY); (6) *safety and security* (Bahrain, Iraq, Kuwait, Qatar, Syria, United Arab Emirates, Yemen Arab Republic); (7) *prosperity* (Bahrain, Iraq, Kuwait, Qatar, United Arab Emirates); (8) *well-being* (Bahrain, United Arab Emirates); (9) *solidarity* (Bahrain, Iraq, Yemen Arab Republic); (10) *unity* (Kuwait, Syria, Yemen Arab Republic, PDRY); (11) *dignity* (Iran, Iraq, Kuwait, Qatar, Syria, PDRY); (12) *virtue and competence* (Iran); (13) *personal development* (Iran, Syria); (14) *stability* (Kuwait, Qatar, United Arab Emirates); (15) *power* (Qatar).

The constitutions also call for the promotion of the following goals: (1) *democracy* (Kuwait, Qatar, Syria, United Arab Emirates); (2) *socialism* (Syria, PDRY); (3) *Islamic brotherhood, Koranic justice, piety* (Iran); (4) *Arab nationalism* (Kuwait); (5)

Arab unity (Bahrain, Iran, Iraq, Kuwait, Qatar, Syria, United Arab Emirates, Yemen Arab Republic, PDRY).

The protection of homes and persons from unwarranted search and seizure is pledged by constitutions in almost identical terms.

"Places of residence shall be inviolable. They may not be entered or searched without the permission of their occupants except in the circumstances and manner specified by law" (Bahrain, Iraq, Jordan, Kuwait, Lebanon, Qatar, Syria, United Arab Emirates, Yemen Arab Republic, People's Democratic Republic of Yemen). The YAR extends the protection also against "surveillance"; and the PDRY prohibits "forceful entry except in connection with punishable acts."

7. *The right to a fair trial.* The constitutional assurance of a fair trial is presented in a variety of ways.

(a) *A commitment to justice.* Justice is declared to be fundamental to government (Bahrain, Qatar). So is "the supremacy of law" (Syria) and "democratic legality" (PDRY not in new draft). No crime is to be established except by virtue of law (Bahrain, Iraq, Kuwait, Lebanon, Syria, United Arab Emirates, Yemen Arab Republic). Judges are constrained to follow "reputable Islamic sources or precedents" (Iran), or "the general principles of the Islamic Shariah" (Yemen Arab Republic).

(b) *Limited detention.* No persons are to be detained except as provided by law (Bahrain, Iran, Iraq, Jordan, Kuwait, Lebanon, Syria, United Arab Emirates, PDRY). Detention is to be only in places specified in prison laws, where health and social welfare are observed and there is supervision of judicial authorities (Bahrain).

(c) *Notice of charges.* The accused shall be notified immediately of the accusation "in written form so that he understands it" (Iran).

(d) *Trial by independent judges.* Judges "shall not be subject to any authority" and "no interference whatsoever shall be allowed in the conduct of justice" (Bahrain, Yemen Arab Republic). They shall be subordinate to no authority but the law and their own consciences" (United Arab Emirates); they shall be "divorced from any unsound relationships and connections" (Iran); they shall have "integrity and impartiality" (Kuwait, Syria) and be "independent" (PDRY).

(e) *An early trial.* A "preliminary file shall be submitted to the appropriate judicial authorities," within a maximum of 24 hours; and "preliminaries to the trial shall be completed without delay" (Iran).

(f) *Defense.* The right of defense is guaranteed (Bahrain, Iran, Iraq, Kuwait, Qatar, Syria, United Arab Emirates, Yemen Arab Republic, PDRY). In Iraq that right is called "sacred".

(g) *Representation.* A counsel for defense shall be appointed with the approval of the accused (Bahrain). If litigants "are not able to select an attorney, legal representation shall be provided for them" (Iran). A criminal defendant may "defend himself either personally or through an attorney" (Qatar). Though an "accused shall have the right to appoint the person who shall conduct his defence . . . the law shall prescribe the circumstances in which the presence of a counsel for the defence shall be obligatory" (United Arab Emirates), and "participation of the advocate in the criminal proceedings shall be compulsory in the cases provided for by law" (PDRY), and the law shall specify when legal aid shall be free of charge (PDRY not in the new draft).

(h) *Public trial.* Trials shall be public (Bahrain, Iran, Iraq, Jordan, Kuwait, PDRY); except as prescribed by law (Bahrain, Iraq, Kuwait, PDRY) or when it would conflict with public morals (Iran) or public order (Iran, Jordan) or decorum (Jordan).

(i) *No forced confession.* Any statement or confession "made under duress, enticement, degrading treatment or threat thereof" shall be null and void (Bahrain, Iran, PDRY not in the new draft). So shall an "oath obtained by force" (Iran).

(j) *Presumption of innocence.* There is a presumption of innocence (in Bahrain, Iran, Iraq, Kuwait, Qatar, Syria, United Arab Emirates, Yemen Arab Republic new draft refers only to misdemeanors).

(k) *No ex post facto crimes.* Criminal offenses shall not be enforced retroactively (Bahrain, Iran, Iraq, Kuwait, Qatar, Syria, United Arab Emirates, Yemen Arab Republic, PDRY). Statutes, however, may provide for ex-post facto civil offenses (Iraq, Syria, United Arab Emirates, Yemen Arab Republic omitted from new draft).

8. *The right to a just punishment*. Constitutions of the Middle East forbid penalties except those established by law (Bahrain, Iran, Iraq, Kuwait, Lebanon, Syria, United Arab Emirates, Yemen Arab Republic, PDRY). In Iran, judges "shall establish punishment according to the Law of God." Punishment is said to be "personal" (Bahrain, Iraq, Kuwait, PDRY) or "individual" (United Arab Emirates, Yemen Arab Republic).

No person shall be subjected to "torture" (Bahrain, Iran, Iraq, Kuwait, Syria, United Arab Emirates, PDRY) or to "degrading treatment" (Bahrain, Kuwait), "humiliating treatment" (Syria), "unhuman treatment" (PDRY), or "physical or moral injury" (Bahrain, Kuwait), or "physical, mental abuse" (United Arab Emirates), or "cruel or inhuman penalty" (PDRY), or to a violation of dignity or honor (Iran), or to an indignity (United Arab Emirates).

Confiscation of possessions may be punishment only as provided by law or when based on a legal ruling (United Arab Emirates).

There shall be no capital punishment except as provided by law and confirmed by the King (Jordan), the President (Iraq), or the Republican Council (Yemen Arab Republic omitted from new draft).

The judicial power shall "punish and rehabilitate the criminal" (Iran). "Prison is for punishment and reform" (Yemen Arab Republic not in new draft).

9. *The right to free movement*. Middle Eastern constitutions provide for freedom of movement within certain restraints.

No restriction shall be placed upon movement inside the country except as defined by law (Iraq, PDRY) or "by a judicial sentence, or in implementation of public health and safety laws" (Syria), or to protect state security or public health (PDRY).

One's residence is recognized at "the place of his choosing . . . except as determined by law" (Iran, Iraq, Jordan, United Arab Emirates).

"No citizen shall be deported" (Bahrain, Iran, Kuwait, Syria, United Arab Emirates), or "exiled" (Jordan), or "banished" (United Arab Emirates), or "expelled" (Yemen Arab Republic). Nor shall a citizen be denied re-entry (Bahrain, Iraq, Kuwait). In PDRY, "the law shall regulate . . . entry to and egress from the country."

10. *The right of suffrage*. The right to vote in elections is guaranteed by all the constitutions in the Middle East.

Reference is also made to conditions or procedures set forth in laws (Bahrain, Jordan, Kuwait, Lebanon, Qatar, Syria). In Iran, the country is to be administered "in accordance with public opinion expressed through elections." In the UAE, each emirate shall determine the method of selection of members of the national legislature.

Elections are required to be "direct and secret" (Jordan, Kuwait, Syria), and by "universal suffrage" (Kuwait, PDRY).

Voting is limited to "citizens (Bahrain, Lebanon, Syria, YAR), "nationals" (Iraq), and such persons over the age of 18 (Iraq) or 21 (Lebanon).

LABOR CODE AND STATUTORY PROVISIONS

In view of the repeated conditioning of human rights by Middle East constitutions with the phrase "in accordance with the law", it would appear that statutory enactments on the subject would be quite significant. There have been many such laws. Generally, they have appeared separately from the labor codes (though not entirely) and they have dealt with national crises or security precautions. Occasionally, statutes or decrees have sought to correct reported abuses of human rights. I have included some pertinent enactments in the listing of all the labor laws I have been able to find in the Appendix. However, since the constitutional provisions on human rights are so pervasive I have foregone the tremendous task of searching for all additional statutes. Several that have received public notoriety will be referred to in comments below.

The Middle East countries that do not have constitutions (Israel, Oman and Saudi Arabia) all profess to observe the Universal Declaration of Human Rights; and they have acknowleged a status of law for such rights in whatever statutes or decrees they have issued.

TREATY PROVISIONS

The UN Covenant on Civil and Political Rights, ratified by Iran, Iraq, Israel, Jordan, Lebanon, Syria, and PDRY, is the principal treaty on human rights. It specifies every one of the rights discussed herein as derived from the inherent dignity of the human person. It establishes a Human Rights Committee, elected by signatories from the nominees of all countries. The Committee is to receive initial reports from governments, and may receive complaints, communicate with the state involved, offer its good offices with a view to a friendly solution, and report to the UN Economic and Social Council and through it to the UN General Assembly.

All Middle East countries, as members of the United Nations, have subscribed to the UN Charter which includes an affirmation of "faith in fundamental human rights, in the dignity and worth of the human person, in the equal rights of men and women." The Charter also charges member states "to promote social progress and better standards of life."

CONSEQUENCES AND INCIDENTALS

The saga of human rights in the Middle East has been lengthy and variegated. Episodes of infringement and personal molestation have been reported by victims and recorded by communal agencies as well as by international organizations, including Amnesty International,[1] the International Commission of

[1] Amnesty International Israel and the Occupied Territories, Amnesty International Concerns in 1988, New York, 1989; Amnesty International, Iran: Violations of Human Rights, London, 1987; Amnesty International USA, Torture in Iraq, 1982-84,

Jurists,[2] and the UN Human Rights Commission.[3] The U.S. State Department has sent an annual report on the human rights situation in every country to the U.S. Congress[4]; and numerous publications have analyzed the human rights policies of Middle East governments.[5] The effect of such policies upon labor law has often been direct and immediate, as in the protection or prosecution of trade union officials for their participation in demonstrations or their advocacy of new labor laws. Over time the governmental policies have slowly and consistently created a social climate in which progress in labor standards has been either stimulated or suffocated.

New York, 1985; Amnesty International USA, Town Arrest Orders in Israel and the Occupied Territories, New York, 1984; Amnesty International, Report and Recommendations of an AIM Mission and the Republic of Iraq, New York, 1983; Amnesty International, Iran Briefing, London, 1983; Amnesty International, Syria, An A.I. Briefing, London, 1983; Amnesty International, Report from Amnesty International to the Government of the Syrian Arab Republic, London, 1983; Amnesty International, Iraq, Evidence of Torture, London, 1981.

2 International Commission of Jurists, Report on Activities: 1981-1985, Geneva, 1985; International Commission of Jurists, States of Emergency: Their Impact on Human Rights, Geneva; International Commission of Jurists, Human Rights in Islam, Report of a Seminar held in Kuwait, Dec., 1980, Geneva, 1982; International Commission of Jurists, Development of Human Rights and the Rule of Law Conference held in The Hague, April 27-May 1, 1981, Pergamon Press, 1982; Jonathan Kuttab, Civilian Administration in the Occupied West Bank, Law in the Service of Man, International Commission of Jurists, Geneva, 1982; Rule of Law in the Areas Administered by Israel, Israel National Section of the International Commission of Jurists, Tel Aviv, 1981; Raja Shehaded, The West Bank and the Rule of Law, International Commission of Jurists and Law in the Service of Man, Geneva, 1980.

3 United Nations, Commission on Human Rights, Report on the Forty-fifth Session, Economic and Social Council, Official Records, 1989.

4 U.S. Department of State, Country Reports on Human Rights Practices for 1988, 101st Congress, 1st Session, Washington, D.C., 1988.

5 Al-Haq, Law in the Service of Man, Demolition and Sealing of Houses as a Punitive Measure in the Israeli-Occupied West Bank, Occasional Paper No. 5, 1987; Armond de Mestral, ed., The Limitation of Human Rights in Comparative Constitutional Law, Yvon Blaes, Inc., Quebec, 1987; America's Watch, Four Failures, A Report on the UN Special Rapporteurs on Human Rights in Chile, Guatemala, Iran & Poland, Jan. 1986; Amer. Friends Service Committee, Lebanon; Toward Legal Order & Respect for Human Rights, Advisory Committee on Human Rights in Lebanon, 1985; George W. Shepherd, Jr., ed., Human Rights & Third World Development, Greenwood Press, Westport, Conn., 1985; David Ott, Politics, Human Rights & the West Bank, Quartet Books, Ltd., London, 1980.

LABOR LAWS IN THE MIDDLE EAST

Recognitions and Violations

A very brief review of the recent state of affairs on human rights in the Middle East may not give sufficient credit to those officials and citizens who have worked steadfastly to preserve human rights (the virtuous are often unacclaimed because they do what is expected of them); but those accused of violating human rights, their strenths and weaknesses, require disclosure if they are to be reformed or overcome. The following account therefore presents highlights of conditions that need attention.

Organization and assembly. Probably the human right most vital to the progress of labor law is the freedom to organize and assemble. In a few Middle East countries, trade unions have been expressly prohibited or officially discouraged (Oman, Qatar, Saudi Arabia, UAE, and until 1985, Iran). In other countries, they have been circumscribed by regulations, such as the prohibition of political acitivity (Bahrain, Iran, Lebanon) or the denial of the right to organize for public employees (Iraq, Lebanon) or a limitation upon voting and holding office in unions by guest workers (Kuwait). In contrast, Israel and the PDRY have officially encouraged the formation of unions and have incorporated their activities in the economic and social programs of their governments.

The right to assemble has been similarly treated in different ways. In Kuwait, any three or more persons desiring to hold a meeting for public discussion or the proposal of resolutions must obtain the approval of the Minister of the Interior. Discreet political discussions are held in homes or social clubs in many countries. Monitoring of organization meetings by unidentified agents is said to be commonplace. Public demonstrations require a government permit, and some are staged by the government.

Free speech and press. Throughout the Middle East certain public utterances are forbidden. In the States ruled by a king, sultan, amir or royal family, citizens have been punished for making offensive remarks about the head of government, or members of his family; or for disputing the objectives and activities of the government (Bahrain, Iraq, Jordan, Kuwait, Oman,

Qatar, Saudi Arabia, UAE). In the countries with representative forms of government, there are other subjects which have been tabooed and made unlawful. In Iran, criticism of the clergy has become a capital offense. In Iraq, self determination for the Kurds has been anathema. In Israel, "inciting support for organizations hostile to Israel . . . or publicly to express support for the PLO" has been declared a crime. In Syria, opposition to the Ba'ath party is not permitted. In the two Yemens, advocacy in one for the other had at one time been deemed treason. The above is not to say that the concept of freedom of speech was not appreciated, even idolized, by the people or statesmen in the countries mentioned; but there are ideas that have not been tolerated.

Limitations upon the printed and pictorial media have been even more stringent. State-owned or controlled newspapers, and radio and television stations have not only refrained from offending the government, but have also omitted or submerged any foreign news deemed critical of their government's official policies. Censorship of the privately owned press has been imposed in all the countries (Bahrain, Iran, Iraq, Israel, Jordan, Kuwait, Lebanon, Oman, Qatar, Saudi Arabia, UAE, YAR, PDRY) and on occasion the Ministers of Information have suspended publication or closed the plants of recalcitrant offenders. Foreign publications have also been routinely censored before distribution. The degree of deletion or obliteration has varied widely; and the publication of different views shared among citizens has produced disparate results, notably a wide range of public dispute in Israel and a dearth of critical opinions in Oman and Qatar.

Freedom of religion. Although freedom of religion is a basic human right for the entire community, it has had special implications for workers as expressed in employment preferances and the denial of opportunities for advancement.

Several Middle East countries have declared Islam to be the state religion (Bahrain, Iran, Iraq, Jordan, Kuwait, UAE, PDRY), and Israel has proclaimed itself a Jewish state. However, all of these governments have announced freedom of religion for other faiths. Nonetheless, qualification for civil service employment, which is substantial throughout the region, is ordinarily weighted strongly in favor of the primary religion. Outright exclusion from that and other forms of employment follows from the banning of a few small religions. Syria denies Seventh Day Adventist Christians (who refuse to take oaths of allegiance to the State) the right to practice their religion in that country. Kuwait does not recognize Hindus, Sikhs, and Buddhists as entitled to protection since they are not mentioned in the Koran. Iran has declared Bahais to be apostates under Islam, and therefore it has not only denied them public employment but has also induced many private employers to discharge them from existing positions. Within all Muslim countries, affiliation with Islamic sects is known and even though there is official acceptance of each other, preferences for members of the majority sect are often asserted.

Proselytizing of devotees of the official religion by other religionists is generally forbidden, and converts away from the dominant creed are objects of social and economic discrimination. Agnostics or atheists, are relativey few in number and are treated as outcasts in Muslim states.

Right of movement. The freedom of Middle East citizens to move about within their homeland, and to depart and return, is widely acknowledged except in security zones. Such restricted zones are established in Iran, Iraq, Israel, Jordan, Lebanon, Oman, Syria, and UAE. Travel restrictions are sometimes imposed upon nationals for domestic reasons such as the limitation of trips to Iran by Bahrain, the posting of bonds to assure return in Iran, and the need of a permit for Kuwaitis to attend Trade Union conferences abroad.

The most pervasive restraint is placed on the migration of workers. Checkpoints for the control of their movement exist throughout the area. Passports, work permits and the requirement of employer sponsorship have supported a tight and confining command over the flow of workers. Not only to and from the oil countries; in the Yemens, it was not until 1988 that they agreed to accept just the display of identification cards for passage between them.

In some Muslim countries, the consent of a male relative is required for the foreign travel of a woman. Intermarriage with nonMuslims has been discouraged by the denial of passports to the undesired spouse or the children of the union.

Arbitrary arrests, detentions and exiles. The arbitrariness of an arrest has often been an issue in Middle East countries. Laws limiting the length of detention and providing review procedures have been safeguards against abuse; but in most Middle East countries, they have been waived in security cases. Holding security prisoners without the filing of charges, and often incommunicado, has been reported in every country. Even in Oman where there has been no recent political dissension, members of the Popular Front for the Liberation of Oman were imprisoned between 1967 and 1975 (those who fled to the PDRY were offered amnesty until 1986). Detentions for days and months have been noted in every country that has been engaged in war or has faced insurgency.

The exile of some adversaries in political struggles has occured in Bahrain, Iran, Iraq, Israel, Qatar and Syria. Deportation of expatriate workers, who have violated immigration or permit laws (or who have been accused by dissatisfied employers to have overstayed their work permits) has been a fairly common occurence. In Kuwait, it is estimated such deportations have numbered 15,000 in 1988 and even higher numbers in previous years.

Arbitrary interference with privacy. Searches and seizures without a warrant have been common in security cases. The law does not require a warrant in such situations in Iraq, Oman, Qatar, Saudi Arabia, Syria, and YAR. The tapping of phones and the opening of mail, for national security, are permitted in most Middle East countries. In Islamic states, marriage with non-Muslims is forbidden, and in Israel, marriage between Jews without the formalities of orthodox rabbis is not recognized.

Torture. No Middle East country admits that it has tortured prisoners; but the security police in every one of the countries have been accused of attempting to secure confessions in many brutal ways. Beatings with fists, rubber truncheons or whips, the application of electric shocks to genitals and other parts of the body, the extraction of fingernails and toenails, dousing with hot and cold water, excessive physical exposure, sexual assaults, threats of death and imprisonment of family members, have all been confirmed by prisoners and others. Such abuses have been reported in too many cases to be considered beyond official knowledge. The extent of atrocities has been concealed by the refusal of most governments to permit relatives to visit prisoners in security cases. Few governments have punished any of its offenders.

Amnesty International has compiled lists of victims with their stories and has submitted them to the governments of Iran, Iraq, Israel, and Syria for further investigation and response. Denials and justifications have been the usual response. However, Saudi Arabia issued a new decree defining proper interrogation procedures. An Israeli Landau Commission reported in 1987 that its security service routinely engaged in physical and psychological mistreatment to obtain confessions, and the government ordered the discontinuance of such methods.[6] The International Red Cross has been invited by Kuwait and other countries to make prison inspections with some benevolent results.

Fair trial. Courts in the Middle East are of several catagories — civil, religious, military, tribal, security, and labor; and they vary in their rules and procedures. All are dedicated to the pursuit of justice, each in its own way. The features that are ordinarily associated with due process of law are at the cutting edge of human rights. Legal safeguards, such as formal notice of the offense charged, opportunity to interrogate accusers, defense by learned counsel, trials open to the public, avenues for appeal or review, all in response to published rules of law, are universal rubrics of justice. They are generally respected, except by offi-

[6] Edy Kaufman and Nadir Tsur, "Walking on a Tightrope", Present Tense, Sept.-Oct. 1989, pp. 39-44.

cials fearful of the loss of national (at times personal) security or advantage.

The denial of some of the usual protections may be rooted in traditional practices that do not necessarily conflict with human rights. Old Islamic trial procedures, whereby attorneys help prepare litigants but do not participate in the trial, or in which there is no jury trial, may or may not be significant. The application of religious principles on marriage and divorce, or the weight to be attached to certain kinds of testimony, found in all major religions, may or may not matter in most cases.

The waiver and denial of early charges, legal counsel, public hearings and appeal procedures do seriously diminish, if not deny outright, the prospect of a fair trial. Such flaws have existed in the special courts set up to handle security matters in Middle East countries, even where they have not been allowed in the other courts of the land. Every Middle East country maintains a court system that offers due process, except in security cases, and every country has held defective security trials at one time or another.

The imprisonment of political activists for crimes connected with their challenge to government policies has usually been covered by charges of treason, terrorism, breach of the peace, or other lawless conduct. The number of political prisoners in custody at any time is rarely announced or admitted. Security trials are secret and records are often not kept. In all Middle East countries engaged in war or public violence, political prisoners have been numerous.

Political killings. For national security, killing has been "justified". Alleged subversives and the measures taken to suppress their activities have at times been publicized. In Bahrain, clandestine political groups linked with Iranian fundamentalists and leftist advocates have been identified as the Bahrain National Liberation Front and the Popular Front for the Liberation of Bahrain. These have been held responsible for an unsuccessful coup in 1981, and punished accordingly. In Iran, the Islamic Republican Party was ordered to disband in 1987; and pro-Soviet groups had been prohibited for some time followed by many arrests, imprisonments and executions. In Iraq, a Da'wa Organization supported by Iranians was targeted for extinction; and in 1987 and 1988, the entire minority population of Kurds was accused of rebellion, many were killed, and thousands were forced to relocate their homes. In Israel, the Palestine Liberation Organization has been declared terrorist and retaliatory deadly missions have been Israel's frequent response. The outlawing of the PLO has been continued even after its recent public acceptance of the Israeli State and its renunciation of terrorism. The intifada demonstration by resident Arabs, with stones and hand bombs, has been countered by shooting and deaths. In Kuwait, bombings have been punished as crimes associated with Shi'a fundamentalists. Public outlawing of entire associations — in Oman, the Popular Front for the Liberation of Oman, in Syria, the Muslim Brotherhood and Communist groups — have resulted in executions.

The killing of human beings in the Middle East has become almost casual. The snuffing out of civilian lives in the wars raging in Iran, Iraq and Lebanon has become so routine it has rarely been described as a human crime. Paradoxically, war is not classified as political killing in violation of human rights. That special verdict is reserved for individual assassinations. Unfortunately, executions by governments, always explained as necessary to prevent or avenge other killings, have occured innumerable times. Apart from the deliberate infliction of death in the well-publicized wars, there have been many political killings in less acknowledged situations. Iraq has killed many thousands of rebellious Kurds, even using poisonous gas in the field and hangings in Bagdad. Between 1982 and 1988, it is reported that the YAR put to death about 250 members of the National Democratic Front, supported by leftist PDRY; and the PDRY, it has been reported, killed 50 of its own citizens plotting for YAR against its national security in 1988. Ironically it appears worthy of special recognition when there has been no recent political killing in certain countries.

Disapperances. The disappearance of persons arrested on suspicion of subversive activities has not been noted as often in the Middle East as in authoritarian countries of Latin America. Statistics of war casualties have probably concealed some deaths in unreported disappearances. In Lebanon, thousands of civilians have been unaccounted for. It is alleged that many have been kidnapped there and detained in Syria and Israel, and many detainees have been released. In the YAR, occasional arrests by secret police have been said to have led to disappearances; and in the PDRY, tribal and factional fighting has resulted in similar reports. The number of alleged disappearances has not demonstrated a continuous Middle East government policy to dispose of subversives in that manner.

Compulsory or forced labor. There has been no indication that any Middle East country knowingly tolerates forced labor. In Saudi Arabia, labor courts have ruled against an employer's requirement of more work than is called for in a contract of employment. In Iraq and Iran, soldiers have been assigned some tasks that would ordinarily be performed by civilians. In Lebanon, militia men have forced common laborers to fill sandbags to be placed around buildings or to clean offices wrecked by bombs; and physicians have been obliged to render services without compensation. Fortunately, such incidents have been rare.

Denial of suffrage. The right of individuals in the Middle East to determine the nature of the government over them has been subjected to many qualifications. That applies to the over-all choice of an absolute monarchy or a democracy or a governmental system in-between; it is true as well for the exertion of pressure to effect basic change in the programs of an administration. There is no right of citizens to vote for public officials in Bahrain, Jordan, Oman, Qatar, Saudi Arabia, UAE, and YAR. Women have no suffrage in Kuwait. Parliament or the National Assembly has been dissolved by rulers in Bahrain, Jordan and Kuwait. In some Muslim countries, the traditional practice of the sultan giving audience to anyone with a grievance has been continued (Saudi Arabia, UAE); and formal consultations are held between the ruler and civilian advisers (Oman, Qatar). It has been argued that political freedom includes the right to choose governmental systems that are traditional, theocratic, or undemocratic; but from the standpoint of the development of labor law, such governments have been resistant or oppressive, and have frequently restricted or denied the human rights of persons striving for the improvement of life.

One of the most distinctive factors in the human rights situation in the Middle East is the attitude taken toward the large number of workers who were imported from other countries. Expatriate workers are regarded as a threat to the purity, status and self-sufficiency of the native population. The alien workers may be a necessary addition, but they have been considered a burden. They have been given more money than they could have earned at home, so it is believed no further attention to their needs is required. If they insist upon other rights they have been replaced; more than that, since they may become a social irritant in the future, they have been treated as temporary residents and closely controlled. Even when guest workers are welcome and receive humane treatment, they are considered and treated as outsiders. They are given privileges, not rights. It is often forgotten that human rights are intended for all human beings.

Documentation of Continuing Controversies

I have endeavored in the foregoing account of the laws and the divergent practices on human rights to limit my statements to what has been confirmed by reputable observers and scholars. Accusations and justifications continue, and may be read in voluminous reports. I shall review two typical controversies, one involving Iraq and the other, Israel.

(1) *Iraq*. Illustrative of the reports on human rights violations and the reactions of the governments involved are the back and forth statements between Amnesty International (hereinafter referred to as A.I.) and Iraq.

In 1975, A.I. sent a letter to the government of Iraq concerning 5 reported deaths under torture. Iraq's response was a categorical denial of the allegations, at the same time asserting that the state had a right to guarantee the security of its nationals and therefore could not "allow corrupt elements to disturb the public order and to expose to danger the security and stability of the state."

In its annual 1975-76 report, A.I. said it had received the names of 43 Kurds who allegedly had died during torture. The reply merely recited Iraq's constitutional provisions prohibiting torture.

A 1981 A.I. Report, entitled "Iraq Evidence of Torture" presented 15 case histories of persons who testified that between 1976 and 1979, among other things, they had been severely beaten on the soles of their feet, forced to run on hot, salty water, jabbed with live electrodes on their faces, breasts, genitals, nostrils or abdomens, suspended by handcuffed wrists from a wall or a step ladder for several hours, and subjected to mock executions (like the pulling of a trigger in an unloaded pistol held to one's head). They were promised rewards if they confessed. Findings of medical men who examined the 15 indicated that all had symptoms and signs, some transient, some permanent, consistent with their allegations, and nothing appeared inconsistent therewith. Iraq described that report as "without foundation."

A.I. requested permision to send a delegation to confer with Iraqi officials. The mission took place in 1983. A.I. issued a report reiterating the earlier charges and others. Iraq replied formally and in detail. Among other responses, it stated that the A.I. memorandum contained falsehoods, that no names of victims or torturers had been given for verification, that there were no "political executions" in Iraq (or the figures submitted were exaggerated and inaccurate), that the party "Al Da'wa", mentioned by A.I. was a fifth column of Iran seeking to invade Iraq and annex its territory (and the humane attitude of the government was demonstrated by a general amnesty given to all detainees of that party, even those sentenced to death).

In its memorandum, A.I. had offered some recommendations that might prevent tortures. Iraq replied, the "A.I. recommendations were phrased in such a way as to seem to be an instruction contrary to accepted forms of international communication and to constitute a blatant departure from the principle of national sovereignty"; furthermore the recommendation that a head of state make a declaration condemning torture would be quite unusual since that was already deemed contrary to all humanitiarian, ethical and legal principles; similarly the recommendation to supply texts of UN Declarations to officials was unnecessary since their equivalents were already in Iraqi statutes; moreover the President's directives to the security forces and numerous Police Department directives had already warned against abuse of power and the police training college had taught the use of proper investigation procedures; in addition, Iraqi judicial practice included safeguards to protect detainees from assault. The reply asked rhetorically how the recommended actions could prove more effective than the letter of the law.

Later, A.I. supplied the names of victims, theretofore mentioned, and 16 more reported to it; and it referred to an earlier publication of a list of 255 Iraqis reported to have been executed in 1978-79. A.I. repeated its opinion that further measures were needed in addition to basic statutes, and it recommended stringent rules on access to prisoners, interrogation methods, supervision of interrogators and prison wardens, and investigation of complaints. It noted that the government had produced no information to suggest that its law prohibiting torture had been obeyed.

In 1985, A.I. published another report, entitled "Torture in Iraq 1982-84". It added many details, supplying names, dates, injuries and medical confirmation, on 5 more cases of torture.

(2) *Israel.* Another example of alleged human rights violations and the responses received from the country involved can be found in the publications on Israeli treatment of Arabs in the occupied territories of Palestine.

The International Commission of Jurists published a report entitled, *The West Bank and the Rule of Law* prepared by attorneys for an IJC affiliate called Law in the Service of Man. Its recitation of Israeli restrictions on basic rights was answered by a publication, *The Rule of Law in the Areas Administered by*

Israel, written by Israeli lawyers who composed an Israel National Section of the IJC. Thus lawyers were pitted against lawyers on the issue of human rights in a focal point of the Middle East.

On the question of what law prevailed in the occupied territories, there was a common recognition that the law of Jordan had preceeded the Israeli occupation; that since 1967 proclamations of the Military Commander governed; and that the Hague Regulations and the 4th Geneva Convention set standards for the control of enemy territory by military rulers. The charge of the Law in Service of Man (hereinafter referred to as LSM) was that military rulers were restricted to regultions required to maintain military security and that after 13 years in which the security forces maintained tight control, the Israeli government had gone far beyond international law in taking charge of all domestic, political, economic and social activities, with the obvious intent of annexing Palestine under an assumed Biblical right to Samaria and Judea. Israel had abolished the local Court of Cassation and substituted its own distant system of courts without maintaining due processes of law.

The Israeli response was that the West Bank was not Jordanian land except by seizure; that it was part of Samaria and Judea; and that the regulations of Israeli authorities still met all the standards prescribed by Jordanian law and the Geneva Convention and the Hague Regulations.

The treatment of specific human rights was then discussed as they affected a wide range of public matters. Since this book is concerned primarily with labor law, I shall limit my presentation to those claims and defenses that relate to several human rights of particular significance to workers and labor leaders.

(1) Limitation on freedom of movement by workers. The LSM stated that under military orders the West Bank was made "a closed area" into and out of which all movement was prohibited without a permit; these were issued within the personal discretion of a military governor and withheld or denied to prevent trade

union activity. The Israeli response was that permits were refused only to avoid action against peace and security.

(2) Prohibition of overnight stay in Israel. The requirement of a permit for an Arab worker residing in the territories to remain in Israel overnight forced such workers to commute long distances with great hardship and a sense of oppression. The Israeli response was that special permits had been issued to accommodate personal needs; in 1979 some 11,300 had been granted; and it should be understood that the majority of those Arabs working in Israel lived within 30 kilometers of their place of employment, many of whom travelled by transport organized by their employers.

(3) The requirement of identity cards. The LSM observed that all workers were required to carry personal identity cards that were frequently asked to be shown to police and soldiers, who could confiscate cards at will; and failure to have a card in one's possession subjected a worker to immediate arrest. The response was that Jews as well as Arabs were obliged to carry cards at all times and that many countries required their residents to do so.

(4) The prohibition of strikes for political change. The LSM made a point of the violent manner in which strikes in commercial establishments and at schools and universities were suppressed. In the former, they claimed soldiers would break locks and open doors by force, or proceed to the homes of merchants and force them at gunpoint to open their shops. Schools were closed with tear gas, shooting and arrests. Specific incidents were identified. A UN vocational training center lost a whole academic year because of closures. The reply was a general statement on the right under international law to restrict a strike which takes on a political character.

(5) The censorship and banning of pro-Arab newspapers and books. The LSM stated that military regulations required licenses to publish; newspapers in Arabic (as well as in Hebrew) were censored prior to publication, no blank spaces were permitted where excisions were made; and critical Arab editors had their licenses suspended and reinstated under continuous threat of rep-

etition. The reply was that Israeli censorship was very liberal; the Arab newspapers cited had published headlines encouraging terrorism and strikes calling for 'armed struggle'; and censorship was applied only to passages that clearly incited hatred and disorder, constituting a threat to security and day-to-day life.

(6) The denial of academic freedom to teachers. The LSM complained of the banning of Jordanian textbooks (listed 55), the official rewriting of books, the placement of informers in classrooms, and the dismissal, at times deportation, of teachers who expressed opposition to the practicies of the military governors. They claimed a failure to build enough schools for the growing population; the overcrowding of classrooms and the arrest and harrassment of scholars who attempted to do research. The Israeli reply presented statistics on the increase of pupils, teachers and classes, the permission given for setting up four private universities and more technical institutions; and the need to screen teachers to prevent the infiltration of persons hired by terrorist organizations with the purpose of inciting to violence and fomenting disorder. Academic freedom, they maintained, did not embrace freedom to disturb public order through demonstrations with burning of tires, blocking traffic on a main road, and throwing rocks, stones and Molotov cocktails at security forces.

(7) The infliction of collective punishment. The LSM attorneys set forth specific instances in which families, neighbors, bystanders and entire towns or villages were punished for crimes committed by extremists, without any trial or any demonstration of connivance or participation by those punished. In those cases, homes were demolished, clearly uninvolved individuals were arrested and detained for long periods of time, and continuous curfews were imposed on villages preventing the care of domestic livestock and the harvesting of crops required for the sustenance of whole communities. The Israeli attorneys replied the homes destroyed had been used to prepare explosives and store ammunition; demolition was used with extreme caution; some rooms were sealed up to be reopened if such practices were discontinued. The LSM cited specific cases of abuse and the reply cited

other cases of proven terrorism.[7]

With respect to every one of the above alleged violations of human rights, the Israeli attorneys quoted passages from the Hague regulations, the Geneva Convention, and Jordanian law that permitted the denial or restriction of such rights in situations in which the occupying authority found it necessary to preserve law and order. The attorneys argued that Israel had exercised more consideration and generosity than were required by principles of international law. The protests of the International Commission of Jurists were based on its belief that the normal guarantees of judicial due process were not observed in ascertaining whether national security had been placed in jeopardy and who was individually responsible for whatever breaches of the peace occured. The LSM attorneys not only challenged the validity of Israeli findings of a threat to national security; they asserted that Israel ignored its obligation to take affirmative steps to protect human rights even in disturbing situations, and that it did so because its real intent was to convert the occupied territories into lands of its own.

In 1983, the ICJ, with the consent of Israel, sent a delegation of educators to visit institutions of higher learning in the West Bank and Gaza. A lengthy report called for a fundamental reappraisal of the relationship between Israeli military authorities and the Palestinian education institutions. It stated that other considerations than legal ones must be taken into account in determining what limitations on academic freedom are proper during an occupation that has lasted for more than 17 years and with uncertainty as to the future of the area.

In 1985, the ICJ published another report prepared by LSM, on torture in the Israeli army prison camp at Al-Fara from May 1982 to May 1984. Twenty affidavits were signed by former

[7] About 800 houses were reported demolished since the beginning of the intifada for offenses ranging from resisting arrest to stone throwing, preparation of incendiary bombs and burning of cars. JPRS-NEA-89-058-27, Gabi Bashan, Collective Punishment, A. Hamishmar (in Hebrew), Tel Aviv, June 2, 1989, p 8. See also, Z. Lockman & J. Beinin, eds., Intifada: The Palestinian Uprising Against Israeli Occupation, May 1989.

detainees; five described harassment, humiliation and indignity with inadequate food and unhygienic facilities; ten described interrogation techniques aimed at procuring a confession; these included isolation in cells awash with filthy water, standing naked in the rain at night, beating on the genitals, kicking with steel-capped shoes, burning with lighted cigarettes, dousing with buckets of urine and cold water and various other forms of extreme humiliation and brutalization; three other detainees attested to a lack of medical care such as the refusal of a doctor unless they confessed or the calling of a doctor only after the signing of a false confession. Israel's Defence Minister described the report as "total nonsense". An Israeli ambasssador attacked the ICJ and the LSM before the UN Commission on Human Rights. However, an army captain was convicted by a military court of an assault on prisoners at Al-Fara's prison. The International Red Cross was allowed to visit the prison camp; but its report has been kept confidential.[8]

Such accusations and official responses have been too numerous to be ignored. In most instances, the violation of acknowledged human rights has been denied by the accused perpetrator. The nature of the dispute over culpability has clearly indicated fears, suspicions, and emotional disturbances that render some governments unwilling or incapable of acknowledging their deficiencies. Many governmental authorities have fashioned justifications for behavior that was abhorrent to their own moral values.

The willingness of some nations to investigate charges of human rights violations themselves or to allow visitations by external organizations has been a measure of their devotion to

[8] In 1988, the Institute for Palestine Studies (Washington,D.C.) issued a revision of the ICJ report on Israel's treatment of human rights in the West Bank (Raja Shehadeh, Occupier's Law: Israel and the West Bank). It repeated earlier statements and added numerous accusations arising out of the resistance to the intifada. The main thrust of the report is the charge that Israel has been endeavoring to absorb the West Bank as its own territory, contrary to international law, that Israeli authorities have misinterpreted well recognized principles of international law and when that failed to convince other countries, Israel has claimed its situation is so unique the old rules do not apply to it.

human rights, or the degree of their sense of insecurity. Bahrain permitted Amnesty International to visit it in 1987. Iran refused permission for an investigation by the UN Commission on Human Rights in 1984, but allowed Amnesty International to come in in 1987. Iraq rejected UN requests to check the use of chemical weapons but cooperated with the International Red Cross and the UN High Commissioner for Refugees. Jordan allowed the Red Cross to inspect its prisons and responded to Amnesty International interrogatories; its bar association has a committee on Human Rights, and it has played an active role on the UN Human Rights Commission. Israel invited the International Labor Organization to conduct a series of investigations of conditions in the occupied territories (See pages 92 - 95 above). The scarcity of such cooperative endeavors may emphasize the fact that the art of diplomacy is still in its infancy.

There are many needs in society, and difficult choices are unavoidable. What benefits one human being often harms another. The UN Declaration of Human Rights, approved by all civilized nations, is an effort to establish standards that should not be breached. The burden of justifying any breach, it would seem, calls for proof beyond reasonable doubt. However, in the Middle East (as elsewhere), reason has vied with nationalistic preferences, with unquestioning acceptance of religious revelations, and with profound emotional loyalties. These have not been amenable to rational argument. Fortunately, there have been human, moral values in all peoples. The mere disclosure of the brutality in flagrant violations of human rights, even when they have been exceptional aberrations, has persisted. Accusations have tended to lead to the discovery of unrecognized horrors, to some restraint upon offenders, and to more positive measures to protect human rights.

Chapter 17

THE SUM OF THINGS SAID

The art of labor law comparison begins with the simple observation that the law of one country differs from the law of others. From then on, the possibilities of interpretation are infinite. One of the possible moves forward is to place the laws in juxtaposition with each other, like hanging similar garments out to dry on a clothes line. That I have done with constitutional, statutory, and treaty provisions, grouped under separate topics of labor law. The presence or absence of contributions from the several Middle East states have been rather obvious, and similarities and differences in the legal texts have also been fairly noticeable. But the details have been quite numerous and before undertaking the more difficult task of commenting upon the significance of the array, it would be helpful to summarize the labor laws on each of the topics studied.

THE STATUS OF LABOR IN THE ECONOMIC AND SOCIAL ORDER

1. *On a Special Role for Labor.* The notion of labor as a distinct focus of law assumes various shades of meaning. In the constitutions of the Middle East there is an expressed concern for labor as an element of the economy in conjunction with property and capital, for work as a social function, for work as a basis of development, and for work as the gratification of personal dignity and the public good. In three countries, Iraq, Syria and PDRY, workers are charged with a socialistic mission. These views underlie codes and other statutes that regulate specific aspects of labor life.

2. *On Slavery and Forced Labor.* Slavery has been condemned so universally, it has seemed unnecessary to announce its prohibition. Only the constitution of the UAE has stated slavery is not to be; however, Iran, Iraq, Israel, Jordan, Kuwait, Saudi Arabia

and Syria have ratified the League of Nations convention to abolish slave trade.

Forced labor, also of ill repute, has received more specific treatment. The constitutions of Bahrain, Kuwait, Jordan, UAE and YAR ban forced labor, with permitted exceptions — for emergencies in Bahrain, Jordan, Kuwait, public health and safety in Jordan, public interest in UAE, YAR, and judicial decision in Bahrain and Jordan. A law in Israel provides for the requirement of labor in prisons and in a labor training program. Labor not agreed upon (with exceptions for accidents, force majeure and essential activities) has been prohibited in Bahrain and Oman. All Middle East countries, except Oman and Qatar, have signed the ILO Convention 29, prohibiting forced labor, but allowing the states to permit forced labor in work of a military character, in normal civic obligations of citizens, in connection with a criminal conviction, in emergencies of war and natural disaster, and in service dictated through community consultation. In prohibiting the "exploitation" of workers, Iran, Syria, and PDRY may have also inferentially outlawed forced labor. The inherent wrong of compulsion has been more difficult to define and prohibit in forced labor than in slavery.

3. *On the Right and Duty to Work.* A right to work is proclaimed by the constitutions of Bahrain, Iraq, Jordan, Kuwait, Qatar, Syria, YAR and the PDRY. Half of those states, Iraq, Jordan, Qatar, and YAR not in new draft, also declare work a duty, and in Iraq, it is called an honor and a sacred duty. The nature of the work to be performed is conditioned by law, morality or Islamic principles (Bahrain, Iran, UAE and YAR) or by one's ability, qualifications and the social interest (PDRY). Labor codes mention the work right and duty only with respect to citizens (Iraq, Saudi Arabia, UAE, YAR, PDRY). Expatriate workers have not been endowed with the broad right to work.

4. *On Freedom to Choose an Occupation.* Career choice or the freedom of the individual to choose his occupation has found legal support in several ways. The constitutions of Bahrain, Iran, Kuwait, UAE, YAR and PDRY proclaim the freedom of choice

(subject to law in UAE, to public order and morality in Bahrain, and to public interest, the principles of Islam, and the rights of others in Iran). Treaty commitments to free choice of occupation have been undertaken by Iran, Iraq, Israel, Jordan, and Lebanon under ILO Convention 122, and by Iraq, Jordan, Lebanon, Palestine ,and Syria under ALO Convention 1 (the latter through its requirement of written contracts of employment). A few countries have sought to protect persons against unwise discretion by prohibiting life long employment contracts (Lebanon), by forbidding contracts to refrain from certain work (Qatar), or by requiring consent to a change in occupation (PDRY).

5. *On Worker Participation in Management.* Worker participation in management has been prescribed in detail only in Israel; but it has been authorized in several other countries by laws declaring certain public policies. Israel has provided for worker representation on the boards of directors of private enterprises. Bahrain and Qatar have provided for Joint Committees of labor and management to promote cooperation (Bahrain) or the raising of standards of work (Qatar). Iraq has called for collaboration based on social solidarity. PDRY has created an obligation on employers to let workers participate in management in order that they may improve the working system and increase production.

6. *On Nondiscrimination.* All the constitutions in the Middle East prohibit some form of discrimination with respect to citizens. The most common unlawful grounds for discriminatory treatment are religion, race, origin, and language. Only three countries (Iran, Qatar and YAR) have constituional bans against sex discrimination. The following list presents the forbidden grounds of discrimination in the constitutions, country by country.

Bahrain — religion, race, origin, language

Iran — race, color, origin, language, sex, tribe, social position

Iraq — religion, origin, language

Jordan — religion, race, language

Kuwait — religion, race, origin, language

Qatar — religion, race, sex

UAE — religion, race, nationality, social position or status

YAR — color, origin, language, sex, profession

PDRY — religion, origin, language, education, social position or status

Statutes prohibiting discrimination against women have been enacted in Iraq, Israel, Syria and PDRY. Israel has also enjoined discrimination based on marriage or parenthood.

Several treaties providing for nondiscrimination have been ratified by a number of Middle East countries. All the countries, except Bahrain, Oman, PDRY, have signed ILO Convention No.111 which prohibites discrimination on the basis of race, color, sex, religion, political opinion, nationality or social origin. The same countries (except Qatar) have signed Convention 100 on Equal Pay for men and women. Conventions providing some protection for special classes of workers have also been signed — Convention 117 on migrant workers signed by Iran, Iraq, Israel, Lebanon, Syria, PDRY, and Convention 107 on indigenous, tribal workers signed by Iraq and Syria. The ALO Convention 5 on Women at Work has been ratified by Iraq and Palestine.

7. *On Development and Planning*. Legal provisions for development and planning are expressions of an overview of a country and an effort to direct how and where it shall progress. Though not spelled out in many plans, workers and their needs are a litmus test of success or failure. The constitutions of Middle East countries identify the kinds of economy desired — private enterprise, socialist, Islamic, or a combination of those. The Iranian constitution is the most insistent on Islamic values; the Iraqi, Syrian and PDRY constitutions are socialistic. All refer to some form of improvement in life. Agencies for planning have been created in all Middle East countries and treaties have reinforced the commitment to social development and planning in some of the States.

SPECIAL CLASSES OF LABOR

8. *On Child Workers*. All Middle East countries have laws to prevent the abuse of child labor: (a) Work of children under

specified ages is prohibited—8 years (on machinery) in Lebanon; 12 years in Iran, Qatar, Syria, YAR; 13 in Jordan, Oman, Saudi Arabia, Lebanon; 14 in Bahrain, Kuwait; 15 in Iraq, Israel, UAE. More generally, work unsuited to age is prohibited in Oman and Syria, and for children who have not completed the first stage of education in PDRY. (b) Night work is prohibited for children under age 15 in Israel, Syria, YAR; 16 in Bahrain, Jordan, Lebanon, Oman, UAE; 17 in Iraq, Qatar; and 18 in Iran, Kuwait, Saudi Arabia. (c) Maximum hours for child labor are set at 6 per day in Bahrain, Jordan, Kuwait, Qatar, Saudi Arabia, UAE, YAR; 7 in Iraq, Lebanon, Syria; 8 in Israel; 4 during Ramadhan in Qatar. (d) Overtime work by children is prohibited in Bahrain, Iran, Iraq, Oman, Qatar, Syria, UAE, YAR. (e) Arduous or hazardous work by children is banned and a medical examiniation is required for children in Bahrain, Iran, Iraq, Israel, Jordan, Kuwait, Lebanon, Oman, Qatar, Saudi Arabia, Syria, UAE. Child labor, however, is expressly exempted from these regulations in agricultural work in Oman, Syria, and on family work in Iraq.

Constitutional provisions directing special care for children are found in Bahrain, Iraq, Jordan, Kuwait, Syria, YAR, PDRY, and treaty commitments for such action have been ratified by Iran, Iraq, Israel, Jordan, Lebanon, Saudi Arabia, Syria, PDRY.

9. *On Women Workers*. Women workers have been the subject of labor laws in all Middle East countries. Constitutions have associated women with the family as a basic social institution (Bahrain, Iran, Iraq, Kuwait, Qatar, Syria, PDRY). They have called for special protection to enable women to combine work with their role within the family (Iran, Syria, PDRY), to restore material and spiritual rights (Iran), and to guarantee the rights and obligations of women under the Shariah (YAR). Special conditions for female employment are also required by the constitutions of Jordan and PDRY. (The Yemeni draft constitution omits these references to women.)

All labor codes prohibit arduous, hazardous or harmful work by women. (Qatar makes no gender distinction in this instance.)

Comfortable facilities for women are required by Iraq, Saudi Arabia, Syria. Night work by women is also prohibited by nearly all countries, with numerous exemptions for special occupations. Work harmful to morals is forbidden for women in Oman, Syria, UAE, PDRY. Saudi Arabia bans work in which women commingle with men. Broad exemptions from the protective legislation for women is made for agricultural work in Oman, Syria; for family work in Iraq, Syria; for charitable institutions in Saudi Arabia, UAE; and for restaurant, hotel, pet care, newspaper, and executive posts in Israel.

The UN Covenant, ratified by Iran, Iraq, Israel, Jordan, Lebanon, Syria and PDRY, provides for equality of the sexes subject to limitations compatible with a democratic society. ILO Conventions restricting the employment of women on underground work, weight lifting, and night work have been accepted by fewer countries. An ALO Convention seeking job opportunities and equal pay for women has been ratified by Iraq and Palestine.

10. *On Agricultural Workers.* Legal attention to agricultural workers in the Middle East has been uncommon and meagre. Some constitutions have expressed a concern for more widespread land ownership (Bahrain, Iraq, Syria); only a few mention agricultural workers — Syria in referring to their exploitation, Iran in establishing worker, farmer, and manager councils, and PDRY in providing for a Union of Peasants and an alliance between the peasant and the working class (omitted from new draft).

Labor codes, covering a range of protective labor measures, often exclude agriculture from their embrace (Bahrain, Iran, Jordan, Lebanon, Oman, Saudi Arabia, UAE, YAR) except for workers in processing and marketing (Bahrain, Saudi Arabia, UAE), or for permanent or long-term employees (YAR, Qatar).

ILO Conventions on the raising of farm labor standards have received few ratifications — on minimum age and workmen's compensation, by Iraq alone, on the organization of rural workers, by only Israel and Syria, and on minimum wages, holidays, and labor inspection, by only Syria.

11. *On Foreign Workers.* All Middle East countries have laws pertaining to the entry and continued residence of foreign workers. Passports and visas are inspected for compliance with designated requirements. Personal qualifications are stipulated, such as good reputation and conduct (Bahrain, Kuwait, Qatar, YAR), physical fitness and freedom from contagious disease (Bahrain) sound morality (YAR), possession of needed vocational and educational skills (Oman, Saudi Arabia, UAE). Israel invites and confers citizenship upon Jewish immigrants. Work permits are required for employment of aliens in all the countries, and in the oil countries contracts must be made with employers who guarantee the worker's compliance with law. Priority in employment is given to citizens (Bahrain, Kuwait, Oman, Qatar, UAE, YAR), second priority to Arab aliens, and a preferential quota to nationals (75% in Saudi Arabia, 90% in YAR).

12. *On Tribal Workers.* Middle East constitutions present somewhat different attitudes toward tribal workers. The Iraqi constitution embraces Kurds and other minorities, and prohibits conduct undermining the national unity of Iraq. The consitution of UAE declares its people a single people, "part of the Arab Nation." PDRY states it desires to emancipate society from "reactionary tribal and clannish inclinations" and urges its citizens to strive against tribal "traditions, ideologies, and customs which conflict with the aims of the national democratic revolution." (Omitted from new draft). Though the official language of Iran is Persian, it requires education in the language of the Koran, Arabic, and allows the use of all ethnic languages in the public media. Arabic Iraq specifies that Kurdish is the official language in the Kurdish region.

Statutes enacted to raise the standards of life and work have had a special relevance to tribal workers who customarily have been among the most deprived. ILO Conventions ratified by Iraq, Israel, Jordan, Kuwait and Syria have established a policy of nondiscrimination on the ground of tribal association.

13. *On Government Workers.* Several Middle East constitutions provide that public employees shall be appointed by the

executive head of state as prescribed by law (Iraq, Kuwait, Lebanon, Qatar Syria, UAE, YAR). The usual qualifications of merit, competence, and citizenship, and the assurance of equal opportunity are noted, and national service is spoken of as in the public interest, or a noble and honorable obligation, or a social trust. In Lebanon, religious sects are to be equitably represented in public employment; only Iran specifies the Islamic religion for such employment. Discipline and discharge are relegated to the executive in accord with law (Kuwait, Lebanon, Syria, Qatar, UAE, YAR). The Iranian constitution restricts all public employees, except teachers, to one job; and the Syrian constitution assures public servants elected to the Assembly a right to return to their jobs.

Nearly all Middle East labor codes exclude public employees from their provisions (Bahrain, Iran, Jordan, Kuwait, Lebanon, Oman, Qatar, Syria, UAE, YAR). Separate statutes on government workers establish comprehensive administrative systems. In Israel, appointments are to be made only among Israeli nationals, on competitive, merit examinations; and a special court adjudicates disputes over discipline. By ILO Convention, Israel and Syria have agreed to provide their government employees terms of employment no less favorable then those afforded by private employers.

14. *On Apprentices.* All Middle East countries have statutes regulating apprenticeship. Most require written contracts setting forth the rights, duties, and compensation of the apprentice (Bahrain, Iraq, Israel, Jordan, Lebanon, Qatar, Saudi Arabia, Syria, UAE, YAR) in the language of the apprentice or in translation. In some countries, the contract must be filed with a labor office. Wages are graduated, but at completion of training no less than the prevailing minimum wage is mandatory (Bahrain, Israel, Sandi Arabia, Syria, UAE, YAR). Training and guidance are required in general terms indicating adequacy. Employers are to be of moral repute; no male shall have a female apprentice or give lodging to a minor apprentice (Jordan, Lebanon, Saudi Arabia). ILO Convention ratifications confirm an obligation for

the progressive development of apprentices in Israel, Jordan, Kuwait and Syria.

15. *On Workers in Cooperatives.* Several Middle East consitutions assert support, protection or encouragement of cooperatives (Iran, Iraq, Kuwait, Syria, YAR, PDRY). The ILO Convention on Social Policy, ratified by Israel, Jordan, Kuwait, and Syria, also commits those countries to form, encourage and assist cooperatives. Employees in such enterprises are benefited inferentially.

16. *On Workers Excluded.* Nearly all labor codes expressly exclude certain workers from their coverage. Domestic workers and family workers are most frequently shut out (Bahrain, Iran, Kuwait, Lebanon, Oman, Qatar, Saudi Arabia, UAE, YAR). Agricultural workers are also often disowned (Bahrain, Iran, Jordan, Lebanon, Oman, Saudi Arabia, UAE, YAR). Temporary workers (Bahrain, Iran, Kuwait, UAE, YAR), casual workers (Bahrain, Iran, Qatar), the military (Bahrain, Oman, UAE), fisherman and dock workers (Iran), and public security workers (Qatar) are also excluded. All employees in small establishments (with fewer than 6 workers in Qatar, and under 10 in Iran, Kuwait, Oman, Saudi Arabia, UAE), are similarly kept out. Labor treaties have usually permitted such deliberate differentiation.

REMUNERATION

17. *On Wages.* All Middle East countries have enacted laws to assure workers proper compensation for services rendered.

All the countries have some minimum wage provisions. The standard for determining the minimum is generally the amount adequate to satisfy the essential needs of a worker. In Iran, Iraq, and Lebanon, the laws include the needs of the worker's family. Other codes or statutes provide also for the consideration of cost of living changes, currency devaluation, employment conditions, and the general economic situation. Minima are set by industry, area or occupation, and at intervals of one or two years, or whenever desired.

The wage setting authority is generally the Minister of Labor; however, Boards including employer and employee representatives are utilized in Iran, Iraq, Jordan, Lebanon, Syria, UAE, YAR and PDRY. In Qatar, the ruling Amir is designated to determine the minimum wage as he "may deem fit".

The actual minimum wages set by the several countries have not been reported in available publications.

Premium pay is provided for overtime in all countries but Kuwait, for night work and holidays in most countries, and for lateshift work in Iran, Qatar and PDRY.

Equal pay for equal work by men and women is required in Iran, Iraq, Israel, Kuwait, and the UAE. Without such a provision, Bahrain, Oman and Saudi Arabia prohibit the payment of higher wages to foreign workers than to citizens.

Severance pay ,in amounts from 15 days to one month's earnings for each year of continuous service, is required in all Middle East countries except Iraq.

Protection that compensation be made in usable currency and at the place of employment is commonly required (except in Kuwait). Some payment in kind or in crop sharing is allowed in Bahrain, Iran, Israel, Jordan, Lebanon, and Oman.

Withholdings from wage payments by an employer are restricted in various amounts. For repayment of loans, the maximum deduction is ordinarily 10% of the wage (35% in Qatar, 25% in Israel and Iran). Similar limitations are placed upon deductions for social insurance premiums, savings, home construction, union dues, damage to tools, and violation of shop rules. Under court attachment, in addition to percentage limits, there are priorities for alimony in Bahrain, Israel, Jordan, Kuwait, Qatar, Saudi Arabia, Syria, and the UAE.

In the collection of money due miscellaneous creditors, wage claims are given priority in Bahrain, Iran, Iraq, Lebanon, Qatar, Saudi Arabia, UAE, YAR, PDRY.

HOURS OF WORK AND REST

18. *On Hours.* Laws regulating hours of work have a sameness

throughout the Middle East. Variations do exist, but they do not appear as significant as the similarities.

The 8-hour day has become standard in all countries. A 7-hour day is ordained before holidays in many states and for night work in Iraq; a 9-hour day is allowed for hotels and restaurants in Jordan, Saudi Arabia, and YAR; and a 10-hour day for hospitals, care centers and essential public institutions in Israel. No specified hours are set for various special occupations or industries in a few countries; and the Minister of Labor is given power to make exemptions in Bahrain, Syria, and Oman.

The 48-hour week is similarly universal. Israel alone has a 47-hour week. For hazardous or arduous work shorter weeks are prescribed in Iran, Iraq, Kuwait, Lebanon, Saudi Arabia, UAE and YAR. However, a lifting of the weekly maximum is provided under a wide range of circumstances in every country except Oman and PDRY.

Periods of rest are provided for in time off and in a limit upon continuous hours of work, and for holidays and vacations. Specified rest periods of one half hour in Bahrain, Jordan, and PDRY are increased to one hour in YAR and range from one half to one and one half hours in Saudi Arabia. Continuous work is limited to 5 hours in Iraq, Jordan, Kuwait, Qatar, Saudi Arabia, Syria, UAE and PDRY; and to 6 hours in Bahrain, Lebanon, and Oman. A Sabbath of rest is observed every Friday in the Muslim countries and on Saturday in Israel. The number of workless holidays is specified as 7 in Kuwait, Syria, and the UAE; 8 in Bahrain and Israel; 10 in Iran, Qatar, Saudi Arabia, and the YAR; whereas "all holidays" are days of rest in Iraq, Jordan, Oman, and PDRY.

Annual vacations are provided, of different lengths — 12 days in Iran, 14 in Israel, Kuwait, Qatar and Saudi Arabia, 15 in Lebanon, Oman, Saudi Arabia, 20 in Iraq, 21 in Bahrain, Jordan, YAR, and 24 in UAE. For work under a year, vacation time is generally prorated, and extra vacation days are added for increases in years of service. Time off is protected against waivers in Bahrain, Iran, Iraq, Saudi Arabia, Syria, and the UAE, and other employment is banned or restricted during vacations in Bahrain, Iraq, Israel, Saudi Arabia, Syria, and the UAE. Special vacations to take a pilgrimage to Mecca are granted in Bahrain, Oman, Qatar, and the UAE.

Hours laws are called for by the constitutions of Iraq, Jordan, Syria and the PDRY. Treaty commitments for the 8 hour day and 48-hour week have also been signed by Bahrain, Iraq, Iran, Israel, Lebanon, Kuwait, Saudi Arabia, Syria, UAE, and YAR.

Despite a wide diversity of economic circumstances and cultural differences, there is a remarkable similarity in the standards adopted by Middle East countries for hours of work and rest. Those laws are directed primarily at industry, commerce and finance in which Western countries are also involved; hence it may not be coincidental that the approach to such regulation has followed a Western pattern. The levels of labor protection have been so well established in advanced industrial nations that emulation would be expected. The agricultural sector, to which the Middle East hours laws are not applied, has also been largely unregulated in the West. Religious and social traditions have not dictated different norms. So on the subject of hours of work and rest, the law of the Middle East is fairly universal.

OCCUPATIONAL SAFETY AND HEALTH

19. *On Safety and Health*. Legal provisions to safeguard the health and safety of workers have been legion, yet adequate funds for the eradication of occupational injuries and illnesses have been lacking. All countries have charged employers with responsibility for safety; most have required employees to be notified of hazards, and have required worker caution and obedience; and all have designated government officials to issue regulations and orders to be observed. Officials have been endowed with extraordinary powers to enter work premises, to interrogate, and to inspect. In Iraq, Israel, Oman, Saudi Arabia, UAE, and PDRY, inspectors may stop work and evacuate unsafe workplaces. Treaties imploring preventive action, education, and enforcement have been ratified by all countries (but Bahrain).

Unfortunately, the dangers inherent in machinery, chemicals, and nature as well as the deficiencies of human comprehension and care have not been eliminated by laws.

EMPLOYMENT

20. *On Employment.* Several Middle East constitutions pledge the state to insure employment; and labor codes and statutes in all states deal with placement services and the protection of jobs. Job creation has been attempted through a wide miscellany of statutes, designed to accomplish specific economic projects not primarily considered with respect to their employment possibilities. Employment generally has been safeguarded by other statutes pertaining to grounds for dismissal, notice, hearings, and severance pay. The variations among such enactments are not as noteworthy as the fact that the subject of job security has evoked universal attention. Peculiar to the Middle East has been the proliferation of laws and administrative regulations on the registration and certification of employees, differentiating expatriates from nationals. These also vary in minor details; but they are stressed in all the countries and they underlie social, as well as legal, priorities in employment.

Treaties calling for full and productive employment have been very general in their statement of a goal, and in steps for implementation. Such treaties setting standards for nondiscrimination or equal opportunities have been ratified by Iran, Iraq, Israel, Jordan, Kuwait, Lebanon, Qatar, Saudi Arabia, Syria, and the YAR.

COLLECTIVE ACTION AND DISPUTE RESOLUTION

21. *On Unionization.* Although unions are afforded legal protection in half of the Middle East countries, there is a quite noticeable absence of such provisions in oil producing countries, Oman, Qatar, and Saudi Arabia.

Freedom to form unions is expressed in some constitutions (Bahrain, Iraq, Kuwait, Syria, YAR, PDRY). It is conditioned in Bahrain and Kuwait on the organizations being lawful and peaceful. The Syria and PDRY constitutions (not in Yemeni draft) spell out union functions more affirmatively, with a socialistic bend.

Codes and statutes in these countries (plus Jordan and Lebanon) assert the freedom or right of workers to organize in order to defend their interests and improve their standards. Iran, YAR and PDRY detail anticipated activities of unions; whereas prohibitions are imposed on political activities in Iran, Kuwait, Jordan, Lebanon, Syria, upon religious involvement in Jordan, Kuwait, Syria, and on financial speculation in Jordan, Kuwait, Syria. Unions are required to register and file information in Iran, Jordan, Kuwait, Syria; but PDRY expressly provides that they are not to be subjected to registration. Dissolution of unions may be ordered in Jordan, Kuwait, Syria, YAR for violations of laws.

Instead of providing for unions, Oman and Qatar authorize the establishment of joint employer/employee councils. Similar enactments for cooperation through joint councils exist also in Bahrain, Iraq, and Kuwait. Employers' associations are given legal standing in Kuwait and Lebanon.

A right to join unions has been affirmed through U.N. Covenants, ratified by Iran, Iraq, Israel, Jordan, Lebanon, Syria and PDRY, also through ILO Conventions ratified by Iraq, Israel, Jordan, Kuwait, Lebanon, Syria, YAR, and PDRY. Unionization of agricultural workers has received special treaty coverage in Iraq, Syria and Israel. ALO Conventions on the right to unionize have been signed by Iraq, Jordan, and Palestine.

22. *On Collective Bargaining*. Although not mentioned in any Middle East constitution, collective bargaining has been given the status of a labor right through the ratification of ILO Conventions (Iraq, Israel, Jordan, Lebanon, Syria, YAR, PDRY) and in labor codes (Iran, Iraq, Jordan, Syria, YAR, PDRY). In Israel, the provisions of several collective bargaining agreements have been extended by government decrees to the unorganized in an industry. In Bahrain, Kuwait, Oman, Qatar, and Saudi Arabia, however, collective bargaining remains without explicit legal

authorization (also technically without legal restraint). In those oil producing countries, the incipient, and government approved, trade unions attempt to influence terms of employment by pleas, protests, and persuasion directed primarily at the government.

23. *On Strikes.* Strikes, as a form of industrial protest or economic pressure, are given legal protection in only a few Middle East countries (Iraq, Israel, Jordan, Syria, PDRY). They are prohibited absolutely in Oman; they are not permitted to present any act of aggression toward employers or non-striking employees in Qatar; and they are banned pending official efforts at conciliation or arbitration in Syria, Jordan, and Qatar. Lockouts are subjected to the same restraints. The UN Covenants and ILO Conventions, seeking to ensure a right to strike, expressly permit restrictive laws.

24. *On Dispute Settlement Techniques.* The paucity of enactments on the legality of strikes is offset by the universality of laws on conciliation and arbitration. Every Middle East country has established agencies and procedures for the exercise of such settlement techniques. A few direct that the government shall arrange for labor/management preliminary meetings to discuss grievances (Iran, Iraq, Oman). All propound voluntary plans, and many provide for legally binding arbitration awards (Bahrain, Iran, Iraq, Kuwait, Lebanon, Oman, Qatar, Saudi Arabia, Syria, UAE). Specialized labor courts have been established in Iraq and Israel.

LABOR'S INTEREST IN SOCIAL WELFARE PROGRAMS

25. *On Social Security.* With commitments to social security in all Middle East constitutions (except the Lebanese constitution), every country in the area has enacted laws that provide systems to compensate for risks of modern life. Such plans cover (a) disability (in all countries); (b) old age or retirement (in all countries but Oman, Qatar, and the Yemens); (c) work-related injuries and diseases (in all countries except Oman and the Yemens); (d) maternity benefits (in all countries but Kuwait and Qatar) with periods for nursing (in Bahrain, Iraq, Israel) and nurseries (in

Iraq, Jordan, Saudi Arabia, Syria); (e) family allowances (in Iran, Israel, and Lebanon); (f) unemployment benefits (in Israel, Bahrain, Iraq, Kuwait); and (g) funeral grants (in Bahrain, Iran, Israel, Kuwait, Saudi Arabia, Syria).

The quantitative benefits have been set forth in the text above so that readers in the Middle East might compare them with payments made in their own countries. An appraisal of the largesse of governments, in light of their resources, is beyond my capability.[1] The absence of specific forms of welfare indicated above is noteworthy. More significant may be the extent of coverage, or the exclusion of certain classes of workers. For pension plans, nearly all employees (with specified exclusions) are covered in Iran, Israel, Kuwait, Lebanon, Syria. For free medical services (such as are available), all residents (with similar exclusions) are made eligible in all the countries. Exclusion from social security is common for domestics, temporary workers, and agricultural workers and employees in small establishments, as are some aliens.

26. *On Housing*. The consitutions of Bahrain, Iran, Kuwait, and PDRY, not in new draft, contain provisions for the state to assist in obtaining housing for their citizens. Statutes require employers to provide suitable living accommodations or adequate living quarters for their employees (in Kuwait, Oman, Qatar, Saudi Arabia, Syria, PDRY). The UN Covenant on Economic, Social and Cultural Rights commits signatories, Iran, Iraq, Israel, Jordan, Lebanon, Syria and PDRY, to recognize the right of everyone to an adequate standard of housing. With the unprecedented migration of workers, housing is still scarce and unfulfilling.

27. *On Education*. All Middle East countries have promoted general education and vocational training. Compulsory and free schooling laws have been directed at the elimination of illiteracy and the development of needed occupational skills. Even university level education has been made available without charge in

[1] Further perspective might be obtained from the publication, U.S. Dept. of Health and Services. Social Security Programs Thruout the World. Washington, D.C., 1989.

Iraq, Qatar, Saudi Arabia, Syria, UAE, PDRY. Vocational training has been sponsored or provided in each of these countries and in Bahrain, Iran, Oman, and the YAR as well. Special laws have provided for vocational rehabilitation and the employment of disabled workers (Bahrain, Oman, Saudi Arabia, Syria).

Traditional denigration of manual work and priorities for education in religion and cultural subjects have left the elite unprepared for managerial, executive, and professional occupations. Regardless of educational efforts to supply such skills among nationals, they have lagged behind the immediate needs.

LABOR'S INTEREST IN CIVIL RIGHTS

28. *On Human Rights.* Legal provisions to preserve human rights indispensable to the development of labor law have been acknowledged and firmly proclaimed, but not without serious qualifications. The advocacy and observance of labor law have flourished or stagnated with the enforcement of these basic rights: 1 - the right to organize and assemble, 2 - the right to speak freely, 3 - the right to print freely, 4 - the right to practice one's religion, 5 - the right to petition for redress of grievances, 6 - the right to personal life and security, 7 - the right to a fair trial, 8 - the right to just punishment, 9 - the right to free movement, and 10 - the right to suffrage. Every one of these rights has been endorsed by constitutions or other laws in all the Middle East countries.[2] Conditions or limitations placed upon human rights however have been critical.

The reservations or limitations upon human rights vary somewhat with the specific right: (a) The freedom to organize or assemble is restricted as provided by law (Bahrain, Iraq, Jordan, Kuwait, Syria, YAR), or to activities that are peaceful and moral (Bahrain, Kuwait), or that are not contrary to Islam (Iran). (b) Free speech is limited according to Islamic principles (Iran), or in line with the Revolution (Iraq), or to expressions that

[2] Since all Middle East constitutions have dealt with these fundamental rights and the three countries without constitutions have indicated their adherence to human rights in other official pronouncements, I have not troubled to follow through with the vast number of statutes bearing upon them.

strengthen the national democratic regime, public ethics and state security without prejudice to the dignity of citizens (PDRY) not in new draft, or to statements that safeguard the soundness of the nation's structure and socialist system (Syria). (c) Publications in Iran are not to be detrimental to public rights, as set by law. (d) The right to hold demonstrations is to be exercised everywhere within the limits set by law. (e) There is a state religion in every Middle East country except Lebanon; but all the countries proclaim freedom for all faiths. (f) All the Muslim countries pledge to promote Arab unity. (g) The right to move about freely may be confined by law (Iran, Iraq, Jordan, Syria, UAE, PDRY), or restricted to protect public health and safety (Syria) or state security or health (PDRY). (h) Various components of the right to a fair trial and just punishment are singled out in the constitutions; but the absence of such a provision in a country does not imply a rejection or limitation of the particular right. Except for the listed provisions permitting restrictions, the principal human rights are affirmed throughout the Middle East. Unfortunately, human rights laws are not self-executing; provisions for enforcement are commonly lacking and abuses are often sanctioned by neglect, insecurity and indifference.

AN OVERVIEW OF THE SPREAD

The foregoing summaries of labor laws in the Middle East merely review constitutional, code, statutory, and treaty provisions. They do not evaluate the respective enactments or attempt to classify countries by their relative perfection of legislative techniques. Only in a remote and indirect fashion do they suggest the social wisdom or circumspection of the countries. They are the naked records of labor laws, with a few irresistible comments. I shall discourse on the art of further comparison and present some personal appraisals in the concluding chapters of this book.

III. OBSERVATIONS AND EVALUATIONS

End Papers. I have been intrigued by the blank pages inserted at the beginning and end of every bound volume. I was told that publishers and librarians call them "end papers" and I imagined they were the swathling blanket and the burial sheet for the birth and death of the book. But the preface usually explains the birth pangs, and concluding chapters lay to rest whatever the author created. In the case of this book, I expect some critical readers to scribble reactions on the blank margins and end papers. Yet I regard the section, entitled the "Gamut of Labor Law", as the hard core of the book's reality, and I wish to add some contemplative discourse that may stimulate further thought on the meaning and future of labor laws in the Middle East.

Any overview of those laws that would consider their constitutional, statutory, and treaty provisions, and attempt to pass judgment upon their relative merits, would be an extraordinarily difficult undertaking. In a way, the arrangement of the laws by subject and the display of their essential terms, as done in the foregoing chapters of this book, have been just a beginning or a foundation for analysis. There are many possible ways to view the significance of such laws. I shall venture here only a few generalizations.

There has been a great confluence of social forces, all of which have left their imprint upon labor law, and though their future influences may only be conjectured, it seems certain they will continue to be impelling and effective. The outpouring of oil wealth has coexisted with a drive for unsatisfied human necessities; the creation of new states has rested upon ethnic assumptions and disputed boundaries; the dominant religious allegiances have asserted themselves relentlessly; and the desires for peace have not dispelled the habits of war. All these factors have gone on simultaneously, interacting among each other and affecting all aspects of life, including labor law. Any consideration of the climate for labor law in the Middle East must bear in mind the intermingling of economic, social, and political forces in the nations of the region; and any prognostication of labor laws should be seen as provisional, dependent upon a miscellany of happenings. I shall endeavor to indicate what appear to be salient forces at work on the trends of labor law in the Middle East.

Chapter 18

ON THE CULTIVATION OF LABOR LAW

The few hundred labor laws planted in the Middle East sustain and embellish life in a myriad of ways. Some are just seeds of promise, suggesting how to overcome noxious child labor or hidden poisons in the workplace. Many bear crops of cash with which to purchase food, clothing and shelter. Others bring forth balms of security in times of disability and unemployment. All of them call for the cultivation of an atmosphere in which the fruits of labor can flourish. These are more than figures of speech. They are realities.

The unwritten and the written. Middle East labor laws were formulated before man recorded them on papyrus or parchment. They arose as spoken advice, directions, or commands, and they lived on for centuries in custom. People responded in impulsive imitation; some articulated changes as they encountered new circumstances. The earliest written labor laws we have found were the startling wage rates in the codes of Lipit Ishtar and Hammurabi; but they obviously did not prescribe the many other norms observed by employers and workers of their days. Written law has always been concentrated upon only selected modes of behavior. And in the field of labor relations, much has been ordered and observed by social forces without benefit of formal enactment by law-giver or scribe.

Many of the ancient legal writings referred to or incorporated existing custom; or assumed that nothing needed to be said about particular aspects of labor relations. The widespread system of slavery was regulated primarily in facets of war or trade until the time when its prohibition was reached. For centuries free labor in the Middle East was governed essentially by individual understanding of custom or by oral agreements. Even with the advent of written indentures, most servants and their masters dealt with each other by word of mouth. It is unknown when and where innovations were made. From time to time laws were enacted, but simultaneously, and even up to the present, employment has been established on terms unwritten. The many vacuums in written law have tended to be filled by custom. Only recently have the Middle East countries resorted to extensive labor codes and somewhat hesitatingly to the supplementing of labor laws with written agreements, individual and collective.

CONSTITUTIONAL DEDICATIONS

Constitutions are distinctive. They are pronouncements to the world of the existence of a nation and an expression of its unique characteristics. They are endowed with a solemnity and in the realm of law they enjoy a position of supremacy. From the particular viewpoint of this book, I hasten to add that all constitutions adopted after World War II (in the Middle East as in every other country) also contain labor law provisions.

The extent to which constitutional provisions are accorded priority over legislative enactments in the Middle East is apparent from the explicit terms of a few constitutions, but also in the deference paid them by courts and heads of state. In Syria, the constitution proclaims it "crowns our people's struggle on the road of the principle of popular democracy," it is a "regulator of the movement of the state and its various institutions, and is a source of its legislation." In Iraq, "Any activity which contradicts the aims of the people defined in this Constitution . . . shall be prohibited." In PDRY, it is written "The Constitution is the organic law . . . measures taken by the state's organizations and the mass organizations must accord with the spirit and content of the Constitution." (not in draft constitution).

A number of constitutions also provide that laws enacted previously to their adoption shall remain in effect if not repealed or amended and if they are not contrary to provisions of the constitution (Bahrain, Iraq, Kuwait, Lebanon, Qatar, Syria, UAE, PDRY).

Iran gives higher priority to its religion, yet preserves the supremacy of the constitution over legislation. "The National Assembly is not empowered to enact laws which contradict the principles and commandments of the official religion of the country, or the Constitution." All laws and regulations "should be based on Islamic principles. This principle will in general prevail over all the principles of the Constitution, and other laws and regulations as well." All proposed legislation is to be sent to a Council of Guardians which shall within 10 days "examine it from the perspective of its adherence to Islamic and Constitutional principles, and in case of conflict, such legislation will be returned to the Assembly for revision. Otherwise, such legislation shall be considered enforceable."

Principles asserted in some constitutions are also protected against possible amendment. They expressly state that there may be no constitutional amendments to the principles of liberty and equality (Bahrain, Kuwait), except to increase their guarantees (Kuwait). The Amiri system of government may not be amended in Kuwait. Nor may amendments change the state religion of Islam (Bahrain, Iran).

In the Middle East countries without constitutions, official pronouncements, referred to above, have indicated a recognition of the special significance of constitutions and a concern over primary principles. In Israel, basic liberties affecting labor relations have been acknowledged by the Supreme Court without legislative enactment. In Saudi Arabia, the reference to Islam as the embodiment of the highest law has been supplemented by the Sheik's endorsement of a basic law on the relationship between the government and the governed, still to be completed. In Oman, the Sultan, after appointing a State Consultative Council in 1981, promised a democracy when he may find his people ready for it. The absence of formal, written constitutions in these countries, when considered in light of the worldwide inclusion of labor principles and specific labor laws in constitutions, poses a degree of uncertainty as to the extent to which the labor laws in those countries are enforceable under changing economic or political circumstances.

Provisional constitutions which are now operative in Iraq, Qatar, and the UAE arose in response to political changes and have not been replaced, but they too contain labor provisions held in the same high regard as provisions in permanent constitutions. In Kuwait, in 1976 and 1986, the National Assembly was dissolved and certain elements of the constitution were suspended so that the country has been ruled during certain periods by decree of the Emir instead of legislative enactment; however, the constitutional labor provisions have remained unchanged.

The labor provisions in the Middle East constitutions have all been adopted in a spirit of accomplishment and national pride, and with an intent to identify social and human qualities with each country. It was expected that all the terms would be followed and fulfilled as is befitting a solemn declaration of State. The words used, however, have influenced the extent to which the provisions have been treated as binding laws. These convey varying legal implications. Some of the labor provisions are clearly general professions of faith; others say they are specific principles for guidance of the government; others are statements of goals to be achieved; others are more definite standards to be incorporated into laws; and still others are discrete declarations of legal rights.

All the provisions pertaining to the treatment of labor are serious and purposeful — none to be disregarded even though they bear different weights. Illustrative of those that raise implications subject to many interpretations are the general references to liberty, dignity, Islam, Arab Unity, the revolution, or socialism. More definite are the statements of goals such as those insuring employment, free choice of occupation, social security, vocational education (Bahrain, Iran, Jordan, Kuwait, UAE); free choice of occupation (Bahrain, Kuwait, Iran, UAE, YAR, PDRY); social security and human rights (all the constitutions). Specific standards to be applied with or without further legislation are found in terms spelling out the qualifications and discipline of public employees (Iran, Iraq, Kuwait, Lebanon, Qatar, Syria, UAE, YAR). Less definitive are the limitations upon the rights of assembly, speech, press, movement (Bahrain, Iran, Iraq,

Jordan, Kuwait, Syria, YAR). To nearly all of these provisions, there is usually added a term indicating action to be taken by the government — protect, care for, support, insure, improve, or assist — which casts further light upon how the constitutional provision is to be interpreted.

The constitutional labor provisions that constitute or have the properties of law in and of themselves, that are not to be violated and that may be sufficient to be enforced directly in courts of law, are those that prohibit actions or speak of rights. Such constitutional provisions have established the right to form unions (Bahrain, Iran, Kuwait, Syria, YAR, PDRY) or have prohibited the employment of children under specified ages. These constitutional provisions are intended to have the force of law with the highest degree of authority; still they have been buttressed by many legislative enactments.

Unfortunately some constitutions provide for emergency powers which may result in the suspension of consditutional guarantees. Such extraordinary powers require a declaration of emergency (Iraq, Jordan, Qatar, Syria, UAE, YAR, PDRY) or martial law (Bahrain, Jordan, Kuwait, UAE), or defensive war (Bahrain Kuwait). The circumstances or rationale under which emergency powers may be invoked are also specified: war (Iran, Jordan, Republic of Yemen draft), defensive war (Bahrain, Kuwait), grave danger, threat to national unity, safety or independence, obstruction to state institutions carrying out constitutional responsibilities (Syria), external or internal security (PDRY), exceptional circumstances (Qatar), force majeur (Iran), necessity determined by law (Kuwait). In a few countries, the duration of the emergency powers is limited: not to exceed 30 days (Bahrain), 30 days (Iran), 3 month (Kuwait). The high esteem in which constitutional guarantees are held is thus marked by the solemnity of their suspension.

STATUTORY PROVISIONS

The spelling out of labor laws in the Middle East has several distinctive aspects. In all the countries except Israel the provisions on the most common subjects of labor law have been grouped together in a Labor Code. Israel has covered the same subjects in separate statutes. From time to time thereafter, in all the countries additional enactments have been made on cognate or new subjects, not originally covered. The codes and the special laws have been given publicity so they might be observed or enforced. In addition, as required for administration, there have been an immense number of regulations or rules (many of which have not been readily available).[1]

Enactment procedures have differed among the countries. In most, a legislature has discussed proposals submitted by the Ministry of Labor and Social Affairs, and it has adopted the provisions which a majority of the body has approved. In Oman and Saudi Arabia, which have no legislatures, laws have been proclaimed by decree of the ruler, after private consultation with his personal advisors (and since the suspension of the constitution in Kuwait, its legislation has been promulgated by decree of its Amir).

Remarkably, all of the countries, despite their differences have created legal norms on the same fundamental subjects of labor concern. Their idiosyncrasies — political, cultural, religious, ideological — have manifested themselves primarily in levels of standards set or in their degree of interest. Notwithstanding great differences in emphasis, there has been a commonality of labor problems among them and a noteworthy similarity in their legislative responses. The basic needs of man are alike and there is a universal desire to satisfy them. Given the tremendous disparities in material resources and the complexities in the cultures people have devised in their lives, it is somewhat surprising that there are so many similar areas and patterns of adjustment in labor relations. The countries of the Middle East (as in all other regions of the world) have set standards for the status of labor: they have chosen to treat workers in separate categories such as

[1] Bahrain has published in English many of its regulations- on various sections of its labor code. State of Bahrain, Ministry of Labor and Social Affairs, The Labor Law for the Private Sector and Legislation Relating Thereto. Manama, Feb. 1986.

women, children, and public employees; they have dealt specifically with remuneration, hours of work, safety and health and collective activities; they have established systems of social welfare, and they have recognized civil and human rights. In these endeavors, individual governments have found or created ways of coping with their problems through labor laws, in greater or lesser degrees, like those of their neighbors.

A few characteristics of Middle Eastern labor law are clearly discernible. Most are reflections of the rapid economic changes that have been encountered in the region. The discovery of oil and the onrush of petrodollars, the unprecedented demand for labor, the burgeoning of cities, transportation and commerce created labor market problems for which there were little or no laws. Manpower needs upset non-oil as well as oil producing countries. Excesses of wealth came to the oil countries faster than they could decide how best to utilize them; they have at times employed more alien workers than citizens; they have been propelled to educate and train new work forces; they have erected barriers and permits to offset disturbances and fears scarcely realized. The non-oil rich countries have lost important skilled nationals and have sought to compensate therefor by the income of wage remittances. These various economic factors have ever been present in the consideration of labor laws in the Middle East; but except for the laws controlling migration and work permits, they took expression more in the levels of standards and budgets than in the creation of peculiarly Middle East labor laws.

We should observe, however, that the countries of the Middle East have an essential component of agriculture, and in that sector labor laws have a significance that they do not carry in the Western world. There is a very large proportion of the gainfully occupied population engaged in agriculture throughout the Middle East. In the countries that have expanded their oil-related, construction, banking, trade and other industrial activities, the numbers engaged in the industrial sector have generally not exceeded one-third of the labor force. Perhaps more importantly, the industrial activity is relatively new and not widely diversified;

only limited capital has been invested in it (foreign investments have been more profitable), and Asian and African markets for products manufactured in the Middle East have not been developed; hence it is not likely that the Middle East will become dominantly industrialized in the near future. In some of the countries, there is an urgent need to increase domestic food production. All of which means that the labor laws affecting agricultural workers in the Middle East have a greater importance than they might elsewhere.

Most governments in the Middle East have become independent rather recently, though they bear age-old traditions. They have suddenly become economically intertwined with their neighbors and with foreign powers. They have found themselves driven by events largely beyond their control. Many of their labor laws have been influenced by their desire to preserve their traditions and to present a unique face in the family of nations. I shall comment below upon the extent to which Israeli, Christian, and Islamic precepts have colored labor laws. Tribal and political rivalries have also affected the enactment or absence of certain labor laws. The brief period following independence has been a shake-down time.

The fact that in the preceding chapters there has been no reference to the enactment of laws by some countries does not necessarily indicate that there is no labor law on the subject in those countries. Broad rubrics of justice or the vagaries of custom often suffice for the application of law in normal dealings, and even in disputes that arise. Statutes make the law more certain or more easily ascertainable; yet law also exists in practice. I have been unable, as an outsider, to gather many nuances of the unwritten law of the Middle East. On the whole, it is clear that the statutory labor provisions in the Middle East have blended into the scheme of Western labor law.

Skeptics are sometimes inclined to regard labor laws as mere scribbles in books few people read. They see them entombed in libraries. Yet they come to life whenever employers take heed and respond, when workers request or demand compliance, when inspectors report observance or violation, or when judges order obedience. Those events occur to the degree that governments appropriate funds to administer the laws and such appropriations never seem adequate. The extent to which labor laws are enforced in the Middle East is an evasive reality, changing from time to time.

TREATY PROVISIONS

Treaties occupy an anomalous position in the labor law of the Middle East. Most treaties affirm principles to be adopted by signatory nations, and set standards to be incorporated into legislation. Usually, they allow nations the choice of a wide range of implementing options. They constitute commitments in good faith and tend to confirm the social advancement and prestige of nations. Few court decisions or other public records are available to indicate how seriously treaties have been observed in the Middle East. Nevertheless, the ratifications of treaties by Middle East countries demonstrate several important facets of their labor laws.

The fact that all Middle East countries, except Oman, have subscribed to the United Nations Charter and have become members of the UN signifies that they have voluntarily sought the approbation of the civilized world, and have pledged themselves to uphold the dignity of labor. The Universal Declaration of Human Rights is a mere statement of principle; but the two UN Covenants, one on Civil and Political Rights, and one on Economic, Social and Cultural Rights, are binding treaties. Both have been signed by Iran, Iraq, Israel, Jordan, Lebanon, Syria, and PDRY. Each covenant contains many labor law provisions. They highlight precepts on which labor leaders and workers often rely, and when rights are not respected, they afford a means for placing the burden of justification upon governments publicly.

The ILO maze of Conventions also promotes general labor standards, and in addition provides an official oversight, objective investigations and technical assistance. Middle East countries have ratified the following Conventions:

Iraq-58 ratifications of Conventions on hours or work, weekly rests, night work, holidays, minimum wages, equal pay, wage protection, minimum age, safety and health and accident compensation, inspection, organization and collective bargaining, discrimination, tribal workers, seamen, forced labor, social security, educational leave, unemployment, employment policy, employment agencies, human resources development, tripartite consultation, labor administration.

Syria-44 ratifications on essentially the subjects listed above, plus Conventions on labor statistics, debt imprisonment and social policy.

Israel-43 ratifications on essentially the subjects listed above.

Lebanon-28 ratifications, on hours of work, weekly rests, night work, holidays, minimum wages, equal pay, wage protection, minimum age, accident compensation, inspection, organization and collective bargaining, discrimination, forced labor, employment.

Jordan-16 ratifications on weekly rest, equal pay, minimum age, safety and health, inspection, organization and collective bargaining, discrimination, forced labor, social security, employment policy, workers' representatives, social policy, human resources development.

Kuwait-16 ratifications, on hours of work, weekly rest, night work, holidays, safety and health, discrimination, organization and collective bargaining, forced labor, inspection, social policy.

Saudi Arabia-13 ratifications on hours of work, weekly rest, night work, equal pay, minimum age, safety and health, inspection, discrimination, forced labor.

PDRY-13 ratifications, on wage protection, minimum age, safety and health, accident compensation, organization and collective bargaining, employment contracts, forced labor, debt imprisonment, public employment.

Iran-11 ratifications, on weekly rest, accident compensation, equal pay, wage protection, discrimination, employment, debt imprisonment, forced labor, seamen.

YAR-11 ratifications, on weekly rest, holidays, organization and collective bargaining, minimum wages, equal pay, debt imprisonment, forced labor, discrimination, workers' representatives, social policy.

Bahrain-4 ratifications, on weekly rests, night work, inspection, forced labor.

UAE-4 ratifications, on hours, night work, inspection, forced labor.

Qatar-2 ratifications, on discrimination, inspection.

Oman-0 ratifications.

An ILO Committee of Experts and a Committee on the Enforcement of Conventions meet annually, or more often, and review signatory reports, correspond with governments on the absence or inadequacy of labor laws, make specific recommendations for corrections, request factual replies and follow through with persistence. The ILO has only the power of persuasion, and it writes to erring or delinquent governments in a tone of extreme diplomatic courtesy. Frequently, it is ignored by offenders; but it does perform a watchdog function. As indicated above, on vital details it has been heeded by some Middle East governments.

Of special significance have been the investigations conducted by ILO experts, at the request or with the consent of signatory governments, and the competent drafting by ILO experts of proposed amendments and new legislation. In addition, the ILO has made available aides to labor law administrators and training courses for management and labor representatives involved in the application of labor laws. Very few of the Middle East countries have taken advantage of these services; but in the present state of international law and international agency budgets, the ILO has made very commendable beginnings in the improvement of labor law among nations.

The Arab countries of the Middle East, in their eagerness to advance unity (professedly the unity of an Arab nation) have formed the Arab Labor Organization, with its own Conventions, largely paralleling those of the ILO. The countries that have ratified ALO Conventions are Iraq, Jordan, Lebanon, Syria, and Palestine. However, the ALO has been underfinanced, as well as the unfortunate victim of dissensions among Arab leaders, so that it has not had the ability to carry forward the formulation or supervision of its treaties.

Realization. An unsolved enigma of labor laws is the puzzle of the law's enforcement. Never is there complete compliance with a law, and no single law is absolutely disregarded. By their very promulgation, labor laws are public commitments, but none is realized in the same fashion. Some are intended to be hortatory, pleas for observance. Others are orders demanding obedience upon severe penalty. In some instances, such as laws on safety and health, it is more vital to educate employers and employees as to the hazards of work and the responsibilities of each participant than to impose fines, and the effectiveness of enforcement is determined primarily by the amount of money spent on administration. Similar budgetary constraints decide benefits or inadequacies in social security programs. In other areas, such as the right to organize or to bargain collectively the operative weight of the laws depends upon the degree of sophistication in management and unions. In the field of human rights almost everything depends upon a sense of security and a dedication to humaneness.

The extent to which individual laws are enforced is rarely measurable. My study of public records has not enabled me to rate the several Middle East countries on their realization of the purpose of labor laws, except for some obvious disparities. With the political changes in the Yemens, the uniting of a capitalistic, market oriented state with a socialistic, planned state (similar to but in many respects unlike the changes now undergoing in Eastern Europe), and the changes likely to occur in the settlement of Palestinian-Israeli conflicts, the effects of labor laws are quite unpredictable. I have attempted to set forth accurately the norms adopted and to report some consequence and incidentals. I suggest that all labor laws must be weighed against the prevailing perceptions of the labor problems confronted.

CULTIVATION OF LABOR LAW

Labor law in the Middle East, through constitutional, statutory, and treaty provisions, is in many respects a record of achievement and promise. In view of its brief history, and the changing processes of development in the region, it may be regarded as the commencement of an effort in tune with world trends. The accomplishments in each country should be considered in light of variant resources and difficulties which I have been able to glimpse and mention only in a passing fashion. In the turbulence of political change, likely to destabilize parts of the Middle East for some time to come, or in the eventuality of new expectations and needs, there will probably arise clamor for changes not yet defined. But foundations have been laid, trends have been started and labor laws promise a progressive concern for the welfare of workers in the Middle East.

Chapter 19

ON THE COMPLEXITY OF COMPARISON

Any presentation of the labor laws of several countries invites a comparison of their terms and their accomplishments. That can be pursued along many lines.

Early law comparatists thought they might discover fundamental legal principles of universal validity. They were guided by religious or ethical precepts or by their own conceptions of social stability. They found philosophical consistencies that led them to conclude there was a law of nature, or a law of God, or a law of justice; but they could not reconcile those findings with the diverse laws desired and adopted by man. So most comparatists have abandoned the search for universal law.

Comparatists influenced by realism or pragmatism have been content to examine laws for what they are, what they are intended to do, and if possible, what they do accomplish. However a law reads, it raises in the mind of an inquisitive reader the question of its merit compared with a law in another country. That question may suffice, but it can not be answered simply.

Should the Middle East labor laws be contrasted in their entirety with the labor laws of the Western World or with the rest of the Third World; should all the labor laws of any one country be compared with all the labor laws of another country; should one law in a nation be weighed against a law on the same subject in another nation? Should not any comparison take into account the needs to be satisfied in the respective societies, the goals set by the governments, and the results achieved? Should not the comparison consider also the extent to which the resources of the countries have been utilized and the plans and promises that have been forecast? All of these objectives are sound and fascinating; and every one requires more information than I have been able to assemble. Still, the urge to engage in some comparative comments on the facts presented in the preceding chapters is irresistible. I shall attempt a few illustrations.

On Topics of Law

On the problems of child labor, all countries have some minimum age requirement. Whether the higher in the scatter of 12, 13, 14 or 15 years of age is the more preferable is probably secondary to the degree of enforcement and the provision of education. The standard of work "unsuited" to age (Oman) or the requirement of permission from a Director of Labor (Qatar) would ordinarily be less effective than the specific age designation. Maximum hours of work are set with little variation. The prohibition of arduous and hazardous work by children is standard; but the requirement of a medical examination for child workers (in all countries except Iran and the Yemens) is more protective in the Middle East than in most of the industrial countries of the world. The coverage of child labor in family work (exempted only in Iraq, Qatar, Syria) and agricultural work (exempted in Oman, Syria) also casts a favorable light upon the remaining Middle East labor laws.

On the problems of remuneration for work done, special provisions make the laws of certain countries only slightly more outstanding than others. Laws provide that a floor for minimum wages be set in most countries (except Bahrain, Kuwait), but the factors to be considered and the administrative procedures to be followed vary widely. Their respective merits can be evaluated only in practice; however, Qatar's law that the minimum basic pay is to be what His Highness the Ruler may deem fit to determine is hardly a model to be emulated.

Premium pay for overtime, night work, and shift work are not extraordinary, and holiday pay is associated as usual with religious and state occasions. Equal pay for equal work which is a threshold issue in other parts of the world seems accepted in Iran, Iraq, Israel, Kuwait, UAE. Laws for severance or termination pay (absent only in Iraq) provide various amounts of compensation, none of which is particularly outstanding. Wage payment and collection laws and laws on withholdings, attachments, and preference among creditors follow similar patterns. Only in the matter of profit sharing (made law solely in Iran) have the wage laws of the Middle East been noticeably innovative.

In dealing with employment, the labor laws of the Middle East have differed from those of the Western World in the absence of laws designed to create more jobs. The oil boom has at least for the present made such laws unnecessary or not critical. The primary employment problems of the Middle East have arisen out of the migration of multitudes of foreign workers into the oil producing states and the emigration of needed domestic workers from the other states. The laws for border checks, recruitment, work permits, citizen sponsors, and training of nationals in new skills have in some respects been unique yet very similar among the host countries. So have regulations for wage remittances and imports in the supplier countries. One aspect of employment legislation, found in the Middle East as elsewhere, has been the preservation of job security — with special concern for national workers and for expatriates needed to expand and stabilize production. Workers have been protected against dismissal without good cause and have been entitled to some compensation to offset the loss sustained in transitional unemployment. The grounds for dismissal have been similar and although the amounts of monetary relief have varied, they have been related roughly to customary levels of income. Differences in administration have reflected traditional ways and levels of budgeted funds.

In social security systems, the Middle East laws have likewise been influenced by tradition and the availability of funds. Traditional forms of aid to coreligionists have persisted, and the enactment of laws for social security institutions in the Middle East has just begun. The development of fiscally sound plans for contributions, benefits and administration has slowly awaited the accumulation of census data on demographic factors; and the indications are that laws will follow patterns established in countries where systems have existed for some time.

These few comparative observations on labor law in the Middle East illustrate the pervasive tendency of modern governments confronted with common labor problems to adopt similar means of dealing with them. Cultural distinctions among the nations have expressed themselves primarily in minor ways. Economic differences have highlighted divergent problems; yet the labor laws dealing with those problems have maintained a remarkable uniformity. It is futile to argue the relative advantages and disadvantages of pluralism. National characteristics will persist, but worldwide means of communication and the example of interrelated countries result in a patterning of labor laws.

Nationalistic commentators have extolled the accomplishments of their own countries. It is easy to observe that certain labor law standards in one country are higher than those of another, and it is desirable that they be studied for emulation or experimentation. But labor laws are not of equal significance to be tallied mathematically. The mere statement of the terms of labor laws does not assess differences in local needs and in the availability of remedial resources. Labor law comparison calls for the comprehension of human needs and their satisfaction. The adoption of a labor law involves the setting of a national goal and its evaluation must be seen in the light of a multitude of social circumstances.

On Systems of Law

One approach to the comparison of labor laws, is that of seeing how they fit into or are affected by the systems of law in which they are embedded. I have been referring to labor laws as specific rules for human behavior in work relationships; but they operate within systems of legal thinking and law institutions. Certain legal systems have, over time, maintained a cohesive or distinct character. Each has had not only a body of rules of behavior, but also a unifying set of principles (philosophies concerning such ends as that which is good, or God‘s purpose, or the destiny of a nation, or social stability, or justice), techniques for the ascertainment of the law (such as following prior precedents, or observing the counsel contained in legal treatises), and specialized personnel for enforcing the law (such as lawyers, procurators, judges, administrators). The primary legal systems found in the Middle East today have been classified as the Common Law and Civil Law systems with an admixture of religious systems. These have produced some differences (a) in the way labor law is discovered or identified, (b) in the manner of applying law to new situations, and (c) in the kinds of practitioners or courts used. These are cultural differences that affect the nature of the labor law applied; but they have not determined the substance of the rules declared to be the law of the land. In the field of labor law, the differences that remain in the Middle East are matters of cultural expression rather than of legal systems.

On Economic Systems

The same might be said of the differences in economic systems. Most of the countries of the Middle East have committed themselves to enterprise economies. Two, Iraq and Syria, have constitutions that extol socialist principles, and one, PDRY, has proclaimed itself a centrally directed communist economy. (The latter requires re-examination under the provisions of the new Republic of Yemen, still to be disclosed.) Those differences have asserted themselves in public policies and programs. In practice, the oil rich countries have made state-owned enterprises of their principal industrial plants and they have adopted, for their citizens, rather extensive social welfare systems; yet they retain essentially private profit economies. Iraq and Syria have some public ownership of utilities and some inclination toward a redistribution of wealth when feasible; but in the upheaval of wars and political rivalries, they have not created predominantly socialist economies. The PDRY stands out as having extended socialist endeavors to socialized farms and to conscious involvement of workers in government and industry; but starting with scarce resources and developing quite slowly, it has still clung to whatever tribal and private enterprise has contributed to its over-all economy.[1] All of these economies have been confronted with labor problems of a similar nature or problems peculiar to their immediate economic needs, regardless of the economic systems they have chosen to establish. They have enacted labor laws dealing with the same topics, in noticeably similar terms.

Comparisons, even of laws that sound alike, may disclose differences when the laws are viewed as measures to serve particular national needs. That is a complicated matter; it may justify the rather elaborate exposition in this volume and may require much more. The tasks of a labor law comparatist are not easily laid to rest; they are constantly reordered.

[1] In a recent interview, the President, Al'Attas stated that private enterprise was acceptable in animal husbandry and poultry raising, and that a new law was under consideration to encourage private investment from the Arab world. The Middle East, London (in English), April 1989, p 19. The draft constitution for a united Republic of Yemen states "The national economy shall be based on the following principles: (i) Islamic social justice as regards social and production relationships; (ii) the establishment of a developing public sector capable of processing basic means of production; (iii) protecting private ownership which shall not be interfered with except in cases of public interest and with the payment of fair compensation . . . ; (iv) directing all such relationships and potentialities to ensure the establishment of a strong and independent national economy and the realization of a comprehensive growth ensuring the creation of socialistic relationships drawing its inspiration from Arab Islamic legacies and circumstances of Yemen's society."

Chapter 20

ON CIVILIZATIONS AND LABOR LAW

There may be some advantage, when observing labor law, to assume a civilizational perspective. The Middle East has been a cradle of civilizations; and stepping back in history offers a long range view of labor law. Regrettably most "civilizationists" (historians, anthropologists, and sociologists who have studied the phenomena of civilizations) have not turned their gaze toward labor law, or for that matter to the entirety of law, as a significant cultural trait. They have given much thought to the classification of civilizations, to the conception of what constitutes a civilization, and to the historical transformations of recognized civilizations.[1] These insights offer a vantage point for an appreciation or understanding of labor law, and the latter may suggest the addition of another element in civilizational study.

The criteria of civilization stressed by many scholars of world history or social behavior have been cultural traits selected by them to illustrate the unfolding of their own observations of mankind. They have found civilization in such clusters of culture as the creation of language, the domestication of crops and animals, the formation of cities, the consolidation of communities into states, or in other cultural achievements such as art, religion and philosophy. The assemblage of such distinctive behavior in certain places and times have been labeled civilizations. Prominent in the classification of civilizations has been the association of cultural traits with political institutions — city states, nation states, empires. Still scant attention has been given to laws or

[1] The early classifiers of civilization, Coulborn, Quigley, Spengler, Toynbee, Kroeber, did not refer to labor law, a miniscule cultural trait; nor do the current writers (see Matthew Melko and Leighton R. Scott. The Boundaries of Civilizations in Space and Time. NY Univ. Press of America. 1987). Their search for a central civilizing force has led them to follow the activities of man, most frequently mentioned by historians, to see what patterns have emerged and what has happened to them.

legal systems (except in expositions of Athenian and Roman civilizations). The peculiarities of labor laws have not been highlighted in the civilizational process.

Regrettably civilizationalists have avoided the definition of civilization, and that has blurred their classification of civilizations. The effort to become objective has induced scholars to omit qualitative factors from consideration. So subjects such as morality and spirituality or the essence of cultural change have escaped some critical analysis. My interest in labor law has led me to include the notion of human betterment — a qualitative advance in culture — as an element of civilization. I find that required in the common usage of the term "uncivilized" as well as "civilized". The element of cultural improvement, as in labor law, should be accounted for in a civilizational perspective.

Difficulty with that arises in the appearance of some uncivilized conduct in every civilization. How should we account for incongruous forms of behavior such as the exposure of female infants to die on a mountain top in some ancient civilizations? More bewildering is how to account for widespread slavery. Developments of such conduct within civilizations must be recognized as basic cultural traits, and the appearance, persistence, or elimination of one of them should be noted in civilizational perspective.

Legal historians and philosophers have not attempted to correlate legal systems with established civilizations. They have presented the development of laws, usually without reference to civilization as such or to the coincidence of civilizational trends. (That has been one of the lesser oversights due to the specialization or splintering of research). Perhaps the fact that the achievements of man have gone off on tangents or with different rates of development in different parts of the world has defied neat classifications of laws and civilizations.

For whatever reason, there has been a stark disparity between the development of labor laws and the development of civilizations. Vital changes in economies, and in labor laws, have taken place at widely varying times within seemingly homogenized civilizations. Such changes as the emancipation of slaves were not aberrations. They were inherent in civilization, even if they complicate our classification of civilizations.

The most fundamental transformation in labor law has been the abolition of slavery. The legal emancipation of slaves was not merely a labor law; it marked a metamorphosis in many social institutions; it was a deep alteration of the conditions of life for multitudes of human beings; it carried a moral principle and norms of human conduct from land to land, worldwide. It was not a sudden invention or a mutation. It emerged from a long development of human culture and should be acknowledged as a very significant example of civilizational transformation. The fact that it was adopted at various times in separate countries under different "civilizations" may have obscured its civilizational significance. (That may also indicate a deficiency in the classifications of civilization that do not account for universal or for randomly occurring cultural phenomena.)

Although social scientists see civilization as a social process in whatever form or substance it is or has had, and without evaluating its development, I choose to emphasize that civilization constitutes a betterment of life, at least as an attempt to avoid the hardships of life and the attainment of more satisfying ways of living. That contains an element of moral judgment on which reasonable persons may disagree. I recognize that a civilization may wander away from its goals, it may fail or it may succeed in small, almost unrelated, things. Nonetheless, inherent in my definition of civilization is the achievement of qualities of life that are better than earlier standards which we have labeled as uncivilized — barbaric, savage, cruel, inhumane, unjust. The dividing line is indistinct; yet the comprehension of civilization compels us to flesh out the differences.

In that respect, labor law has helped. The origins of labor law have not been preserved in writing. The earliest written codes (Hammurabi and Lipit Ishtar) contained labor law — wage rates, legalized by rulers with the assertion they were so authorized by Gods. We do not know how considerate, how just, those wage rates were. We merely have indications that they, and other rules of employment and other labor relations became established by custom or agreement. In time, as rules of conduct made their way into written labor legislation, they have become recognized as adjustments to improve the nature and conditions of labor, thus as evidence of advancing civilization.

In the long run, labor law has served at least two ends. It has helped to buttress our economies and it has made the lives of workers more comfortable and satisfying. Whether the economy has been feudal, capitalistic or communistic, whether it has been agricultural, commercial or service oriented, we have fashioned labor laws that have supported the system. At the same time, we have designed laws that have reduced personal hardship and enhanced enjoyment of life. Such laws may not have been identified as criteria of civilization; but they have been an indispensable element of the civilizing process.

Though there is some disagreement among the classifiers of civilizations as to whether the Judaic and Islamic cultures in the Middle East should be regarded as two separate and distinct civilizations, labor laws have weathered alike in both. None of the current labor laws in the Middle East has been found incompatible with any of the precepts that have been identified as norms of labor relations in the Bible and the Talmud or in the Koran and the Sunna.

There have been many significant religious attitudes toward rules for workers and their employers. Both the Judaic and Islamic laws were regarded as sacred axioms or commandments; and modern laws, even when they have repeated the same or similar words, have been considered secular; the former were God made, the latter man made. In early commentaries concerning the sacred texts there were debates over the extent to which rulers were permitted to add laws and the duty of the religious to obey them. Islamic scholars, although insisting upon the completeness and exclusivity of the Muslim law, still differentiated five categories of admonitions in the Koran and the Sunna; various religious rules were distinguished as obligatory, recommended, indifferent, blame worthy, or forbidden. That made it easier for Muslims to consider unspecified rules for secular behavior more openly. In the development of Muslim law, flexibility was acquired by reliance upon custom, analogical reasoning, and inventive adaptation. Likewise, in Israel, although extreme orthodox sectarians have sought to be guided solely by the Torah, the Talmudic characteristic of answering all questions by commenting "on the one hand, and on the other hand", has encouraged an inquisitive attitude in secular lawmaking. The political decision in Middle Eastern countries to allow Muslims, Christians, and Jews to be governed by their separate religious precepts in matters of family relationships, inheritance, and religious practices preserved religious law in those fields, but also tended to free the way for the development of labor law as secular law.

In the matter of slavery, there was a major departure from early Judaic, Christian, and Islamic labor law. Abolition of slavery, now the law throughout the Middle East, was a repudiation of the early acceptance of slavery. There was in all those faiths a basic affirmation of the brotherhood and equality of all human beings (unfortunately also religious texts that appeared to sanction differentiations). The fact remains that the adoption of modern laws prohibiting slavery, coming only after years of religious disputation, constituted a fundamental change in the labor laws observed by Jews, Muslims, and Christians in the Middle East.

The civilizing process in Middle East history has brought forth many new labor laws. In the millennia of traditional livestock raising, farming, and trade, there was little cause for change; but with the infiltration of Western colonialism, independence, and economic transformations, conditions of labor changed and new adaptations were required. The discovery and exploitation of oil threw the entire Middle East into disarray. In a brief span of time, modes of life were uprooted; the area was exposed to the industrial world, to new social aspirations and to new political opportunities. The Middle East was undeveloped, poverty was extensive, and the need for helpful legislation was urgent. Exemplary labor laws were abundant in other countries, and Middle East countries copied them in essence if not in exact words.

The explosive introduction of a Hebraic state into a Muslim land has raised special problems; but except for the refugee exodus and the later occupation of Palestinian territories, the problems of labor have remained essentially unchanged. Legal approaches to their solution have been readily available, and the adaptation of labor law has been primarily a matter of administration. New labor laws have been added, patterned to a large extent upon the laws on migrant workers in other lands. Specific terms or standards of law have varied, but they have been adopted within universal categories. Motivations or philosophical commitments in law have differed; but they have produced remarkably similar labor laws. Despite Judaic, Christian and Islamic civilizational differences, a body of similar labor laws throughout the Middle East presents evidence of civilizational convergence.

In the flow of human history, the labor laws of the Middle East bear traces of cultural history transformed by adaptation to new economic and social conditions, not only conditions peculiar to the region but also to patterns of behavior from around the world. At the time the Mesopotamian civilizations (including the Hebraic and Muslem) were formed, agriculture, handicrafts, barter and trade changed slowly. Labor roles and relationships were determined by family and tribal leaders in response to the availability of land, domesticated animals, and water that remained essentially the same for centuries. The early states, Hebew and Muslim, were dispersed over wide territories and their peoples enountered new ideas but their economic activities were altered little. The Industrial Revolution arose under other states, and the European empire builders were content to exploit the Middle East for exportable materials that could be produced in traditional ways. Slave trading introduced some new practices but even it did not significantly change other prevailing labor relations. Only in recent years, with the opening of the Middle East to new governments and with oil booms that shook them out of their customary economic activities came forces impelling them to rearrange their traditional labor relations. By then, the outside world had moved on to new civilizations and new forms of labor relationships. The civilizational heritage of the Middle East was challenged not only by new ideas but also by examples of economic efficiency and prosperity that were irresistable and that made civilizational change and new labor law unavoidable.

Chapter 21

ON WEALTH AND WESTERNIZATION

Traditionalists in the Middle East have been disturbed both by wealth and by Westernization — the former an irresistible lure to dream, and the latter, a confounding awakening. Even in the field of labor law, both are manifestations to be taken into account.

Wealth and Westernization are not necessarily linked together; yet they seemingly have had an innate affinity toward each other. Oil has spouted forth from the bowels of the earth without design and the thirst of the industrial West for more energy has been unquenchable. The epicenters of those phenomena have been far apart and in a less volatile world, they could conceivably remain apart. Suppliers of other raw materials, particularly under the control of colonial exploitation, changed little. The Middle East, however, has been greatly transformed and the effects of oil wealth and Westernization call for further analysis.

Tributary streams toward Westernization appear, push forward, are diverted and meander around traditions that stand in the way. A trickle may have been started with the sending of sons and daughters to complete their education in foreign universities. The surge of Western technology came with the importation of engineers, accountants, doctors and teachers, brought in to supply skills and techniques that were not present and that successful outsiders had to offer. Their Western attitudes were augmented in the training of nationals, intended to diminish dependency upon British and American managers and perversely they have transferred alien practices to native executives. The infusion of Westernization was obviously made lasting with the modern methods of exploiting oil; and it has been extended as more and more new industries have been made integral parts of the local economy. Accompanying these innovations have come

Western attitudes that accept industrialization, banking, commerce, investment and market manipulation as a way of life. All of these influences have pulsed forward with the influx of oil wealth.

By no means have they infiltrated into all aspects of Middle East thought and action. Native cultures have always resisted change, and a great many indigenous traits and institutions have stubbornly survived. The languages, Arabic and Persian, as well as tribal tongues and their numerous dialects, have remained relatively untouched; and old Hebrew has been revived. Judaism, Christianity and Islam, in their many sects, have asserted themselves, each claiming eternal validity. Modes of pastoral existence among Bedouin tribes have persisted and traditional forms of agriculture still are the mainstay of food for millions of people. These deep seated cultural factors have shown signs of adaptation to economic changes, but they remain prominent characteristics of the Middle East and will continue to rebuff and modify whatever alien inroads are made.

In the section above on Development and Planning, I have indicated various efforts of Middle East countries to enhance their well-being. In almost every instance, attention was directed to activities in which the Western World had set standards to be emulated. Economic gains could be made through almost any measure of Westernization. Whether it was in the use of air transport, which had become universalized, or in investment in building construction, which had undergone high-rise modernization, or in irrigation and fertilization, which offered great yields, the way to improvement lay in the use of Western technologies. The basic technique of development planning itself was borrowed from abroad. The difficult questions were where and how much Westernization should be encouraged. The nations differed in their answers.

In the wide range of official attitudes toward Westernization, the extremes are perhaps most clearly seen in Iran and Israel. The violent revolution against the Shah of Iran was a positive repudiation of his modernization program and an emotionally charged assertion of Shi'ite fundamentalism against the influence of a Satanic West. That did not deter the purchase of state-of-the-art military equipment to repel the Iraqi invaders or the use of Western technology in industry; but the spiritual condemnation of Westernization has remained firm. By contrast, in Israel, there has been an intense desire to identify the state with the Western World, as a democracy and as a willing recipient of all the scientific and technological knowledge that might be available. Israel's Jewishness has had its own spiritual overtones, but its secular activities have been deliberately eclectic.

The other Middle East countries have also looked inward toward their own traditions and outward to the Western World. Without delving into the many facets of their individualities, a few observations may illustrate how every one of them has responded to wealth (or the lack of it) and to Westernization.

The small oil producers, Bahrain and Kuwait have chosen to become mercantile and banking centers for the Middle East and so have eagerly accommodated themselves to Western business practices. Populous Saudi Arabia has insisted upon preserving its traditional Muslim character; but its overflowing wealth has resulted in a splurge of modernized industry, construction and social welfare programs for its nationals. Oman, Qatar and the UAE have also clung steadfastly to old sheikdoms; but they have begun to plan their economies with an increasing openness to Western influences.

Iraq and Syria have been beset with domestic difficulties that have preoccupied their leaders and that have not readily lent themselves to foreign remedies. Their protests against Western colonialism took expression in socialist principles — still patterned after Western thought. Their industrial development has proceeded slowly, yet along Western lines.

Lebanon, early on, decided to open its city doors to the commerce and education of the West, but internal warfare has forced them closed. Its farming hinterland where traditional cultures survive has also been ravaged so that the country looks in all directions for a new identity. The agricultural Yemens, somewhat on the fringe of Middle East activity, have not had the resources or income to take much advantage of Western mechanization except to bolster irrigation, home building, and domestic pursuits that have not markedly altered their societies. Ironically, the Marxist ideology of the PDRY is a Western influence in a traditional agricultural economy.

Westernization in the Middle East has gone ahead in many ways, with some unpredicted twists and turns, but with a persistence wherever petrodollars (and incidental remittances from migrant workers) have been received. What effect has this phenomenon had upon the enactment of labor law and what influence will it be likely to have in the future? Several observations seem significant.

For workers in the Middle East, Westernization has meant new employment opportunities and new problems. Many openings at attractive wages became available. Some on-the-job training helped in the acquisition of required skills. But many jobs were located in distant places, and housing, particularly for families, was quite inadequate. In time, wages lagged behind cost-of-living increases. The influx of expatriate labor brought problems of job insecurity and unsatisfactory work conditions. There were clear distinctions between native workers and in-migrants, between Arabs and Asians, between contract laborers who were supervised and sent home at a project's completion and those who came and remained, many illegally. Discriminatory treatment was common. Grievances were frequently ignored or disposed of arbitrarily. Labor laws were enacted to facilitate adjustments made necessary by such problems. The laws have helped and the fact that they have not eliminated all difficulties calls for more laws—likely to be influenced by Western example.

The wealth that has accompanied Westernization has been distributed very unevenly. Workers in certain Middle East countries have been bypassed entirely, except for some slight spillover in the remittances of migrant family members. More importantly, within the oil rich countries, there have been large numbers of workers who have not been direct recipients of their nation's largesse. Notwithstanding the fact that initial salaries paid workers in industrialized enterprises were higher than earlier customary earnings, few of those employed have experienced a lasting sense of affluence, and substantial numbers of people in the labor force have remained poor. Westernization has meant television and air travel which have raised expectations in life without supplying the means for their realization by all. It seems certain that Middle East traditions will linger, perhaps forever, but that Western attributes of work and leisure will continue to be irresistible and unflagging.

It is striking that labor law, despite the wide diversity in the kinds and levels of work in the Middle East, has followed rather uniform patterns. The problems of wages, hours and conditions of work have been approached similarly, and the norms established country after country have varied in degree more than in substance. That may be due, in part, to the convergence of legal systems in the West, or to a sameness in employment and work in the modern world. Some credit for the creation of similar laws and labor standards, I think, must be assigned to the International Labour Office, which has communicated with all countries whatever their character and needs. Pluralism may dominate the assertion of nationalities at the time of this writing, but one world-forces also exist and have a salutary influence. In the field of labor law, Westernization (and a few auguries of universalization) has helped shape the Middle East.

Chapter 22

ON LEADERS FRAUGHT WITH RELIGION

In the lands where great religions — Judaism, Christianity, and Islam — were born, believers are still vying with each other for the approval of God and man. Each religion professes a holy mission which can be fulfilled only by its followers. It preaches a gospel and fortifies its efforts through principal shrines in the Middle East. It offers Eternal salvation to those who abide by a creed, ritual, and good deeds. Included in the good deeds are acts of compassion toward workers, whether required by law or not. But above and beyond that, each religion, or sect thereof, claims to possess an essential element of faith, which demands a primacy in loyalty.

So transcendent is each religion, so important is its image, so impassioned is its spirituality, that many of the faithful are prepared to devote their lives to it. Even when tolerant of other creeds, the believers identify themselves with their own coreligionists and are less caring for outsiders. When they perceive a threat to their religion, in unfriendly treatment such as discrimination in labor relations, they become militant self-defenders. When they face a defiance to their separate existence, believers are ready to lay down their lives to preserve their religious institutions and possessions. Most unfortunately, that has been the common perception of religious observance in the Middle East. At the same time, a goodly number of theologians, and their disciples, have expressed their faiths in more constructive ways.

Islam. Islamic thinkers have drawn attention to their religious precepts that mandate the oneness of the community and the treatment of every human being with equal regard; that make personal service a religious imperative; that require the contribution of an individual's surplus wealth to the community (the Zakat) with the right of the less fortunate to partake of it; and that declare it a sin for one person to take advantage of another. These sacred principles they draw from the Koran and the teachings of Mohammed. No more guidance is thought needed. The essence of Islam applied to labor law, as in these views of pious writers, gives to the law the legitimacy and strength of eternal truth. Yet not all Muslims think of their religion in the same way.

The emergence of Shi'ite fundamentalists, from the revolt of Iran against Westernization, has rung a note of challenge throughout the Middle East. The Iranian Shi'ites have elevated religious leaders to the highest positions in government, and they have infused orthodox Islamic concerns into most social relationships. Their traditional concepts of separation of the sexes and of the proper role of women do affect the freedom of women to participate in the workplace and do color their Islamic recognition of equality between men and women. But women in Iran have been asserting themselves, by speech and silent action. Fundamentalists face greater challenges to their traditional rules for family relations, land ownership and inheritance than they have with the laws or mores that affect terms and conditions of work. The struggle of the Islamic clergy for dominance over the Muslim community has risen to a crescendo in Iran, that is viewed with alarm and determined resistance in other states.

The principal Islamic schools of law — the Shafi, Hanafi, Maliki, Hanbali — have not dictated the nature of labor laws; nor have the differences among Muslim sects shaped labor laws. The more active rivalries (and hostilities) between the Sunnis and the Shi'ites have expressed themselves wherever politically expedient; but they have not chosen to find in labor law a vital forum for battle.

There is another voice among some Islamic writers who present still another religious and philosophical outlook on labor law.[1] They use the phrase "origin is destination" to indicate their

[1] Sayed Hassan Amin, Islamic Law in the Contemporary World, Royston Ltd., Glasgow, 1985; Duncan MacDonald, Development of Muslim Theology, Jurisprudence and Constitutional Theory, Darf Publishing, London, 1985; Noel J. Coulson, Conflicts and Tensions in Islamic Jurisprudence, Univ. of Chicago Press,

total commitment to the determination of all phases of life through Islamic precepts. They have applied their views not only to theological considerations, but also to secular matters. They disown both capitalism and communism and propose a global economic system in which the primary motivation is the observance of teachings found in the Koran and the Sunna. They stress the liberal precepts referred to above, precepts they believe will alleviate the suffering of the working underclass. They do not object to labor legislation; but they think faith and devotion to Islamic principles are indispensable to and sufficient for economic justice.

Deviation from traditional expresions of Islam appears not likely to become a force in current affairs; yet laxity of observance or indifferent neglect among many Muslims seems to be a concomitant of industrialization and Western education. That does not suggest the collapse or disappearance of Islamic influences upon the enactment or enforcement of labor law; but it may temper the emotional force of the devout in the commercial centers of the Middle East.

Christianity. The Middle East has had a special attraction to Christians as their holy land, even though they have been unable to establish dominion over it. After the division of Christendom between Rome and Byzantium, the few resident Christians formed an outpost of their Middle Eastern devotees. Even today, the Maronites, Armenians, and Greek Catholics are principal Christian activists in the region, and though Protestants are present, the older, orthodox churches are the outstanding keepers of the faith. Their primary activities have been concerned with the preservation of Christian creeds and not secular matters. Except for a brief involvement in the British mandate, their only attempt to control a State has been in Lebanon. There they have for a time maintained a peaceful legal system in alliance with Muslims;

Chicago & London, 1982; Joseph Schact, An Introduction to Islamic Law, Clarendon Press, 1959; Joseph Schact, The Origins of Muhammadian Jurisprudence, Clarendon Press, Oxford, 1950.

however, for a long time Christian militia have been embattled with Islamic militia.

Neither Christianity nor Islam has fashioned a labor law more characteristic of one faith than the other. Both have offered spiritual and some material support for workers. Officials designated as representatives of the two religions in Lebanon have dealt with coreligionists, who have had all the various economic interests in the population, and they have adopted labor laws without particular religious traits.

It appears that Christians in the north of Lebanon have prospered more than the populous Muslims in the agricultural south; but so have Muslim Sunnis when compared with rural Shi'ites. Demands for material relief have arisen in all sectors of the country and have fueled political rivalries. Religious identification has become so pervasive that economic protest and open warfare have proceeded along religious lines. The animosities, however, have not intruded into the sponsorship of laws affecting labor.

Judaism. Israel has undergone unique and paradoxical religious experiences. As a homeland for Jews denied freedom to practice their faith in many lands, it has consecrated itself to the ingathering of Jews from all over the world. Those who have made the homecoming (called the alliyah) have not had identical religious views and practices. A rather small number of extremely orthodox settlers have clung to their belief that secular matters, even the existence of a Jewish State, is irrelevant to their religion. All that matters is that Jews continue to live by the words of the Bible until the Messiah comes to release all humanity from worldly ties. The preponderant majority of Israelis, however, respond to nationhood as a refuge for their oppressed and feel an emotional need to protect all those who embrace Judaism regardless of their idiosyncrasies. How Judaism is expressed in labor matters is to them a secular concern.

In the proliferation of political parties in Israel, there are a few small parties referred to as the religious parties. Although they have polled a very small fraction of votes, they have exercised considerable influence on public policies affecting Judaism. In the past decade or so, neither of the major political parties, the Labor or the Likud, has been able to enlist a firm majority of the populace, and in order to stay in power, the plurality winner has been obliged to form a coalition including small religious parties. The latter have been primarily concerned with public practices that breach orthodox Jewish tenets. Certain laws of Judaic import such as the law which confers citizenship upon all immigrating Jews and the law declaring the Sabbath on Saturday have posed complications. The religious parties have insisted upon no work on the Sabbath — no transportation, no commercial entertainment, no business activities from sundown Friday to Saturday evening. Both the Labor and Likud parties have resisted demands for such legislation, but passionate advocacy has erupted in some violent disturbances. Though other interpretations of Judaism, primarily over who is a Jew and whether only orthodox rabbis may perform official functions, have also been the subject of disquieting disputation, their impact upon labor law has been remote.

There have also been a significant number of Israelis who are not strictly religious. They partake of religious holidays and Jewish traditions without theological commitments. Part of their traditions are associated with the labor movement, as exemplified in the Histadrut, and with labor legislation that they do not view as religious. On questions of statehood and national security, the preservation of Judaism may be regarded as indispensable, but on labor law, the non-observant Israelis have treated religion as an irrelevant factor.

The over-all impact of religion upon labor law in the Middle East has been more confessional than pragmatic. Sacred sources are revered; but their broad moral teachings have been kept open, more and more, to lay interpretation. Religious practices have tended to be held aloof from the labor market. In Arab countries that have special councils to screen legislative proposals for consistency with the Shariah, I have been unable to find any rejection of a proposed labor law. In Israel, a Justice of the Supreme Court who is reputed to like to include Biblical or Talmudic references in his decisions, has apparently not seen it necessary to do so in any significant case involving labor relations. That is not to say that the prevailing religions have had no influence upon labor law. All religions in the Middle East have expressed an abiding concern over the poor and the oppressed; yet no sectarian group has distinguished itself as a special sponsor of labor legislation, nor has it called for measures that could not readily be approved by all faiths. Fatalistic or messianic attitudes that discourage striving for betterment have been attributed to some devotees of Judaism, Christianity, and Islam; but that has not been characteristic of any of those faiths. Concentration on institutional structures, striving for hierarchical prestige, and observance of rituals have dominated religious activities. Labor laws have been spared their sectarian differences.

At the same time, religious leaders in all faiths in the Middle East have been involved in sectarian activities inconsistent with the peaceful enjoyment of those benefits that labor laws have sought to accomplish. Under the rationalization of defending their religions, believers have participated in conduct that defies their spiritual and moral values. The massacre of Islamic Kurds by coreligionists in Iraq or Iran violates basic precepts ordained by Allah in the Koran. The killing of some Christian militiamen by other Christian militiamen in Lebanon desecrates the fundamental Christian credo of brotherly love. The bombing of Palestinian camps or communities housing innocent children by Israeli forces breaches commandments holy to Judaism. Pleas of self-defense do not conceal the wanton disregard of the sacredness of human life and the abandonment of the moral edicts of all religions. The widespread denial of lesser human rights, even to protect one's self against the injustices of others, sacrifices moral and social values inherent in all the religions. The benefits of labor law are too often obliterated or forgotten in other religious pursuits.

Chapter 23

ON DEFENDERS OF STATEHOOD AND TERRITORY

Nationalist goals of Arabs and Jews have probably had a greater bearing upon their labor laws than have their religions. The attainment of independence meant the creation of new law-making governments. Each had a history that came to a new juncture, and each government sought to demonstrate its legitimacy and to display its character through a system of laws. Some of the current Middle East states had their territories defined with some ambiguity so that the extent of their sovereignty has remained somewhat in question. All of these matters have been of relatively recent happening and several have had to be defended against challenges. Labor laws have been chits of authority and respectability in maintaining statehood and territory.

Despite their claims to ancient origins, the governments now ruling the Middle East have recent credentials. Their first constitutions, that pre-eminent certificate of national identity, bear the dates 1906 and 1979 in Iran, 1921 in Iraq, 1930 in Syria, 1943 in Lebanon, 1946 in Jordan, 1961 in Kuwait, 1965 in the YAR, 1970 in PDRY and Qatar, 1971 in UAE, and 1973 in Bahrain. The three countries without constitutions came into existence with the approval of world powers, Saudi Arabia in 1932, Israel in 1948, and Oman in 1970. In historical perspective, all have had relatively few years in which to enact labor legislation.

The boundaries established by or for these countries—and consequently the people subject to their laws—have been marked off in recent years accompanied by considerable dispute. The territory occupied by Kurdish tribesmen was split amongst Iraq, Iran, Syria, Turkey, and the Soviet Union, without any provision for a Kurdish state.[1] Other Islamic tribes had been dispersed or cast asunder in the creation of Middle Eastern states with less turmoil. The states themselves have had border disputes. Such conflicts erupted between north and south Yemen in 1972 and again in 1979 to 1982; and though a common cultural background has led to negotiations for unity between the Yemens, they only recently permitted free transit of their workers across their line of separation. Saudi Arabia has had boundary disputes with Kuwait and UAE — fortunately settled peacefully. The most intractable dispute has arisen out of the creation of Israel and the dismemberment of Palestine.

After the defeat of Germany and its allies, the United Nations issued mandates to England and France for the government of several sections of the Middle East. The British in Palestine were unable to mediate or squelch the rival claims of Jews and Arabs; and the United Nations resolved to divide Palestine, part to a new State of Israel and part to the recently formed Hashemite Kingdom of Jordan. War declared by all the Islamic countries was successfully resisted by Israel and an uneasy truce was maintained over the territory allotted to Israel. Many thousand Palestinians fled into neighboring Arab countries. Refugee camps were built to keep alive their demand to return to a revived Palestine; and they have so remained, supported by the UN and Arab sympathizers, for over 40 years. Terrorist attacks upon Israelis and retaliatory assaults upon Palestinians in Lebanon prolonged animosities. A pre-emptive strike by Israel brought on a war, and in 1967 Israel defeated the Arab forces and occupied Arab territories in the West Bank of Jordan and in the Gaza strip of Egypt.

To the basic dispute over the presence of a Jewish State in the land set aside by the United Nations, there was added a new territorial dimension. It started with a military occupation by a victorious army, and it has escalated into a dispute over the

[1] Chas. G. MacDonald, The Kurdish Question in the 1980s. Ch. 14 in M.J. Esman and I. Rabinovich, Ethnicity, Pluralism and the State in the Middle East, supra.

permanent settlement of Israelis in the Biblical lands of Judea and Samaria.

Widely scattered terrorist attacks and reprisals between Arabs and Jews erupted into a war in 1973, followed by an invasion of Lebanon in 1982. They inflamed religious passions which had dominated political policies throughout the Middle East for decades, but the dissension has now concentrated upon the West Bank and Gaza.

Tens of thousands of Arab workers in the occupied territories see themselves humiliated and oppressed by discriminatory practices. They may have more employment, more income and more schools than they had before; but they have enumerated their misfortunes and have attributed them to arbitrary and abusive policies of Israeli authorities. Palestinian leaders outside the territories had not secured them relief and they decided to act for themselves. In November, 1987, they started an uprising (the intifada), and with stones and shouts they attacked Israeli soldiers. Arrests and indefinite detention did not stop them. Burning tire barricades and gasoline bombs were met with shootings, deaths, and communal punishments. Commercial strikes and boycotts followed. Women and children taunted soldiers with rocks and epithets. Detention, deportation and the destruction of homes increased anger; tear gas, rubber bullets and fatal shootings intensifed hatred and prompted more protests. Stones and home-made bombs with open defiance, the strangling of informers and the occasional killing of an Israeli became an irrepressible form of modern combat, lasting now more than two years. And the stumbling block toward peace appears to be a dispute over the relinquishment of territory.

The Palestinians of the intifada call for self determination of their nation on land they have occupied for a great many years. The Likud-Labor government of Israel insists upon the right of Jews to dwell on that land (as part of historical Judea and Samaria) and believes it must assure them that right through its governmental power. Extremists among the Arabs would drive the Israelis into the sea and extremists among the Israelis would expel the Arabs from their homes in Israel. Both sides have had recourse to religious texts, one to the Biblical promise of Jehova to provide a homeland for Jews in Judea and Samaria, and the other to the Koranic words of Allah for the holy to spread Islam to all mankind. It is unlikely that a territorial solution will be found in their religions.[2] Political compromise may be induced by the external world powers which once did set boundaries for the State of Israel and for other Middle East states.

In the meanwhile, labor laws are determined by states and their scope and effectiveness are beset with the vagaries of statehood and territory.

[2] Perhaps it is yet to be decided whether the voice of Yeshayahu Leibowitz is quixotic or prophetic. The orthodox Jew and iconoclastic philosopher has cried out from the very beginning of the West Bank occupation that Israel's efforts to embrace all of Judea and Samaria have unavoidably led to a fascistic police system and has become an idolatry of land in flagrant violation of the first commandment. Far more vociferous have been the Gush Emunim who have interpreted the Bible differently. Matthew Nesvisky, "Social Critic or Prophet?", Present Tense, Vol. 17, no. 3, March, 1990.

Chapter 24

ON SEARCHERS FOR SECURITY AND PERPETRATORS OF WAR

At times, labor law in the Middle East seems submerged in a fog of insecurity. Oil rich Saudi Arabia, Kuwait, and Bahrain abide in fear of possible subversion by immigrant foreign workers; so the powerful rulers impose upon hundreds of thousands of impotent laborers servitude under work permits, sponsorship and threats of expulsion. The subversive activities have not materialized, but the insecurity still overshadows both sides. Little Oman fears to emerge from its old isolation and refuses to join the UN or the ILO under the pretext that its tribesmen are not ready (for the dignity of citizens in a free world?). Israel has been so traumatized by past persecution of Jews that many Israelis subordinate the protests of Palestinian workers to their own quest for security. In various contexts, Sunnis feel threatened by Shi'ites, Iraqis by Kurds, Christians by Muslims; and the fears are reciprocated. Extremists, Arabs who want to push Israelis into the sea and Israelis who want to drive Arabs out of Jerusalem or Judea and Samaria, fan the flames of insecurity. Every Middle East nation cries out for security and they have stumbled and sloughed through wars to find security — without feeling they have found it.

Deep seated fears are seldom dispelled by reason or logic, and I am under no illusion that whatever I write can dissuade insecure masses of their hysteria or aberrations. On the other hand, the wisdom of Middle East leaders has failed them. Of all the conceivable ways to allay or eliminate their insecurity, they have resorted to the most dangerous and costly measures — war, terrorism, and armed deterrence.

In the most pervasive insecurity, the Arab-Israeli confrontation, there has been a complete miscarriage and a harrowing impasse. The conflagration of 1948 led only to a truce, and except for lapses into more death and destruction and the expenditure of millions for unused armaments, there is still only a truce, interrupted almost daily by more killing and no feeling of security for either Jews or Arabs.

I pause to comment fragmentarily on certain realities, not often acknowledged. The area of the Middle East is so small that missiles now available to all parties can fly across any border; and no known system of interdiction can prevent some hits with horrendous consequence. There is no security in a first strike or in retaliation. Increases in armaments merely increase the insecurity. The deterrence of opposing forces could be just as effective at a lower level of fire power as at a higher level, yet the drive for more fire power continues. No stand-off of military might has brought anyone a sense of lasting security.

So entrenched is the popular dependence upon armed deterrence that regardless of my conviction that it is a delusion, I shall not argue its validity. I am resigned to the terrible waste of resources for armaments in place of expenditures for human needs. If that gives antagonists a bit of comfort, so be it; they will have it whatever the cost. I am more concerned with what additional measures can be taken to cultivate peaceful and cooperative relations. And there, the ways in which labor laws have been dealt with offer possible help and encouragement.

I think there is no assurance for peace without the actual commingling of people, face to face, learning to know each other for whatever they may be, and having the opportunity to voice their aspirations and grievances to each other. Hatreds paralyze the afflicted and fears of the unknown hide the possibilities of rapprochement. To break through to human communication requires a degree of courage and self confidence that only a few possess. And once the flow of understanding begins, it will take a very long time to overcome the hurt of past suffering, the lingering doubts and suspicions (and the setbacks of emotional flare-ups). To dissipate the insecurities that now exist in the Middle East, it is essential to take advantage of every available point of agreement, every form of human empathy, every means of cooperative effort. Such common grounds and mutual understanding exist in labor laws.

The process of considering, debating and drafting labor laws (in the Middle East as well as in the developed countries of the world) has been a process of reconciling conflicting interests and insecurities. Unsatisfied, raw needs have given rise to demands, at times explosively. Fears of the organization of workers, their radical proposals and their occasional disruption of production have been common. Such social quandaries have been stabilized in large part by labor laws. That is experience that can be expanded.

There are multitudes of human beings who seek eagerly to improve their lives and the lives of others in any way available. There are also many empathetic and tireless individuals who strive for the betterment of society despite difficulties in their way. The enactment and enforcement of labor laws have given them a sense of security and fulfillment. The recognition that similar achievements are being accomplished in unfamiliar countries leads to a feeling of commonality among peoples who see themselves differently.

I am suggesting that there are several ways in which the use of laws of direct interest to labor can quiet national insecurities and stimulate peaceful relations among different peoples. Some of these have been experienced — not so much in the Middle East as elsewhere — and they can be elaborated and utilized in improved ways. There are existing international agencies and techniques that can be employed with significant impact, and given a little innovative thought they can be strengthened to bring peace and security in some places where they do not exist today.

The UN and its agencies, particularly the ILO, are now dedicated to the cooperation of nations for the peaceful enhancement of life, and if their operations are augmented in several respects, even within their present charters, they could accomplish much to overcome the insecurity and bellicose reactions prevalent in the Middle East. That would require only a commitment to (a) keeping alive and up to date the information on labor relations in all countries, (b) receiving and disseminating the grievances of nongovernment agencies, private organizations and individuals with respect to labor conditions, as well as the responses of governments thereto, (c) monitoring pertinent developments and providing technical assistance designed to alleviate labor problems, and (d) stimulating combined participation of governments, employers and workers in all matters of mutual interest. In a very limited measure, all of these things are now being done. With the expenditure of a small percentage of current military budgets (without disturbing funds thought necessary for defensive military needs) the designated commitments could be carried forward to very significant accomplishments.

(a) The educational function could be extended to the provision of reliable data, not now available, on labor conditions and labor law in every Middle East country. There are now no comparable statistics on employment, income distribution and other labor facts in most of the region. There are some Gross National Product indexes, but no index of social well being for the Middle East (as has been started by the Organization for Economic Cooperation and Development for other countries). Such information would not only assist in the formulation of necessary laws, but would also make countries aware of how they compare with and are seen by their neighbors. The disclosure of comparable social facts would be a foundation for sympathetic understanding and cooperation.

(b) The deposit of grievances and requests for relief, accepted from Non-Governmental Organizations of the UN, from labor organizations, and from individuals, would constitute an extension of the services being performed by UN Committees and the ILO. That would provide an opportunity for dispelling fears and misunderstandings. Some governments might resent being involved, but they also would be able to present their views. Although much of the information would probably be a monotonous repetition of unverified complaints and self-justifications, there are therapeutic social benefits from public ventilation of opinions and there is no way to screen or silence opinions if justice is to be done. The persistence of complaint may be annoying and unfair, yet it is essential to the location and remedying of real problems.

The investigations and reports by UN monitoring agents would cast light upon countless matters that now fester in darkness. They would not only demonstrate what has been in dispute or unknown; they would also indicate the concern of the outside world and promote cooperative dealing among peoples.

(c) The offer of technical assistance to governments and private individuals would supply expert aid to those who wish to serve themselves and their fellow men. There is a large reservoir of intelligence and experience in the world that can be put to work. The oil producing countries have learned to take advantage of it in industrial techniques; and they and the less endowed nations of the Middle East should be induced to do the same in other public activities. It offers a hands-on treatment for any sort of insecurity.

(d) The promotion of tripartite cooperation (government, management, and labor) would activate remedial measures among the persons most concerned over labor problems and the most to benefit from mutual understanding. Participation in such joint efforts on labor law administration has had a contagious effect carrying over to many other community problems.

These measures are not unfamiliar, though seldom resorted to in the Middle East. They need not await the millennium for adoption. They can be put into operation even without the prior or full approval of every government. They do require funds which have not been easily forthcoming for many peace-keeping activities; but the diversion of even a little from existing budgets could make a substantial difference. Any increase in the support and completion of the proposed tasks would produce tangible gains. The fact they would be concentrated on labor problems and labor law would not confine their benefits. The field of labor relations is a pervasive source of insecurity and fear, and cooperative habits formed in that area would carry over to dealings on other matters as well.

These proposals for easing out of insecurity through the stimulation of common interests and cooperative activities on labor law would not be a panacea. They alone could do no more than strengthen the human, personal interaction that is required for peace in a tormented Middle East. However, the proposed steps on labor law (even a few of them alone) could have some curative effect in societies now riven with insecurity. The fact that they would be confined to the tiny area of labor law has the advantage that they would be in a field of concern not divided by religious differences or dissents. Instead, they would deal with matters widely approved as promising individual and social betterment.

No one questions the need for some action to uproot the insecurities of the Middle East and the choice is not between courses of action, either of which is likely to succeed. The perpetration of war is a foregone disaster. The balancing of weaponry is the most costly and perilous of postures. If national insecurities in the Middle East are to be overcome, some other ways must be selected to accomplish that end. The utilization of the labor law process with international sponsorship is a rational and feasible alternative.

As deeply convinced as I am of the soundness of the thoughts I have just expressed, I am not sanguine that the leaders of Middle East governments or the purse wielders in the Western world are prepared to do what is proposed. Many thoughtful individuals have compatible ideas and in so far as they are concerned with labor law, they may be encouraged to press for labor law activities that would give nations a greater sense of security. But I realize the world powers are motivated in other ways. The foreign policies of most nations are moved, above all else, by the criterion of what best serves their own interests and labor law is very low in the list of their priorities. Even my own government has on occasion abandoned its powers of persuasion and resorted to financial pressures in dealing with the UN and ILO when other member nations have dared to disagree with it. However, there is an inventiveness that leads human beings to find ways to accomplish rational action. War is not one of the ways. Nor is insecure detente acceptable. Per chance in the pursuit of labor law some persons will find ways to nourish security.

Chapter 25

LOOKING TO BASIC NEEDS AND HUMAN POTENTIAL

Labor laws are life sustaining in ever changing scenes. The ancient Middle East migrants who drove their sheep and goats, and carried their children into strange valleys in search of a place to toil and dream, were mindful of the scarcities as well as the bounties of nature and the presence of friends and foes. Their descendants, many still migrating, have sorted out new complexities of existence and are finding new ways to cope with them. By no means have the basic needs of food, clothing, shelter, recreation and a yearning for betterment been satisfied for all. Not alone in lands parched and fallow; also in lands overflowing with nature's oil wealth, there are human beings who feel the sting of material and spiritual want. The needs of the Middle East have been transformed and continue to change in an endless procession. Labor laws help to satisfy those needs but, as they do, other human appetites and expectations crop out anew.

In the few decades since the commencement of the modern oil era, the Middle East has barely begun to legislate for the welfare of workers. The region has been characterized primarily by upheaval and madness, in the midst of which men and women of intelligence and compassion have tried to map out some sensible developments. They have been endowed with traditions that have distilled centuries of experience; yet they were plunged into currents they could not control. Unpredictable nature unleashed outpourings of oil in random places, in overpowering proportions. Foreign powers injected political forces that upset and rearranged established state and spiritual relationships. Fast changing circumstances have bred fears and violent reactions, tempered only slightly by the innate rationality of man, even under stress.

In this ambiance of wealth and opportunity, of perplexity and passion, the workers in the Middle East have posed a multitude of problems. Traditional attitudes of first protecting oneself, then enriching oneself and then caring for the unfortunate have prevailed; but the magnitude of the possibilities and their difficulties have been not thoroughly appreciated.

When workers are in need of food or clothing, their plight is readily recognized. In the Middle East, that has been seen most often among agricultural workers in remote rural areas, and assistance has been forthcoming in making more arable land available or in providing better irrigation or improved seed. Remittances from family members who have gone into gainful employment elsewhere have supplied more help. Except for the feeding and housing of the unemployed in over-crowded towns, the problem of basic needs has been amenable to correction by social assistance.

For workers engaged in industry or commerce, there have been minimum wage laws keyed to their basic needs. Fortunately, the employment opportunities in the growing Middle East economies have provided the minimum essentials and more, for native workers and for most expatriate workers who were hired. Development plans have also attended to some of those needs. To the extent that basic needs have not been met, as has been the case for workers not covered by labor laws, charity within traditional forms has ameliorated suffering.

Labor laws in the Middle East have recognized basic human needs and have gone beyond food, clothing and shelter. They have served in various ways to elevate standards of living. They have freed hours of work for family life and recreation. They have helped preserve healthy bodies in frequently hostile work environments. Latterly, they have also provided some compensation to offset the tolls of disability, old age and involuntary unemployment.

The distribution of these social benefits has been mired in Middle East political and religious containments, in animosities and wars, and in the fear of future disturbances. Masses of alien workers have walked a narrow line between cushioned care and callous rejection. Within immigration regulations, their basic essentials have been assured; but the status of Asian and non-Arab guest workers in the oil states and Palestinian workers in the Occupied Territories is still unresolved. Arabs in the oil producing states and Jews in Israel have experienced a special welcome and preferential treatment. Labor laws that have proclaimed equal sharing of the good things in life have not been widely realized.

Still, some labor laws have been designed to enable workers to achieve a dignified role in the conduct of their lives. At an elementary level, they have permitted and facilitated worker involvement in political action. In more sophisticated ways, labor laws have sought to promote workers' participation in the making of management decisions and in the fashioning of work processes that might be enjoyable as well as productive. Not many countries in the Middle East have adopted or envisioned such labor laws; yet they have persistently moved toward new frontiers. A current goal of labor law, as perceived throughout most of the world, is to provide the opportunity for every human being to fulfill the totality of his or her capabilities — not only to satisfy basic needs but also to achieve his or her human potential.

The laws of no Middle East country have reached that stage of perfection. Few statesmen have clearly declared an intent to achieve that goal. In some respects there are elementary improvements to be made. Much is still to be done to embrace all workers within the ambit of existing protective laws. Many areas of acknowledged interest are still left unattended. In no state have enough resources been devoted to the administration of enacted laws and the exploration of new needs. On the other hand, all Middle East states are aware of their labor problems, all have made solemn commitments to improve their conditions, and all have started to do so. If not paralyzed by religious animosities or insecurity paranoia, and if not emasculated by war, they will have an opportunity to accomplish all that labor laws promise.

The perception of labor problems in the Middle East lights up ways still to be traversed. Many consequences and incidentals following the enactment of labor laws reveal progress. Occasional retrogression in the preservation and enforcement of human rights is woefully frustrating; but their value is undenied and is attainable. Labor laws in the Middle East have moved from the satisfaction of basic human needs toward a gratification of the potential in every human being. Such is the transit from tradition to modernity.

Appendix I

Selected Labor Statutes

Bahrain

1947	Workers Compensation
1957	Ordinance: Bahrain Labour Ordinance
1976	LABOR LAW

Iran

1957	Workers Compensation
1959	LABOR CODE
1960	Social Insurance
1963	Profit Sharing
1965	Fair Labor Standards Act
1975	Social Security
1977	Holiday and Leave Pay — Agricultural Workers, Settlement of Disputes

Iraq

1932	Strikes
1937	Workers Compensation (occupational diseases)
1940	Civil Pension Law
1946	Employment Service
1954	Conciliation and Arbitration
1958	Agrarian Reform Law
	Social Security Law
1961	Employment of Women and Children, Seafarers (conditions of work)
1964	Social Security
1970	Labor Code
1971	Copyright Law, Retirement, Social Security
1973	Employment — Foreign Workers
1975	Non-Discrimination (Equality of Women)

1977	Youth Training, Remuneration and Discipline of Workers
1981	Vocational Training, Employment of Iraqis Abroad
1982	Cooperatives
1983	Employment (work card in private sector)
1984	Social Security (pensions for laborers)
1987	LABOR CODE, Social Security, Women Labor, Maternity Leave, Pensions, Cooperatives

Israel

1945	Accidents & Occupational Diseases Ordinance, Dentists' Law, Pharmacists Law
1946	Factories Ordinance
1947	Medical Practitioners Law, Midwives' Law
1948	Days of Rest, Palestine Government Employees Ordinance
1949	Emergency Regulation — Cultivation of Waste Lands, Compulsory Education Law, Discharged Soldiers' (Reinstatement in Employment) Law
1950	Fallen Soldiers Families (Pensions and Rehabilitation) Law,
1951	Hours of Work and Rest Law, Night Baking (Prohibition) Women's Equal Rights Law, Annual Leave Law
1953	Apprenticeship Law, State Education Law, Youth Labor Law, National Insurance Law
1954	Employment of Women Law, Labor Inspection (Organisation) Law
1955	State Service (Benefits) Law
1957	Collective Agreements Law, Penal Law Revision, Settlement of Labor Disputes
1958	Wage Protection Law, Engineers & Architects Law
1959	Employment Service Law, State Service (Appointments) Law, Restrictive Trade Practices
1963	State Service (Discipline) Law, Severance Pay Law

1964	Male & Female Workers (Equal Pay) Law
1967	Restrictions on the Use of Agricultural Land & Water Law, Emergency Labor Service Law
1968	Licensing of Businesses
1969	Labor Courts Law, Public Service (Restrictions After Retirement) Law
1970	Emergency Work Volunteers
1971	Medical Professions (Fees for Licenses & Permits) Law
1972	Guard Services and Private Investigators' Law
1976	Dentists' Ordinance, Sick Pay Leave
1977	Artisans' Licensing Law, Psychologists Law
1980	Assurance of Income Law
1981	Employment Equal Opportunities Law; Public Land (Removal of Squatters) Law, Male & Female (Equal Retirement Age) Law, Acquisition of Undertakings by Employees Law
1987	Minimum Wage Law
1988	Equality of Opportunity at Work Law

Jordan

1947	Workmen's Compensation Ordinance
1953	Trade Unions Law
1956	Social Security
1960	LABOR CODE
1971	Labor Code (amendments)
1978	Social Security
1984	Public Employees (pensions)
1987	Child Labor

Kuwait

1959	Foreign Labor (amended through 1987)
1961	Legal Relations with a Foreign Element
1962	Labor Code, Cooperative Societies Law
1963	Public Meetings, Processions and Demonstrations
1964	Labor Law — Special Provisions for the Oil Sector
1973	Vocational Training

1975	Decree re Employment of Young People, Powers & Duties of Officials Responsible for Enforcing Labor Legislation
1976	Women's Night Work, Vocational Training, Social Insurance Act
1977	Cooperatives
1979	Employment (work permits for foreign workers), Cooperatives, Safety & Health, National Employment Service, Labor Inspection
1980	Vocational Training (women), Employment (conditions of work), Health & Safety (on board ship)
1981	Social Insurance, Conciliation in Collective Labor Disputes, Cooperative Associations (supervision and inspertion)
1983	Retirement Pensions
1984	Child Labor, Work Permits (non-Kuwaiti workers), Women's Night Work (repeals 1976 law), Occupational Safety and Health
1989	Employment Placement

Lebanon

1946	LABOR CODE (AMENDED 1975)
1964	Cooperatives, Collective Agreements
1966	National Labor Council
1971	Social Insurance
1972	Cooperatives, Trade Unions, Minimum Wage (manual and office workers), Medical Benefits (teachers)
1980	Labor Disputes (individual)
1981	Remuneration (minimum wages for manual & non-manual workers)
1982	Social Security
1983	Remuneration (minimum wages)
1984	Property rights (commercial & industrial), Safety and Health
1987	Minimum Wages, Social Security

APPENDIX I

Oman

1973	LABOR CODE
1976	Compensation for Occupational Injuries & Illnesses
1978	Vocational Training

Qatar

1962	LABOR LAW, Labor Courts
1963	Regional and Local Labor Courts
1987	Labor Inspection, Workmen's Compensation & Work Related Injuries, Religious Courts

Saudi Arabia

1969	LABOR CODE
1970	Social Insurance
1971	Civil Service
1973	Public Employees (retirement)
1983	Arbitration Law

Syria

1946 Labor Code	
1949	Contracts of Employment, Strikes & Lockouts
1950	Cooperatives
1952	Compulsory Labor
1955	Vocational Education, Annual Leave
1958	Agricultural Labor
1959	LABOR CODE, Contract of Employment (Seafarers)
1961	Social Insurance
1962	Trade Union Officials, Dismissals
1964	Co-management
1965	Labor Inspection
1968	Trade Unions
1969	Peasants' Associations
1970	Dismissal (individual workers)
1971	Labor Inspection (night work)
1972	Trade Union Schools, Lawyers' Retirement Fund

1973	Public Employees, Hours of Work (overtime), Health and Safety, Employment (mine workers)
1975	Agricultural Vocational Training, Safety and Health, Dismissal
1976	Job security (protection of trade union representatives against unlawful transfer)
1977	Cooperatives, Occupational Safety
1978	Family Allowances
1979	Remuneration (public employees), Health Insurance, Women's Labor (remuneration & a children's allowance)
1980	Public Employees (pension, remuneration), General Amnesty for Persons Guilty of Abandoning Their Work, Employment Service
1981	Hours of Work, Work Permits for Foreigners, Safety and Health; Public Employees (pensions)
1982	Child Labor (prohibit work under 12 years), Trade Unions, Employment of Handicapped, Public Employees (settlement of disputes), Cooperatives
1984	Social Insurance, Public Employees (wages), Vocational Training

United Arab Emirates

1980	FEDERAL LAW TO REGULATE EMPLOYMENT, Permits for Foreign Workers, National Employment Service

Yemen Arab Republic

1970	LABOR CODE

People's Democratic Republic of Yemen

Laws of Aden

	Contracts of Employment —Indigenous Workers, Domestic Servants, Women, Young Persons and Children, Ord. Cap. 31, 54, 55, 84
1956	Apprenticeship Training Ordinance

APPENDIX I

1958	Employment in Shops, Trade Unions, Trade Disputes, Arbitration and Inquiry, Ord. Cap. 150, 152
1960	Wages Council Ordinance
1967	Notification of Vacancies Ordinance
1969	Settlement of Labor Reduction Disputes Law, Deduction of Workers' Contributions from their Wages Law
1972	Civil Service Law
1973	Yemen to Socialist and Non-Socialist Countries for Study and Training
1978	LABOR LAW

Index

INDEX

E

F

H

INDEX

M

O

P

R

S

T

U

W